PATTERNS
IN
PRACTICE

PATTERNS
IN
PRACTICE

Selections from the
Journal of Museum Education

MUSEUM EDUCATION ROUNDTABLE
Washington, D.C.

Museum Education Roundtable, Inc.
P.O. Box 23664
Washington, D.C. 20026–3664

First edition published 1992
Printed in the United States of America
Library of Congress Catalog Card Number 91–066484
ISBN 1–880437–00–7

Publication of this book was made possible by a matching grant from the Institute of Museum
Services, Professional Services Program, Washington, D.C.

Cover: Japanese stencil design

Contents

Preface   *Susan K. Nichols*   *xi*

COMING OF AGE

Introductions
The Museum's Role in a Multicultural Society   *Claudine K. Brown*   *3*
Evolution of the Field: Historical Context   *Barbara Franco*   *9*

Afro-American Museums: A Future Full of Promise   *Amina J. Dickerson*   *12*
The Growth of a Program: From Childhood through Adolescence
    Alberta Sebolt George   *20*
On Interpretation and Historic Sites   *Suzanne B. Schell*   *27*
To Realize Our Museums' Full Potential   *Joan C. Madden*   *35*
Educators Respond to *Museums for a New Century*   *41*
        Some Limitations   *Susan Stitt*
        Implications for Museum Educators   *Danielle Rice*
        Key Issues   *Anna Slafer*
        Internal Growth   *Carol B. Stapp*
The Uncertain Profession: Perceptions and Directions   *48*
        Introduction   *Carol B. Stapp*
        A Questionable Attitudinal Survey   *Lonn Taylor*
        Strength in Ambiguity   *Judith White*
        Our Work Is Good for People   *Danielle Rice*
        Key Issues   *Judith Landau*
        Eisner and Dobbs's Generalizations
        Eisner and Dobbs's Recommendations
Professional Standards for Museum Educators *American Association of*
        Museums Standing Professional Committee on Education   *60*
        Preface   *Patterson B. Williams*
MER at Twenty: Some Observations on Museum Education
    Kenneth Starr   *66*
Museums and the Future of Education   *Joel N. Bloom and Ann Mintz*   *71*

"Excellence and Equity: Education and the Public Dimension of Museums"
   American Association of Museums Task Force on Museum Education   79
      Introduction   *Bonnie Pitman*
      "Excellence and Equity:" Excerpts from the Report
      The Diverse Potential of Education in Museums   *James Affolter*
      Education: *A* Responsibility or *the* Responsibility?   *Nina Archabal*
      Museum Education and Ideals   *Edmund Barry Gaither*
      The Importance of "And"   *Elaine Heumann Gurian*
      Museum Literacy and "Visitor Literacy"   *Paul G. Heltne*
      Museums in Cultural and Temporal Context   *Roger Mandle*
      Museums' Social Contract   *Scott T. Swank*

REFLECTING ON THINGS AND THEORY

Introductions
Looking   *John Fines*   97
Were Those Indians Hit by Cars?   *Robert Sullivan*   99

Object Knowledge: Every Museum Visitor an Interpreter
   Thomas J. Schlereth   102
Defining Museum Literacy   *Carol B. Stapp*   112
      Afterword
Object Contemplation: Theory into Practice   *Patterson B. Williams*   118
Responses to Schlereth, Stapp, and Williams   123
      From What to Why   *Joan C. Madden*
      Unhanding the Visitor   *Ken Yellis*
Interpreting History through Objects   *Barbara G. Carson*   129
      Afterword
The Missing Link: The Role of Orientation in Enriching the Museum
      Experience   *Robert L. Wolf*   134
      Afterword   *Barbara L. Wolf*
Vision and Culture: The Role of Museums in Visual Literacy
   Danielle Rice   144
      E. D. Hirsch's Art Terms in *Cultural Literacy*
Museums and Knowledge: The Responsibility to Open Minds   *Lisa Roberts*   153
Naive Notions and the Design of Science Museum Exhibits
   Minda Borun   159
Passionate and Purposeful: Adult Learning Communities   *Luke Baldwin,*
   Sharlene Cochrane, Constance Counts, Joan Dolamore, Martha McKenna,
   and Barbara Vacarr   162
Museum Visitors and the Development of Understanding
   Eleanor Duckworth   168

Sending Them Home Alive   *Anita Rui Olds*   174
Museum Multicultural Education for Young Learners   *Joseph H. Suina*   179

CONSIDERING THE MUSEUM EXPERIENCE

Introductions
New Directions for Research   *Judy Diamond*   187
Evaluating Visitors' Conversations with Exhibits   *Mark St. John*   191

Back to the Future: A Call for Coordinated Research Programs in
   Museums   *Mary Ellen Munley*   196
   Afterword
Visitor Participation in Formative Exhibit Evaluation
   Patricia A. McNamara   204
Do Museums Have "Curriculum"?   *Valorie Beer*   209
The Family Museum Experience: Implications from Research
   Lynn D. Dierking   215
   Afterword
The Family Museum Experience: A Review of the Literature
   Marcia Brumit Kropf   222
Beyond "Aha!": Motivating Museum Visitors   *Marlene Chambers*   230
Understanding Demographic Data on Zoo Visitors   *Barbara A. Birney*
   and Carolyn Heinrich   233

PUTTING PLANS INTO PRACTICE

Introductions
Ideas on Informal Learning and Teaching   *Susan M. Mayer*   243
Inviting the Public to Learn in Art Museums   *Vasundhara Prabhu*   246
A Personal Viewpoint   *Zora Felton*   249

Decentralizing Interpretation: Developing Museum Education Materials
   with and for Schools   *Peter S. O'Connell*   251
Education Programs for Older Adults   *Elizabeth M. Sharpe*   262
   Afterword
Case Studies: Museum Programs for Older Adults   268
Learning about Reptiles and Amphibians: A Family Experience
   Judith White, Dale Marcellini, and Sharon Barry   276
Student Interpreters: Narrowing the Gap between Visitor and Exhibit
   Karen A. Hensel with Merryl Kafka   279
The University Gallery as a Field Setting for Teacher Education
   Marian L. Martinello and Mauricio Gonzalez   286

Master Teaching in an Art Museum *Philip Yenawine*   *294*
Addressing Community Needs: The Pontiac Art Center *Ann Treadwell*   *299*
    Afterword
Role-Playing in Children's Museums *Jim LaVilla-Havelin*   *307*
Theater Techniques in an Aquarium or a Natural History Museum
    Patricia Rutowski   *312*
Current Approaches to Interpretation in Zoos
    edited by Janet S. Jackson-Gould   *317*
        Designed to Be Interpreted *Sharon Kramer and John Gwynne*
        An Integrative Process for Exhibit Design *Jon Charles Coe*
        High-Tech Interactive Exhibits *Howard Litwak*
        Low-Tech Interactive Exhibits *James F. Peterson*
        The Use of Humor in Zoological Interpretation *Linda Taylor*
        Entertainment and Education: Antonyms or Allies? *Catherine Tompson*
        Theater in a Zoo? *Rosemary Harms*

THINKING ABOUT OURSELVES AND OUR FIELD

Introductions
On Professional Knowing *Teresa K. LaMaster*   *331*
Your Private Temple: Fighting Change *Richard Mühlberger*   *334*

Getting It Down on Paper *Ken Yellis*   *337*
Education for Excellent Interpretation *Robert C. Birney*   *346*
    Introduction *William Tramposch*
Concept, Method, and Professional Exchange *Candace T. Matelic*   *351*
Training for Museum Education Professionals *Nina Jensen and*
    Mary Ellen Munley   *355*
    Afterword *Nina Jensen*
Preparation for Empowerment *Diane Brigham*   *362*
The Whole Audience Catalogue   *368*
    Introduction *George E. Hein*
    Questioning Premises *Carol B. Stapp*
    Touchstones *Dennis O'Toole*
    Teaching and Learning and Being *Mary Worthington*
    A Visitor's View *Arminta Neal*

Contributors   *375*
Index   *383*

Preface

Since 1973, the Museum Education Roundtable (MER), an organization of professionals dedicated to the use of museums and cultural institutions as educational resources, has published a professional journal, originally called *Roundtable Reports* and renamed the *Journal of Museum Education* in 1985. In 1984, MER published its first book, *Museum Education Anthology, Perspectives on Informal Learning: A Decade of Roundtable Reports, 1973–1983.* That benchmark publication, which became a best-seller, was a significant accomplishment for the field of museum education in general and for MER in particular. The enthusiastic reception the anthology received from all corners of the museum profession reflected the growing interest in museum education thought and practice.

Since the publication of that first anthology, MER has matured as an organization. It celebrated its 20th anniversary in 1989. Once an all-volunteer group, MER now has paid administrative staff, and the *Journal of Museum Education* is professionally edited and designed. MER's development has paralleled that of the field of museum education. Soon after the *Museum Education Anthology* was issued, the American Association of Museums (AAM) published *Museums for a New Century,* which focused renewed attention on learning in museums. Then, in 1989, the AAM Standing Professional Committee on Education adopted "Professional Standards for Museum Educators" (see page 60). This year, the AAM has issued *Excellence and Equity: Education and the Public Dimension of Museums,* a major policy document to guide museums in the years ahead (see page 79).

This second anthology, *Patterns in Practice: Selections from the Journal of Museum Education,* reflects the maturation of our field, reports on its evolution, and reminds us of our diversity. Introspective essays challenge us to reexamine our goals, our attitudes, our work, and our audiences. With passion and insight, the authors encourage us to rethink our philosophies and take a fresh look at the important work we do in our museums. The liveliness of the pieces in this volume mirror the vitality of our field and the energy of our colleagues.

Patterns in Practice was made possible by a number of those colleagues. Members of the MER Board of Directors, 1984–91, marshaled the resources to ensure continuous publication and increased professionalization of the *Journal of Museum Education.* Mary Alexander, Judith Landau, Ken Yellis, and I formed the committee that coordinated the anthology. Baiba Sube Lennard, Steve Pike, Sarah Ridley, and

A. T. Stephens headed the fund-raising and public relations activities. Jane Lusaka, MER's administrative consultant, deftly handled many organizational details. Letitia Doggett, Randi Korn, Judith Landau, Teresa LaMaster, Karen Luetjen, Jane Lusaka, Britt Raphling, Sarah Ridley, and Amy Singel assisted with the tedious but necessary task of word processing. Christopher Buchanan performed yeoman service proofreading the index. Publication costs were supported by the Institute of Museum Services Professional Services Program, which provided matching funds.

We are especially grateful for the professional services of three individuals: Ann Hofstra Grogg and Ellen Cochran Hirzy, who edited the articles and generously shared their extensive experience with the anthology committee, and Polly Sexton, who designed the book and related promotional materials.

Patterns in Practice is dedicated to Suzanne B. Schell, a beloved friend and colleague to many journal contributors and readers. Her untimely death in 1989 diminished the immediate world of those who knew her and the larger world of museum education. Suzanne was associated with the Museum Education Roundtable from 1970. By her example, she challenged her colleagues on the journal's editorial committee to greater clarity; her broad experience with history museums resulted in two of the journal's finest issues, "Interpreting Historic Sites and the Built Environment" (vol. 10, no. 3 [1985]) and "Heritage Education: Teaching a Preservation Ethic," (vol. 13, no. 2 [1988]). As a MER board member, she guided the organization's inaugural long-range plan from concept to implementation; her wry humor and sly grin lightened many meetings. We miss her.

Ten years ago in *Roundtable Reports* (vol. 7, no. 2 [1982]), John Fines wrote about his evolution as a teacher, describing his philosophy and his stages of development:

> Beware, dear reader, of assuming that because . . . programmed behaviours may be learned that you can put them into action without first analysing what *your* [beginning stage] is. For it will be different, it should be different, and will involve many different patterns and sequences of learning. I, in describing [my stages of development as a teacher], am not setting up a model to follow, but a framework whose constituents are variable, a way for you to examine how you might work out how you work and how you might work better.

We who worked on this anthology challenge you, dear reader, to use it to measure your own work, to guide you as you lay out your plans, to frame your thoughts, to refresh your spirit. Consider it a reference, a directory to others with experience and vision. We hope *Patterns in Practice* will encourage and stimulate you as you "work out how you work and how you might work better."

Susan K. Nichols
Chair, *Patterns in Practice* Committee
December 1991

COMING OF AGE

INTRODUCTION

The Museum's Role in a Multicultural Society

Claudine K. Brown

Culture in a societal context is the integrated pattern of human knowledge, belief, and behavior that depends upon a person's capacity for learning and transmitting knowledge to succeeding generations. Museums in American society are primary repositories devoted to the procurement, care, study, and display of cultural artifacts and objects of lasting interest and value.

As we approach the 21st century, museums around the globe are beginning to examine whose culture is being preserved and whose is not, from whose point of view the story is being told and whose point of view is being suppressed or distorted, whose culture is being respected and whose culture is being demeaned. In this country we are confronting these issues head-on as we watch the face of the nation change. We are living with the knowledge that by the year 2000 the word "minority" will have a completely different meaning, and we are espousing the notion of a cultural plurality.

The primary issues for museums of all types are cultural equity and equal access. In confronting these issues, the many cultural institutions that purport to interpret American life and the artistic endeavors of American people are beginning to reexamine the entity we call "the community."

Who Are Our Communities?

I have been concerned for some time at the easy codification of "the community." By definition, a "community" is an interacting population of various kinds of individuals in a common location. These individuals often share a common history or common societal, economic, or political interests. The community is not solely an ethnic group, a neighborhood, or the residents of a defined area. From the moment that we are born we find ourselves integrally involved with one community or another and with many different communities simultaneously.

In museums, the term "community" often refers to that audience whose needs we are not meeting: the poor, or in some instances specific ethnic groups. In truth, a community is any group of individuals who have the potential of being members of an institution's visiting public. As Barry Gaither and many others have recommended, if we were to draw concentric circles around our institutions, we would be able to identify potential visitors by their proximity.

Once we have identified groups with fairly easy access to our institutions who are not attendees, we must concern ourselves with whether our offerings are of interest to them and concurrently whether they have reason to believe they would be welcome at our institutions.

How Do We Presently Serve Diverse Communities?

Over the past few years, many of us have tried a variety of methodologies to engage the interest of a wide range of ethnic groups and to encourage their visitation of our institutions. We have done special mailings and advertising for culturally specific exhibitions and programs to targeted communities; we have initiated collaborative programs with schools having a particular ethnic makeup. We have sponsored cultural festivals and special events; and we have offered outreach programs in underserved communities. We have convened focus groups, advisory boards, and in some instances brought non-European Americans onto our boards of trustees. We have hired more diverse staffs and recruited minority interns.

We have nonetheless often seen only minimal progress; and we have also witnessed some disturbing trends. Often these new audiences come to our institutions for programs and exhibitions that reflect their own cultures, but they do not return for other high-quality programs concerning other cultures. Some institutions have engaged in major membership recruitment efforts and targeted ethnic social organizations. The results have more often than not been most discouraging. Additionally, if the entire staff of an institution is not made aware that a particular underserved audience is being courted and should be made welcome, we have sometimes faced a situation in which the vision of management is not shared by the support staff and target audiences are the unwitting recipients of ill will on the part of guards, information desk staff, food service employees, and other service providers. Our efforts have frequently been hit or miss and seasonal, and the responses of our desired new audiences have been similar.

I suggest that we can attribute this lackluster response to our efforts to two distinct factors. The first is inconsistency. When an institution only programs for African Americans during Black History Month, it is no surprise that the largest turnout of black Americans is in February. I have also heard colleagues complain that when they do programs with signage for the deaf, deaf audiences rarely attend. There is a certain arrogance at work when a public program staff member does one program each month with signage, assuming that of all the institution's offerings this is the only program that appeals to deaf audiences. And as most programs with signage do not solicit response, we often assume that attendance is poor when in fact it may not be. If we begin not with black history or signage as a goal but with the notion of community within the context of social and human development, we will be able to define approaches to audience development that acknowledge ethnic and ability differences while taking into consideration similarities that grow out of the human experience.

The second issue that affects our inability to maintain "ethnic" audiences once we have gotten them through our doors involves our very limited way of viewing these groups. Our seduction of and newfound love for a new ethnic group each season gives rise to what one of my colleagues calls the flavor-of-the-month syndrome. This syndrome also suggests that there are easy ways of programming for these groups because their issues are simplistic. Often the scope of our programming involves booking a dance company, doing hands-on ethnic crafts workshops, having a great ethnic icon speak, and arranging for bilingual interpreters. While I don't seek to diminish these programs, I do fault the programmers for frequently failing to represent more than one point of view, for dealing with the issues of these cultures in isolation and not as they affect others, and for being reluctant to listen to youthful and radical voices.

Alternative Ways of Viewing Communities

It is our inability to view non-European persons within the broader community context that most hinders our efforts in the area of effective audience development. With this in mind, I would like to consider four types of communities that are representative of the broader American experience. Though not bound by ethnicity, these groupings enable us to identify ethnic enclaves within a social, historical, and developmental context. Further, these groups give credence to the complexities of the human experience and enable us to look at Latino men as fathers, Asian women as managers, Caribbean men as educators, and African-American women as union organizers. This method for considering our communities allows us to look at ethnic groups by examining the many roles that they play in the many communities they find themselves in. The four communities I will focus on are the family, peer groups, educational communities, and the neighborhood and workplace.

Family as Community

The community of family imparts the fundamental body of learning that shapes our formative years. Within the context of families we learn speech, how to stand upright, social interaction with others, and common courtesy. Our families can of course include the many individuals who contribute to our well-being, who are also known as our extended families.

While many museums have family programs, most don't look to these types of programs as endeavors geared toward increasing participation by more diverse audiences. Family programs are ideal for this purpose, but they must be reconsidered in terms of their structure if they are to become mechanisms for audience development. These programs must be responsive in terms of time, space, cost, and logistics so that they can accommodate family groups having different types of life-styles and needs. Types of programs I recommend include:

■ parent-child programs in which parents have briefings alone as well as time with their children so that they can take a competent leadership role in the shared experience

■ foster grandparents co-parenting programs in which children interact with seniors and single adults who function as interpreters or facilitators in regularly scheduled programs

■ special programs for noncustodial parents that facilitate their understanding of their children's needs in a nonthreatening interactive manner

■ programs for volunteers and interns that provide child care.

All these programs look at ways of serving families that recognize parents and children in the role of teacher and/or learner. They are also programs that see museums as service providers as well as places where visitors can come to learn, be entertained, or just relax.

Peer Group Communities

Peer groups can be educators who are off during the summer, adolescents doing a class assignment together, or friends just looking for something of interest to do together. They can be seniors from senior citizen centers, tourists, docents from other institutions, or Brownie troops engaging in activities that will help them get badges. Peer groups often share particular commonalities. They are often of similar age; they have shared interests, commitments, or purposes; and they sometimes have similar expectations based upon their common orientation to our institutions.

Within ethnic communities there are social clubs, civic organizations, service organizations, and block associations that attend to the articulated needs and concerns of their members. There are also many types of informal gatherings of neighbors and friends who form peer groups as a result of proximity, common purpose, and shared interest. The interests and concerns of these formal and informal groups need to be identified and considered as they relate to the mission, collections, and programmatic possibilities of an institution. They can then be translated into viable programs and exhibitions that can be culturally specific, cross-cultural, and cross-class.

Educational Communities

While museums have enjoyed continued success with school groups, mostly with elementary school audiences, there are other age groups and educational constituencies we know are neglected or underserved. There are many successful programs for adolescents, and most museums offer internships for college students. I would nonetheless suggest that the term "educational institution" needs to be more broadly defined and the mechanisms for collaboration need to be reconsidered and expanded on.

Educational institutions serve a wide variety of audiences, many of which are overlooked when we engage in audience development initiatives. Special attention should be given to continuing education and certificate programs. Often large segments of underserved communities have not had opportunities for educational advancement, and they are frequently in programs that take place after work hours. Efforts need to be made to accommodate these groups.

There are other natural collaborations we should consider. American history museums are ideal venues for new immigrants who are studying to meet citizenship requirements. Teachers in these programs should be invited to use our institutions. College professors should be encouraged to teach sessions or entire courses in museum galleries, and they should be offered classroom space when it is available. Alliances should be made with community centers, especially where there is an underserved population that does not speak English. Museums should make an effort to have ongoing foreign language programs that address issues of importance to these groups in their new communities. Such programs can provide historical understanding of the environment new immigrants find themselves in and can offer them an opportunity to share their traditions with their neighbors.

Neighborhood and Workplace

While we are making sense of our place in a school community, we have the concurrent responsibility for coming to terms with our neighborhood community. In our neighborhoods we begin to deal with definition of personality that is influenced by our race, class, and age; by our proximity to and interaction with other communities; and by our overall neighborhood personality. Neighborhoods are imbued with personality when we ascribe the following terms: urban or suburban, inner-city, middle-income, or gentrified. All of these factors help to shape one's sense of self and the role one plays in a neighborhood community. Our school and neighborhood communities represent those places where we spend the greatest amount of time and make bonds that last for a lifetime. Accordingly, every museum should see itself as a neighborhood museum. If an institution is not accessible to the individuals who must of necessity pass by its portals each day, then it is not a truly public institution.

Once we reach adulthood, there are a number of environments that can become communities and affect how we perceive ourselves. The primary entity that affects us in this manner is our work environment. But we might also be strongly influenced by other environments that we might find ourselves exposed to as a matter of personal choice or need, or necessity, or societal determinant. These might include hospitals, recreational facilities, correctional facilities, religious institutions, recreational facilities, and cultural institutions. In many of these places, we learn a language, a culture, rules, and sometimes a specific way of dressing. Our very survival is dependent upon our effective mastery of the tasks set before us and our grasp of the political situations that we find ourselves in.

Our Communities Are Not Homogeneous

In the world of work we find ourselves confronting issues daily that are often the premises for museum exhibitions, but these exhibitions are not pitched to us as workers. Exhibitions that deal with process, history, collecting, recording data, creation, and interpretation are all issues we face in the workplace. New materials in the construction and technology industries have found their way into art museums. Political issues being interpreted in history museums have antecedents in contemporary issues. Common objects we use today were preceded by similar objects made from different materials. Societies throughout the world have created mechanisms and systems for solving problems that have applications in the world today. Objects of beauty and wonder transcend ethnicity, race, and class.

What I am saying in a more concrete way is that:

■ African-American children from Southeast Washington, D.C., would come to see "Dinosaurs Alive"

■ workers of all ethnic backgrounds would find something of interest in a Jacob Lawrence or Lewis Hine show

■ anyone with an interest in nature or the environment might see something worthwhile in a painting by Albert Bierstadt or Vincent Van Gogh.

There is no validity in programming for the homogeneous Latino community or a singular African-American community, because no such animals exist. Often when you target a people living in an area, you exclude persons of the same ethnic background from different classes and with different ideological and political points of view. Be wary of the community representative who purports to speak for all persons of that ethnic group, for while he or she may be an accepted leader in the community, no community is so simplistic that only one point of view prevails.

Pose thoughtful questions that speak to the human experience. What are the primary issues facing this community? (At one point in the Anacostia neighborhood of Washington, D.C., it was the rat, and that issue became the subject of one of the most innovative exhibitions of the past few decades.) How does this community view the museum? How can the museum meet the needs of the community? How do we provide means of access that allow human beings of every age to understand how the museum can serve them and how they, in turn, can serve the institution? Museums are public institutions. They receive substantial support from public sources. It is our mission to preserve, exhibit, and interpret these collections for the public—not some of the public, but all of the public. Though we can't give all of the public what they want all of the time, we can provide more of the people with an honest representation of their achievements and contributions in this society. The time to begin is yesterday, and the place to begin is where you stand.

INTRODUCTION

Evolution of the Field: Historical Context

Barbara Franco

Museums are changing. This statement is as true today as it was 25 years ago when I first began working in a museum. I suspect it will be equally true 25 years from now. In some respects, change seems antithetical to the notion of museums as venerable institutions housed in granite and marble buildings that store permanent collections. We are keepers and preservers. On the other hand, museums are cultural institutions, and recognizing that culture is always in flux, it is appropriate that our institutions and profession continue to change. Frank Oppenheimer, quoted in the essay by Joel Bloom and Ann Mintz, states, "It is a mistake to think that preserving culture is distinct from transmitting it through education." Oppenheimer, founder of the Exploratorium, defines museums as cultural institutions that both preserve and transmit culture, and in doing so he identifies the inherent duality in the mission of museums.

Duality of mission—preservation and education—has existed from the beginnings of our profession and is reflected in most institutional mission statements. As Bloom and Mintz point out, most institutions have education as a basic element in their charters, but the meaning of education as it is carried out can vary considerably. The "public" museum has encompassed the role of museums in setting and maintaining cultural standards, expressed by Benjamin Ives Gilman of the Boston Museum of Fine Arts, as well as John Cotton Dana's vision of broad public participation in museums. The writings on museum theory throughout this century reflect similar tensions that are expressed in a variety of juxtapositions: inside versus outside; warehouse of valuable objects versus educational institution; professionalism versus community involvement; formal versus informal; expert role versus public service. The most recent expression of this juxtaposition of values is the dual public responsibility identified in *Excellence and Equity: Education and the Public Dimension of Museums,* a report of the American Association of Museums Task Force on Museum Education, completed in 1991. Most discussions of museum theory and practice return to this dual mission. These polarities of values and purposes appear to be a constant in our profession, and the changes that have occurred and continue to occur can be seen as movement back and forth between the roles of expert, keeper, authority at one end of the spectrum and public servant, communicator, community participant at the other.

The changes taking place in museum education can be understood within the larger context of an evolving museum environment in which the current trend is toward an expanded public service role. Museum education in recent years has also moved toward greater public service. Many museum education departments established in the 1960s and 1970s were structured to convey expert information through formal programs, mainly aimed at organized school groups. Exhibits were assumed to be authoritative but inaccessible to the nonexpert. Education departments became the public interpreters of expert curatorial knowledge through guided tours, lectures, and school programs. Educators were not expected to have expertise but to communicate it. Operating in an institutional culture that valued expertise above communication, education departments, as my friends in museum education always reminded me, were relegated to the basements of most institutions.

As museums generally move toward a greater public service role, an obvious shift is taking place in museum education as well. Formal tours are giving way to informal programs; cognitive learning objectives are being replaced by affective learning; school tours are being joined by programs for families and the adult general public. Some of these changes are responses to demographic trends that include the increased numbers of adults over 65 and the life cycle of the baby boom generation. They also reflect changes in educational theory that incorporate new research and validate multiple learning styles. Museum education is also responding to changes in the definition of education in our society from something that only occurs early in one's life in a formal school setting to continuing, lifelong learning in self-directed, informal settings that include museums, media, and communication technologies.

External factors are responsible for many of the changes taking place in museums. Cultural diversity and multiculturalism have entered our professional vocabulary and challenged museums as cultural institutions to reassess our reference point from a single dominant culture to a composite of diverse and distinct cultures. In this process, Amina Dickerson's comments suggest the important role that Afro-American and other community-based museums play in our profession as models. Along the spectrum of expert versus public service, these museums cluster at the public service pole. Their strength lies in their responsiveness to their communities. Mainstream museums can learn from them how to reach out to new audiences and be inclusive of community and public. Conversely, these community-centered museums are challenged to move toward greater professionalization by expanding collections, encouraging scholarship, and developing expertise in their subject areas. Afro-American museums are changing as well, but they are moving toward a more expert role.

Recognizing the essential duality of our profession, the current and future changes in museums can be seen as shifts between two poles. The current shift in museums toward the public service role is changing the nature of museum education. Education staff are increasingly incorporated into the exhibit development process as exhibits become learning environments with greater opportunities for self-directed, affective learning that includes visitor participation. Rather than viewing education programs as add-ons to make otherwise inaccessible expertise understandable, museums increasingly view education as integrated into all programs. A shift to external orientation in many institutions explains our new interest with audience. Audience surveys, evaluation, and community advisory committees are some of the many ways that museums are looking outward for direction as well as depending on internal expertise. Within institutions, education staffs are moving toward greater professionalization and expertise, while curators are being asked to be communicators who are public oriented.

Change can be both liberating and frightening. If we can accept change as a constant in museums, we can begin to understand the nature of the changes and how to manage them as they affect our institutions. The challenge to museums now, as always, is to harness the energy and creativity produced by the inherent tension of our dual purpose as we learn to balance competing goals, continue excellence and high standards, but remain responsive to our public audience.

Afro-American Museums: A Future Full of Promise

Amina J. Dickerson

There are an estimated 100 Afro-American museums in the country, a fact that surprises many people. They are located in such unexpected places as Wilberforce, Ohio; Omaha, Nebraska; Orangeburg, South Carolina; and Providence, Rhode Island, as well as major metropolitan cities. They collect everything from paintings and sculpture to archeological remains, utilitarian objects, and historical memorabilia. They present an exciting array of interpretive programs: tours, workshops, lectures, dramatic presentations, and seminars. Their staffs vary in size from 25 full-time paid employees to a sole director/tour guide/board chair. Some obtain funds from local school systems or arts funding agencies; others rely on the salary of a dedicated bibliophile who has committed his or her meager funds to keep a dream alive. Still others receive direct appropriations from city and state governments as well as grants from the National Endowments for the Arts and the Humanities. More than collections of curiosities or Pantheonic buildings, people are their priority.

The tradition of Afro-American museums is not new, despite the lack of public awareness. Their histories extend back more than 100 years to institutions founded on the campuses of black universities in the South. That history continues today with the recent establishment of Afro-American museums in Philadelphia and Los Angeles, with more planned for New Orleans, Atlanta, and other cities.

This article explores Afro-American museums in the United States, their methods of collecting and of interpretation, and some of the challenges they will encounter as they enter the new century.

Mission and Philosophy

The concerns black museum professionals have are, in many instances, common to the field: lack of staff and funds, inadequate space, a desire for capital expansion, a need for better collections management and more research. So what makes them different? Perhaps it is their Afro-centric, activist point of view. The number and range of these institutions clearly illustrate the long-standing desire of Afro-Americans for institutions that are controlled by and responsive to the needs expressed by the unique communities in which they reside. Such museums have the

Roundtable Reports 9, nos. 2–3 (Spring/Summer 1984): 14–18.

means of making people more aware of the black presence in the world, as articulated by Afro-Americans.

Thus, the role of interpretation is essential for these institutions: it is their raison d'être. Black museums provide unique opportunities to reexamine, and in some cases redefine, history, culture, and the arts. Utilizing the "new scholarship" in black history, Afro-Americans—be they curators, historians, educators, or audience—are able to place the events of the past, significant or mundane, in a context in which they can be critically examined or validated. In the museums, black creative and intellectual expressions combine to promote a black esthetic while providing an environment in which it is manifest. They function not only as archive, repository, and exhibition center but also as gathering space, community forum, and cultural refuge. Within and outside of their communities, they generate an understanding of Afro-American historical origins and the vitality and continuity of these cultural traditions. Barry Gaither, director of the Museum of the National Center of Afro-American Artists in Boston, said in an article in *Museum News* in February 1982, "Our presence informs and reforms our neighborhoods."

In a traditional view, the scope of the program, some of the interpretive methods, even the subject matter of the exhibitions may not be considered appropriate. However, it is just this control of choices and priorities that Afro-American museums hold precious. Most of them do fulfill basic museological functions: they collect, preserve, exhibit, and interpret the material evidence of the complex black past. But even within their special universe there is a sentiment that the traditional reputation of museums does not communicate what Afro-American museums do. Marta Vega, director of the Caribbean Cultural Center, has often maintained that "museum" may not be an appropriate term for the lively, community-conscious approach of black museums. They provide a link, as poet Larry Neal said, "to the deepest and most profound aspects of our ancestry." This ancestry reinforces communal obligations.

Afro-American museums sense in their work an opportunity to reshape the role of museums and their relationships with the public. Their growing numbers and long history attest to their ability to do so.

History
The earliest recorded Afro-American museum was founded at Hampton Institute, Hampton, Virginia, in 1868. The College Museum was started by Samuel Chapman as part of his overall goal to provide higher education and economic survival skills for freedmen of color. Its outstanding collection of art and ethnographic materials includes objects from sub-Saharan Africa, Oceania, Asia, and Native American Indian cultures as well as works by contemporary African-American artists (including the prestigious Harmon Collection from the Harlem Renaissance period). Of particular note is the 1,400-object African collection acquired in 1911 from Dr. William Sheppard. Sheppard, an

explorer and missionary, had collected the materials between 1890 and 1910 in present-day Zaire, in central Africa. Today, the museum collection is a primary resource for scholars as well as an important source for loans of Afro-American and African material culture and artworks.

In Washington, D.C., the Moorland-Spingarn Research Center at Howard University has a history nearly as long. Its earliest acquisitions included antislavery materials donated by Lewis Tappan, a New York abolitionist, in 1873. It was not formally incorporated into the university's programs until 1914. Later, under Dr. Dorothy Porter, a pioneer in identifying and acquiring materials on the peoples of the African diaspora who headed the center for more than 25 years, the holdings were increased substantially, elevating the collection to international stature. Similar museum collections exist at Fisk University in Tennessee, Atlanta University in Georgia, and Tuskegee Institute in Alabama, among others.

Another form of museum activity was generated by Afro-Americans organizing displays and exhibits for national and international expositions beginning around 1895 and continuing until 1940. The historian Stephen Jones reports that large exhibitions of black technological, scientific, and commercial endeavors were organized in separate "Negro" halls in Atlanta in 1895, Nashville in 1897, and Charleston, South Carolina, just after the turn of the century. These displays were fully representative of industrial activity of Afro-Americans at the time. The largest exposition of black material took place in Jamestown, Virginia, for the 1907 tercentenary. More than 50,000 displays were mounted in the largest public presentation of Afro-American material culture ever amassed. It took 50 agents more than a year to gather material for this landmark event, coordinated by the National Negro Business Association. Further, one of the finest American artists of the day, Henry O. Tanner, had his work exhibited in Paris in 1900, in the Pan-American Exposition of 1901, and in the St. Louis Exposition of 1904.

During the era of the Harlem Renaissance, private collections grew to great dimensions and were made public. The most famous assemblage resulted from a personal vision of a Puerto Rican immigrant, Arthur A. Schomburg. This immense collection was made part of the New York Public Library in 1926 and has served scholars the world over, including Langston Hughes, W.E.B. DuBois, Alex Haley, and Leon Damas. The gallery at the Schomburg Center for Research in Black Culture features changing exhibitions of the permanent collections of paintings, sculpture, photographs, and artifacts, and it organizes a full schedule of public lectures and tours. Perhaps its most important function, however, is as a research center because of its rare materials on Africans and their descendants in the New World. The Amistad Collection in New Orleans and the Western States Black Research Center are other examples of the museum-cum-archive approach.

Black churches such as Philadelphia's Mother Bethel African Methodist Episcopal (AME) are pillars of the sociopolitical fabric of black America. They have maintained historic records and documents, most of which are used to serve their discrete congregations. Hence, they have received little attention from the general public.

During the late 1950s and extending through the civil rights movement, a new crop of Afro-American museums was founded. Some of these institutions came about as a reaction to a history "either ignored or misrepresented." Others were more concerned with social problems than the muses. All of them sought direct involvement in their communities. Commenting on the period, Duncan Cameron stated, "One of the most visible trends in the 'museum revolution' in North America has been the creation of nonmuseums, by which I mean activities concerned with public education through the medium of exhibits but without dependence on collections of original material."

The founders of these museums were not as concerned about museological practices as they were with a well-defined purpose and audience. This was in sharp contrast to other museums that during the same era were accused of "wandering aimlessly toward undefined goals" by Lothar Witteborg and a host of others assessing the field at the time. In Detroit, Dr. Charles Wright began the Afro-American Museum in 1961, preceded by Margaret Burroughs, artist and educator, who founded the DuSable Museum in Chicago in 1959. The Bicentennial also inspired new museums, such as the Afro-American Historical and Cultural Museum in Philadelphia.

Today, this body of museums is mostly devoted to history and the arts, although one includes a planetarium. The Black American West Museum in Denver is dedicated to black cowboys and blacks in the pioneer movement. Syracuse, New York, has the Community Folk Art Museum, and Washington, D.C., has the Bethune Museum and Archives of Black Women's History. These are but a few: the list is long and continues to grow.

Trends in Development

Despite honorable intentions, meeting social and professional standards is a continuing challenge. In some instances, institutions have not fulfilled their potential. They manage to survive because of the sheer determination of a founding civic leader or local bibliophile, but have not yet managed to put their museums on sound financial and intellectual footing. Others have received levels of local and federal funding, but rarely, it seems, do the amounts compare favorably with awards made elsewhere. Still, they survive.

In the last six years, an organization devoted to providing assistance to black museums and professionals has become an important force representing these institutions. Indeed, without its pioneering work there would be no formal mechanism for communication among the diverse membership. The African American Museums Association (AAMA) is an advocate of institutions committed to the support of African and African-derived cultures. "It defines a relationship for them within the national museum community; it seeks to strengthen them through improved communication, shared resources, technical aid and assistance, and through fund-raising guidance." Joy Ford Austin, executive director, emphasizes that the association's work is just beginning. "At present there is no definite or even comprehensive study on black museums," she said at a recent meeting in Washington, D.C. This is evident from the lack of statistics on staff size, annual budgets, nature and size of collections, and membership—even an accurate count of the number of museums.

AAMA provides workshops and development counseling and initiates advocacy efforts to increase national visibility and funding for these institutions. With grant assistance from the National Endowment for the Humanities, AAMA conducted studies of six representative institutions in 1982–83 in an attempt to get a reading on the status of black museums. Together with an independent two-year study conducted at the Afro-American Historical and Cultural Museum in Philadelphia, some trends are discernible:

■ *Many museums are reevaluating their mission statements and are defining more narrowly the geographic and interpretive scope of their work.* Philadelphia and Detroit, as examples, will be giving less attention to national and international exhibitions and will place more emphasis on state and local research and acquisitions.

■ *The role of research is being given more priority.* Partnerships are being forged with art and cultural historians on an ongoing basis. Consulting scholars are being included more prominently in exhibition planning and research phases, with enhanced scholarship in label copy, catalogs, and conceptual approaches as a result. Partnerships are also providing these scholars, mostly black, with new vehicles for exposure of their own work.

■ *Strong efforts at museum career counseling and professional in-service development have been initiated.* Increased attendance of Afro-Americans and other minorities can be noted at the workshops and seminars of the AAMA, Smithsonian, American Association of Museums, American Association for State and Local History, and regional or local associations. In addition, formal programs, such as internships at a host of museums and the Smithsonian Office of Elementary and Secondary Education's program on museum careers targeted for secondary students, are creating interest in museum work among people who may not have considered such job options. A recent AAMA survey elicited some 300 responses, indicating increased involvement in the museum profession by Afro-Americans. Growing numbers of blacks are enrolled in museum training programs around the country.

■ *The challenge of developing collections is being addressed through more narrowly defined collections policies and aggressive efforts to collect contemporary material culture and archival memorabilia.* Faced with limited to nonexistent funds for acquisitions, Afro-American museums are placing greater emphasis on collecting materials from the 20th century, because they are more readily available than 18th- or 19th-century artifacts and are often less expensive. Also, more attention is being given to refining collections management practices so as to improve the standard of care given the existing collections. At present, there are no figures available on the average size of Afro-American museum collections: they are estimated to range in size from 500 or so objects to the well over 8 million documents being cared for by the Amistad Research Center in New Orleans. Donors are being cultivated, and, as the work of the museums becomes better known, gifts are increasing.

■ *There is greater sophistication in fund-raising and management practices.* Practical experience, seminars, workshops, graduate programs, and greater awareness of museum practices are paying off for Afro-American museums. In Detroit, the city council has appropriated some $3 million for a new building. The Afro-American Historical and Cultural Museum in Philadelphia was recently awarded a $345,000 William Penn Foundation grant to support continued development and staff training, and the Studio Museum in Harlem has a $3.5 million challenge grant campaign under way. These activities demonstrate the growing experience and skill that museum administrators are bringing to bear on their institutions.

Interpretive Programs

Joy Austin will hasten to note that the greatest strength the studies revealed is the "imaginative programs" produced by black museums. Often built on "ideas rather than objects," the museums have developed a strong rapport with their communities through the range of activities they sponsor: tours, workshops, lectures, film programs, concerts, curriculum development, outreach, and others. This work is conducted by museum educators supported by a host of volunteers, students, and museum teachers, although the 1983 directory of black museum professionals lists only three dozen educators. Because the context is one with which they are familiar, youth and adults alike react positively.

At the Anacostia Neighborhood Museum in Washington, D.C., programs not only stretch minds and sharpen critical thinking but also develop cognitive skills. The director of education, Zora Felton, works in close collaboration with local teachers and parents. One result has been bold, simple labels suitable for slow learners as well as those with poor eyesight. A local history project, "A Walk through Old Anacostia," was used in primary grades of nearby schools as part of their curriculum on communities. And because of the involvement of teachers and students in researching and designing the materials, the impact was that much stronger and more long lasting.

After-school programs, like those produced at the Museum of the National Center of Afro-American Artists in Boston, not only supply important learning experiences for children but also provide constructive activities that ease the burden on working parents. At the Studio Museum in Harlem, the education curator, Schroeder Cherry, has developed a junior docent program. Trained to use puppets to orient school groups visiting the museum, these teenagers are given release time from their individual schools to work with the museum. They also assist with tours and workshops. Such a program gives these teenagers professional work experience as well as an opportunity to observe role models. In another program, the museum was awarded contracts by the New York City Board of Education to provide artists-in-residence to selected schools for minimum 12-week periods throughout the year. Not only does the program provide meaningful work for the artists and exposure and training for the students, it strengthens the museum's role as intermediary between artists and the public.

Philadelphia's Afro-American Museum conducts an outreach program, "Museum Roadways," which brings objects, slides, and hands-on activities to the classroom in preparation for a museum visit. At the National Museum of African Art in Washington, D.C., the Education Department has developed informative, attractive orientation materials for teachers that provide information and activities to be used to prepare and reinforce museum visits. Finally, the I. P. Stanback Museum and Planetarium in South Carolina provides special presentations on the cosmos and the creation using slides, music, videotapes, and film. Some of these methods are fundamental to museum education. Others are new twists or approaches to traditional techniques. Still others are experiments that Afro-American museums are attempting to better meet the needs of their audiences.

The Future

The trends seem to indicate the path of the future for Afro-American museums. Cultivating greater resources within their communities is one of the first tasks. This involves building membership—black and nonblack—and making the resources of black museums available to the public at large. Certainly, collections development will present a major challenge, especially since Afro-American museums have only actively entered the collecting game in the last 30 years, too late to compete for some of the more valuable artworks, books, and memorabilia. Unfortunately, such material often languishes in the basements of other museums. Increasing staff size, professional practices, and their public profile will require diligence and hard work.

But perhaps the biggest challenge will be to maintain their responsiveness to black communities. As the emphasis on professionalism grows, great effort must be employed to enable them to remain flexible and open to the ideas presented by their constituents while fulfilling the needs that collections and research will present. Museums are instruments of social change, vehicles for the exchange of ideas, and centers that facilitate communication among people because of the "things" they care for. Afro-American museums also have a responsibility to care for the ideas of the past, to help their constituents prepare for the future. The constant juggling of internal and communal priorities will only become more complicated for black museums in the new age. Judging from their own past, we should expect that they will almost certainly create new solutions.

> We must invent and we must make discoveries—for ourselves and for humanity. We must work out new concepts and try to set afoot a new man.
> —*Frantz Fanon*

References

African American Museums Association. *Blacks in Museums.* Washington, D.C.: African American Museums Association, 1983.

————. *Reports of Self-Study Evaluations of Six Museums: The Afro-American Museum of Detroit, Great Plains Black Museum, I. P. Stanback Museum and Planetarium, African-American Cultural Center, San Francisco Historical Museum.* Washington, D.C.: African American Museums Association, 1982.

"What Lies Ahead for Black History Museums?" *History News* 36, no. 2 (February 1981): entire issue.

Austin, Joy Ford. "Their Face to the Rising Sun: Trends in the Development of Black Museums." *Museum News* 60, no. 3 (January/February 1982): 29–32.

Battle, Thomas C. "A Browser's Guide to Black American Museums." *Black Enterprise* 14, no. 6 (June 1983): 266–68.

————. "Research Centers Document the Black Experience." *History News* 36, no. 2 (February 1981): 8–11.

Burgard, Ralph. "Cultural Cooperation." *Museum News* 61, no. 6 (August 1983): 20–25.

Findlay, Ian. *Priceless Heritage: The Future of Museums.* London: Faber and Faber, 1977.

Harding, Vincent. *Beyond Chaos: Black History and the New Land.* Atlanta, Ga.: Institute of the Black World, 1970.

Hudson, Kenneth. *Museums for the 1980s.* New York: Holmes and Meier, for UNESCO, 1977.

Lewis, Samella. "Beyond Traditional Boundaries." *Museum News* 60, no. 3 (January/February 1982): 41–44.

Linder, Bill R. "Black Genealogy: Basic Steps to Research." Technical Leaflet 135. *History News* 36, no. 2 (February 1981).

Pitman-Gelles, Bonnie. "Beyond Outreach: Museums and Community Organizations." *Museum News* 61, no. 6 (August 1983): 37–40.

Rhodes, Bertha N. *An Afro-American Guide to Museums, Galleries and National Historic Sites.* Baltimore: Bertha Rhodes Press, 1982.

Rushing, Byron. "Afro-Americana—Defining It, Finding It, Collecting It." *Museum News* 60, no. 3 (January/February 1982): 33–40.

Williams, Nancy Anita. "Afro-American Museums: Merging Past and Present." *National Leader* 2, no. 10 (February 1983): 8–9.

Wittlin, Alma A. *Museums: In Search of a Usable Future.* Cambridge, Mass.: MIT Press, 1970.

The Growth of a Program: From Childhood through Adolescence

Alberta Sebolt George

Old Sturbridge Village, an outdoor museum less than 40 years old, has always addressed education as one of its primary functions. In many ways, the focus and thrust of the museum's educational program have grown from seeds planted by the founding family, who consciously included education as a major priority. As they began to conceptualize a plan for the museum, they were guided by criteria that encourage active learning. That direction was reflected in subsequent decisions about site selection, exhibit setting, and mode of presentation. While the museum has a complex history, the focus of its educational mission was shaped by a commitment to provide opportunities for museum visitors to experience the past through participation.

Old Sturbridge Village began as a personal collection that has been strengthened over the years to become an excellent representation of the material culture of rural New England. The collection's primary emphasis is on the common men and women who lived in this region during the nation's first half century, 1790 to 1840.

In the museum's formative stages, the goal of exhibiting objects in contexts as close as possible to their original situations naturally gave rise to a second major area of collecting—historic buildings. The buildings were chosen, studied, moved, and restored at Sturbridge in an effort to complete the museum's statement of community life as it was during the Federalist years.

A third major area of collecting followed that focused on work processes such as blacksmithing, coopering, shoemaking, printing, tinsmithing, basketmaking, and pottery as well as spinning, weaving, and various other women's hand skills. Preservation of the tools of these processes and demonstration of the appropriate skills allowed the museum to go beyond the *what* of history to help people understand the *how* and the *why*. Thus, the learner was directed into the past through the re-creation of authentic period settings and with the assistance and skill of well-trained and costumed staff who breathed life into each exhibit. As we interpreted work processes, historical farming, and household patterns further, we drew more deeply upon the collection of objects and buildings to explain their relationship to the functions they served and the people who used them.

As in many museums, other educational programs developed from these early

Roundtable Reports 9, nos. 2 and 3 (Spring/Summer 1984): 19–22.

collection decisions, and today at Sturbridge a wide variety of creative strategies are employed for presenting the past. All the elements of the museum—the collection (objects, manuscripts, and buildings), the historical landscape and interpretive programs, the historical hand skills and special demonstrations—set the "living history" scene and focus the design of educational programs.

How did this growth happen? In the beginning, the powerful support of Ruth Wells, the museum's first director (and now trustee) served to keep the attention well focused on educational objectives. As a member of the founding family, her tireless efforts, expressed partly in successful fund raising, have helped to bring to fruition the education program as we know it today. The support of subsequent museum directors (Frank Spinney, Alexander Wall, and Crawford Lincoln) and the leadership of administrative staff such as Barnes Riznik pressed the program development in the direction we now know.

Moving beyond these immediate developmental forces, it is important to place the growth of the Sturbridge program within the context of the larger world of the 1960s and early 1970s. The impact on the field of education by the advance of Sputnik in the late 1950s, the influences of educational psychologists and theorists, federal grant monies for research and development created by the Elementary and Secondary Education Act in 1965, and the establishment of the National Endowment for the Humanities and the National Endowment for the Arts (also in 1965) all converged to create a positive climate for the changes that were to emerge in this educational program as well as in others.

The influence of John Dewey and other educational theorists was clearly evident as educators in schools began to ask questions about the nature of teaching and learning, the nature of curriculum materials, the effectiveness of nontraditional learning environments, and the structure and organization of the learning day. Museum professionals were also feeling this influence as they analyzed approaches to teaching, questioned their methods of presentation, focused on the nature of their museums as learning environments, and began to look critically at the relationship of their resources to school programs. In the mid-1960s, both schools and museums were searching for points of intersection at which they could best meet learner needs through creative use of museum resources. The time was right for growth and change.

The archive of program announcements at Old Sturbridge Village confirms that in the first stages of the museum's development, concerns were fairly basic and centered on ways to organize the movement of students through the museum. Here, as elsewhere, students and teachers were welcome to "plan a visit." The museum tried to assist them in arranging their day, organizing their "tour" within the museum, and avoiding interference with other museum visitors. To some extent, the plan was to provide assistance for (and protection from) children as learners. It is no surprise that museums reflected the posture of formal education, which was unsophisticated in the design of field studies.

During the 1960s, the societal climate encouraged both museum and school programs toward integration of theoretical constructs of learning with the subject matter of the museum. This trend had a major impact on program design. As educators and museum professionals sought and explored ways to provide effective learning experiences, they addressed pedagogical issues that formed the basis for programs.

At the time, I was working in a public school system that was deeply involved in curriculum revisions. The impetus for this undertaking had emerged from a concern for the teaching and learning processes. As teachers, we were searching for more effective approaches in our task of helping students to learn. If our students were to develop higher-level thinking skills, we needed more than the resources of our classroom. The real world offered an important and available option.

As we ventured forth to explore field laboratories and plan well-structured field studies, we found Old Sturbridge Village a willing partner. In the mid-1960s, staff at the museum were opening the door to collaboration, asking us to help them learn about our goals and to define the ways in which our curriculum objectives intersected with their museum resources.

In retrospect, I view this as a decade of planning and scene setting. It was time for decision makers to clarify their roles and to define the philosophical direction for programs that were to be tested, revised, implemented, and refined in the 1970s.

The next 10 years provided a time to explore the variables that influence how museum exhibits communicate to the learner. With a surer knowledge of the student audience, the task became one of exploring the ways in which the audience and the museum environment might come together.

Where did we turn? Years of research in education, focusing on both the cognitive (mental operations) and the affective (feelings and values) processes, produced some indicators that were useful to us in developing the philosophical base for our program plan at Old Sturbridge Village. Soon we had several principles that formed the basis for modifying our teaching strategies, not the least of which was the premise that students at every level need to be involved in the learning process in some active way.

While our planning was governed, of course, by the body of knowledge incorporated in Old Sturbridge Village, we worked to integrate that knowledge with effective teaching strategies. The actual experience of the students would determine whether a strategy was effective. Our commitment to field-based education and its significance for strong museum programs grew from this position.

Viewing the field trip as a "field study" allowed us to explain and strengthen the experience because it combined many approaches to learning. Museums such as ours seem to be a natural for this approach, as the collection in context often helps learners form connections. Museums and other field sites encourage students to draw upon a combination of senses in support of their inquiry. These uncommon environments give students an opportunity to strengthen their thinking skills and can be a powerful force in motivating them to extend the depth of their inquiry. At Old Sturbridge Village, the most productive investigations are those that give students an opportunity to explore workable solutions to real-life problems.

By now, the depth of our analysis, and sometimes agony, as we conceptualized a rationale for this program must be evident. However, our frustrations as we observed student groups bewildered by the strangeness and silence of the museum environment prodded us to find a better way. The growth of the museum had made it impossible for students to see all of the village in one day. For student groups that tried to visit each exhibit, the experience seemed to generate only confusion and fatigue. One solution to this problem appeared to be a structure that provided a focus for the day's visit. For example, if students could study the ways in which a farm family satisfied most of its own basic needs, perhaps they would then be prepared to view the general store as the source of other goods and not simply as another collection of unfamiliar objects. The work of family members could serve to focus the study.

By the mid-1970s, after several years of trial, it was recognized that thematic tours were successful approaches to this historical community. Concepts such as family life, work, community decisions, and the like became commonplace. The thematic approach became the major program strategy, with artifact study and room reading the means for gathering data with which to solve problems. The museum teacher's role in these tours was to stimulate the group's own inquiry into the thematic problem and to provide flexible and resourceful assistance to students in their efforts to make sense of the environment.

Ten years later, the themes are still present, although they sometimes disappear as the group's day is tailored by pretour planning with the teacher. This approach helps students understand why they are coming to the museum and which questions to ask while exploring this rich environment. Today, we suggest variations within themes of family, work, and community as starting points for exploring life in the early 19th century.

As you can imagine, the success of this in-depth approach often caused tensions within exhibit spaces. What we needed was a 20th-century space where we could encourage participation, extend our directions, and provide the support necessary to achieve the instructional objectives.

In 1974, we dedicated a new education building that provided this environment. With its architecturally open plan, this building of wood, brick, and glass provides several teaching areas, or studios, linked by a series of ramps and steps. Each studio serves a thematic focus and is equipped with appropriate artifacts (diaries, account books, recipes, maps, farm tools, kitchen wares, spinning wheels, and looms) to provide the teacher with tools and the learner with avenues to the past. This multilevel building moves students through a series of activities in which to explore aspects of the life of the early 19th-century New Englander. Typical tasks such as spinning wool and weaving, grinding and flailing corn, winnowing grains, fence building, open-hearth baking from recipes of the period, wood graining, stenciling, and printing engage the learner in discovering the past. Role-playing as members of the early 19th-century community, participating in re-created school lessons, and discussing issues faced by families in that era are frequently used techniques. It is our experience that these strategies increase the chance that students will be able to articulate generalizations about history.

The most significant audience for us in the area of program development has been classroom teachers. Paramount in everything we have done in the design of teaching spaces or educational programs is our work with teachers in helping them make more effective use of our resources. Teachers needed to be brought into the planning process if the program was to mature and, in fact, have any long-term impact on students.

In 1971, I joined the museum staff to develop a model teacher training program that would integrate our resources into the learning process for all students at all levels. This program, now [1984] in its 14th year, has trained students throughout Massachusetts and New England and in scattered areas across the country. As our skill matured, we involved other museum professionals in our annual training session and have often traveled to their sites to help build and extend this process of training teachers.

We have worked with a broad range of experienced and new teachers, including many with little knowledge of how to use these uncommon resources. Our work is continually sharpened by an awareness of the changing directions or emerging issues in public education. We have worked hand in hand with teachers' organizations and professional associations to avoid isolating ourselves from the primary world of formal education.

It was only through teacher involvement that we attained the concept of field study. The classroom teacher's role in prefield preparation and postfield synthesis took on a new reality and added balance and wholeness to the investigation. From this vantage point, our materials development program emerged. As a learning environment, the museum's buildings, objects, and demonstrations of work processes are supported by the research collection of manuscripts and other primary sources. These not only provide documentation for our interpretive presentation but also are important sources in our teaching. Teachers and students frequently asked for additional data. Primary sources, such as land use maps, diaries, letters, account books, landscape paintings, and portraits, provided the evidence to assist their inquiry.

Originally available as resource packets, these sources now constitute an extensive materials program. The materials are distributed nationally to teachers of history and the social studies. They present new ways to use the museum's collection and challenge students in their inquiry.

The impact of our work with teachers can be felt in every aspect of our program. Every document or activity has successfully evolved from an intensive pilot program in a teacher's classroom. More important, teachers have served us as consultants or "adjunct faculty," often developing a special area of expertise that has been mutually beneficial in future training sessions.

For example, one of our teacher consultants has done extensive research on gravestones. His interest moved from the conceptual level to assisting his students in extending their knowledge of people in the early 19th century by studying gravestones. Each year, this teacher directs a session of our teacher workshop, providing background material on gravestones as a data source and leading a field study to a local cemetery.

While we are conscious of the dangers of merely adding new wrinkles to the program, our experimentation has frequently reflected pervasive issues in the education community. Teachers of environmental education, civic education, or consumer economics caused us to look at our resources in new ways. Newly defined client groups increased our awareness of objectives and teaching strategies and sharpened the sequence of activities. Today, the interest and growth in adult education add a new dimension that is certain to continue through the 1980s.

Over the years, we have worked and continue to work with inner-city groups, rural students, the gifted and talented, and special-needs students. For example, the museum was able to overcome the usual barriers some special-needs students feel in situations that primarily rely on reading and writing. Efforts have been made to make the museum's resources accessible to each student's distinct needs. Although the daily three- to four-hour field study for students remains our main concern, as the program has grown we have also designed programs for these special client groups. As they have tested the viability of the museum's purposes, they have encouraged our continuing evaluation of teaching strategies.

Each year new staff, changing exhibits, or the needs of a particular client group may produce a new twist. The programs that have survived over the years, however, are ones in which museum-school collaboration was strong and the classroom teacher had developed sufficient control over the field study to retain it as part of the curriculum.

From time to time, the challenge of an expressed need may tempt our "urge to create." It is crucial that we not lose track of our priorities or compromise the objectives of the institution. Lasting programs of worth will emerge when we are clear about our mission, understand our educational philosophy, and are attentive to the potential of available resources. Moreover, the museum education programs that will most likely mature from childhood through adolescence to adulthood are those that reflect the nature of knowledge and the knower and place a priority on the process of learning. Finally, as a program matures, the nature and quality of leadership are crucial to its growth.

Further Reading

Gottleib, Elaine. "Students Live 1830s History at Sturbridge Village." *Boston Sunday Globe,* July 10, 1983.

Rich, Leslie. "Old Sturbridge: Past Indicative." *American Education* 14, no. 10 (December 1978): 18–22.

Rothman, Ellen K. "The Worcester Sourcebook." *Museum News* 56, no. 4 (March/April 1978): 31–37.

Sebolt, Alberta P. *Building Collaborative Programs: Museums and Schools.* Sturbridge, Mass.: Old Sturbridge Village, 1980.

———. "The Community as a Learning Laboratory," *Educational Leadership* 29, no. 5 (February 1972): 410–12.

———. "Family, Work and Community: The Museum Education Experience." *Rural Visitor* 19, no. 3 (Fall 1979): 8–10.

———. *A Guide for the Development of a Curriculum Model.* Sturbridge, Mass.: Old Sturbridge Village, 1980.

———. "Museums and Learning." In *Museum-School Partnerships: Plans & Programs,* ed. Susan Nichols Lehman and Kathryn Igoe, pp. 13–16. Washington, D.C.: Center for Museum Education, George Washington University, 1981.

———. "Old Sturbridge Village Teacher-Training Program." In *Museums, Adults and the Humanities: A Guide for Educational Programming,* ed. Zipporah W. Collins, pp. 313–37. Washington, D.C.: American Association of Museums, 1981.

———, ed. "Using the Community to Explore 200 Years of History." *Social Education* 39, no. 7 (November/December 1975): 454–81.

On Interpretation and Historic Sites

Suzanne B. Schell

Historic sites are important cultural resources that preserve and re-create a historical context for the tangible remains of the past as evidenced in historical environments, architecture, and artifacts. Their potential for interpreting American history has evolved slowly.

Historical Perspective

Beyond preservation, which frequently was an end in itself, America's historic sites initially were saved for the didactic purposes of inspiring patriotism and inculcating civic virtues. Early preservationists established historic houses as shrines to the nation's Founding Fathers and marked battlefields and graves as monuments commemorating war heroes. Patriotic reasons led the New York State legislature in 1850 to acquire the Hasbrouck House in Newburgh, which had served as General Washington's headquarters.[1] This monument to the "Father of Our Country" and the American Revolution was the first historic site preserved and opened to the public. In 1859, Ann Pamela Cunningham and her fellow female philanthropists, the Mount Vernon Ladies' Association, succeeded in their crusade to save Washington's home as a shrine where "mothers of the land and their innocent children might make their offering in the cause of greatness, goodness, and prosperity of the country."[2] Patriotism and filial pietism continued to be major motivating forces for preservation nearly 75 years later when the Thomas Jefferson Memorial Foundation solicited funds from elementary school students to preserve Monticello as "a Patriotic Shrine for the Children of America."[3] Likewise, Colonial Williamsburg was founded in 1926 to tell the story of America's patriots. This nationalistic interest in America's heritage during the late 19th and early 20th centuries coincided with a wave of immigrants who, according to some preservationists, needed to be Americanized.[4]

Besides association with historical figures and events, historic buildings were preserved by virtue of their antiquity. For example, the first or oldest structure in a town was saved by many local preservationist groups in New England. As appreciation of America's tangible heritage grew in the early 20th century, esthetic considerations became another justification for preserving historic buildings. The Society for the Preservation of New England Antiquities, established in 1910 by

Journal of Museum Education 10, no. 3 (Summer 1985): 6–10.

William Sumner Appleton, saved historic houses for their architectural merit.[5] Similarly, the Pennsylvania Museum (now the Philadelphia Museum of Art), under the leadership of architect Fiske Kimball, restored historic houses in Fairmount Park "to illustrate the evolution of American art," representing "the very finest of their respective periods and types."[6] Thus, artistically outstanding examples, but not necessarily representative examples, of American architecture were preserved.

Gradually, a more strictly educational purpose emerged for historic sites. The Essex Institute in Salem, Massachusetts, was the first museum to install American period rooms. George Francis Dow furnished these three period rooms (still intact) "to heighten the illusion of actual human occupancy" by casually arranging objects such as an 1800 Salem newspaper and a pair of spectacles.[7] Two years later, he moved the endangered John Ward House from its original site to a lot behind the museum where it could be preserved. It was furnished "to present a truthful picture of an interior of the year 1700" with original artifacts and, where necessary, reproductions to give "the atmosphere of livableness."[8] Other historic structures were added to the Essex Institute site, making it the first American outdoor museum, where Dow sought to illustrate the everyday life of America's forefathers.[9] Following in this vein, Henry Ford, in 1929 at Dearborn, Michigan, dedicated Greenfield Village to reproduce "American life as lived."[10] Like present-day material culture historians, Ford believed that we can learn about the past from "the things people used." However, his was a nostalgic and idealistic view of the past—the good old days. Ford also celebrated the Common Man and modeled Greenfield Village after Skansen, Stockholm's open-air living folk museum, founded in 1891 by Arthur Hazelius.[11] Colonial Williamsburg and its patron, John D. Rockefeller, Jr., also pioneered the outdoor museum concept by attempting to re-create the historic environment of that 18th-century Virginia capital and to portray the lives and times of its political leaders.[12] Other open-air museums were established during the following decades, some of them beginning as generalized colonial or pioneer villages with historic buildings moved from original sites to an architectural park for preservation. The most noted of early reconstructed villages include Lincoln's New Salem in Illinois, Conner Prairie Pioneer Settlement in Indiana, the Farmer's Museum in Cooperstown, New York, and the Shelburne Museum in Vermont.[13]

Laurence Vail Coleman, in *Historic House Museums* published by the American Association of Museums in 1933, documented that there were more than 400 such museums at the time, a number which had grown from a mere 20 historic houses open in 1895 and nearly 100 in 1910.[14] Coleman attributed this proliferation to increased leisure and the popularization of the automobile, which made it possible for people to visit scattered historic sites. He observed that "people are asking that houses be explained, as well as saved" and provided insightful suggestions for "interpretation."[15] Guides had made their appearance as early as 1876 at the Centennial Exposition in Philadelphia where costumed ladies conducted visitors through the reconstructed New England Farmer's Home.[16] At Mount Vernon, the resident director showed visitors around the mansion and grounds or the guard at Washington's tomb talked to tourists; a visitor handbook was published in the early 1870s.[17] Later at the Essex Institute, women dressed in homespun costumes of the period acted as custodians, showing the John Ward House to visitors.[18] At Colonial Williamsburg, William Goodwin advocated "interpretation" to inform visitors "about the people who lived in Williamsburg," and in 1932 the first costumed hostesses greeted visitors to Raleigh Tavern.[19] These hostesses and tour guides were the forerunners of today's historic site interpreters.

Historic Sites Today

Of the estimated 5,500 museums in the United States surveyed in 1978 for the Institute of Museum Services, half were history museums and, among these, historic sites were the most common.[20] Historic sites include domestic structures (city dwellings and farms of both prominent individuals and common people); communities (neighborhoods, villages/towns, utopian settlements); industrial and commercial sites (factories, mills, trading posts, taverns, general stores); transportation sites (trails, canals, railroad depots, ships); military and governmental sites (battlefields and forts, courthouses and town/city halls); educational and religious structures (schools and churches); monuments and cemeteries; prehistoric and Native American sites; and historic landscapes and environments. Historic site museums encompass historic houses, living history farms, architectural parks, restored villages, folk parks, and open-air museums. William T. Alderson and Shirley Payne Low distinguish three categories of historic sites paralleling the historical evolution of these museums: the documentary site associated with a historical event or person; the representative site depicting a period of history or a way of life; and the esthetic site displaying exceptional examples of furnishings in period rooms.[21] Despite their diversity, these historic sites share a number of unique characteristics related to environment, collections, and interpretive methods.

Philosophical Perspective

Historic sites exhibit artifacts arranged in the context of a preserved or re-created environment to communicate something significant about the past. A historic structure and its furnishings must be considered an integral part of the whole site, including its surroundings. The Historic Sites Committee of the American Association of Museums Accreditation Commission recognized this unique synergetic character of historic site collections when it observed that the historic structure is an artifact itself and "functions as the prominent feature of the collection."[22] A historic site consists not only of its structures but encompasses its total environment, including gardens, fences, and roads. The landscape, whether rural or urban, reflects the historical relationship between people and land. Together these elements form a macroartifact.[23] Objects in a historic site collection do not necessarily have intrinsic value but may be utilitarian in nature without special esthetic merit. The historical significance of these artifacts is in their arrangement and relationship to one another.[24] Frequently, historic sites have living collections—plants and animals; sometimes the latter eat the former, as is the case when livestock consume crops. Because historic sites and their collections must be considered in their context of a total environment, interpretation becomes paramount.

The National Endowment for the Humanities, some years ago, defined interpretation as "the bridge between the object and the observer."[25] The role of the interpreter is to create a dialogue between artifact and visitor. The AAM Historic Sites Committee defined the word more specifically for historic sites: "Interpretation is a planned effort, to create for the visitor an understanding of the history and significance of events, people and objects with which the site is associated."[26] The unique nature of historic sites has made passive interpretive methods, such as exhibit labels and what I call "this is" tours, largely ineffective except as a supplement to a more active mode of interpretation. Functional interpretation of how and why objects and structures were used is much more meaningful to the public. At historic sites, usually an interpreter is the key to explaining the past and relating it to the life experiences of visitors.[27] For this reason, historic sites have pioneered innovative educational methods such as living history and first-person interpretation, in which an interpreter (or an actor) role-plays a historical character dressed in period clothing. Less dramatic, but perhaps more realistic, are interpretive programs and craft-process demonstrations conducted in third person by an interpreter also dressed in period clothing. Some sites invite visitors to participate in live-in programs, where they perform historical activities themselves. At the very least, historic site museums with limited resources rely on tour guides to interpret the site, giving visitors a personalized experience. Through the inductive educational method of inquiry, traditional tours can be enlivened for visitors by encouraging them to "read" objects, structures, and the environment. Freeman Tilden's "Six Principles of Interpretation," progressive when they were first published for the National Park Service in 1957, still constitute useful guidelines for interpreters.[28]

But interpretation at a historic site does not begin for visitors when the guide greets them, or even when they read a brochure or see an audiovisual orientation program. There is the phenomenon of nonverbal interpretation derived from sensory perceptions initially experienced by visitors. Even before they set foot on the site, visitors form a mental image of the past. Through the unique contextual environment and its sensory experience—what Edward P. Alexander calls the "fourth dimension"—historic sites can mentally transport people back in time.[29] It is this feature that makes historic sites powerful educational tools for interpreting history. Accuracy of detail in restoration and furnishing, therefore, is essential if this visual image of the past is to be correct. Since no sites appear today exactly as they did in the past, modern intrusions and anachronisms must be dealt with interpretively so that visitors understand what they see. Changes in scale, land use, and landscape should be explained. For example, many historical farms are only scale models used for demonstration purposes compared to the original working farms.[30] It is equally important not to impose 20th-century values, standards, or esthetics on the past. A historic house, for example, should reflect the taste and housekeeping practices of its own time period, not ours.[31]

Many historic sites and open-air museums are ideally suited for interpreting the social history of ordinary people and their everyday life. During the last decade, research findings of social historians have provided new insight for interpretive programs. By using demographic data to reconstruct history from "the bottom up," museum educators have generated profiles of average people.[32] When combined with research about folk traditions, this becomes the basis for interpreting daily life experiences of common folk—family, foodways, shelter, clothing, rites of passage, education, work, community, and values. In order to treat a culture as a whole and avoid a false, nostalgic view of the past, negative as well as positive aspects must be interpreted, such as disease, death, poverty, crime, and conflict.[33] To transcend merely descriptive "pots-and-pans" history or "show-and-tell" demonstrations, artifacts and mundane activities must be interpreted in the broader context of social, political, economic, religious, and cultural phenomena. It is necessary to explain *why* these activities were done and *why* events occurred in the past. At living history museums, experimental archeological techniques are used to simulate historical processes such as farming methods, food preparation, and building construction techniques. These re-created historical processes are as vital as the collections.[34] Some historic sites interpret a specific time and place. A more difficult goal, particularly for time-capsule restorations, is the explanation of the dynamic forces—continuity and change—that transformed communities over time.[35]

Through an interdisciplinary approach to material culture, historic sites interpret the social, political, economic, religious, and cultural influences, trends, and events in American history. For example, historic houses can serve as "learning laboratories" for cultural anthropology, folklife studies, social psychology, cultural geography, art and architectural history, literature, environmental studies, and the sciences.[36] Techniques of archeological inquiry have been successfully applied above ground to "read" historic sites and the built environment of the cityscape.[37] A holistic approach to history is achieved by relating material culture to ideas.[38]

Research is the key to creating a credible interpretive program. Information about material culture and life-style must be based on thorough research. At living historical farms, agricultural research is necessary to backbreed plants and animals authentic to the period represented.[39] If historic sites are to avoid an inaccurate homogeneous view of American history, this research must entail a study of regional, economic, ethnic, and racial differences.[40] Finally, it is necessary to admit that our knowledge of the past is limited and based on incomplete records.[41] Historic sites only represent our current interpretation of the past, subject to revision by future historians. Truth in interpretation is essential; anything less is to mislead the public.

Practical Considerations

Key words in the AAM Historic Sites Committee's definition of interpretation are "planned effort." The AAM's "Supplemental Accreditation Questionnaire for Historic Sites" goes on to establish that a written interpretive plan is a professional standard.[42] Initially, this is a conceptual document that derives from the museum's mission, inventories the site's cultural resources, and defines interpretive objectives. Based on this foundation, it develops the site's storyline by identifying specific themes to be interpreted. Then the plan outlines how the interpretive message will be conveyed to the public by determining the type of programs to be offered. This requires decisions about interpretive methods to be used, ranging from passive self-guiding materials to interactive living history. The nature of the interpretive strategies selected may necessitate policies regarding the costuming of interpreters, the inclusion of living collections, and the use of reproduction artifacts. For example, reproduction period clothing must be accurate in all details, including accessories. To be appropriate to the historical period being interpreted, plants and animals at the site usually must be backbred varieties. Replicas should be used in place of original artifacts for hands-on education programs or demonstrations to avoid deterioration or destruction. This planning process should include audience research for the prospective programs. The second half of the interpretive plan must deal with the reality of implementation by identifying the resources needed: finances, personnel, facilities, and equipment. The economics of personal interpretation dictate that methods using tour guides or interpreters are costly because they are labor intensive, compared to passive alternatives. Provisions must be made in the plan for developing a formal program to recruit and train interpretive staff or volunteers. Visitor orientation must be addressed in the plan, indicating whether written materials, audiovisual programs, or interpretive exhibits will be employed to provide visitors with historical background, orient them to the layout of the site and the pattern of circulation, and prepare them for the method of interpretation they will experience. The mode of interpretive program selected will have implications for all aspects of historic site operation, including security, care of collections, visitor services, maintenance, and site development, which must be taken into consideration. Lastly, the plan must establish a mechanism for periodic, formal evaluation.

In the 135 years since the first historic house was opened to the public in the United States, historic site museums have evolved from patriotic shrines to centers for learning about American history with standards established by the museum profession to guide their operation. These recent efforts to self-monitor and set professional standards are only the latest steps in an intriguing and complicated institutional history. If, as we are advised in Shakespeare's *Tempest,* the past is prologue, then we can anticipate more changes in historic site interpretation as the profession matures.

Notes

1. Charles B. Hosmer, *Presence of the Past: A History of the Preservation Movement in America before Williamsburg* (New York: G. P. Putnam's Sons, 1965), pp. 35–36.

2. Quoted in Edward P. Alexander, *Museums in Motion: An Introduction to the History and Functions of Museums* (Nashville, Tenn.: American Association for State and Local History, 1979), p. 84.

3. Hosmer, *Presence of the Past,* p. 187.

4. Michael Wallace, "Visiting the Past: History Museums in the United States," *Radical History Review* 25 (1981): 67.

5. Hosmer, *Presence of the Past,* chap. 10.

6. Ibid., pp. 234–35.

7. Dianne H. Pilgrim, "Inherited from the Past: The American Period Room," *American Art Journal* 10, no. 3 (May 1978): 18.

8. Hosmer, *Presence of the Past,* pp. 214–16.

9. Ibid.; Jay Anderson, *Time Machines: The World of Living History* (Nashville, Tenn.: American Association for State and Local History, 1984), p. 27.

10. Alexander, *Museums in Motion,* p. 92.

11. Ibid.; Anderson, *Time Machines,* p. 28; Wallace, "Visiting the Past," pp. 72–73.

12. Alexander, *Museums in Motion,* pp. 91–92; Anderson, *Time Machines,* p. 30.

13. Candace Matelic, "Through the Historical Looking Glass," *Museum News* 58, no. 4 (March/April 1980): 40–42.

14. Laurence Vail Coleman, *Historic House Museums* (1933; reprint, Detroit: Gale Research, 1973), p. 18.

15. Ibid., p. 99; see also chap. 10.

16. Pilgrim, "Inherited from the Past," p. 6; Anderson, *Time Machines,* p. 25.

17. I am indebted to Ann Rauscher in the library of the Mount Vernon Ladies' Association for information about early forms of interpretation at Mount Vernon.

18. Hosmer, *Presence of the Past,* p. 216.

19. Anderson, *Time Machines,* pp. 30–31.

20. Lee Kimche, "American Museums: The Vital Statistics," *Museum News* 59, no. 2 (October 1980): 55; National Center for Education Statistics, *Museum Program Survey, 1979* (Washington, D.C.: U.S. Department of Education, 1981), p. 8.

21. William T. Alderson and Shirley Payne Low, *Interpretation of Historic Sites* (Nashville, Tenn.: American Association for State and Local History, 1976), pp. 11–14.

22. Historic Sites Committee of the Accreditation Commission, *Accreditation and Historic Sites* (Washington D.C.: American Association of Museums, 1982); Randi R. Glickberg, "Historic Sites and Accreditation," *Museum News* 60, no. 2 (November/December 1981): 42–49. Also see Historic Sites Committee, *An Annotated Bibliography for the Development and Operation of Historic Sites* (Washington D.C.: American Association of Museums, 1982).

23. Edward L. Hawes, "The Living Historical Farm in North America: New Directions in Research and Interpretation," *Association for Living Historical Farms and Agricultural Museums, Proceedings of the Annual Meeting* 2 (1976): 50.

24. William Seale, *Recreating the Historic House Interior* (Nashville, Tenn.: American Association for State and Local History, 1979), chap. 10.

25. National Endowment for the Humanities, *Humanities Projects in Museums and Historical Organizations Guidelines* (Washington D.C.: National Endowment for the Humanities, 1979), p. 6; Martin Sullivan and Cheryl McClenney, "The Theory and Practice of the National Endowment for the Humanities," in *Museums, Adults and the Humanities: A Guide for*

Educational Programming, ed. Zipporah W. Collins (Washington, D.C.: American Association of Museums, 1981), p. 368.

26. Historic Sites Committee, *Accreditation and Historic Sites,* p. 1.

27. Rosemary Troy Krill, "Working toward Effective Guiding," *Museologist* 16, no. 167 (Spring 1984): 14.

28. Freeman J. Tilden, *Interpreting Our Heritage,* 2d ed. (Chapel Hill, N.C.: University of North Carolina Press, 1967), chap. 1.

29. Edward P. Alexander, "A Fourth Dimension for History Museums," *Curator* 11 (December 1968): 264.

30. Darwin P. Kelsey, "Historical Farms as Models of the Past," *Association for Living Historical Farms and Agricultural Museums, Proceedings of the Annual Meeting* 1 (1975): 37.

31. Ralph H. Lewis, *Manual for Museums* (Washington, D.C.: National Park Service, 1976), chap. 13.

32. Cary Carson, "From the Bottom Up: Zero-Base Research for Social History at Williamsburg," *History News* 35, no. 1 (January 1980): 7–9; Barbara G. Carson and Cary Carson, "Things Unspoken: Learning Social History from Artifacts," in *Ordinary People and Everyday Life: Perspectives on the New Social History,* ed. James B. Gardner and George Rollie Adams (Nashville, Tenn.: American Association for State and Local History, 1983), pp. 180–203.

33. James Deetz, "The Link from Object to Person to Concept," in *Museums, Adults and the Humanities,* p. 31; Mary Lynn Stevens, "Wistful Thinking: The Effect of Nostalgia on Interpretation," *History News* 36, no. 12 (December 1981): 10–12; Roger A. Fortin, "The Challenge of a Humanities Approach," in *Museums, Adults and the Humanities,* p. 21; Larry R. Gerlach, "Making the Past Come Alive: *History News* 30, no. 9 (September 1975): 222–25; Peter S. O'Connell, "Putting the Historic House into the Course of History," *Journal of Family History* 6, no. 1 (Spring 1981): 29; Albert Eide Parr, "History and the Historical Museum," *Curator* 15, no. 1 (1972): 58.

34. Hawes, "Living Historical Farm," pp. 49–50; Anderson, *Time Machines,* chap. 9.

35. Cary Carson, "Living Museums of Everyman's History," *Harvard Magazine* 83 (July/August 1981): 29.

36. Thomas J. Schlereth, "Historic House Museums: Seven Teaching Strategies" and "The Historic House Museum Village as a Cross-Disciplinary Learning Laboratory," both in Schlereth, *Artifacts and the American Past* (Nashville, Tenn.: American Association for State and Local History, 1980), pp. 91–129.

37. John L. Cotter, "Above-Ground Archaeology," *American Quarterly* 26, no. 3 (August 1974): 266–74; David R. Goldfield, "Living History: The Physical City as Artifact and Teaching Tool," *History Teacher* 8 (1975): 535–56; Thomas J. Schlereth, "Above-Ground Archaeology: Discovering a Community's History through Local Artifacts," in *Artifacts and the American Past,* pp. 184–203.

38. Fortin, "Challenge of a Humanities Approach," p. 21.

39. Hawes, "Living Historical Farm," pp. 50–51; David O. Percy, *Living Historical Farms: The Working Museums* (Accokeek, Md.: Accokeek Foundation, 1981), chap. 4; Darwin P. Kelsey, "Outdoor Museums and Historical Agriculture," *Agricultural History* 46 (1972): 118–22.

40. Thomas J. Schlereth, "It Wasn't That Simple," *Museum News* 56, no. 3 (January/February 1978): 40.

41. Robert D. Ronsheim, "Is the Past Dead?" *Museum News* 53, no. 3 (November 1974): 62.

42. Historic Sites Committee, *Annotated Bibliography.* For more information on interpretive planning, see Edward L. Hawes, "Planning Living History Programs and Facilities," *Association for Living Historical Farms and Agricultural Museums, Proceedings of the Annual Meeting* 4 (1978–80): 22–27; Percy, *Living Historical Farms;* and John A. Veverka, Sandra A. Poneleit, and David E. Traweek, "Standardized Planning Forms for the Development of Interpretive Planning Documents," *Interpreter* 4 (Spring 1980): 12–26.

To Realize Our Museums' Full Potential

Joan C. Madden

Museums have yet to realize their full potential as educational institutions. We believe a new approach to learning in museums must be developed, one that does justice to the unique learning environment they provide.
—*Museums for a New Century*

Of the 25 million visitors who come to the Smithsonian Institution's museums each year, fewer than 1 million take a tour, hear a lecture, attend a seminar or a series of classes, listen to a concert, or see a demonstration. In other words, less than 4 percent of our museum visitors have an experience in which a museum staff member, paid or volunteer, provides some kind of educational service or program. The other 96 percent visit some portion of the institution's exhibits. We know from studies that have been carried out over the years that a Smithsonian visitor may spend anywhere from 30 minutes to three hours in a museum; we know something about his or her socioeconomic status, education, age, and whether he or she comes to the museum alone or with another person or group. These statistics provide descriptions of the average visitor as well as the extremes, but they tell us nothing about particular visitors. And they tell us nothing about whether visitors, on the average, learn anything in museums.

What is true about the Smithsonian is probably true for other museums and their visitors. For argument's sake, let's raise the figure on the percentage served by the nation's museum education programs to 10 percent of all visitors. The question to be posed in this essay is, How can museum educators improve the chances that their museums are rich learning environments for the walk-in visitor? The answer lies not in programs, publications, and special events for 90 percent of the visitors, but in the exhibits. If a museum expects to realize its full potential as an educational institution, the effectiveness of its exhibits is of paramount importance. That is, literally, where the action is for the visitor. Museum educators have an important role to play in assuring that the public areas of museums are learning environments.

In the recent past and, for some of us, perhaps even in the present, exhibits were conceived by curators and prepared by designers. A finished product was delivered, and, at that point, the museum educator began to plan programs and publications.

Journal of Museum Education 10, no. 4 (Fall 1985): 3–5.

In the last three years, a trend toward including museum educators in the "team approach" to exhibit development has been reflected in sessions at the annual American Association of Museums meetings and in seminars offered by various universities and museums. The team, as usually described, is composed of curators, exhibit specialists, and educators. In some instances, the team is curators or scientists, exhibit designers, and evaluators or psychologists whose interest is measuring the effectiveness of exhibits. For the purposes of this essay, the team will be considered to include museum educators. The question that museum educators should then be asking themselves is, If I am to be part of the team that conceives and develops exhibits, how well prepared am I to do this job?

Museum educators are inveterate visitors to museums other than their own. Each of you takes time out on holidays, during conferences, and on your travels to visit museums of all varieties. On these museum visits, you are usually a "walk-in visitor" and experience the museum as other casual visitors do. True, you may bring more knowledge and skill in looking at objects than the average visitor does, but if the selection of exhibits is broad, your experience is apt to be similar to that of any other visitor. Out of these cumulative experiences comes a clearer understanding of what works in an exhibit. Does the exhibit please the eye and use placement, lighting, and color effectively? These are design factors. Are the labels readable, well placed, and large enough for ease of viewing? More important, do the labels answer your questions about the object? Are you comfortable? Are you engaged by the exhibit? Can you find your way easily? Are you able to learn what you wanted to learn?

Through our own experience as part of the museum public and through familiarity with exhibits in the museums in which we work, we have sharpened our intuition about what makes a good exhibit. In assisting school groups and adults through museum lessons and tours, we have become acquainted with successes and failures in exhibit development. Whenever we find ourselves explaining what a particular exhibit *intended* to show, we identify an exhibit that has failed. If an oral introduction to a major exhibit must explain a time frame or explain where in the world the objects come from or what the major theme of the exhibit is, because those pieces of information are not clearly presented, we know that an important part of the communication in the exhibit plans has not succeeded.

We need, however, to have more than a good intuition about exhibits. We need to familiarize ourselves with the critical elements of exhibition planning so that when we have the opportunity to be part of an exhibit development team, we can function effectively in that role.

What are our resources? There have been many studies carried out during the last 20 years, in all kinds of museums, on the effectiveness of museum exhibits. Minda Borun, Chandler Screven, Robert Lakota, Harris Shettel, A. E. Parr, and Ross Loomis are some of the important writers (see References). Their publications make interesting and illuminating reading. Robert Wolf and Barbara Tymitz carried out numerous evaluations, using what they called "naturalistic evaluation" techniques, in the Smithsonian museums. The results are descriptive of what happens to visitors in exhibit areas and what their perceptions are. R. S. Miles and M. B. Alt of the British Museum (Natural History) have carried the evaluation of exhibits one important step beyond learning what happens to the visitors *after* the exhibit is complete. They are testing reactions of visitors to elements of new exhibits *before* they are finally installed. Their book, published in 1982, *The Design of Educational Exhibits,* although suffering from the lack of a tough editor, is a gold mine of ideas about exhibit development for educational goals.

Another recent publication, Lothar Witteborg's *Good Show: A Practical Guide for Temporary Exhibitions,* published by the Smithsonian Institution Traveling Exhibition Service in 1981, offers such practical advice to the exhibits team as:

> Important questions to answer for putting on more effective exhibits are:
> 1. Who makes up the audience? What are they interested in? What are their objectives?
> 2. What are your objectives? Do you have information to convey, attitudes to change, or both? Has anyone tried to specify them?
> 3. How best can you reach your own goals and objectives and those of your audience? What content and what media are most appropriate? How much time, money, talent do you have to work with?
> 4. Once you put an exhibit together, does it really work? If it doesn't where is the problem? Can it be fixed? Can you pretest an idea before putting a lot of money into it?
> 5. What have you learned from your experience that would help yourself and others to do even better next time? Did you document and share your findings?

In addition to becoming familiar with the literature on the planning and evaluation of effective exhibits, educators should be familiar with scholarly writings in behavioral and educational psychology. Great minds have devoted entire lives to trying to understand how individuals learn and to describing the means by which individuals can be assisted in the learning process. Shettel wrote in *Museum News* in 1973, "One of the most powerful principles to emerge from the general field of behavioral psychology and its application to instruction has been the idea that active participation heightens the acquisition and retention of information." The development of science centers, discovery rooms, and learning labs and the use of participatory elements in otherwise static exhibits demonstrate an awareness on the part of museum professionals that manipulation and problem solving can enhance learning. It may have been the influence of the still-fabulous Deutsches Museum in Munich that stimulated this whole trend, starting with the Museum of Science and Industry in Chicago and the Exploratorium in San Francisco. Both of these museums and dozens of children's museums and science centers design their exhibit units around the idea that "doing it yourself " helps one to learn.

But active participation is not the only road to learning. There are other characteristics of effective learning environments with which we should familiarize ourselves. Miles, Alt, and others write that exhibits have to *attract* and to *hold* the visitor's attention before any learning can commence. The attractive power of an exhibit depends on the medium used, color, light, nearness of other exhibits, and many other factors, most of which come under the heading of design. But *holding power* has more to do with communication and an individual's perception of what the exhibit is about. The visitor wants to know: What will I learn if I pursue this course? What does it have to do with me and my interests at this moment? How is this exhibit organized? Most visitors will not give more than a few seconds of their time to find the answers to those questions and, if they are not easily available, will turn away.

The comfort of the museum visitor affects his or her ability to learn and to enjoy exhibits. Comfort here refers to more than a place to rest. It refers to the ambience, level of noise and light, style of language, and variety of information. Our visitor surveys show us that the range of visitors' education and experience is widening as museums make themselves more appealing to broader audiences. As we are successful in attracting minorities, persons from varied ethnic backgrounds, and persons with differing abilities and skills, our exhibits must be planned in response to what we learn about our audience. Of course, not all exhibits appeal to everyone. But in most museums there should be enough diversity in exhibits to meet the needs of this widely diverse public.

The commission report, *Museums for a New Century,* charges us in its sixth recommendation to place a high priority on research into the ways people learn *in museums.* At least one educational psychologist with whom I have talked doubts that this can be accomplished in any meaningful way. There are too many uncontrollable elements in the population and the environment to be studied. If those elements are controlled, then the population and the environment are no longer those of a museum. Possibly there are aspects of informal learning that can be studied which, if better understood, would cast light on planning exhibits. Museum educators will be well advised to keep abreast of such progress in educational and behavioral psychology as reported in the professional journals of the disciplines.

No matter what the limitations on research on learning in museums, research and writings on learning as a lifetime of experience can be used to determine how exhibits should be structured. The contribution of museum educators can be to assure that an exhibit provides the means by which visitors can build upon past experience. John Dewey's creed applies. He wrote, "Education must be conceived as a continuing reconstruction of experience: the process and the goal of education are one and the same thing." Estes, Shiffrin, Simon, and Smith write:

> Comprehension is based on knowledge. People understand the new in terms of the old, and memory organization is thus the cornerstone of comprehension. This principle's major implication for education is that new information should be presented in a way that ensures maximum contact with prior knowledge. Educators must determine what

knowledge schemas individual students [read "visitors"] already have, and structure new information so that it best matches these old schemas.

And finally, John Holt recently said in an informal lecture, "Learning takes place all the time, in every aspect of one's life. . . . Learning does not necessarily involve instruction. Learning is not the product of teaching. The learner has to want to learn. Knowledge comes from curiosity, activity, observation, wonder, speculation, and theories about how things work." I am quoting him only approximately, but his comments were wonderfully appropriate for museums and the kind of informal learning that they hope to encourage.

I do not intend, by what I have written above, to indicate that I think educational programs and publications, which have become the most recognized products of museum educators, are without value. Most of the easily recognized efforts of membership and education offices are courses, lectures, films, field trips, tours, self-guides, festivals, concerts, and a myriad of other events and publications based on the collections, exhibits, and human resources of museums. The very popularity of these programs is ample proof of their value to our clients. The point is that we are missing one of our most important responsibilities if we do not bring what is known about learning to bear on the conception and design of exhibits. This is where learning takes place for most museum visitors if it takes place at all. This is where the potential lies for museums to be institutions for learning. This is where the museum educator must play an active role.

I advocate that museum educators extend their influence in museums beyond the planning and presentation of programs and publications to include an active role in the planning and development of exhibits as a regular part of their responsibilities. The best way to make this an accepted part of their museum role is to demonstrate that they have something valuable to offer. Some museum educators have already achieved this goal and are valued members of exhibit teams. Others of us may still be on the outside, looking in, and still others are on the threshold of acceptance. Being prepared to fill the role effectively is the prerequisite to being made a member of the team. Gaining knowledge, experience, and expertise in the several fields of communication and educational and behavioral psychology that can be applied to exhibit development will be the passport to entry.

Mark Lilla, in the *New Republic,* wrote while trying to analyze the role of the modern museum, "The museum is an 'empowering' institution, meant to incorporate all who would become part of our shared cultural experience. Any citizen can walk into a museum and appreciate the highest achievements of his culture. If he spends enough time, he may be transformed. This is precisely what the museum founders had in mind when they brought great collections to their own cities." Lilla is writing about art museums, but what he says applies to all museums and to their potential as "educational institutions" for the people who come to them.

References

Borun, M. *Measuring the Immeasurable: A Pilot Study of Museum Effectiveness.* Philadelphia: Franklin Institute and Association of Science-Technology Centers, 1977.

Borun, M., and M. Miller. *What's in a Name? A Study of the Effectiveness of Explanatory Labels in a Science Museum.* Philadelphia: Franklin Institute, 1980.

Dewey, J. "My Pedagogic Creed." *School Journal* 54 (January 1897): 77–80.

Estes, W., R. Shiffrin, H. Simon, and E. Smith. "The Science of Cognition." In *Outlook for Science and Technology—The Next Five Years: A Report of the National Research Council.* San Francisco: W. H. Freeman, 1982.

Lakota, R. *The National Museum of Natural History as a Behavioral Environment.* Washington, D.C.: Smithsonian Institution, 1975.

———. *Techniques for Improving Exhibit Effectiveness.* Washington, D.C.: Smithsonian Institution, 1976.

Lilla, M. "The Great Museum Muddle." *New Republic,* April 8, 1985, pp. 25–29.

Loomis, R., and P. Elliott. *Studies of Visitor Behavior in Museums and Exhibitions: An Annotated Bibliography of Sources Primarily in the English Language.* Washington, D.C.: Smithsonian Institution, 1975.

Miles, R. S., et al. *The Design of Educational Exhibits.* London: Allen and Unwin, 1982.

Museum Reference Center. *Bibliography on Exhibits.* Washington, D.C.: Smithsonian Institution, 1981.

Commission on Museums for a New Century. *Museums for a New Century.* Washington, D.C.: American Association of Museums, 1984.

Parr, A. E. "The Time and Place for Experimentation in Museum Design." *Curator* 1, no. 4 (1958): 36–48.

Shettel, H. "Exhibits: Art Form or Educational Medium?" *Museum News* 52, no. 1 (September 1973): 32–41.

Witteborg, L. *Good Show: A Practical Guide for Temporary Exhibitions.* Washington, D.C.: Smithsonian Institution Traveling Exhibition Service, 1981.

Wolf, R., and B. Tymitz. *Whatever Happened to the Giant Wombat: An Investigation of the Impact of the Ice Age Mammals and Emergence of Man Exhibit.* Washington, D.C.: Smithsonian Institution, 1978.

——— and ———. *The Evolution of a Teaching Hall: You Can Lead a Horse to Water and You Can Help It Drink: Study on the Dynamics of Evolution Exhibit, National Museum of Natural History.* Washington, D.C.: Smithsonian Institution, 1981.

Educators Respond to Museums for a New Century

The moment *Museums for a New Century* was published [1984], it prompted a wide variety of reactions from museum professionals. Educators took special note of chapter 3 and convened panels and presented talks at local, regional, and national meetings to discuss their reactions. Others formed groups to make plans for action. The following articles are samples of some of these early responses.

Susan Stitt was one of the first reactors. Just a week or two after the report was published, she spoke (her article is derived from that talk) at the Northeast Museums Conference annual meeting in Syracuse, New York. The pieces by Danielle Rice and Anna Slafer outline responses made at two Museum Education Roundtable program meetings held in Washington, D.C., this past year [1984]. Carol Stapp's article goes beyond being a single personal reaction. In her memoir she describes a process that began as a response to the report and continues today.

Some Limitations
Susan Stitt

Since 1982, when the Commission on Museums for a New Century began its work, many of us were vaguely aware of the endeavor but not involved. During 1982, the too-brief exposure to some of the futurists consulted for the project at the Philadelphia meeting of the American Association of Museums whetted our appetite and aroused our curiosity through thought-provoking forecasts of trends. The AAM Council received reports on the activities, but not the thought process, of the commission. In January 1984 the Council was briefed on the production schedule but not informed of observations that the report would make.

Thus, for two years we knew about Olympus, saw stray lightning flashes, but the plain of our lives had not been illuminated. In situations of such secrecy, perceptions inevitably develop that reflect the concerns of the uninformed viewer and perhaps only dimly mirror the reality of the situation. We wondered about the criteria of selection for the commission members, described as the future leaders of museums. Were they? Who said so? In many ways museum workers are almost innately democratic, perhaps because primary data and public service are the substance of our

Journal of Museum Education 10, no. 4 (Fall 1985): 6–9.

work. We have struggled for years with uncomfortable questions of status. For example, why aren't educators considered as important as curators? To discuss these issues we often create a hierarchy, which we are then forced to question by our own impulses rather than its inadequacies. So, too, the commission's objectives could have been addressed by only a small group. Still, as professionals whose business is the identification, preservation, and presentation of information and knowledge, in reading and absorbing the report we must acknowledge its limitations.

For example, only four of the 24 commission members were women. The museum data base is inadequate, as the report observes, but there is substantial evidence that over half of museum workers are women. If the premise for commission selection was future leadership, then I fear we must conclude that the museum leaders key to the commission selection process did not see women as future leaders. But quotas are a political issue, aren't they, and there are more subtle forces at play here than the eight women who weren't selected. Those women who were selected were very senior: one described as emeritus and two very senior arts personalities who died in the course of the commission's two-and-one-half-year existence. One midcareer female represented a significant segment of the field, and there is no reason to assume that she was conscious of an advocacy role. Even more subtle is the fact that the staff were all women, a circumstance common to professional associations.

In raising these points again, as I did at the January 1984 AAM Council meeting, I don't want to cloud the integrity of the commission but simply to make the point that most of us learn from what is done as well as from what is said. There are some negative messages in this commission's actions.

I have been asked not to review but to react, so let me briefly review my reactions. The report is clearly written and easily gets the reader's attention, especially a reader involved in museums. It is stimulating and thought provoking. Its reassuring and important emphasis on mission will serve as an affirmation of personal professional goals for the majority of its readers.

My favorite points in the commission report are the recommendations that efforts begin on the systematization of related collections; that institutions within a collection area begin to determine shared priorities and individual emphases; and that the characteristics of museum learning be studied in order to better understand how individuals benefit intellectually and personally from museums. The recommendations should stimulate fascinating and useful inquiry and experimentation within the field.

From the perspective of my work in and with museums, I found some critical areas not stressed in the commission report. Board development and the cultivation of leaders for voluntary assistance to museums are not emphasized. Nor is the mobility of certain professions key to museums such as development and public relations. The amount of time many of us spend daily on museum marketing and on developing or seeking marketing skills is second only to keeping our facilities adequate and capable of satisfying demanding curatorial and educational standards. Buildings and their endless physical deterioration do not appear as a problem for the museum field in the commission report.

The years of work and thought of the commission and its able staff will provide years of value to the museum field. The report provides confirmation for professionals in the field and an articulate restatement of standards. The easily handled book provides a communication tool for museums in staff development; for the functional groups within the field, such as curators and educators, it presents priorities and challenges for thought; and for the community at large, it presents a rationale and justification for the institutional goals of museums within American society.

Implications for Museum Educators
Danielle Rice

The following are my responses to key ideas from the commission report with regard to their implications for museum educators:

Examination-Reorganization of Museums' Internal Structures
What does it mean when the commission recommends a new internal organization of museums? Let's look at the context of the discussion. First, the distinction between learning and education. The commission report states that "Learning in museums is a spontaneous, individualized processes; it cannot be imposed upon the visitor. When museum education emphasizes teaching and verbal communication, it does a disservice to the museum as a learning environment." Further, the "intellectual isolation of the learning function from exhibitions, research and other museum activities with which it should be inextricably joined" is detrimental to museum functioning. Concluding, "If learning is to remain at the philosophical core of museums, we believe its place in the internal structure of museums must be reexamined."

The commission suggests one model that includes an organizational structure whereby the category of "programs" absorbs education, exhibition design, and publications. Although useful, the combination of areas such as exhibitions with education and publications maintains the separation between curatorial and educational functions in the museum. This suggestion provides excuses for museum administrators to eliminate educators from the arenas of power and influence.

Moreover, the distinction between learning and education reminds one of the old attitude that mere seeing equals understanding and that museums need only to display objects with a few judicious labels for learning to occur. Many factors in our culture contribute to making learning from objects virtually impossible. Consider the discrepancy between the way we use our eyes to watch television as compared to the visual skills required to look at paintings. In addition, museum educators must guard against the trend to perceive their work merely in terms of "programs." Teaching remains a vital task to be performed in museums.

Research into Learning Theory and How People Learn in Museums

The report asserts that "confusion over the learning function of museums stems in part from the failure of museum professionals to articulate, to the satisfaction of all involved, the nature of the learning experience. . . . There is no accepted philosophical framework."

This poses a dilemma for most museum educators. To undertake this kind of research they must have a commitment to learning theory. Yet, in most museums, they are already devalued because they are not specialists in the museum's content area.

National Colloquium

The commission recommended the establishment of a national colloquium of museum and educational professionals. Will the real educators have a voice in this? Too often the "national" implications of policy invite input from a certain stratum of the profession that seldom includes the rank-and-file educator. Museum educators must start moving up to the level of policy making within the museum organization or they are likely to be left out of the real decision making.

Recommendations for Action

1. Educators must acknowledge their responsibility to educate the museum staff about the public.

2. Educators must attain positions of power by taking charge in areas that may not have the title "education" but then work from within to initiate change.

3. Educators have to become specialists in several areas.

4. Respect for curatorial work is a must. Demand respect in return. The nature of the information focused on by educators and curators is different.

Key Issues
Anna Slafer

Robot docents and moving walkways may be some images that spring to mind upon hearing the title of the commission report, *Museums for a New Century.* However, as Ellen Hicks, project director for the commission, stated, the purpose of the report was not to take a "crystal ball" approach and make predictions of what the ideal museum of the year 2000 would be like but rather to look at the "role and future of the museum as a popular institution in a complex world" by examining the issues that shape and define it.

The March Museum Education Roundtable meeting at the Woodrow Wilson House entitled, "*Museums for a New Century:* Discussion of Findings and Implications for Museum Education," brought together three of the key participants in the development of the report. Ellen Hicks was joined by Mary Ellen Munley, research coordinator for the Commission on Museums for a New Century, now on the faculty of the George Washington University Museum Education Program, and Richard Fiske, director of the National Museum of Natural History and a commission member.

The role of learning in the museum surfaced as a key issue during the commission process. As Mary Ellen Munley pointed out, the commission felt that although "education" has always been an accepted, highly touted, and much-appreciated contribution museums make to society, what has been lacking is a clear definition of what makes learning in the museum unique. This lack of definition has contributed not only to confusion over the role of learning within the museum but also to impeding museums' connecting effectively to the rest of the formal and informal educational system in this country.

A variety of frustrations were voiced by museum educators during commission discussions, Munley noted. A typical concern focused on the observation that museum professionals operate with a very narrow view of the potential of museum education. Specialists from outside the museum, on the other hand, offered a larger view of museum learning possibilities.

Another common issue touched upon the unhappy "legacy" associated with museum education. This legacy defines a museum educator as a museum "teacher," and since teachers teach things to children, museum education is, perforce, something that really happens only for school children.

A further finding brought commission members across the board to acknowledge the isolation of education departments in the museum's organizational structure as a serious flaw. The insufficient subject matter expertise often attributed to museum educators contributes to hindering their involvement in the "real work" of the museum. Museum education suffers, therefore, from a tradition as an adjunct function of the museum as opposed to being central to its mission. This situation has left museum educators feeling out of the mainstream, both in the museum and in the world of "education."

The commission made a conscious effort to reframe the emphasis in the report to focus on "learning" in the museum rather than on "education," Munley reported. Commission members found that adopting the word "learning," which has a broader, less restrictive connotation than "education," engaged a similarly broader spectrum of people in discussions about the museum as a learning environment.

Audience members uniformly wanted to know how to implement the commission recommendations on museum learning. The consensus of the panel was that the report is now in the hands of the profession; individuals have the ability to make changes, and the report can serve as an opportunity to initiate discussion. All the panelists agreed that the first step is to have all members of the museum community read the report thoughtfully and carefully. Clearly, the report's emphasis on the role of learning puts museum educators in a position of strength.

At the same time, since the report was developed by the whole museum profession, its recommendations carry the necessary weight to enable museums to employ the report as an advocacy tool within their communities.

Since panelists found that they themselves were transformed by the commission process, they hoped to see "mini-commission" experiences and summer institutes that would bring people together for serious work to formulate action agendas. Richard Fiske described how he came away from the commission process with a new sense of mission: to make the entire National Museum of Natural History into a "learning factory." He developed a heightened awareness of the connection between the "museum's public face, research, collections, and the process of learning that magically takes place." He suggested that a pragmatic step for individual directors to take would be to emulate the changes he instituted at the National Museum of Natural History to improve the Office of Education within the museum's hierarchical structure. He elevated the head of the Office of Education to the level of assistant director for education, and he modified Natural History's hiring policy. His museum is now seeking "broad-spectrum" curators who are interested in working with the education department.

Beyond individual efforts to implement the commission recommendations, the AAM accreditation guidelines should be changed to accentuate public programming. And finally, a sense of commitment and a source of money must be directed toward research on museum learning. Ultimately, until museums can state what the unique or "magical" process of museum learning is all about, museum educators will be unable to contribute their specific expertise to the educational endeavor within and outside the museum.

Internal Growth
Carol B. Stapp

We met for the first time in August 1984, at the National Museum of Natural History, to talk and to decide if we wanted to meet to talk again. "We" are a small group of museum educators (variously composed of Gretchen Jennings, Visitor Information and Associates' Reception Center, Smithsonian Institution; Joan Madden, National Museum of Natural History; Caryl Marsh, National Archives and Records Service; Mary Ellen Munley, George Washington University; Betty Sharpe, National Museum of American History; Judy White, National Zoological Park; and myself) who were puzzled and provoked by a train of events associated with the then-upcoming publication of the report of the Commission on Museums for a New Century. We were aware of Elaine Gurian's "talking paper" on midcareer training for museum educators; indeed, some of us had been solicited directly by Elaine to comment on the first draft, and some had been invited to attend the special discussion with Larry Reger, executive director of the American Association of Museums, concerning this proposal at the 1984 AAM annual meeting in Washington, D.C.

What brought us together for the first time, then, was a vague but shared disquiet about what we perceived as a potentially one-dimensional response to the commission's extremely important pronouncements on learning in the museum. We came together to clarify our individual thinking and to formulate our personal perspectives on this highly significant philosophical and practical matter. It was immediately apparent that our singular grapplings could be multiplied exponentially by a concerted, congenial effort to come to grips with the implications of the commission report. Once we identified our common objective, we moved rapidly to an agenda for action. Rather than propose a sweeping, national initiative, we sought to enhance our own competence, using ourselves to advance the concept of the centrality of learning in the museum. Spurred by Marcella Brenner's remarks at the 1984 EdCom reception, we concluded that no amount of politicking or advanced degrees either in our collections-related disciplines or in conventional education training would substitute for genuine competence in the particularities of learning in the museum. We recognized that, as the voice—both within the museum profession at large as well as inside specific institutions—for the centrality of learning, museum educators are obligated to command an armada of skills and knowledge, the flagship of which is the capacity and taste for continual professional self-development.

Consequently, we settled upon a *modus operandi* that nurtures internal growth as the necessary precursor to external change. The questions we posed for ourselves— What are our personal basic assumptions about how learning takes place? What theories and philosophies of education are influencing our attitude and daily practices?—have led to a decision to undertake a long-term, in-depth exploration of educational philosophers (in the original text) from Plato to Piaget. We meet regularly for about two hours, we rotate leadership, we generate abbreviated "minutes," we share resources and thoughts. As we gain further intellectual mastery through this process, we strengthen our abilities to discern the appropriate ways to implement the commission's recommendations.

The Uncertain Profession: *Perceptions and Directions*

Introduction
Carol B. Stapp

In the spring of 1986, the Getty Center for Education in the Arts published a report that has generated a good deal of interest—and controversy. The Elliot W. Eisner and Stephen M. Dobbs study, *The Uncertain Profession: Observations on the State of Museum Education in Twenty American Art Museums,* has been the subject of a number of articles, letters to the editor, and panel discussions in museum periodicals and at meetings. This spring [1987], the Museum Education Roundtable assembled a panel of museum professionals representing a variety of perspectives to weigh the merits of the study's findings and elicit the response of museum educators.

By way of background, Eisner and Dobbs (professor of education and art, Stanford University, and professor of creative arts, San Francisco State University, respectively) interviewed the director and the person in charge of museum education at 20 art museums across the country, from the Art Institute of Chicago to the New Orleans Museum of Art. The hour-long, tape-recorded interviews—gathered over five months in 1984—were the basis for the authors' construction of "a picture of the views and attitudes" of the 36 interviewees and the authors' interpretation of "those views in light of their meaning for the field."

Eisner and Dobbs's eight recommendations (see page 58) range from a multiweek institute for museum educators, curators, and directors, to a small grant program to stimulate research, to the establishment of a refereed publication. The authors stress that these are not in order of priority.

To bring matters up to date, the interviewees' responses to the study's findings were solicited and made available. In the summer of 1986 the Getty Center sponsored a two-week institute as recommended in the study. *The Uncertain Profession's* generalizations and recommendations were excerpted in the fall 1986 issue of *Museum Studies Journal,* and an overview of the study was published in the December 1986 issue of *Museum News.* (The review by Terry Zeller and the letters from Philip Yenawine and Patterson Williams in the February 1987 *Museum News* are also of interest.)

Journal of Museum Education 12, no. 3 (Fall 1987): 4–10.

The three panelists whose remarks are reprinted here addressed *The Uncertain Profession* from three distinctive angles:

■ Lonn Taylor, assistant director for public programs at the National Museum of American History, represents the viewpoint of both the history museum professional and the relative newcomer to the report. As a first-time reader, Lonn brings a fresh eye to the definition of the issues in the study.

■ Judith White, chief of the office of education at the National Zoological Park, represents the viewpoint of both the science museum professional and the professional who is conversant with the report. As a member of the D.C. Museum Education Study Group, Judy brings a measured response born of a year-long dialogue about the report's findings.

■ Danielle Rice, curator of education at the Philadelphia Museum of Art, represents the viewpoint of both the art museum professional and the panelist most familiar with the study. As one of the interviewees and a participant in subsequent Getty-sponsored events, she is intimately acquainted with the report's implications.

After the panel presentation, there was a lively and stimulating audience discussion, summarized here by Judith Landau, assistant director of the Museum Education Program at George Washington University. MER's contribution to the continuing dialogue about *The Uncertain Profession* proved that for *certain,* museum educators are one active and reflective lot as they contemplate and refine their professional identity.

A Questionable Attitudinal Survey
Lonn Taylor

First, I should explain that I am not a museum educator by training, but a historian who was a curator for many years and is now an administrator whose responsibilities include museum education. However, I am both an enthusiastic advocate of the field and one who believes that everyone who works in a museum has educational responsibilities. I originally went into museum work because I thought museums were better places to teach history than classrooms.

Since I lack any special expertise or credentials in museum education, I am going to approach *The Uncertain Profession* as a book reviewer. The first thing that struck me about the study is that it is strangely skewed, so that it fails to deliver what its introduction promises. The introduction, written by Leilani Lattin Duke, director of the Getty Center for Education in the Arts (which commissioned the study), states that the authors' work focuses "on how the potential of museum educators might be more fully realized, rather than on how education can become a more museum-wide responsibility." On page 1, the authors themselves list a series of questions that "were among the driving motives of the study":

> What role can a museum play to enable its visitors to have artistic experience with those objects we call works of art? Who within the museum is to perform such a function, if

it is to be performed at all? How shall such an undertaking be most effectively accomplished? In short, what can a museum do to help works of art live in the experience of those who encounter them?

These are good questions, but once raised they are simply left around the front door as architectural decoration by Eisner and Dobbs. The study itself is pure *reportage,* an attitudinal survey of the opinions of art museum directors and educators about their own and each other's work.

As such it is absolutely fascinating. I found myself appalled by the director who said that he didn't know what museum education departments were supposed to do, excited by the director who compared his museum to an urban university, and sympathetic to the educator with the room full of audiovisual equipment and no one to operate it. Most of all, I found myself surprised by how closely many of the directors' attitudes about museum education paralleled my own—that is, until I began to work with museum educators, and the scales fell from my eyes.

Which brings me to a second point: this report is very much that of an outsider, and it shows a thin understanding of the structure and workings of the museum world. It is as if a team of anthropologists decided to study a much-examined and well-documented culture in order to search for new insights but neglected to read any of the previous literature on their subjects. This lack of understanding appears most nakedly in the authors' recommendations, several of which are for programs and publications that already exist. (Others, however, are excellent; I am especially taken by the idea of a handbook on museum education, but it would be a crime to restrict it to art museum education.)

Although this report has been much discussed by museum educators in general, the authors limited themselves to art museums, and, within that branch of the museum world, to 20 institutions, an extremely narrow sample of this country's art museums from which to draw generalizations, as they do, about art museum education in general. Their strategy, the attitudinal survey, did not permit them to look at substantive matters such as budgets, staff sizes, audiences served, or any of the other institutional issues that might help provide answers to their initial questions. More troubling, their strategy did not permit them to explore the larger cultural context within which art museums operate, playing, as they do, an ambiguous role in a culture that cannot decide whether they are educational institutions or warehouses of valuable objects. The attitudes of both directors and educators are functions of this ambiguity. Is it possible that the low esteem accorded educators by some directors and curators is an aspect of these professionals' own insecurities in a culture that values commercial success above all else? Nor are the authors able to examine the general role of art education in American culture. Surely the ways in which both elementary and secondary schools deal with art education have considerable relevance to the task of the art museum educator.

The authors' recommendations, while helpful, suffer from this same narrowness of vision. Art museum educators share many intellectual and practical problems with educators in history and science museums, and many of those problems, as the authors point out, flow from the lack of a body of knowledge about communication and learning in the museum setting and from a lack of resources to generate this body of knowledge. Summer workshops and journals are all very well, and do in fact exist, but the establishment of model year-long programs at the academic institutions that are already grappling with these problems might, in the long run, achieve more. Such programs could be operated in conjunction with a wide variety of museums. After all, it is the audience, not the contents of the museum, that should be the constant factor governing our research. We have a great deal to say to each other, and we need to focus that knowledge and experience, and our unanswered questions, in order to define a series of actions that will advance the field of museum education in general. Perhaps Eisner and Dobbs have challenged us to do that.

Strength in Ambiguity
Judith White

I approached *The Uncertain Profession* as something of an outsider. I work in a zoo education department, not in an art museum, and I was not familiar with the background of the study or the politics of art museums. On the other hand, I do keep in touch with many museum educators, so I have a fair understanding of what goes on in the field. I found that the Eisner-Dobbs report applied very well to educators in zoos and other kind of museums. At times, in fact, I forgot that I was reading about art museums and felt the report was describing my own situation. Four points in particular struck a chord in me. The first two, which museum educators have discussed at great length, are by now old hat:

■ "There is a lack of consensus among museum professionals regarding the basic aims of museum education."

■ "Museum educators perceive themselves to be without much political power."

But two others were newer ideas and gave me cause for thought:

■ "Museum education lacks a sufficient intellectual base and theoretical foundation, including that of scholarly models in the universities."

■ "Museum educators have little or no technical training in research or evaluation methods relevant to their professional tasks."

These last two points seem particularly valid, and in fact they might help explain the lack of power and sense of diffusiveness in the profession, which Eisner and Dobbs commented on. I found myself comparing museum educators with curators. In contrast to the powerless, unfocused museum educators, I pictured zoo curators, all of whom have Ph.D.s in a particular field and all of whom have been contemplating and doing research in their fields for years. By the time they become curators, their senses of self—as professional herpetologists, geologists, or entomologists—are well formed, and they have been immersed in research so the impetus for that continues in their museum jobs.

Although I agreed with the authors' comments on professional training and research, their recommendations, on the whole, disappointed me. A videocassette, a handbook, a summer institute—all these ideas are merely Band-aid solutions. What I felt was needed was to go to the source of the problem: there are no Ph.D. programs in museum education. Only with such a program could we be comparable to curators. We need time to study the philosophical themes of informal education and time for research in our field.

A group of colleagues with whom I occasionally meet and discuss museum education agree with me. We went so far as to draw up a theoretical curriculum for such a degree program. We talked about our idea with other colleagues; we pondered some more. Then we began to see flaws in our proposal, and we had second thoughts. One disturbing thought was the frightful image of a horde of postdoctoral students, descending on museums armed with a philosophy and conducting research on visitors. We wondered if the emphasis on scholarship and research would make the profession too academic. What about innovative program development?

So I began to realize that research and scholarship are only one part of museum education. Think about outstanding museum educators; you will realize that not only are they multifaceted people but that their approaches vary. Some are excellent researchers; others are excellent administrators; others are creative program or exhibit inventors. They are writers or artists or thinkers, and so on.

So where does this leave me? I still agree that we should devote more time and thought to research and to the intellectual and theoretical foundations of our profession, but I am unclear as to how we achieve that (perhaps "informal education" rather than museum education is the subject area we should all identify with). We must not forget those other skills needed in museum education as well—writing, "inventing," and so forth. And we must make allowances for various avenues into the profession. A Ph.D. is only one way.

As to the issue of political power, I have now given that one up as a nonproductive issue to discuss. The routes to power seem various and sometimes elusive. Competence and expertise are sometimes one route. But there are many others—serendipity, charisma, and social contacts. What's more important to being a successful rock star—an excellent voice or an excellent agent? (I hope we spend little time discussing "museum educators and power" at future meetings.)

Rather than apologize for the amorphous, "unclear" nature of our profession (Eisner and Dobbs's first point), perhaps we should realize that this ambiguity is part of our strength. In museum education we are dealing with complex issues for which no one has clear answers. We are challenged to invent creative programs that no one has even thought of yet. We do wear lots of different hats, and that's important. This last point became even clearer to me as I searched for a role model when I found the curators didn't fit. Then I found one that did. Guess who in the museum most resembles the museum educator? The director. Here is a museum professional who has some of the same qualities as a museum educator, but no one criticizes these qualities. The job of director and educator both require a diverse range of skills and allow for different approaches. The jobs are not always well defined, but this ambiguity allows for creativity. It can be a strength. We just have to work to make it stronger.

Our Work Is Good for People
Danielle Rice

I will first review the events that have occurred since the publication of the Eisner-Dobbs report and conclude with some thoughts regarding the responsibilities of museum educators.

The Getty Center for Education in the Arts first circulated a draft of the Eisner-Dobbs report in the summer of 1985. In November of that year, the Getty Center brought together in Toledo, Ohio, a group of 11 museum directors and educators who had been interviewed for the study to discuss the report's findings before publication. After much debate regarding Eisner and Dobbs's portrayal of the museum profession, the group urged that the Getty Center publish and distribute the proceedings of the Toledo meeting with the report. This was done, and *The Uncertain Profession,* along with the Toledo commentary, was published in the spring of 1986.

The Getty Center then decided to test Eisner and Dobbs's hypothesis that museum professionals are unfamiliar with educational research and theory that could prove beneficial to art museums. Eleven institutions participated in a summer colloquium by sending an educator, a curator, or the director of the museum to study with Elliot Eisner at Stanford for two weeks. Nine educators, one chief curator, and one director took part in this experiment.

The colloquium failed in most respects to meet the participants' expectations. It was pitched at much too naive a level and revealed Eisner's lack of understanding of the needs of museum professionals. Nevertheless, the experiment had its merits. The group of colloquium participants convened in February 1987 in Malibu and began investigating alternative ways of helping the museum education profession through colloquiums that would be organized by the museum profession for the museum profession.

Through my continued involvement with the Getty, I became more aware that, in fact, art museum educators had not sufficiently articulated for themselves and their peers the most important belief that motivates them. It is my contention that, in spite of the diverse theories and ideas driving the actions of museum educators, one deeply felt belief unites all of us.

I am referring to the sense that our work is good for people. Many of us are driven by a missionary zeal that allows us to ignore even the realities of low status and low pay. We have self-sacrificing tendencies that a colleague ruefully described as a

"Florence Nightingale/Depression mentality," a state of mind that makes us willing to endure almost any hardship because we know that it is for the benefit of the public.

The notion that art is good for people is commonly accepted in Western culture. This notion underlies museum educators' conviction that if they can facilitate and inform the interaction between people and art objects, they will be performing an important public service. But the philosophy behind this conviction is seldom articulated.

Why is art good for people? And what are the goals of informing people about art? In other words, what is the nature of the service that museum educators provide? To answer these questions for myself, I found that I needed to develop an ethics of museum education, that is, a theory of what is good and bad for the museum public and what the museum's obligations and responsibilities are to that public.

Museums as we know them are largely the product of the political and economic revolutions that took place two centuries ago. Like many other institutions in our culture, they are fraught with contradictions. On the one hand, they make art that had been privately owned available to a larger public; on the other, they bear witness, through their very existence, to the marginality of art in our culture. The artifacts they house were often produced for quite different purposes by cultures for which the very notion of art or art museums did not exist. Far from being the neutral, transparent, natural vehicles for presenting art that they are often assumed to be, museums are the product of a set of beliefs particular to modern, urban, industrial, Western culture.

Two notions of art are common to museum cultures. One is the concept of art objects as valuable pieces of property. The other is the assumption that seeing equals understanding, or that one has merely to look in order to appreciate art. Both of these notions deny the strong conceptual and theoretical frameworks that define art. In the museum setting the curator stands in honorary "owning" relationship to the objects under his or her care. The administrative functions of the institution are coordinated to reflect the importance of maintaining that "owning" relationship. The emphasis is on acquisition of objects, even in institutions where storerooms are filled to capacity.

The focus on vision as the primary activity in the museum setting is evident from the reluctance of many curators to provide extended labels. Museum educators are often accused of trying to trivialize esthetic experience by attempting to explain objects with words. The irony of people who devote their entire lives to studying art proposing that one has merely to look at art in order to understand it is not lost on museum critics.

Inequalities between curators and educators, where they exist, are not due to the museum educators' lack of training or to the curators' greater mastery of the discipline of art history. These inequalities stem primarily from the value system underlying the structure of museums, the value system that places art as property over art as idea and art as record of human achievement. But art is art not because of any intrinsic characteristics. Art consists of objects made by people and assigned an art value by them. Its importance lies in being a tangible record of human experience and creative endeavor, a means of knowledge and a source of inspiration. The history of taste easily demonstrates that the values that make some objects masterpieces and others junk are far from stable and absolute. Modern artists, beginning with Marcel Duchamp, have continually questioned where the notion of "artness" resides, thus pointing to the relativity of the values assigned to art objects and to the systems and institutions required to maintain these values.

If we begin from the premise that art is primarily about ideas and that museums, as institutions devoted to preserving art as property, inadvertently obscure this concept of art, the moral duty of the educator takes on a special significance. For the task that falls to the educator is to navigate through institutional contradictions in order to bridge the gaps between the value systems of the scholars who collect and exhibit art and those of the visitors who come to the museum to look at and perhaps to learn about art.

In my opinion, it is the educator's ethical responsibility to represent from within the institution the position that art is valuable because of ideas conceived by human beings about what constitutes value. It also falls to the educator to gently remind museum professionals and visitors alike that these ideas are neither universal nor absolute. The values that our culture holds dear are as mutable as those of other cultures whose artifacts the museum displays, and they may seem foreign to people who believe differently from the way we do.

It is precisely because of their diverse collections of art by many individuals and from many periods and civilizations that I am optimistic about museums. For all its contradictions, the museum is an ideal forum in which to teach the human value systems underlying institutional structures. In revealing the ideas behind the objects, we contradict what anthropologists call "phenomenal absolutism"—the tendency most people have to assume that everyone else sees and thinks exactly the same way they do. In teaching people discernment, museum educators are not just teaching them to know what is good in art (the artist's value system), but also revealing how decisions about what is good are made (by curators, collectors, dealers, and art critics), so that they can eventually make informed decisions for themselves.

Key Issues
Judith Landau

Following the presentations by the panel members, the meeting was opened up to the audience for comments and questions. Throughout this lively discussion, which ended too soon for all to be heard from, three key issues surfaced repeatedly: the role museums, art and others, play in American culture and the museum educator's connection to that role; the hierarchy of power in the administration of American museums and the museum educator's place in that structure; and the professional training of museum educators. Several additional points of interest were also raised.

Panel member Danielle Rice articulated perhaps the most profound issue in her comments about the value system inherent in art museums, "the value system that places art as property over art as idea and art as record of human achievement." Ken Yellis, curator of education at the National Portrait Gallery, was quick to comment, noting that changes are occurring in the museum world and in society that necessitate a fresh look at the meaning of the term "museum" and the development of a new "theory of museums." "Museums are essentially introspective," he said. "We always work from the inside out," focusing on collections first and developing programs from there. To formulate a new "theory of museums," institutions "need to work from the outside in," emphasizing service to the public. Yellis eloquently stated that the evolving "theory of museums . . . has to do with what the public's expectations and needs are and the services and products and interpretive view of reality that we should be providing in museums and aren't."

Caryl Marsh, project director of the American Psychological Association's Traveling Psychology Exhibition, reminded the audience "not to separate out the science museums from the art museums." She underscored the need to "understand the role of museums in our society" and summarized some of the apparent changes occurring over the last 20 years. Marsh characterized many museums today as "big businesses," indeed doing "business on a multinational scale." She sees American museums as "significant centers of informal education in a variety of communities in a variety of ways," offering services to an international public. Given this growing significance, she encouraged museum educators to continue to work toward their goals as advocates for the public.

The role of the museum educator in the changing museum world was touched on repeatedly by the panelists. Judith White identified the museum educator as "the conscience" of the museum. In Danielle Rice's view museum educators put the emphasis on people and human concerns rather than on collecting. Lonn Taylor defined the role of the museum educator as that of a generalist and synthesizer and one who concentrates on the audience.

A progression from the first two-part issue led naturally to the next: how the museum educator can become a more powerful force in his or her institution. Here there was a flurry of comment and concern. Isaiah Kuperstein, director of education, United States Holocaust Memorial Museum, faced the issue head-on. He was struck by the "power in numbers" represented by the MER meeting and questioned how "we make those who have power take notice of our numbers." Lonn Taylor answered that effective programming is the best way to attract a director's attention. Judy White that "inventing" new programs and having fun doing it is what counts. Danielle Rice advised educators to take opportunities to keep those with power informed about what you do; be aware and knowledgeable about the museum world; and make efforts to humanize the relationships among staff members, communicating on a one-to-one level as often as possible.

Kuperstein pressed further, saying that these answers were characteristic of the problems museum educators face. He was impatient with the inability of those within the profession to use the strength of their numbers to assert themselves. Judy White emphasized writing and publishing as power-building activities. Jennifer Gerlach, former curator of education, Children's Museum in Houston, recommended that museum educators attend board meetings to keep members informed of their activities. Russell Sale, director of education, National Gallery of Art, advised museum educators to pay attention to numbers. Since large museums often measure their success in terms of the size of their audiences, museum educators should observe and keep records of the numbers their programs attract and make that information available to directors. Shirley Cherkasky, museum programs coordinator, National Museum of American History, remarked that "our first job is to improve the quality of museum visitors' experience," although measuring that quality is admittedly a challenge. She saw a more pertinent measure of the strength of museum educators in the value of their programs to visitors than in the numbers of visitors.

The third key issue of the discussion was the appropriate education and training of museum educators. Gretchen Jennings, deputy director of the Visitor Information and Associates' Reception Center, Smithsonian Institution, cited museums as multidisciplinary institutions and stressed the importance of a solid liberal arts education as a prerequisite for the job of museum educator. Museum educators have to "have a sense of history, . . . a sensitivity to other cultures as well as to their own, . . . a sense of esthetics." Bea Taylor, former curator of education, Capital Children's Museum, and currently a doctoral candidate "putting together a degree in museum education," had words of encouragement for those seeking advanced training. She spoke of a growing trend in universities to establish interdisciplinary Ph.D. programs that allow students, with plenty of hard work, creativity, and political maneuvering, to design programs that enhance the museum education profession. Dianne Stillman, director of education at Baltimore's Walters Art Gallery, commented on the variety of skills and backgrounds necessary to the museum education field and saw the need for some "commonality." She felt that, in an art museum, the commonality still has to be art history. Judy White asked if one could substitute "informal education" as the commonality instead.

Ultimately, the meeting ran out of time but not out of energy. Indeed, while *The Uncertain Profession* did antagonize many museum educators, it has also served as a catalyst for discussion and perhaps for action. In Ken Yellis's words, "Professionalizing is an institution-building process. It is about the future." As museum educators we need to be focusing on that future. We have a lot to think about, talk about, and do for ourselves and the public we serve.

Eisner and Dobbs's Generalizations

1. There is a lack of consensus among museum professionals regarding the basic aims of museum education.

2. There are widely different attitudes toward museum education and museum educators among museum directors.

3. There is a need for museum curators and museum educators to reorganize their complementary functions.

4. Within any single museum, innovative ideas about museum education are limited.

5. Museum educators perceive themselves to be without much political power and at the bottom of the status hierarchy in museums.

6. Museum educators require recognition and acknowledgment as making a specific and indispensable contribution to the work of the museum.

7. The career opportunities for museum educators are limited.

8. Museum education lacks a sufficient intellectual base and theoretical foundation, including that of scholarly models in the universities.

9. Museum educators regard art history as the intellectual core of their field and have given it the highest priority in their own professional preparation.

10. Many museum professionals don't know the field of education and make assumptions about it which are counterproductive to the museum's attainment of its educational objectives.

11. Adequate resources have not been made available for professional preparation in museum education.

12. The staffing of museum education is generally not adequate for the diversity and demand for educational services.

13. Museum educators and directors are divided in their views about the benefits of various technologies available for educational programs.

14. There is no viable network of communication and contact which reaches all museum educators and provides exchange of ideas and program resources.

15. Museum educators have little or no technical training in research or evaluation methods relevant to their professional tasks.

16. Museum educators would like a place where empirical questions about audiences and their experiences with works of art might be studied.

17. The relationship between museum education and other educational services and institutions in the community has been inadequately conceptualized.

18. Museum educators seem to lack a well-defined vision of their responsibility and the methodologies necessary to develop new audiences for the museum.

19. Museum educators vary widely in their perceptions of the usefulness of volunteers and the degree of preparation necessary to work in educational programs.

20. Museum educators have relatively little contact with those persons who shape museum policies, as represented on boards of trustees.

Eisner and Dobbs's Recommendations

1. The Getty Summer Institute in Museum Education
2. Handbook for museum education (theory, research, and practice)
3. Annual conference on museum education
4. Research studies in museum education
5. Visiting fellowships in museum education
6. Journal of museum education
7. Videotape cassette series
8. Collaborative program development

Source: Elliot W. Eisner and Stephen M. Dobbs, *The Uncertain Profession: Observations on the State of Museum Education in Twenty American Art Museums* (Los Angeles: Getty Center for Education in the Arts, 1986).

Professional Standards for Museum Educators

American Association of Museums Standing Professional Committee on Education

Preface
Patterson B. Williams

The publication of *Museum Ethics* in 1978 marked the first time in more than 50 years that the American Association of Museums had issued a statement on ethics for museums and museum professionals. In the decade since, we have seen a renewed attention to professional standards and practices, as the museum community has thoughtfully engaged in the continuing self-examination that appropriately characterizes any profession in this complex world.

Today there is a strong consciousness that museums as institutions and museum professionals as individuals have far-reaching obligations to their public and their collections, obligations that are not to be taken lightly. A revised statement on museum ethics is in progress, a sign of the firmly held commitment to setting standards for our profession that are consistent with both the traditional functions of museums and the tenor of the world in which they operate.

This statement on professional standards for museum educators complements both *Museum Ethics* and the International Council of Museums' *Statutes/Code of Professional Ethics* (1987). It represents the fruit of an ongoing dialogue among museum educators about museums' mandate as public educational institutions and museum educators' responsibilities as practitioners who help fulfill that mandate. It too is the sign of a firmly held commitment—a commitment by museum educators to strive for excellence in the service of the public. As the first statement of professional standards in our field—and the first to focus on the museum's educational obligations to its public—it is a hallmark in the evolution of museum education.

In the spirit of the museum profession, the preparation of this statement has been a collaborative effort. Educators in the Southeast region, led by Karen King and Nancy Glaser, created a draft that was a major step toward realizing the final product. Groups of educators around the country, at regional and local museum meetings, offered thoughtful critiques of the document-in-progress. More than 40 individuals took the time to study it and make substantive suggestions; Diane

Journal of Museum Education 14, no. 3 (Fall 1989): 11–13.

Brigham, Barbara Henry, Kate Johnson, Teresa LaMaster, Joan Madden, Gordon Murdock, Susan Shaffer, and Bret Waller were especially helpful. Mary Ellen Munley incorporated all of these comments into a revised draft. Mary Alexander, Nancy Glaser, Elaine Heumann Gurian, Mary Ellen Munley, Carol B. Stapp, and I worked as a committee with editor Ellen Cochran Hirzy to produce the final document. The entire Education Committee approved it by a vote of members.

We hope that all museum professionals will see this statement as an affirmation of the vital mission we share: helping to make museums places of inquiry, discovery, and learning for all.

Introduction

Every museum has an educational responsibility to the public it serves. Museums offer a unique encounter with objects and ideas for people of many ages, interests, and backgrounds. Museum education strengthens that encounter by building bridges between visitors' experiences and expectations and the experiences and ideas that emanate from a museum's collection.

To fulfill the educational mandate of their institutions, museum professionals must work together to ensure the following:

■ the integrity, authenticity, preservation, and quality of the objects the museum presents;

■ the accuracy of information disseminated to the public;

■ the intelligibility and usefulness of such information to the museum's audiences;

■ the quality of its presentation; and

■ the recognition of the diversity of audiences and the importance of intellectual integrity in the exchange of ideas and in the collection and presentation of objects.

This statement of standards is intended to encourage museum professionals to strive for excellence as they carry out these important responsibilities. These standards provide reminders of the variety of public service obligations that all members of the museum profession assume, benchmarks against which the educational responsibilities of museums can be measured, and guidelines to help museum educators can examine their own professional conduct.

Although this is a statement by and for the members of the American Association of Museums Standing Professional Committee on Education, its principles apply to all museum professionals, paraprofessionals, and volunteers who are involved in helping visitors have an enriching experience in the museum.

Defining Museum Education

Museums collect, preserve, present, interpret, and conduct research on tangible objects of cultural, historical, scientific, and esthetic value. Each of these functions is part of a museum's relationship to its audiences, but presentation and interpretation figure most prominently in the domain of museum education.

Museum educators serve as advocates for museum audiences. Their primary responsibilities are to assure public access to the museum's collections and exhibitions and to create both the environment and the programs that encourage high-quality experiences for all visitors. Public education in a museum is accomplished through the thoughtful application of audience analysis and principles of teaching and learning to the processes of interpretation, exhibition, and—where appropriate— to collecting and research.

The Museum's Obligations to Its Public

The museum's role as an agent of education carries with it certain obligations to the multifaceted public it serves.

Audience Diversity

Museums should be well integrated into their communities and accessible as educational resources and places of inspiration. Museums should seek to expand their audience base by actively extending into their communities with efforts and activities designed to build new audiences. Not every museum need serve every potential audience. Decisions about audiences, however, should be consciously made and carefully examined to ensure that they do not, by default, exclude those who traditionally have not felt welcome in museums. As a general rule, each museum should strive to make itself and its collections accessible—physically, emotionally, and intellectually—to the widest possible audience.

Audience Needs

To meet their responsibilities to a diverse public, museums must reflect a knowledge of their audience and a sensitivity to the varied capabilities and experiences visitors bring with them. The museum audience is a heterogeneous blend of publics that have both unique needs and common interests. The exhibits, programs, and services that a museum offers should attract and serve a diverse audience and stimulate the spirit of inquiry at all levels of capability, mastery, and interest.

Diversity of Perspectives

Research, exhibitions, publications, programs, and other forms of interpretation are powerful mediums of expression, even more so because the public vests museums with considerable authority. A museum's interpretive practices should acknowledge clearly the variety of cultural, esthetic, and intellectual perspectives that can legitimately contribute to the visitor's understanding of a given exhibition, program, or collection. The integrity of the objects, the freedom of museum staff to express informed points of view, and the freedom of visitors to discover ideas and form opinions all deserve respect in the interpretive process.

Education within the Museum Structure

The magnitude of museums' educational responsibilities requires a commitment on the part of each museum to afford education a major place in the institutional policy-making and planning structure.

Education Policies and Plans

Service to a diverse audience and creation of a responsible interpretive program are important functions that require creativity, knowledge, skill, and dedication. Just as well-managed museums have formal, written policy statements to guide their collecting activities, so should they have formal, written policies that set out their educational purposes, identify audiences to be served, and give direction to education programs. The success of a museum in meeting its educational mission should be measured against these policies.

Education Resources

A supportive institutional structure and an appropriate commitment of financial and human resources are essential to creating and sustaining high-quality educational services in museums. This commitment entails hiring experienced and highly trained education staff and providing compensation commensurate with job responsibilities, experience, and education.

Institutional Structure

The process of presenting and interpreting museum collections is enriched by collaboration among professionals with a variety of skills and talents. Museum staff with knowledge of audiences and expertise in education theory and practice should actively participate in the formation of all policies and practices that affect visitors' experiences.

The way in which an object is exhibited and interpreted powerfully influences the kinds of perception and learning that take place. The museum educator's role in the early stages of exhibition planning is to identify audiences and articulate clear educational objectives in order to develop appropriate communication and interpretive strategies. These strategies can then be employed to create links between visitors and objects so that curiosity is fostered and exploration of ideas, topics, or objects is encouraged.

Knowledge from outside the museum can be an important ingredient in program development. Therefore, museum educators should involve others in the community who can contribute to the interpretive process and provide bridges between the museum and its public.

Responsibilities and Competencies of the Museum Educator

Every museum educator brings a blend of experience and skills to his or her position. For all museum educators, however, certain responsibilities and competencies are necessary.

Knowledge

Museum educators help visitors see, understand, and respond to objects in museum collections in intellectually, aesthetically, and emotionally rewarding ways. Museum educators must have the skills to encourage interaction between the visitor and the objects on exhibit, at whatever level the visitor requires. To do this effectively, educators must know both their museum's audiences and their museum's collections. This means having a demonstrated knowledge of developmental psychology, philosophy of education, educational theory, and teaching, especially as related to the kind of voluntary and personal learning that takes place in museums. Equally important are a solid grounding in the history, theory, or practice of a field of study relevant to the areas in which the museum collects, as well as the ability to identify and cooperate with scholars and specialists in the appropriate fields.

Advocacy

As advocates for museum audiences, museum educators must have thorough knowledge of and sensitivity to the audiences their museums serve. Museum educators must also express a willingness, and demonstrate an aptitude, for expanding the museum's audience over time. Toward this end, educators must understand the trends, issues, and changing attitudes and demographics in the museum's immediate community and in contemporary society.

Communication

Museum educators should facilitate communication both within the museum family and between the museum and its communities. Effective oral and written communication skills—for teaching, volunteer and staff training, public information functions, and internal management—are needed by the museum educator.

Evaluation

Museum educators must understand how to assess the effectiveness of exhibitions and programs, both from the museum audience's point of view and in light of the museum's educational mission and the distinctive nature of museum learning. The ongoing evaluation of exhibits and programs should be used to ensure that the museum's educational objectives are being realized.

Management

Museum educators should have a clear understanding and appreciation of the museum's philosophy and mission and be able to articulate and foster it in those with whom they work. Furthermore, museum educators share responsibility for the economic health of the institution. Museum educators should demonstrate skills related to the management of fiscal and human resources needed to accomplish the museum's educational goals.

Collaboration

Museums are just one part of a universe of formal and informal educational institutions. Museum educators should develop sound working relationships with other museums and cultural institutions, schools, universities, and community organizations to provide the best possible public educational experience for the visitor.

Dissemination

Museum educators should share their knowledge of the principles and practice of museum education with others in the museum field and in the educational community at large. This can occur through workshops, publications, and participation in state, regional, and national conferences.

Professional Development

Recognizing that learning is a lifelong pursuit, museum educators should persistently seek opportunities to expand their own expertise in education methods, knowledge of their museum's collections, evaluation, and management. Museum administrators and educators should create an atmosphere that encourages this professional growth and development.

MER at Twenty: Some Observations on Museum Education

Kenneth Starr

It is an honor to be invited to join you in celebrating the 20th anniversary of the Museum Education Roundtable, which through massive amounts of sustained work by many of you over the years has made signal contributions to museum education, far beyond the District of Columbia, all on the solid foundation of being actual "do-ers" of education.

Apart from the actual educative function, you also have contributed in two other respects. One, you have given heightened meaning to the word "cooperation," for you have dealt with your common challenges in concert, and that is not always easy in local situations, given the twin green-eyed demons of individual and institutional competition. Two, you also have given substance to the word "volunteer," for you have achieved your successes through the giving of your own personal time and energies.

As a perquisite of being a bit older than some of you and of having weaved my way through the busy highways and quieter side roads of our marvelous museum world, I would like to make some observations about five aspects of museum education that relate to your concerns, regardless of discipline. Those observations are distillates of my own experience and thinking, and so represent only my personal perspective. Little of what I shall say will be new, and some of it will echo comments that some of you made in the sessions this morning. Most of it will have meaning, or should have meaning, not only for all of you as working educators but also for trustees, directors, and other staff, all of whom should consider themselves educators as well.

Resources
The first aspect has to do with the resources at our disposal, and in that regard we are fortunate beyond measure in having access to awesome resources, both human and material. Apart from having access to curatorial staffs—and having begun my museum career as a curator I am quick to add that not all curators are equal, with

Journal of Museum Education 15, no. 1 (Winter 1990): 18–19. This essay was originally a talk presented at the Museum Education Roundtable's 20th anniversary celebration in September 1990 in Washington, D.C.

some more equal than others as regards their feelings of responsibility to you and the public—you also have access to books and, most particularly, to collections that speak of all of nature and human invention. Your potential for sharing the magic, the absolute magic, of those objects and of all that they represent is limited only by your creativity and your ability to communicate that sense of magic. There is not a single object in your collections, no matter how humble or plain, that does not have its mind-exciting tale to tell, its soul-satisfying qualities to share.

Communicating with Your Audiences

In telling that tale and in sharing those soul-satisfying qualities, personal and professional ethics are first and foremost: we must have integrity of content and integrity of presentation, for we are in the business of education, not indoctrination and not entertainment. Sometimes it is difficult to hold to that principle, for, on one hand, we feel strongly about many issues, some of them socially sensitive, and, on the other hand, admittance revenues increasingly are a factor in our decisions.

Of but slightly lesser importance is the need to "know your stuff," whatever that "stuff" is, and to balance fact with concept, and both with the encouragement of thinking. There also is the need to balance quality and quantity, not sacrificing the quality of what we present in order to win more people and more dollars. For many of us who are educators there is a constant intellectual tension between wanting to move many people a little way and wanting to move the few a long way. As a professional I still have not resolved that tension, but as an individual I always have found museums to be intensely personal experiences. Whether from a professional or an individual view, however, I remain nervous about moving too far in the direction of mass experiences, especially when the process is dollar driven. We of course should strive to educate as broadly and as deeply as possible, but never at the expense of quality.

We also should seek creativity in our teaching, using our heads—*really* using our heads—to think of *truly* fresh and imaginative approaches to communicating our subjects in ways that challenge the mind and please the spirit without trivializing the substance. It is not easy to move beyond traditional patterns—many of which, incidentally, are practical, time-tested, and eternally effective—but whatever we do it is vital that we always remain open to new ways of thinking and of dealing with our ever-growing, ever-changing challenges. Such efforts take extra work, both brain and back, and for one's pains in trying to initiate change one often meets with active resistance, polite disregard, or, at best, unenthusiastic acceptance. In my former incarnation as a museum director I urged my staff members to take a small part of their time and dollars to experiment with new ideas and approaches, but I met with only partial success, for it was difficult for some of them to change. Old ways are easier and more comfortable.

Closely related to encouraging new ways is evaluation, which in its many manifestations is one of the most fruitful approaches that has come into the museum world in recent years. Its use in education is no less important than it is in exhibits, analyzing our programs in order to ascertain how effective, or ineffective, they are in relation to their purposes. The technique is particularly valuable in assessing education programs, for with the flexibility of museums, at least compared with more rigid school systems, one more easily can modify education programs on a continuing basis. The expression, "different strokes for different folks," is very important to keep in mind in our increasingly diverse contemporary world, for it should move us to consider our widely differing audiences and to adapt our presentations to match.

Professional Relationships

Guidance and support must come from the very top of the museum organization, and if educators are to be successful in devising and implementing their programs they must have access to their directors and be able to persuade them of the importance of the education component. Given the fact that most directors have their training and experience in other areas of museum endeavor—and, alas, more frequently, nonmuseum endeavor—such persuasion is not always easy, but citing Norman Cousins in another context, "The only thing greater than the difficulty is the necessity." The times are on our side, for there is growing attention to education throughout the country, with particular emphasis on science education. We can but hope that "the education president" will put his money where his mouth is and, further, that he will include museums on his education agenda. "Take care of your men" is a military dictum, but it also applies to heads of museum education departments. Support and speak up for education and your educators in every way that you can, including being right up there in front when the director makes budget allocations for programs and hands out salary increases, constantly reminding him or her of your value to the museum and its constituencies.

In like way, support and help your volunteers. The relationship between paid and volunteer staffs should be a symbiotic one wherein you gain in additional human resources and your volunteers gain in satisfaction from self-advancement and from being part of an extremely important enterprise. As with all human relationships, those between staff and volunteers are built on needs, and so long as there is mutual satisfaction of those needs the relationship will remain strong. There has to be something in the relationship for everyone.

Societal Aspects

Here, the overriding concern is for women and minorities. My awareness of this concern has been heightened by my experience at the National Science Foundation, where there is a strong thrust toward bringing greater numbers of women and minorities into science. The same urgent need continues to exist in our museum world at all levels, including boards of trustees, directorships, and senior positions. Such especially is the case with respect to minorities, a cause for concern in virtually every professional situation. When I left the AAM Accreditation Commission last year I composed a letter to my fellow commissioners in which I urged the commission to add to the accreditation questionnaire questions about the numbers of women and minorities on museum boards and in senior positions. Given the diversity of our audiences, especially in major urban centers, and the critical importance of the matter for our nation, it is incumbent upon us to bring about a similar diversity in our own institutions, including especially the education staffs, who are our public face. As Mark Twain observed about the weather, however, everyone talks about minority representation, but no one does anything about it. In way of personal but highly relevant comment I take the opportunity of noting that when John Kinard, director of the Smithsonian's Anacostia Museum, died recently, we lost a good friend and dedicated fellow professional.

Incidentally, before I leave the subject of equity, and in puckish but also serious manner, I once again was reminded this morning, as I studied the group of attendees, that there is a reverse need among museum educators for more men.

The Schools and the Children

As for the schools, over the years I have wrestled with the challenges of how to deal most effectively with the formal school system and to strengthen the mutually fruitful relationship between schools and museums. It of course is useful to appeal to the teachers themselves, but only the more imaginative and dedicated of them tend to respond, and even those who do respond have to contend with rigid structures that make it difficult, and in some cases impossible, for them to use museums in a consistent and effective way. Heightening that difficulty is the fact that some school administrators do not understand, or perhaps do not want to understand, the nature and contributions of museums as education resources, and often look upon them either as threats or as "second-class citizens." Alas, as in too many other areas, I have no answers, but I would suggest that if you are striving for heightened cooperation with the schools you might increase your contacts at the top with school boards, superintendents, and assistant superintendents, especially those responsible for curriculum, impressing upon them the distinctive, complementary, and important contributions that museums make to the educational process.

As for the children, in two different sessions this morning I heard ever so thinly disguised negative comments about dealing with children in museums. In one session an individual referred to the stereotype of museum educators as dealing with children, as though that somehow was an unimportant or lesser responsibility, while in another session I heard reference to shifting from the focus on children. Now, even though I have a 10 percent hearing loss, I am reasonably sure that I heard correctly. Do not neglect the children, for as Kahlil Gibran so perceptively wrote, "They are not your children, they are the children of tomorrow." They also are the adults of tomorrow, and if you do not make your museum a rewarding place for them to come as children today, they will not come as adults tomorrow.

Thank you again for inviting me to join you this evening. You and the Museum Education Roundtable now mark 20 years of cooperation and success, with everyone gaining: you yourselves as individual professionals, your institutions, your profession, and your publics. In a recent conversation between us, Michael Templeton opined that pound for pound MER has had a more sustained impact on museum education than any group in the country, and that comment is right on the mark. Borrowing from Tiny Tim and *A Christmas Carol,* I end my observations by saying that you all can be very proud, "every one."

Museums and the Future of Education

Joel N. Bloom and Ann Mintz

In late 1989, the American Association of Museums established the Task Force on Museum Education and charged it with describing the critical issues in museum education and recommending action to strengthen and expand the educational role of museums in today's world. In his letter of invitation to the distinguished members of the task force, AAM President Joel N. Bloom noted that "the museum community has long been concerned with education. Many institutions have education as a basic element in their charters, and some in fact see education as their primary reason for existence."[1]

The two dozen task force members shared a commitment to and involvement in museum education, but their first meeting revealed some significant—though not surprising—differences of opinion about just what museum education is and what it should be. The fact is that once we move beyond truisms, education becomes a tricky issue and consensus is difficult to attain. Even within the museum field, the very word "education" can mean different things to different people. There are conflicts of opinion about the relationship between preservation and interpretation, about the relative priority of collections and education. As a result, apparent agreement can vanish when we seek to define our terms.

Given the complexity of the issues involved, why should the Task Force on Museum Education venture into these murky waters? Because literally nothing is more important. Our future as a nation depends on the decisions we make about how to educate our children to face the challenges of the next century.

The Current Crisis in Education
Our society puts great emphasis on education. Universal free public education, described by Thomas Jefferson as a "crusade against ignorance," is central to the American dream. Our system of government is predicated on the existence of an informed citizenry that is capable of participating in important decisions. These are lofty educational ambitions. Yet it is increasingly clear that there is a significant shortfall between expectation and performance.

The picture is complicated. More Americans are finishing high school and pursuing higher education than ever before, but the quality of that education is

Journal of Museum Education 14, no. 3 (Fall 1990): 12–15.

questioned. Every day new horror stories are reported in the newspapers. College students cannot place the Civil War in the proper half-century. Design students think that Frank Lloyd Wright was one of the Wright Brothers. An alarming percentage of adults persists in the belief that the sun revolves around the earth. International studies document that our students, compared to those in other countries, score somewhere between the bottom quarter and dead last. Even this is not the grimmest aspect of the picture. A child born in the United States today has one chance in 432 of becoming a doctor, one chance in 350 of becoming a lawyer, one chance in 107 of becoming a teacher, and one chance in five of growing up illiterate. By the time that child enters the work force, the average job will probably require 14 years of education—a high school diploma and two years of additional schooling. One-fifth of our population will be virtually unemployable, unable to participate in the democratic process, unable to help educate their own children. This situation is particularly troublesome, since the most significant single indicator of educational performance is the educational attainment of the parents, especially the mother.

The failure of our educational system puts our future at risk—our economic future, our future as a nation, our personal futures. There is considerable urgency to the role of museums as a community of educational institutions. Frank Oppenheimer, founder and director of the Exploratorium, said it well: "The whole point of education is to transmit culture, and museums can play an increasingly important role in this process. It is a mistake to think that preserving culture is distinct from transmitting it through education."[2]

Education as the Spirit of Museums

Education has long been a hallmark of our nation's museums. In its 1984 report, the Commission on Museums for a New Century cogently described the importance of museum education:

> Many consider public education to be the most significant contribution this country has made to the evolution of the museum concept. . . . If collections are the heart of museums, what we have come to call education—the commitment to presenting objects and ideas in an informative and stimulating way—is the spirit.[3]

Although 19th-century museum pioneers emphasized the significance of education, they defined it in terms very different from ours today. "Education" usually meant formal programs; the more a museum program was like a school, the more "educational" it seemed. Early museum educators believed that the public should be educated on the museum's terms, on the museum's turf. That turf was often a park on the outskirts of a city, chosen as the site in keeping with the "city beautiful" concept that reigned in city planning but often isolating the museum both geographically and spiritually from its community.

Today, "education" has an expanded definition both within and outside museums. The increasing importance of informal learning in our lives has led us to emphasize the broad educational significance of the museum visit. The concept of informal education encompasses the many ways people learn beyond the classroom—by reading books and magazines, watching television or movies, observing the natural world, or visiting a museum.

Still the old model retains much power, and we ourselves can be defensive about the educational impact of museums. "Museum education" often refers to structured classroom experiences in the museum involving a teacher and a group of students. Thus, discussions of museum education often founder on different definitions of the term itself.

But there is general agreement that museums are unique places of learning. A museum offers direct, one-to-one experience with real objects. Even in this media-saturated "information age," there is no substitute for the power of reality. A museum visit is self-structured. Visitors can browse until they find something that inspires focused attention and return again and again to whatever interests them. There are no performance standards in a museum visit. Visitors need no prior experience to participate in what a museum has to offer, and they are free to explore without fear of judgment or failure.

The museum visit has educational significance in both the affective and the cognitive realms. In fact, many specialists believe that the affective aspect of museum learning may be more significant than the cognitive. A museum can inspire a visitor to ask questions and pursue a newfound interest independently. This type of learning may well have a greater long-term impact than the nuggets of information gleaned from an exhibit.

Museums must learn how to assess the power of museum education. Serious investigation of the way people learn in museums will document the impact of museum education and reveal how we can become even more effective. Such studies have revealed that museums stimulate kinds of learning that are not possible in the classroom. Current research indicates, for example, that object-based learning using specially designed interactive exhibit devices is particularly effective in countering erroneous beliefs about the physical universe. These so-called naive theories of science are very difficult to eradicate in the classroom setting.

Research into the dynamics and impact of museum learning will serve another purpose as well. Museum professionals often speak of the need to change the perception of museums and to expand public understanding of museums' importance. In this era of diminishing public support and increased competition for the corporate and foundation dollar, we compete for funding with programs for the homeless, treatment and prevention of substance abuse, teenage pregnancy, and high school dropouts. Cultural institutions may provide touchstones, inspiration, reminders of the magnificent potential of the human spirit. Unfortunately, they are often seen as luxuries that many communities can ill afford. Education, on the other hand, is widely accepted as an important part of a solution to our most pressing problems. Surely it will be more effective to reinforce our identities as educational institutions than to change the public perception of the value of cultural institutions. Museum education is thus strategically important as we move toward the next century.

The New Educational Environment

In recent years, as public concern for the state of education in America grows, museums are taking more and more initiative. They are playing an active role in their communities, forming broad-based partnerships to address educational issues, and working with school systems and the private sector to improve public education.

In the future, partnerships between schools and museums will flourish, but the educational arena will expand. Museums will provide even greater opportunities for the adult learner. The "shelf life" of an education is getting shorter, and career change is becoming the norm rather than the exception. As a result, lifelong learning will be increasingly important. In the United States today, adult participation in education is growing. More than one-third of the students enrolled in higher education institutions are adults. In fact, education is one of the most popular uses of discretionary time.

Museums have an important function in this new educational environment. We can expand our informal educational offerings, work more closely with schools, and provide professional development opportunities to educators. We may also find ourselves involved in a new type of education. One factor that drives the increasing concern about the quality of American education is that corporations often find it difficult to recruit qualified workers. As a result, many businesses are becoming directly involved in education, providing professional development for senior staff or remedial education for entry-level workers. This new form of continuing education may offer an opportunity for museums.

Cultural Pluralism and the "Proliferation of Voices"

The importance of museum involvement in education at every level, for every age group, cannot be overstated. Yet as museums deepen their commitment to education, we will increasingly confront another set of challenges. We are educational institutions, but who are we educating? What are we teaching? How should we make decisions about educational mission and content?

These are not simple questions. They relate to complex factors that are shaping the future for us all. Two interrelated forces of societal change are involved, both of which were identified by the Commission on Museums for a New Century and are active today: the growing recognition and acceptance of cultural diversity and the rise of participatory decision making at all levels of our society.

For 19th-century museum pioneers, the concept of cultural pluralism did not exist. There was very little question about the primacy of the mainstream culture.

As recently as two decades ago, our cultural ideal was the melting pot—the loss of Old World identities and the creation of a new American identity. Today we no longer aspire to the melting pot. We celebrate our diversity and no longer seek to submerge it. Increasingly, we recognize and accept that cultural pluralism is a distinctive element of our national character. It should be reflected in all our institutions, including museums.

Cultural pluralism has many implications for museums and museum education, and the Task Force on Museum Education will address them in its report. The internal implications of staffing and governance are as significant as the implications for collections policies, programs, and exhibitions. How will we assure that our boards of trustees, our staffs, and our volunteers truly reflect the diversity of the communities our museums serve? How can we encourage the expression of diverse values and viewpoints in our programs and exhibitions? And how can we engage a more diverse spectrum of the public in all that museums have to offer? It may be that until our profession reaches consensus on such questions, we cannot truly be effective players in the world outside our walls.

The second force of change that has profound implications for museums is a new kind of populism—a "proliferation of voices," as the Commission on Museums called it—that has resulted in a fundamental change in decision-making processes. It is inextricably connected to the growing acceptance of a multicultural America. In this new populism, traditional hierarchical structures are being modified so that decisions can no longer be handed down from the top. Many more players demand and are being given a role. In the workplace and in society as a whole, there is a broader base of participation.

Evidence of this new style of decision making can be found in the growth of special-interest politics, the move to participatory management styles, and the search for "win-win" conflict resolution. Every voice asserts a right to be heard. A Midwestern woman is offended by the language and subject matter of a television program. Not long ago, she would have changed the channel and forgotten about it. Today, she begins a campaign that leads to the cancellation of half the advertising on the offending show.

The confluence of these two forces of change has profound implications for museums. One of the most obvious expressions is in the growth of ethnic museums and arts centers. Philadelphia, for example, has a Swedish-American museum, an African-American museum, a museum of Jewish-American history, a Puerto Rican arts center, and an institute for ethnic studies.

But such specialty museums are only the beginning. Many American museums are hearing the voices of a pluralistic community and developing programs and exhibitions to reflect those voices. A few years ago, the Philadelphia Museum of Art presented an exhibition on Nigerian art that included a full-scale African marketplace. The Chicago Museum of Science and Industry recently organized an exhibition called *Black Achievers in Science* that focused on the accomplishments of that community. The American Museum of Natural History in New York City has exhibited ritual objects from Harlem along with their African counterparts.

The Challenges of Inclusiveness

Despite efforts to expand the perspective of museum exhibitions and programs, mainstream culture still pervades our institutions. Just ask the Native Americans who are fighting to rescue what they believe to be their cultural heritage and their ancestors. Ask women and minority artists, who believe that they have been systematically, if unconsciously, excluded from the mainstream. Thirty years ago, René d'Harnoncourt of the Museum of Modern Art pointed out that there is no such thing as a neutral museum exhibition. An exhibition is the result of myriad decisions, major and minor. Museums are widely perceived as standard-bearers of culture, arbiters of quality. The decisions we make will be scrutinized closely by the mainstream as well as by vocal minorities.

These are not simple issues. It has proved difficult indeed to forge a compromise between Native Americans and the legitimate scholarly concerns of anthropologists and archeologists, difficult to acknowledge the historical primacy of the mainstream as well as the cultural significance of the disenfranchised. Regrettably, such conflicts often become political footballs, and resolution becomes yet more difficult.

No decision can satisfy all the stakeholders. Further controversy seems inevitable. How can we juggle these apparently irreconcilable demands? How do we decide what we include and what we leave out? Whose side of the story should museums tell? Who decides? What criteria do we apply? What standards do we use when we select artifacts and works of art for exhibitions? What cultural biases shape our decisions?

The educational community has confronted such issues for some time. Are SAT tests a fair assessment of intellectual potential, or do they confer an unfair advantage on middle-class students? Should Latino students submit their school work in English or Spanish? How should American history be taught? What literature belongs in the English curriculum?

The recognition of cultural diversity and the proliferation of voices have politicized education. Ironically, confronting societal issues has resulted in a retreat from controversy, not a balanced exploration of opposing views. Today many educators deplore the blandness of their textbooks. Publishers prefer to avoid offense; no matter how balanced the treatment of a difficult issue, extremists are likely to object. Unfortunately, it seems that if something is designed to offend no one, it is unlikely to interest anyone either.

As a community, we are moving toward a stronger definition of museums as educational institutions. If we expand this role, museums will be subject to the same pressure from diverse communities as formal educational institutions have felt. These communities will expect to be represented in our institutions and participate in our decisions. Inevitably, there will be objections to some of these decisions. It would be tragic indeed if we, too, retreated from controversy and opted only for the safe, the sanitized.

We cannot underestimate the impact we may have. We must not forget that the child who stands silent before Picasso's *Guernica* may feel more strongly about human rights for the rest of his or her life. We must understand that Anselm Kiefer's work is among the most powerful arguments against another Holocaust, that iron slave chains may teach more about black America than any textbook.

The politicization of museums has already begun. We can see it in the controversy over the repatriation of Native American remains and artifacts, in the recent addition of slave quarters at Colonial Williamsburg, in the demands of African Americans that their lost heroes be included in history and science museum exhibits. More problematic are the demands by evangelical Christians that "creation science" be included in earth science and paleontology exhibits and in planetarium shows.

In addition to the central issue of cultural diversity, another kind of diversity merits mention. It is the diversity of values, which has raised difficult issues for those who decide how public money should be spent in support of the arts. This is a period of transition for America's museums. Traditionally, we occupy the "high ground" and thus have never been subject to the same degree of scrutiny as other institutions in this open society. Now we are seeking to define ourselves as central to society, and market forces are forcing us to become market driven.

We cannot have it both ways. Either we are above the hurly-burly or in the thick of it. We cannot both transcend the world and respond to its demands. This dilemma is not unique to museums. For literally thousands of years, questions have been asked about the proper relationship of art to society. Thoughtful, decent people often have radically different opinions, because thoughtful, decent people do not necessarily share identical values.

As we expand and deepen our definition of museum education, we must address issues of values in a rational way. Age-old questions are embedded in these issues. What is the relationship of the individual to society? Should we always aspire to the "greatest good for the greatest number"?

Our society likes answers. Uncertainty is difficult for us to accept. Yet we must learn to live with it. Beneath the issues of cultural diversity and the "new populism" are fundamental questions—questions about our nature as human beings, about the role of art in society, about the nature of morality. Education raises these questions because through education, culture is transmitted. By tackling the issue of museum education—what it is and what it should be—the Task Force on Museum Education has taken on a challenging task.

We must continue to ask difficult questions, even though we may never agree on the answers. As museums move into an ever more complex, option-filled future, we can serve society by providing a place to explore these questions. The future will not be a simple place to live. Yet we will spend the rest of our lives there. No matter how complicated the world becomes, there will always be a place for museums and for the special kind of learning that takes place in them. Museums can light a spark that burns for a lifetime. This is the unique role we can play in meeting the educational demands of the future.

Notes

1. The report of the Task Force on Museum Education is available from the American Association of Museums.
2. Frank Oppenheimer, "Exploration and Culture: Oppenheimer Receives Distinguished Service Award," *Museum News* 61, no. 1 (September/October 1982): 39.
3. Commission on Museums for a New Century, *Museums for a New Century* (Washington, D.C.: American Association of Museums, 1984), p. 55.

"Excellence and Equity: Education and the Public Dimension of Museums"

American Association of Museums Task Force on Museum Education

Introduction
Bonnie Pitman

In September 1989, Joel Bloom, president of the American Association of Museums, asked me to chair a task force concerned with the educational role of museums. Our charge was to articulate the critical issues in museum education and recommend action that will strengthen and expand the educational role museums play in today's world. Finally, we were charged with outlining an ongoing role for museums, professional associations, and other appropriate organizations. The intention was to ensure that the task force's recommendations would be carried out.

The work of the task force is an outgrowth of the AAM's 1984 report, *Museums for a New Century*, which states, "If collections are the heart of museums, what we have come to call education—the commitment to presenting objects and ideas in an informative and stimulating way—is the spirit." The report described and the Task Force on Museum Education affirmed the powerful capacity of museums to contribute to the richness of the collective human experience.

The task force's report, *Excellence and Equity: Education and the Public Dimension of Museums*, identifies 10 principles with attending recommendations for consideration and action by the museum field. These principles are reflected in three key ideas:

■ First, we assert that education is a primary responsibility of museums. The commitment to serve the public must be clearly stated in every museum's mission and central to its activities.

■ Second, we believe in the potential for museums to be enriched and enlivened by the nation's diversity. As public institutions in a democratic society, museums must achieve greater inclusiveness. Trustees and staff must acknowledge and respect our nations's diversity in race, ethnic origin, age, gender, economic status, and education, and they must attempt to reflect that pluralism in every aspect of museum operations and programs.

■ Third, we stress the need for dynamic, forceful leadership in museums and throughout the museum community. Strong leadership on the part of individuals, institutions, and

Journal of Museum Education 16, no. 3 (Fall 1991): 3–17.

organizations will provide vision, inspire broad-based commitment, and generate resources; it is the key to meeting the challenges and fulfilling the promise expressed in this report.

Excellence and Equity represents the thinking of a diverse group of individuals who addressed a range of significant issues for the museum profession. It focuses on the strengths and weaknesses of museums and helps define the museum's role as an educational center in its community.

Members of the task force willingly engaged in open and challenging discussions about topics that often touched the core of their beliefs and feelings about the profession. They were not always in agreement. Sometimes we had extended discussions over the use of single words such as "a" or "the." But we took care to listen to each other and to develop a clear understanding of the meaning of each other's ideas. Together, we came to a consensus about the principles and recommendations expressed in the report.

Twenty-five individuals representing different kinds of museums, areas of the country, types of professional and volunteer positions, and years of service served the AAM on the task force. Producing the report moved much more slowly than anyone had expected and required a personal commitment of almost two and one-half years from task force members. Ellen Cochran Hirzy's expertise with words and patience through numerous drafts helped us achieve a thoughtful and coherent document. The report was reviewed three times by the AAM Board of Directors. The task force received written and verbal comments from the board as well as from the AAM's standing professional committees and affiliate organizations. In addition, drafts of the report were discussed at most of the regional meetings. The final draft was approved by the AAM Executive Committee and board in spring 1991 and presented to the membership at the annual meeting in Denver in May. It will be published this winter [1992].

Recognizing that the report is a statement by a group of individuals who worked to articulate the issues, the task force asked participants in the annual meeting to join in a town meeting to discuss the next steps: What should the museum profession do to help promulgate the report? Participants suggested strategies for making trustees, foundations, and education and business leaders aware of the report, as well as ways to reach registrars, curators, and directors within the museum community, all with the goal of convincing them to implement the recommendations in their institutions and communities. The town meeting format continued the task force's dialogue about diversity, education, and leadership at a national level.

The following essays offer readers of this journal an insight into the thinking of 18 members of the task force (the other seven were unable to contribute due to scheduling demands). [Note: Seven essays are reprinted in this volume.] They testify to varied and passionate concerns. Whether the focus is on the roles of education or diversity, the humanity of museums, the importance of scholarship and master teaching, or the unique role of museums in working with schools, each essay elaborates at least some of the ideas that were critical to the thinking of task force members and to the development of the report.

The individuals who so ably served on the task force must be acknowledged for their tremendous contributions to our field. In addition, I want to extend my thanks to Ellen Hirzy and to the AAM Board of Directors and staff for their support, guidance, and many thoughtful comments.

Excellence and Equity:
Excerpts from the Report

The educational role of American museums has been central to their history, evolving through the years in relationship to the changing public dimension of museums. The creation of the American Association of Museums Task Force on Museum Education in September 1989 signaled the profession's desire to advance the dialogue about museums and education and to inspire new solutions for challenging times. . . .

As the task force considered museums and education against a backdrop of global change, a central question arose repeatedly: How can museums—as multidimensional, socially responsible institutions with a tremendous capacity for bringing knowledge to the public and enriching all facets of the human experience— help to nurture a humane citizenry equipped to make informed choices in a democracy and to address the challenges and opportunities of an increasingly global society? Museums can no longer confine themselves simply to preservation, scholarship, and exhibitions independent of the social context in which they exist. They must recognize that what we are calling the public dimension of museums leads them to perform the public service of education—a term we use in its broadest sense to include exploration, study, observation, critical thinking, contemplation, and dialogue.

Museums have a dual public responsibility suited to today's world. One element of this responsibility is excellence: A hallmark of museums is intellectual rigor, a tradition that must continue to be applied in the context of a wider public dimension. The other element is equity: In reexamining their public dimension, museums must include a broader spectrum of our diverse society in their activities. Museums must fulfill both elements of this dual responsibility—excellence and equity—in every aspect of their operations and programs. . . .

The task force has identified 10 principles with attending recommendations for consideration and action by the museum field. . . .

1. Assert that museums place education—in the broadest sense of the word— at the center of their public service role. Assure that the commitment to serve the public is clearly stated in every museum's mission and central to its activities.

2. Reflect the diversity of our society by establishing and maintaining the broadest possible public dimension for the museum.

3. Understand, develop, expand, and use the learning opportunities that museums offer their audiences.

4. Enrich our knowledge, understanding, and appreciation of our collections and of the variety of cultures and ideas they represent and evoke.

5. Assure that the interpretive process manifests a variety in cultural and intellectual perspectives and reflects an appreciation for the diversity of museums' publics.

6. Engage in active, ongoing collaborative efforts with a wide spectrum of organizations and individuals who can contribute to the expansion of the museum's public dimension.

7. Assess the decision-making processes in museums and develop new models that enable an expanded public dimension and a renewed commitment to excellence.

8. Achieve diversity among trustees, staff, and volunteers to assure a breadth of perspective throughout the museum.

9. Provide professional development and training for new and established professionals, trustees, and volunteers that meets the needs of the museum profession so that museums may carry out their responsibility to their diverse public.

10. Commit leadership and financial resources—in individual museums, professional organizations, and training organizations and universities—to strengthen the public dimension of museums. . . .

The issues the Task Force on Museum Education has considered go to the very core of what museums are all about: How can museums, which have so much to contribute to the collective human experience, welcome the broad spectrum of our society? How can they enrich and empower citizens from all racial, ethnic, social, economic, and educational backgrounds? How can we, as museum professionals and trustees, effect the serious and lasting institutional and professional change necessary to resolve these issues? The complex challenges at hand require time, resources, and continuous review and assessment, but above all they require commitment.

The community of museums in the United States shares the responsibility with other educational institutions to enrich learning opportunities for all individuals, to nurture an enlightened, humane citizenry that appreciates the value of knowing about its past, is resourcefully and sensitively engaged in the present, and is determined to shape a future in which many experiences and many points of view are given voice. In this endeavor, museums will play a powerful, beneficial role for the people of the next century.

Source: *Excellence and Equity: Education and the Public Dimension of Museums* (Washington, D.C.: American Association of Museums, 1991).

The Diverse Potential of Education in Museums
James Affolter

All of us who participated in the Task Force on Museum Education brought our own sets of experiences and biases to the table. As one who works primarily with living collections, my perspective may be different from most. What follows are some personal observations stimulated by the discussions at task force meetings and by the final report.

If education is the primary mission of a museum, it follows that decisions to add or subtract specific objects to or from the collection should reflect the educational goals of the institution. How many museums permit their education staffs to play a primary role in determining new acquisitions? How many collections grow instead in the direction of staff or donor interests or in response to windfalls? Museums should develop clearly articulated statements of educational goals, which can then be used as a standard for assessing the value both of existing elements in the collection and of potential new acquisitions.

Museums with living collections may be able to adapt the content of their collections to their educational objectives at a more rapid rate than museums whose collections are relatively static. Compared to paintings of the Italian Renaissance and artifacts from ancient Greece, Himalayan rhododendrons and South American armadillos are fairly easy to obtain. Living collections are also in a constant state of change, as specimens die or are discarded and new ones acquired to take their place. Museums with a higher rate of turnover have a greater opportunity to adjust their collections by controlling patterns of replacement and change; long-term educational objectives should provide the blueprint.

The task force report asserts that "museum missions should state unequivocally that an educational purpose is imbedded in every museum activity." Thus museums should be transparent in the sense that their inner workings, not only their objects, should be on display. Visitors can learn as much from an explanation of how an exhibit is assembled or maintained as they can from the exhibit itself, particularly in museums with living collections, where care and maintenance of specimens are an intensive process. Many visitors to botanical gardens, for example, are avid gardeners. They have as much interest in knowing how a bed was prepared for planting as they have in the plants themselves. Museums devote considerable resources to acquiring and propagating their living specimens, but information about these processes is not accessible to the museum's audience unless an effort is made to communicate it.

One way museums can attract and serve a more diverse audience is to interpret their collections from a greater variety of perspectives. A tour guide leading visitors through a formal herb garden can discuss the exhibit from the perspective of garden design, human history, evolutionary adaptations, or ethnic cuisine. A visitor with little interest in horticultural characteristics of a particular plant species (e.g., hardiness, growth form) may be fascinated by an explanation of the natural chemical defenses it employs to foil its insect predators.

The report observes that objects exist in a complex social and intellectual context. This statement is true not only for human artifacts but for plants and animals as well. While on the staff of the University of California Botanical Garden at Berkeley, I was involved in the development of a garden of plants used in traditional Chinese medicine. What fascinated me as I led groups through this collection was that I spent relatively little time discussing the plants themselves but got into lively discussions concerning the differences between Chinese and Western medical philosophy, the efficacy of acupuncture, and the limitations of the scientific method.

Finally, museums are a place where families can learn together. The report states that we all bring our own sets of preconceptions and experiences to the interpretation of objects. Museums provide a setting for sharing these perspectives in response to new experiences. Our traditional educational institutions were not designed to facilitate family learning, nor do they necessarily encourage communication among different age groups. With so many forces in our society placing stress on the family unit, museums can play a unique role in providing an environment in which communication is encouraged and family members can share the excitement of discovery.

Education: A *Responsibility or* the *Responsibility?*
Nina Archabal

The warning that it is unwise to raise a question unless you are prepared to hear the answer applies in a big way to the American Association of Museums and its Task Force on Museum Education. The charge to the task force was straightforward enough:

- to describe the critical issues in museum education
- to recommend action that will strengthen and expand the educational role of museums in today's world
- to outline an ongoing role for museums, professional associations, and other appropriate organizations in ensuring that these recommendations are carried out.

The effort grew out of the 1984 report *Museums for a New Century* and could have been confined safely enough within one of the quarters of museum life—the museum education department. In our common parlance we have come to use the phrase "museum education" narrowly to refer to some of the activities of our museums. It brings to mind lines of yellow buses and groups of elementary school children arriving for a museum lesson or a guided gallery tour. With a little stretch of the imagination, the adult learner comes to mind participating in some special workshop or attending a lecture offered by the museum's education department. Contrasted with the museum's long-established curatorial and exhibition functions, the museum education function as defined within a discrete department is a relatively new phenomenon. And the denizens of those departments, while large in number today, have struggled over the last decade for status in the field.

Beginning with the first meeting of the task force, the members began to extend the meaning of museum education. Our discussion developed in the context of growing awareness, both in the field and in the larger society, of the cultural diversity of our nation's peoples and of the accountability of museums to an American public that is anything but homogeneous. Quickly we broadened our focus from the museum education department to a perspective that encompassed the entire institution. We had clearly moved the discussion to the level of institutional mission.

The report as approved by the governing board of the American Association of Museums asserts that education is *a* primary responsibility of museums. In earlier versions drafted by the task force, the document asserted that education is *the* primary responsibility of museums. As our discussions progressed, the task force members developed a picture of all the museum's activities in the context of a broader societal mission to educate. *Museums for a New Century* counterpoised the museum's collection as its heart, education as its spirit. The task force went beyond this state of equilibrium to look at the museum in society. While acknowledging that not every museum can be all things to all people, the task force found that the collective responsibility of museums should be first and foremost to educate, to give public service.

The adoption of the report by the American Association of Museums was certainly a milestone in the development of our field. But there is a difference between regarding education as *a* primary responsibility and as *the* primary responsibility. The significance of that difference is reflected in the reactions of three of my colleagues at the Minnesota Historical Society to the draft report.

One colleague, upon reading the report, asked me what all the fuss was about. He observed that most "outsiders" have always assumed that education is the primary responsibility of museums. This colleague has been in the field for less than five years but has been a lifetime user of museums. From his perspective museums exist first and foremost to educate. To achieve their purpose, they conduct such activities as collecting, preservation, and research. He scribbled the words "obvious or self-evident" in the margin opposite the task force's premise that every area of museum activity contributes to museums' public dimension and to the important public service museums provide.

Reading the same version of the report, another colleague who has been in the museum field for many years observed that making education and public service a central part of every museum's mission may require adjustments of institutional goals rather than new mission statements. From her perspective the juxtaposition of excellence and equity, of expert and public service, of quality and outreach is a recurring theme in museums as they look to the future.

A third colleague reading the same report took issue directly with the assertion that education is *the* primary responsibility of museums. Citing other institutions that provide education as their primary responsibility, she observed, "Museums were developed as repositories for our culture . . . and without that aspect of their mission, museums would not be distinguishable from other educational bodies." For this colleague the collections-based nature of museums is central, and issues of accessibility and context follow.

Indeed, what is all this fuss about? In my estimation it is about the fundamental question of identity, of what museums are and why they exist. There are good reasons to ask this question at this moment. The answer we give must make sense in the context of a pluralistic society and incontrovertible evidence that our schools do not fulfill by themselves our society's need for education. Fundamental changes in institutional culture and in who governs and works in the nation's museums will require extraordinary leadership in a field that is conservative by nature. What is called for is not a minor adjustment but a major change in the course of many of the nation's museums.

The reactions of my colleagues will probably mirror the reactions of the museum field. For some, the concepts of the report will suggest nothing new and the recommendations will not go far enough. Others will see challenges, especially in developing the leadership and vision needed to achieve change. Finally, some will approach the report cautiously and warn us not to sacrifice excellence for equity.

I hope it is not too much to assume that the report will be read widely and discussed within the field. I hope, too, that each institution will find appropriate ways to convert into practice our shared mission as articulated in the report. There is surely something here for everyone.

Museum Education and Ideals
Edmund Barry Gaither

I think that work in the museum field proceeds on three levels simultaneously. It is important for us to embrace an intellectual framework consistent with our missions. Only through such a framework can we gain a clear notion of where we need to go and why it is important to go there. It is also necessary to create structures that allow us to advance toward our goals, or at least to evaluate our progress. And finally, it is necessary to implement programs guided by our ideals and tempered by our real experiences.

The Task Force on Museum Education provided an opportunity to discuss education in ways that fostered the development of a shared or common intellectual and philosophical framework. Moreover, by suggesting such a framework, it presented a context for the emergence of bolder education leaders who could shape programs of increasing effectiveness and daring. Without discounting the very specific differences in missions, publics, goals, and institutional histories, the task force sought to promote a sense of broad common purpose among museums. I saw my contribution as helping shape a framework within which the broadest consensus could be achieved. I hoped that we could find mutually satisfying reasons for being in this field, reasons that reached beyond our personal circumstances and aspired to affect the larger social setting in which we all find ourselves. Engaging issues in such a way seemed a very important thing for us to do.

After 21 years in the museum world, I found it useful to reexamine my own motivations. And in doing so, I wanted to share my view that museums are ultimately human institutions. They belong to the body of institutional structures that communities created to serve perceived needs—to serve people. So museums exist as specialized social institutions within a larger social fabric. They exist in an inescapable social contract. And even if the public support—particularly the governmental support that ought to be there—wanes, the nature of the contract itself does not change. Not even a crisis such as we face today can invalidate that museums are social institutions existing in a reciprocal relationship with the public at large.

What do I mean in asserting that museums are in a social contract with the public? I want to suggest that museums take on themselves a responsibility to provide education *in the most expansive sense* to the broadest public possible, and, in exchange, they expect and merit support from that public and governmental entities, which are vehicles for the corporate expression of the public will. That's a fair contract and a good equation.

What do I mean by providing education *in the most expansive sense?* In a society like ours, with its fractures, profound injustices, distorted values, and the like, we are both challenged and imperiled by the structures and systems that don't work, yet we don't have the option of another world.

Although we have a variety of institutions fundamentally committed to education from various perspectives—schools and colleges, religious centers, homes, cities and states—museums distinguish themselves by proclaiming that objects from previous human experience are rich vehicles for exploring the meaning of the human enterprise. Museums propose that by encountering and examining such objects, we can promote a dialogue in which the objects—while central—lead us to reflect on deeper values that we as humans share. A fundamental educational role for museums thereby becomes fostering humane values—tolerance, acceptance of difference, understanding—by focusing attention on objects rooted in shared human experience and trying to draw lessons from them. This role is possible because all humans, giving vent to their creative impulses, have made stuff. That stuff—art, artifacts, and countless other manifestations—exists as evidence of our creative will from the beginning of the human family up to the present. So each museum, with every object and each visitor, has a new opportunity to pose questions about fundamental human values associated with cultural and historical objects. This opportunity is not a function consigned to a department within the museum. It is a pan-museum matter. The dialogue sought is one that engages multiple parties from multiple perspectives focused on common issues or concerns. Museums are called upon to enlist and encourage the widest possible participation of their publics in such a dialogue. That commitment underpins the public dimension of museums.

Now if museums accept the commission of increasing knowledge and engaging people in dialogue around humane issues, they will recognize almost immediately that the scope of this magnificent mission is impossibly large. Thus it becomes clear that museums, to be effective educators, must regard this work as a shared mission. Different museums have different opportunities and responsibilities according to their histories, missions, and specialties, and yet, with wise use of the task force report, all can work within an overarching consensus of the importance of advancing humane values through their programs. So I would like to think that the report has given us a broad philosophic direction underscoring the degree to which museums *must be involved in education and the formation of humane values* in a society such as ours in which social wholeness should be a major objective of the social contract between museums and society.

Addressing the great task before us will require our institutions to strive to reflect more completely—in their staffing, governance, and programs—the diversity that is the most remarkable aspect of America's cultural and social fabric. We must also recognize that it is not sufficient for us simply to achieve great diversity within the majority of institutions; it is essential to have a diverse community of institutions that share responsibility for reshaping the world in which—for better or worse—we will live the rest of our lives and which we give to those who follow us.

The Importance of "And"
Elaine Heumann Gurian

We, as Americans, have consistently believed in the idea of the winner. "There is no such thing as second place" is an adage we have all heard. The childhood game of "King of the Mountain" has trained our youngsters to believe that at the top of the pyramid there is only one "king."

This simple idea—that there are only single winners—affects our intellectual life as well. The idea that two equally weighted ideas could both be "primary" has not been tolerated; one must be supreme. A group discussion in which more than one idea is presented usually leads to a discussion of priorities.

"And" is a word we learned to read in the first grade and one we used orally much earlier. We all know the meaning of "and"—it is a linking word between equally weighted ideas or objects. Yet, in the arena of ideas, we consistently behave as if "and" means "or."

The Task Force on Museum Education report—*Excellence and Equity*—uses "and" in the title. This is a report in which there was a concerted attempt to accept the two major ideas proposed by factions within the field—equity and excellence—as equal and without priority. After much discussion in which each proponent attempted to "win" the group over, the task force decided to go forward with both rather than the usual one idea.

These formerly contested ideas were linked together with "and."

However, for the museum field to go forward, we must do more than make political peace by linking words. We must begin to believe what we have written, namely that complex organizations must and should espouse the coexistence of more than one primary mission. Still more revolutionary, we must begin to believe that such organizations can and should espouse these multiple priorities even when the inherent actions are potentially conflictive.

The intent of the task force was that we must collectively incorporate the real meaning of inclusion—the acceptance of multiple ideas and the notion of power sharing—within the institutions and the professions that we love. For example, we can have both ethnically focused museums *and* generic museums that are inclusive in their respective presentations. We can simultaneously be citizens of the country, even the world, *and* be functioning members of our specific community. There can be an intellectual canon of the Western tradition that is valuable for all of us to learn, *and* we should simultaneously learn about the glories of the rest of the world. Research *and* public service can both be primary if the museum administration wishes it. Can equity *and* excellence exist side by side without one diminishing the other? Of course!

One can postulate that the fight for idea primacy was not one of intellect but rather one of implicit resource allocation. To be truthful, that is correct. To have a museum hierarchy that includes more than one primary idea—more than one department at the top—assumes that the institution plans to fund these fundamental ideas more or less equally.

The task force report raises the issue of money rather obliquely, but the task force intended that fundamental ideas should have dollars commensurate with their place in the mission hierarchy. Realistically, to fund ideas equally is either to garner lots of new money or to reallocate what funds there are among programs in the new hierarchy. That step will diminish the monetary hegemony of the former winners and engender anxiety and anger among the previously funded.

An inevitable shifting of resources is probably the most uncomfortable consequence of the report. The haves will argue that to give up anything is to diminish the quality and thereby the excellence of their work. And in fact, some diminution of quality or scope may occur temporarily in response to an altered resource landscape. But we cannot proclaim the task force report a success without acknowledging that implementation actions—even difficult budgetary ones—should follow. In public service, both excellence *and* equity can occur in each of our museums if we so wish it, and public service itself can become one of the primary missions of each of our museums if that becomes our collective intention. The task force hopes it has persuaded the field and that there will no longer be only single winners.

Museum Literacy and "Visitor Literacy"
Paul G. Heltne

Central to the commitment to excellence and equity is the service museums provide to our casual or school visitors. Museum services center around our primary mode of information delivery—our exhibits. The quality of a visit will depend on the visitor's ability to engage successfully with the exhibit as a medium. The success of the visitor measures the success of the museum.

So at the heart of excellence and equity is the visitor. Where is the visitor in terms of the ability to enjoy a museum? We know that visitors are at many levels of expertise with respect to "reading" exhibits, that is to say, visitors are at many levels of museum literacy. As museum professionals, we are all convinced that once a person has experienced the thrill of discovery at a museum, that person will come back again and again. In many instances, however, the design of museum programming has restricted that thrill of discovery to persons who have, *a priori,* a significant level of museum literacy. This kind of programming may be a primary barrier to achieving our aims. To be successful, we must devote diligent programming attention to novice museum-goers, especially reaching out, again and again, to those with low or negative levels of museum literacy.

Museums, then, must become at least as expert at reading the visitor, and his or her level of museum literacy, as the visitor is in reading the museum. I believe that recognition of the following two factors is fundamental to the museum's need to develop its "visitor literacy."

The first factor governing museum literacy, and all literacy for that matter, is the recognition that human beings are primates. Being a primate means that our first impulses in a new (and not over threatening) learning situation are to glance at, stare, touch, feel, heft, and, by putting our hands around a thing while looking at it, to get an experience of its dimensionality. As primates, we learn by exploring and imitating. Most exhibits, perhaps every exhibit, should afford these opportunities as a way of reaching the novice.

The second factor is that most of our human evolutionary history has been spent as hunter-gatherers, a term that itself may explain why we have collections and why they are endlessly fascinating. As hunter-gatherers we learn by trying things; we need to try them in intimate groups, at our own pace; we need to tell stories about what we encounter; and we need to have these stories validated. Initially, anyway, what is important is the story the visitor forms, not necessarily the details of a scientific concept, the reasons for a war, or the names of donors of a work of art. Museums must validate the visitor's story and then offer a partnership to build on that story.

In some ultimate sense, a museum is about building the visitor's own story. To achieve equity we must become excellent in helping the visitor to that magical point between boredom and anxiety, at which the new challenges can be designed in a partnership with the visitor—wherever that visitor is.

Museum literacy requires a dynamic combination. On the museum side it requires educators with a commitment to the visitor, an eye for design, and a hunger for subject matter knowledge; exhibition designers with artistic brilliance, real knowledge of the topic, and concern for learning; and subject matter specialists with an interest in the exhibit medium and an excitement about communicating.

If all the other equities are satisfied but the visitor is not enriched by the museum experience, our efforts will be notable but the exercise futile. For tax revenues require citizen support, and citizens are unlikely to support what they do not value. If the visitor experience is enlivening, it will be perceived as valuable, and our society will generate the energies for achieving full equity in the museum world.

Museums in Cultural and Temporal Context
Roger Mandle

The report of the Task Force on Museum Education will be much read and discussed in the museum community. Its greatest usefulness, however, will be outside the field. It should be validated by the positive responses of the communities served by museums and by the individuals responsible for education policy development and funding.

It is a verity that museum are reflective devices of society. The very mandate of museums is to be conservative because they save material culture and examples of the natural world. Museums are also reactive; they analyze issues and ideas of value emanating from created or found objects. The fundamental truth of museums, however, comes from the objects themselves and not necessarily from contemporary interpretation of them out of historic or environmental context. This relativism of meaning is manifest in the place, time, and cultural perspectives of the individuals responsible for the interpretation of these objects. Curators and educators are not only influenced by their own background and training but also by the economic and social conditions of the institution and its collective sense of purpose.

To what ends does the institution put the objects in its care? To what audiences are these purposes directed? What influence does the history of the institution have over the current uses and interpretations and audiences for the objects?

There is always a temporal context for the objects, which in the main has been ignored as a factor in the interpretation of them by the institutions showing them. This temporal context reflects the impermanence of a museum's perspective, not of the objects themselves. No curator likes to face the idea that his or her perspective, developed through four years of training and research, could possibly be subject to another, perhaps equally valid but opposing interpretation, or that in time the cultural or scientific evidence upon which that perspective is based could be viewed as archaic or invalid. The current collective wisdom of institutions will also be challenged over time by other assumptions outside their walls.

These challenges, the task force report maintains, are to be welcomed. But what should be done with these so-called new assertions? These perspectives are more than background noise as museums position their messages to the public or draft the language of a label for their visitors. The issues the report seeks to address are the cultural and temporal contexts for assessing the validity of museums as a place for various kinds of learning opportunities. While a museum or an exhibition cannot be all things to all people, new considerations of audience diversity are recommended by the task force as essential for the institutional perspective on learning. Further, the whole museum is invited to participate in the development of these opportunities for the public.

The ultimate focus of experience for museum visitors is the object itself, which has been placed in invented surroundings and sequences with other objects to provide contexts for learning. That contemporary attempts at interpretation change the meaning of objects is understood in our field. Less understood is the shift of meaning our museums have created by their stated and implied attitudes toward our diverse public. These attitudes can sometimes express, we are now learning from focus group interviews and other kinds of audience surveys, signals to our visitors of which we may be oblivious. We have come to know how much we need additional perspectives in our attempt to comprehend our own point of view.

Perhaps museums have just passed through a stage in their development analogous to that of the Roman Catholic church during the Counter-Reformation, when it attempted to reestablish the relevance, if not the validity, of its mission by interpreting gospel text, architecture, music, and art in a new way in order to inspire people from all walks of life. The church moved to respond to its adherents on their terms, to take into account their needs in its reinterpretations. The only path to a broader engagement of the public with museums, however, is first to have a thorough understanding of museums' intent. Otherwise, reinterpretations will be hollow testimony about the objects, put in terms that engage but also confuse the public about their current meaning or historical status.

Museums can reconsecrate their missions by taking a closer look at the objects in their care to find the core meaning that links them to both contemporary and historical ideas of value to humanity. These objects are thus part of a continuum of knowledge potentially significant in myriad ways to the interests of a diverse public, to which we are becoming more alert. The cultural issues inherent in objects are therefore fundamental to our assumptions about the current nature and process of museums as institutions. The key to the realization of the higher value of museums lies in the receptivity of those responsible for objects to new interpretations of their roles. It does not lie in new technologies of presentation, which are useful tools only after the current meaning of the objects has been confirmed in their relationship to current audiences.

Just as contemporary perspectives on objects change their meaning, current methodologies of presentation affect their meaning as well. Exhibitions of European and American art have concentrated to a large extent on style and esthetic issues in their historic contexts, while ethnographic exhibitions have mainly attempted to place art in the broadest cultural context. More recently, however, some art exhibitions have attempted political, social, and economic interpretations. In these cases, the objects have been used as supportive evidence of nonesthetic issues that seek to mold contemporary public perceptions. Interpretive exercises such as these try to demythologize the past, but in doing so, remythologize it by ignoring the layers of subsequent critical literature that would place the objects and their makers in a continuum of opinion and perspective. While these interpretive exhibitions may aid the public in seeing objects and history from a new point of view, they should seek also to instruct viewers about their own time and place with respect to the objects.

The museum field must not be frightened by investigations into the meaning or the history of interpretation or by attempts at understanding institutional relevance to current audiences. The two seemingly shifting reference points for the museum professional—on the one side for the object and on the other for the viewer—have always been in a state of flux. The responsibility of museums as places to be, both for staff and for the public, is based on the inevitable tension between knowledge and the means available to describe usefully the relationship between what we know and what we think we know about the objects, and about ourselves.

Whether we choose to recognize it or not, museums are a part of, as well as about, history. Paradoxically, this perspective of temporality comes not from a dispassionate distance from these institutions but rather from an intense engagement with them through objects and people. The sense of history and place we acquire through this effort should be reassuring evidence of the lasting value of those objects we are charged with saving and of the changing nature of the museums we are charged with shaping.

Museums' Social Contract
Scott T. Swank

Excellence and Equity, the report of the Task Force on Museum Education, provides an opportunity for museums to take stock and prepare for the social realities of cultural life in the 21st century. Museum response to the report will determine how centrally museums are positioned in the structure of a rapidly changing society.

Centuries ago, when museums were private cabinets of curiosity for aristocratic families and monarchs, most people were excluded from the treasures of the past except as those treasures survived in the form of the built environment, such as cathedrals. In the 18th century, museums such as the British Museum were formed by combining private collections and making them available by special permission to the "right kind" of people, that is, those of aristocratic birth or career distinction. Over time the right kind of people won the privilege to enter museums without petition or reservation. By the late 20th century, most museums have accepted the democratic principle that all people—of all classes, ages, races, and ethnic origins—have the right to share the cultural patrimony available to them.

Throughout the centuries of the democratization of museums there was a constant factor underlying the changes. Private collectors and museum professionals usually determined what should be collected, preserved, displayed, and interpreted. Generally this internal control also determined what would be presented and in what manner. Consequently, from princes to professionals, proprietary paternalism was still the governing principle of museums.

The task force report, for me, represents a landmark in the historical development of museums, for it affirms that American museums, whether public or private, are public educational institutions. By virtue of their social contract with democratic government, museums acknowledge public control. The situation is no longer one of the public's "right" to come when museums choose to invite. Museums now have an obligation, under the social contract governing their existence and tax-free status, to collect, preserve, display, and interpret for the benefit of the public. Museums also have an obligation to mirror social reality in terms of their future collecting, board and staff composition, and public programming.

The logical implication of this revolution is that all museum functions should be shaped by a dialogue with the public, however that public dimension is defined for each institution. Each museum should be responsible to its publics for keeping pace with social reality. Democracy will finally enter board rooms, collection storage areas, exhibition galleries, and classrooms. In the process, we hope that museums will move to the center of American cultural life.

Many blue-ribbon reports gather dust more quickly than they generate change. To facilitate implementation of the educational imperatives of *Excellence and Equity,* the Advisory Committee of the AAM's Museum Assessment Programs has developed a new program called Public Dimension Assessment, or MAP III. The committee has worked with the Task Force on Museum Education to prepare a self-study questionnaire and assessment tools that correlate with *Excellence and Equity.* MAP III, therefore, though a small program, can provide one avenue for implementing the goals of the task force report. Moving on parallel tracks, these two initiatives reached their final destination in Denver at the 1991 annual meeting. The next steps are up to each of us, as well as to the museums and publics we serve.

REFLECTING ON THINGS AND THEORY

Looking

John Fines

Hello again, the U. S. of A.! How nice of you to invite me to contribute to your second volume of selections; I am honored. I remember with delight the cultural riches of your museums and galleries of Washington, Chicago, and Atlanta that you let me use, and with much greater delight the far richer endowment of children who came with me to look. I have read all the essays that follow carefully and diligently, and I do most warmly recommend them to you. They are about important matters, and people have stretched their brains in your interests, so read them. It would be an insult to the authors for me to try some quick summary, so instead I will try to give you a footnote, perhaps a slightly critical one (aren't I ungrateful to do so!).

It seems to me that you are all into quite long words. We need them sometimes, but they do not by themselves endow us with grace. Simplicity is a virtue in the business of explanation, and I worship it to excess. You also trust in research, and of course research can be a great help to us, but I always find it has limits, and they should be defined first—to say how long a ride it will take us, when we have to get off and walk for ourselves. Finally, you yearn so strongly for a theory as a self-validating activity that I get worried sometimes. For, to tell the truth, I have never had a good idea in a study in my life (because of course I am not often in one and fidget so when there that I am soon out). Every good thing has come to me on the floor, working, in action. I unashamedly believe in practice. Now many kind people who watch me work talk about my "creativity" and "lateral thinking" and that's nice, but in my heart I know that my winning trick is my inner silliness, which prompts me to do odd things to see whether they will get the ball rolling, to make things happen. Sometimes they do; sometimes they don't.

Let me illustrate. I live in a town with an ancient cathedral, and that place bores the pants off thousands of child visitors a year. When I take children round I say to them: "Now look, any fool can find old things here—that's no problem. But a cathedral is growing just like you, every day. So come round with me and see who can find the *newest* thing. I am not going to be that interested in anything else, so don't pester me with old things." So as we go round I rely on the basic disobedience of all good kids everywhere, and they have muttered conversations that occasionally rise into questions: "What's that?" and I reply, "Oh that's no good at all; it's about the oldest thing in the place. It's about a dead man coming out of his grave by magic—actually it was probably made even before the cathedral was built—

hopeless for our quest. *Do* come on." And they do unwillingly, and they cast secret glances and mutter about it all, so that when we get back in school the one task I have set them is easily done with, and then I can say, "Did anyone see anything else, then?" and out it all comes: "There was this dead man, and I think it was Jesus, maybe, well anyway, he was so tall, and the dead man was coming out of the grave, and it was a thousand years old and on the label it said it had been turned to the wall to save it from Henry VIII and only found when the spire fell down, and they looked in the rubble and . . .". I don't have to do any work any more—inspired silliness has set it all up for me. Okay, you say, does this all come from God, instinct, or what? I want an address. Yes, a lot comes from God, a lot from adrenalin, but there are some helps. Here are seven clues I wrote for an American audience last year, appropriately enough:

1. Economize. Concentrate, focus down on one item. Stick with it and dip ever deeper. Ignore the siren calls of all the rest.

2. Approach from around the corner; don't try to go direct (is that a translatable expression?) Snake your way to your objective—for it will change as your lesson grows, anyway, according to the children's interests and performance that day.

3. Establish a context or point of view within which children can work, and give them a role to help them look. I may ask children to help me check out the number and type of colors an artist is using, because I think it might be significant. As they become my helpers in this research, so they begin to look.

4. Watch and listen to the children, not the object you are looking at. You know the object well, and it won't change, but the merest wriggle of a child may tell you something about how he or she is growing in relation to that object.

5. Accept all that you receive and say thank you. I say thank you to a child who merely grunts in response, because that is a beginning, but I also praise, for your prime job is to build a raft of self-confidence for these children to stand on so that they can begin to make critical and analytical statements (big words for a big event).

6. Talk fast and keep the pace going hot, but really go slow: questioning, excavating, pondering, taking everything seriously, not moving on until everyone is ready.

7. Admit that your promise to the children, your responsibility, is to make it all work in the end, to so put it together that the children know they have arrived somewhere. The teacher must conduct, must assemble, must show.

And of course, forgive yourself when it all goes wrong and you have to say, "Sorry, kids, we've just got to start again because I fouled it up." Best wishes!

INTRODUCTION

Were Those Indians Hit by Cars?

Robert Sullivan

> Sometimes the best teacher teaches only once to a single child or to a grownup past hope.
> —*Anonymous*

I will never forget my first day "on the floor" of the Rochester Museum and Science Center. I had just given a rousing hands-on, inquiry-based, multi-sensory, object-centered (and several other trendy, hyphenated teaching strategies that I have long since abandoned) lesson in front of our Iroquois longhouse reconstruction. A timid six-year-old raised her hand and pointed at the manikins in the case just behind me and asked, "Were those Indians hit by cars?" Twenty years later I am still considering that question, and I resurrect it whenever I feel tempted to become too earnest or self-serious about the nature or purpose of museum education. In that opening moment of my career, the dilemma that has driven me for 20 years was framed: How can museums achieve serious social and educational purposes while still being fun places to visit? How can we take advantage of the natural links that have always existed among play, curiosity, magic, art, and science? Let me suggest a way.

Paradigms Lost and Found: Inventing the Future

> However rich a collection may be, it has to be re-interpreted for every new generation, and by that, I do not mean sand-blasting the facade of the building and re-decorating the galleries. I mean taking a profound new look at the purpose of the institution, at the attitudes of the community and its needs, at the methods whereby the gap between them may be bridged. Imagination, enthusiasm, understanding: all these have parts to play in stirring up again the ferment of creativity out of which most of our museums grew.
> —*Jan Finlay*

Museums are now standing on the edge of nothing less than a cultural fault line. Almost all the great natural history museums emerged in late 19th-century cities in the lengthening shadow of the Victorian paradigm of ascending progress. At the pinnacle of that ascending spiral was rational, logical, scientific, technological, Western man. With quasi-religious fervor and divine sanction, natural scientists roamed the world collecting, categorizing, and classifying creation and sending it back to urban institutions that groaned under the load of nature's hold. The public face of these first natural history museums presented a fragmented, "ologized," exotic natural and cultural world, normally hanging or mounted or stuffed with Darwin's evolutionary theory. But even this theory was misused and forced into the vertical paradigm of progress with nature, itself, "treeing" upward from the simple to the complex, while cultures were seen to advance from the primitive to the civilized, with Western technological man crowning the pinnacle. In an increasingly urbanized, pretelevision, preautomobile, prejetliner world, natural history museums represented the primary place to tangibly contact nature: the exotic, the bizarre, the primitive, the curiosities of the world that lay beyond the city limits.

This Victorian vertical paradigm of progress has been shattered and is rapidly shifting to a horizontal, interconnected, globally interdependent one. We have lived to see the technology hailed as a savior by one generation become the horror of the next. We are in the midst of a shift to a horizontal paradigm of the very place people hold in nature. No longer viewed as the vertical masters of a natural order over which we are given divine dominion, Western peoples increasingly view themselves as participants in a horizontally interconnected ecological system and an interdependent, pluralistic cultural system. The urgency and vulnerability of both natural and cultural systems have transformed the nature of our interests in them. In an environmentally degraded world, natural history and science museums can no longer be passive scholarly institutions, merely curious about how the world works. We must be engaged institutions committed to the necessity for global and human survival.

In an increasingly confident, assertive, pluralistic cultural world, the intellectual, cultural, ethnographic authority and primacy of Euro-American, Western society are being challenged everywhere. The ascendant vertical search for "truth" itself has gone horizontal, with all truths, including anthropological and scientific, now viewed as contingent, contextual, relative. Multiple ways of knowing, explaining, being in the world are now the expected norm. Museums can no longer be merely scholarly, curious, detached observers of cultures; we must be active champions of cross-cultural respect, empathy, tolerance, and equity.

Communication media, especially television, and global travel have altered our world and the fundamental ways we perceive it. The exotic seems immediate and familiar while the familiar has become exotic and distant. Ironically, visitors very likely know more about the lions of the Serengeti and Australia's Outback than they know about their own house cats and what's "outback" in their yard.

As they whiz through their world at a mile a minute, their immediate environment is an anonymous blur of green. How many can identify even the most common trees, plants, insects, or birds in their immediate surroundings? Most visitors have little tangible contact or comprehension of the ecosystem they live in and depend upon. This is where the collections, ideas, information, staff passions, and assertive conclusions have an educational and leadership role to play. To move visitors from their current state of passive curiosity to a state of active engagement with our collections, exhibits, and, as important, staff, we must not only satisfy their need to encounter the exotic celebrities of our collections but also enable them to see, and perhaps recognize for the first time, the utterly familiar. What is the ecosystem of a house? How are highways habitats? What is the mystery of a meadow? What are the esthetic judgments or ecological decisions you make in the grocery store?

The educational mandates of the 21st-century museum will not be about curiosity; they will be about survival. So what ought we do?

Learn that which we love so that others might learn to love it, too. That is the heart of good museum teaching for me. As sensual, intellectual, and emotional educators, museum exhibits and programs need to be more than just accurate, factual, and up-to-date with the latest teaching strategies. They must be passionate, personal, moral, filled with respect and affection for both subject matter and learners. Ultimately we are change agents, changing our users' minds, hearts, lives, environment, relationships. No matter how accurate, beautiful, strategically up-to-date our products are, if visitors leave unchanged, or worse, indifferent, then we have failed. We must be active partners in an educational effort that will generate a new conservation ethic in this nation. We must make that message personal and particular and pointed at empowering people to change their own and their communities' behavior. First and foremost, we must show that it is in their best interest to preserve the resources and diversity of nature.

But morality begins where self-interest ends. And our exhibits and programs must also understand the moral principles that inform and undergird conservation of both natural and cultural diversity: cross-cultural empathy and respect, social and economic justice, responsibility to posterity, the value of all life, and the belief that knowledge and understanding are the gateways to respect, love, and preservation of our world.

Object Knowledge: Every Museum Visitor an Interpreter

Thomas J. Schlereth

My brief for museum literacy begins with a personal definition of the museum. I would define the museum as a site where people learn about people (including themselves) primarily through objects that people have made, used, or found meaningful.

In my definition there are several commonplace but crucial ideas. The first is the emphasis on people. In my judgment, a museum is conceived of by people, exists for people, and is made up of people—people who staff its departments, people who visit its exhibitions, and people whose skill and spirit are still embedded in its collections.

Museums, I also believe, exist primarily to promote learning, a claim bolstered by the *Oxford English Dictionary's* acknowledgment that the earliest—although now admittedly obscured—meaning of museum was "scholar's library" or "study for learning."[1]

But I also cannot conceive of a museum without objects; they are crucial to the institution's basic identity. Since the subject of my argument here is the object, let me propose that we consider the subject of the object in two ways. The first is the way we normally think of objects in a museum, that is, as museum collections or *museum objects.* The second way, which we might label the *museum-as-object,* would view the entire museum site as an intriguing assemblage of material culture evidence also worthy of interpretation. Museum visitors ought to have the opportunity to learn more about both types of objects, and museums ought to help foster such object knowledge. Therefore I want to suggest a few ways that museums might assist the visitor in acquiring or expanding a special type of literacy that would enable them to read both the museum's *collections* and the museum's *context* with greater interest and insight. Such an acumen might also help visitors look, and look again, at the universe of objects—the domain of material culture, that part of the physical world that we have shaped according to a culturally dictated plan—in an entirely new and different perspective.[2]

In suggesting how we might think about these questions, I would first like to review some museum activities that I have observed, primarily in American history

Roundtable Reports 9, no. 1 (Winter 1984): 5–9.

museums, where the museum has encouraged the average visitor to become his or her own interpreter; I call this section: "An Eclectic Sampler of Ideas Worth Trying." Since the evidence for this category must be more widespread and diversified than my sample, I would welcome additional examples that might be found in science, art, and technology museums. My second category, whimsically titled "A Future Agenda of Quixotic Ideas Possibly Worth Entertaining," is composed largely of my own speculations, offered as a few ideas that might be implemented in making museums centers for object study. Here, too, I would appreciate hearing of your own fantasies.

An Eclectic Sampler of Ideas Worth Trying

How have museums taught visitors to read objects? One recent instance has been the development of an 18,000-square-foot open study collection of 19th-century material culture in the Margaret Woodbury Strong Museum in Rochester, New York. In an area eventually to contain 20,000 objects, there are to be several reference data stations containing the files of computer-generated index cards that will provide visitors, amateur and connoisseur alike, with the exact research data found within the museum's own catalog about each of those objects.[3] With such institutional resources, the visitor can almost take an introductory course in museum methodology and basic material culture research. Questions of provenance, typology, nomenclature, and registration techniques can all be explored.

Since the arrangement of objects in the Strong's study collection will be systematic rather than thematic, logical rather than historical, the visitor will be able to compare this method of object display with other exhibition strategies employed elsewhere in the museum. The study collection, primarily a creation of the curatorial staff, can be compared with thematic galleries, a creation of exhibit designers. In addition to learning from the often different ways in which curators and designers work at understanding objects, the visitor can formulate his or her own classification systems in order to satisfy individual research questions and intellectual curiosity. By becoming his or her own typologist, the visitor acts as interpreter.

A similar experience will be possible in the new orientation gallery currently being discussed by the staff of the Studebaker National Museum (formerly the Discovery Hall Museum), a city museum of 19th-century Midwest industrial history and working life, located in South Bend, Indiana.[4] In order to assist visitors in their self-guided tours of the institution's permanent exhibits, the staff and I have entertained constructing a Visitor's Workshop at the entrance to the permanent galleries. The term "workshop" is meant not only to evoke the world of work depicted throughout the museum's exhibits but also to suggest the type of research work that must be done in order to understand the objects that survive from that bygone world.[5]

In the Visitor's Workshop, therefore, people will have the chance to learn how to extract information and insight from data like company records, patent models, census tracts, and mail order catalogs. Reproductions of photography (especially commercial studio work, aerial photography, and family albums) and cartography (business atlases, fire insurance maps, city plans) will be stocked in the workshop, along with guides and primers explaining how to use such data as cultural evidence. Perhaps exercises will be devised especially to enable the school children to work at learning the different skills of the interpreter's craft. They might be rewarded, as they master various levels of the material culture trade, with a certificate designating their advance in status from apprentice to journeyman, and on to master of historical interpretation.

Of course, there will be a series of original artifacts in the shop. The series will probably change as new combinations of objects are thought appropriate to new interpretive questions. At present, the curators are thinking of including an early 20th-century Studebaker farm wagon; three different kitchen ranges made between 1880 and 1920; a highly ornate plow handcrafted for the 1876 Philadelphia Centennial, and two Singer sewing machines, one from the late 19th century, the other from the early 20th. All visitors will have complete access to these objects. In their encounters with those examples of material culture, visitors will have the opportunity to learn something about research techniques like seriation, reasoning by analogy, and the concept of manifest and latent functions. Here again the objective is to introduce the visitor to a few of the actual concepts frequently used in thinking about things, in order not only to enrich their museum experiences in South Bend but also to make their daily encounters with the objects of everyday life more exciting.

In the past two decades museums have become increasingly interested in the objects of everyday life. For example, the Museum of Man in Ottawa, Canada, in its program for "Collecting the Future," has involved curators and visitors in an innovative fieldwork project requiring research into contemporary material culture.[6] This project enlisted volunteers to help work out an appropriate policy for deciding what objects of contemporary life—prepackaged foods, pocket calculators, disposable diapers, plastics and synthetics of all kinds—would be the most useful as cultural data for researchers of the future. Since to collect is to interpret, this project gives the museum visitors a perspective on interpretation as well as collection development. In having some sense of what collecting entails, visitors also acquire an idea of what recollecting ("re-collecting") involves.

In these instances, museums are encouraging visitors to acquire object knowledge on their own. Other museums promote such learning by showing the visitor how their professional staff interprets objects. From the visitor's perspective, the latter approach might be called learning by watching, as compared to the former, which is learning by doing. Both have their uses in assisting every visitor to become his or her own interpreter. Some instances of the learning by watching approach will illustrate how this can work.

Craft demonstrations, living history reenactments, and any activity involving the making, using, or reusing of objects are typical ways visitors learn about artifacts by seeing something done to or with them.[7] When done well—and when visitors are permitted some significant role in the process—such demonstrations can prompt one to muse about one of the most exciting facets of all object study: the why and wherefore of human creativity. Why do humans create? Where does the impulse— termed variously by material culture scholars as "the mental template," "the artificial grammar," "the craftsman's competence of mind," "the scientist's aesthetic"— originate?[8] Are the creative ideas of the cobbler, the industrial designer, the architect, or the weaver the same? different? the same *and* different? How are creative ideas, intuitions, and insights actually translated into leather or steel, stone or textile?

Several contemporary students of objects—Brooke Hindle in technology, James Deetz in archeology, Henry Glassie in folklore, to mention but three who have worked in museums—have been fascinated with the complex processes of creativity and what a systematic study of it through objects might reveal.[9] The Boston Museum of Fine Arts exhibit, *New England Begins: The Seventeenth Century,* particularly the section devoted to "Mentality and Environment," is one recent example of how research on the bases of creativity might be explored in a museum; another is Cyril Stanley Smith's *From Art to Science: Seventy Objects Illustrating the Nature of Discovery,* first displayed at MIT's Compton Gallery.[10]

But many another museum exhibit has attempted to look at an object as it resided in the mind before the mind drove the muscles to create and to produce it in the tangible world. Such evidence of mind both in and over matter would include early sketches, prototypes, preliminary models, patent drawings, even doodles. More careful examination and more widespread exhibition of the "material culture of creativity" might help us better understand the processes of creativity, which many philosophers and psychologists hypothesize are often highly nonverbal, frequently visual, and even esthetic, difficult to translate into conventional written or spoken prose.[11] Exhibits attempting to explore this complex phenomenon should keep in mind Isadora Duncan's remark, "If I could say it, I would not have to dance it."

In fostering museum literacy, however, we should not neglect speech. Indeed, there is at least one instance where speech patterns were crucial to leading the visitors to consider themselves as interpreters. When the staff at Plimoth Plantation in Massachusetts thought it worth learning to speak in 17th-century East Anglian dialect in order to do first-person interpretation on their site, they came, using good anthropological parlance, to call themselves "informants" and the museum's visitors "interpreters." It was as if the visitors to the outdoor living history museum were anthropologists doing fieldwork, going into an exotic community and attempting to elicit whatever information they could from an alien culture. Unfortunately, these visitors to Plimoth did not always take away a sense of how carefully the museum staff had studied 17th-century speech patterns and vocabulary. Had they acquired this sense, linguistics, another tool in the contemporary material culturist's kit bag, might have been added to the visitor interpreter's as well.

Yet there are other examples of how museums let us in on how they exhibit or how they arrive at their interpretations. Curators at the National Museum of American History (NMAH) at the Smithsonian in Washington, for instance, have been willing to let visitors learn how object research fieldwork is done, demonstrated by the section of the *Buckaroos in Paradise* exhibit devoted to a display of researcher's field notebooks, photographs, sketches of artifacts, and oral history interviews. They have also disclosed how exhibit designers and curators exchange ideas, reach compromises, and decide on exhibit content and design, as evidenced by the display of the original storyboard that had been used in the fabrication of the Smithsonian's Electricity Gallery as a permanent component of the final exhibit. From that storyboard, the visitor can partially reconstruct how the curator of electricity and the exhibit designer traded marginalia, revised concepts, contested each other's ideas, and even indulged in a bit of graffiti as they created the exhibit. A final NMAH example, a nine-minute video presentation titled "The Past in Your Future: Changing Perspectives on the Eighteenth Century," done by the Center for History, gives us a powerful sense of the debates surrounding the changing historiography of colonial America: it also shows the role that new paradigms and new material culture evidence will play in the major exhibition planned for the Hall of Everyday Life in the American Past, scheduled to reopen in fall 1984.[12]

But whether NMAH will also retain a portion of its previous interpretation of early American life, assembled in the 1960s by anthropologist C. Malcolm Watkin and the museum staff, remains to be seen. If they do, future Smithsonian visitors would gain an appreciation of how and why historians, in museums and academies alike, change their minds and their interpretations. The visitor has been able to acquire similar historiographical savvy at places like the Shelburne Museum in Vermont, the Hagley Museum in Delaware, and the Camron-Stanford Historic house museum in Oakland, California. In the Camron-Stanford house, for example, the curators have deliberately retained earlier interpretations of their site and its objects so that the visitor recognizes that one generation's orthodoxy often gives rise to another generation's revisionism. Parenthetically, a greater awareness of the interpretive potential of previous exhibits might also stimulate more museums to recognize the importance of keeping more comprehensive documentary, photographic, and, where possible, artifactual records of their own intellectual and institutional history.[13] Museums that labor diligently to collect and conserve the creativity of others treat their own creations with callous indifference.

A Future Agenda of Quixotic Ideas Possibly Worth Entertaining
Thus far we have been looking at a small sample of data, suggesting the desirability of offering museum visitors some, not necessarily all, exhibits that contain healthy doses of participatory self-learning, awareness of historical relativism, and methodological pluralism. Unlike these instances, however, the next set of

examples has not been tried in an American museum, so far as I know.

In my recent attempt to give some form to the diverse components of *Material Culture Studies in America,* I have tried to sort out the various conceptual models by which American researchers are currently gaining knowledge from objects. In that book, I proposed nine possible paradigms: art history, symbolist, cultural history, environmentalist, functionalist, structuralist, behavioralistic, national character, and social history.[14] Each of these nine perspectives interprets objects in different ways, asking different questions and emphasizing different characteristics in order to learn from the physical data.

Of late, I have been experimenting with applying the nine conceptual frameworks to a single object, a 1922 Dutch Colonial Revival tract house that also happens to be my present home—and almost identical, even to the green and white exterior color scheme, to the one Sinclair Lewis, writing in the same year, fashioned for Babbitt. My objective has been to develop an interpretive scheme, applicable to many objects, that would show beginning students of material culture how enormously informative—and often equally enigmatic—a single object can be when studied from several angles of vision. As I have pursued this heuristic task, I have also pondered whether this sort of analysis could be done for a typical historical house museum. Would it not be useful to show visitors how to think about the concept of shelter, say from a functionalist *and* and environmentalist perspective, a symbolist *and* a structuralist point of view, and so on? Might not a museum try this multiple interpretive approach to a single artifact—like the Gateway Arch in St. Louis, the Chicago Water Tower, or the Los Angeles Freeway? Indeed, the general concept could also be applied to a museum *site* as well. For example, an exhibit in a zoological or botanical museum, a state park or an outdoor living history museum might be built around geographer D. W. Meinig's provocative model, "Ten Ways to Look at a Landscape."[15]

While much material culture research attempts to comprehend people through the objects that they make or use, there is another body of literature that suggests that we also consider what objects make of people. A future museum exhibit might explore what Mihaly Csikszentmihalyi and Eugene Rochberg-Halton have done in a new book titled *The Meaning of Things: Domestic Symbols and the Self.* The thrust of this research is how and why contemporary Americans relate to objects in their immediate home environments. Or, to put it another way, which things mean the most in people's definitions of who they are, have been, and wish to become?[16] Object researchers might likewise inquire if there are certain things to which people are especially attached, say in childhood or adolescence, middle or old age? Is there a category of things especially meaningful for each of Erik Erikson's eight stages of human development?[17] These are some of the intriguing questions worth pursuing in object research both in the museum and in the academy, among researchers and with museum visitors.

To date, however, despite all our collection and classification of objects, little is known about the reasons for human attachment to them or about the various personal ways by which they become incorporated into people's goals, experiences, and very identities. The Csikszentmihalyi–Rochberg-Halton study, especially the section on "The Most Cherished Objects in the Home," is one avenue of investigation; the insights found in novels like Marilynne Robinson's *Housekeeping* (1980) or W. D. Wetherell's *Souvenir* (1981) are another for helping us think through what the presence or absence of furniture, visual art, photographs, books, stereos, musical instruments, televisions, sculpture, and plants mean as part of what Csikszentmihalyi and Rochberg-Halton call the "possessions of selfhood." Data gathered empirically from contemporary Americans about their attachments to specific objects might also help museums explain more effectively the role of similar artifacts in earlier periods of American history.

In our quest for new object knowledge, we might also help visitors understand better contemporary environments and their objects. Could we not, for example, devise techniques for analyzing more thoroughly the material culture of 20th-century institutions like the supermarket, the shopping center, and the automobile suburb? For instance, might it be possible to apply Claude Levi-Strauss's concept of "the cooked and the raw" to the artifacts of the modern supermarket? Would it be appropriate to think of the shopping plaza as the "New American Main Street" in the new type of urban form the geographer Peirce Lewis calls the "Galactic City?"[18] And is not the automobile suburb an excellent example of what the archeologist Michael Schiffer calls "the archaeology of us?"[19] Museum exhibitions have been done on suburbanization and the strip, but I think the supermarket and the shopping center have been neglected. So have other emporiums of American consumerism: discount houses, sporting goods stores, electronics outlets, souvenir shops, and, of course, museum stores. And to return to a point suggested earlier, that is, the sharing with visitors of some of the theory and practice of museum exhibitions: Why not do a comparative exhibit in which the art of museum exhibiting is contrasted with other genres of object displays like department store windows, trade shows, and world's fair pavilions?

If you grant the premise that museums should help us recognize and understand the inordinate abundance of material things that our contemporary culture produces, what Mary Douglas calls *The World of Goods*,[20] then it follows that we might also look at the profusion of objects our society throws away. Prompting people to think how many 20th-century objects have a planned—or unplanned—obsolescence might be the beginning of an exhibit design idea that explores the material culture domain of personal waste disposal (e.g., waste baskets, trash compactors, compost heaps, garage sales) and of public waste removal (e.g., county landfills, auto graveyards, metropolitan incinerators, toxic waste depositories). This proposal amounts, of course, to the very reverse of what was suggested above: that is, it may be as culturally significant to know what objects people decide to chuck as to cherish.[21]

Jim Deetz once promised to do an exhibit at the Lowie Museum at Berkeley on the coal-mining town of Somerville in northern California, where he has been doing an archeological dig for several years. Deetz's semiwhimsical plan was to shovel heaps of everything, including garbage, that the archeologists had dug up into a rank or so of exhibit cases in the museum. In one alcove there were to be some 125,000 objects on display in whatever haphazard way they happened to fall from the forklift. Photographs and extensive quotations from oral histories taken from former miners who worked the site were to be displayed as well. One entire wall was to be plastered with documents and ephemera (e.g., mail-order catalogs, advertisements, newspaper clippings) about 19th-century objects. Jim conceded, "In one little section off in a corner we will tell how we started thinking about these objects, to kind of give people a lead into the experience," but, he insisted, "we will not give a single interpretive statement."[22] Of course, the desire to do a strictly noninterpretive exhibit is itself a type of interpretation. Deetz's proposal does, however, speak directly to the issue of the visitor as his or her own interpreter—as well as to a playful bit of museum anarchy.

In this irreverent spirit, let me put a final item on the agenda for expanding museum literacy. Realizing that a number of museums have already begun to do so, I suggest that many more assume the responsibility for increasing the public's skill at interpreting public sites and structures.[23] At present, there are approximately 5,000 museums in America; they make up a significant part of the built environment of our public and communal life. These institutions have an opportunity to play a wider role in helping visitors interpret the meaning of a museum's spatial, historical, and cultural context through walking tours of their locale; by publishing guidebooks to their neighborhood's public art, sculpture, and architecture; as well as by developing exhibits on the economic, real estate, geographic, and political history of the area of which their physical plant is a part.

In short, museums might show their visitors how to do what some of us have called the "above-ground archaeology of the museum."[24] The Delaware Art Museum, the Cincinnati Historical Society, and the Indianapolis Museum of Art have created just such programs and even extended their purview beyond the immediate neighborhood of their institutional setting to include their entire metropolitan areas. Since American architectural history has, to date, largely emphasized research into the single-family house and the commercial skyscraper, American museums might assume the initiative in promoting investigation of all types of public structures—their architectural style, their iconography, their relations to other public edifices, their place in city planning, their position in political, economic, and cultural decision making, and their meaning in our communal and personal lives.

Of course, this final type of inquiry—knowing the meaning in our communal and personal lives—is the primary reason for attempting to know an object, be that object a 19th-century Carleton Watkins photograph of the Yosemite Valley or the present 20th-century physical site of Yosemite National Park. In material culture studies, it is only the understanding of the culture that is behind, within, and around the material that makes the enterprise worthy of our time and our talent. Museum literacy, at its core, is but another form of human literacy, another mode of knowing, another grammar of understanding for reading others and ourselves.

Notes

1. *Oxford English Dictionary,* 6:781; see also *Webster's Third International Dictionary Unabridged,* p. 1490.

2. James Deetz, *In Small Things Forgotten: The Archaeology of Early American Life* (Garden City, N.Y.: Doubleday Anchor, 1977), pp. 24–25.

3. William T. Alderson, "Right from the Start: The Strong Museum Opens Its Doors," *Museum News* 61, no. 2 (November/December 1982): 52.

4. For a description of the work of the Discovery Hall Museum, see Geoffrey Huys and Marsha Mullin, "Industrial History on Exhibit," *History News* 37, no. 5 (May 1982): 12–16.

5. A useful anthology of how historians work with documentary resources is L. P. Curtis, ed., *The Historian's Workshop: Original Essays by Sixteen Historians* (New York: Knopf, 1970).

6. Barbara Riley, "Contemporary Collecting: A Case Study," *Decorative Arts Newsletter* 4 (Summer 1978): 3–6.

7. Jay Anderson provides a succinct overview of such museum activities in "Living History: Simulating Everyday Life in Living Museums," *American Quarterly* 34, no. 3 (Summer 1982): 289–306. Anderson, in relating his own work at Colonial Pennsylvania Plantation, notes that the museum attempted to interpret "not just the *content* of colonial history but the methods of *researching* colonial history. . . . Historiography itself was the exhibit" (p. 300).

8. These synonyms for the creative force behind the making of objects can be found in theorists like Henry Glassie, *The Folk Housing of Middle Virginia* (Knoxville: University of Tennessee Press, 1975); Eugene Ferguson, "The Mind's Eye: Nonverbal Thought in Technology," *Science* 197, no. 4306 (August 26, 1977): 827–997; Cyril Stanley Smith, "Materials and the Development of Civilization and Science," *Science* 148 (May 14, 1968): 908–17; Andrew Harrison, *Making and Thinking* (Indianapolis: Hackett, 1978); and David Pye, *The Nature of Design* (New York: Reinhold, 1964; reprint, 1978).

9. Brooke Hindle, *Invention and Emulation* (New York: New York University Press, 1981); Glassie, *Folk Housing of Middle Virginia;* Deetz, *Invitation to Archaeology* (Garden City, N.Y.: Natural History Press, 1967).

10. *New England Begins: The Seventeenth Century,* vol. 2: *Mentality and Environment* (Boston: Museum of Fine Arts, 1982); Cyril Stanley Smith, *From Art to Science: Seventy-Two Objects Illustrating the History of Discovery* (Cambridge, Mass.: MIT Press, 1980).

11. Eugene Ferguson has long been a proponent of this line of object research; see, for example, *The Various and Ingenious Machines of Agostino Ramelli* (1588), ed. and trans. with Martina Teach Gnudi (Baltimore: Johns Hopkins University Press, 1976), and "The Nature of Technologic Invention: Play and Intellect," paper presented to the Symposium on Technology and Evolution of Culture, American Anthropological Association, Washington, D.C., 1980.

12. "The Past in Your Future," exhibit handout accompanying a video presentation at the National Museum of American History, March 19, 1983. Another example of a museum's interest in showing visitors the methodology behind the exhibit's research is the Yale University Art Gallery's *Work of Many Hands: Card Tables in Federal America, 1790–1820,* summarized in a museum catalog of that same name published in 1982 by the gallery.

13. Carole Schwartz, "Keeping Our Own House in Order: The Importance of Museum Records," *Museum News* 61, no. 4 (April 1982): 38–50.

14. Thomas J. Schlereth, *Material Culture Studies in America* (Nashville, Tenn.: American Association for State and Local History, 1982), pp. 32–72.

15. D. W. Meinig, "The Beholding Eye: Ten Versions of the Same Scene," in *The Interpretation of Ordinary Landscapes,* ed. D. W. Meinig (New York: Oxford University Press, 1979), pp. 33–50.

16. Mihaly Csikszentmihalyi and Eugene Rochberg-Halton, *The Meaning of Things: Domestic Symbols and the Self* (Cambridge, Eng.: Cambridge University Press, 1981).

17. Erik Erikson, *Childhood and Society* (New York: W. W. Norton, 1950).

18. Peirce Lewis, "The Unprecedented City," in *The American Land* (Washington, D.C.: Smithsonian Exposition Books, 1977), pp. 118, 119.

19. Richard A. Gould and Michael B. Schiffer, *Modern Material Culture: The Archaeology of Us* (New York: Academic Press, 1981).

20. Mary Douglas, *The World of Goods* (New York: Basic Books, 1979).

21. William Rathje, "Le Project du Garbage," in *Historical Archaeology and the Importance of Material Things,* ed. Leland Ferguson (Columbia, S.C.: Society for Historical Archaeology, 1977), pp. 36–42.

22. James Deetz, "The Link From Object to Person to Concept," in *Museums, Adults and the Humanities: A Guide for Educational Programming,* ed. Zipporah W. Collins (Washington, D.C.: American Association of Museums, 1981), p. 33.

23. One model is put forth by Carol Duncan and Alan Wallach, "The Universal Survey Museum," *Art History* 3, no. 4 (December 1980): 448–69.

24. Thomas J. Schlereth, "Above-Ground Archaeology: Discovering a Community's History through Local Artifacts," in *Artifacts and the American Past* (Nashville, Tenn.: American Association for State and Local History, 1980), pp. 184–203.

Defining Museum Literacy

Carol B. Stapp

"Museum literacy" represents a recent coinage in the lexicon of the museum professional, yet it refers to a recurrent concept in the classic literature on museums. New phrase yet old idea, museum literacy summarizes a philosophy of museum accessibility with profound implications for museum policies and practices. To define museum literacy is, in effect, to articulate a previously unarticulated posture on museum accessibility.

But perhaps to define museum literacy it is best to resort to an analogy. "Computer literacy"—or even "library literacy," if I may take the liberty of using a seemingly redundant verbal formulation—connotes competence in using a complex system of information storage and retrieval. Competence comprises mastery of the language appropriate to that system as well as familiarity with its institutional environment. True literacy, of course, far exceeds basic literacy. The truly computer literate or library literate person operates at a high level of proficiency, autonomously exercising his or her critical faculties. For example, basic library literacy means competence in reading books, but full library literacy signifies competence in drawing upon the library's holdings purposefully and independently.

By analogy, basic museum literacy means competence in reading objects (visual literacy), but full museum literacy signifies competence in drawing upon the museum's holdings and services purposefully and independently. Museum literacy therefore implies genuine and full visitor access to the museum by virtue of mastery of the language of museum objects and familiarity with the museum as an institution. In a word, the museum literate visitor is *empowered*.

Without recourse to the actual phrase, arguments for the importance of museum literacy abound in museum literature. The rationale for the recurring call for museum literacy can frequently be located in the invocation of the oft-quoted, never attributed aphorism, "Museums represent with libraries the two halves of the public memory." As equal and parallel repositories of public memory, the library and the museum have public responsibilities, especially in the light of American democratic ideals of an informed populace.

But there is a major difference between the mandates of these two public institutions. Traditionally, libraries have not been charged with the obligation of

Roundtable Reports 9, no. 1 (Winter 1984): 3–4.

ensuring user competence. Our system of schooling focuses on developing the knowledge, skills, and attitudes for library literacy (and, more recently, computer literacy). The knowledge, skills, and attitudes for museum literacy enjoy no comparable cultivation within the schools.

Perhaps this neglect of museum literacy arises from an assumption that command of the language of objects is spontaneous and innate. A number of students of the museum have sought to correct this misunderstanding. According to Pierre Bourdieu, visitor competence in the museum reflects culturally learned behavior, not natural proclivity or sensitivity. Bourdieu explicates his argument by referring to language acquisition. Exposure within the family circle to more complex language enhances the ability to take advantage of opportunities in language enrichment and refinement. Similarly, childhood exposure to "cultural goods" increases the capacity to benefit from opportunities in cultural enrichment and refinement.[1]

Nelson Graburn, too, strives to dispel the myth of inborn museum literacy. He refers to a theory of "symbolic estate" to argue that in our pluralistic society the beliefs and behaviors of some socioeconomic groups are more likely than those of other socioeconomic groups to encourage museum literacy.[2]

Both the sociologist Bourdieu and the anthropologist Graburn would no doubt endorse Alma Wittlin's tart comment on the opening to the public of formerly inaccessible collections during the revolutionary ferment of the later 18th century. "The minds of most visitors," Wittlin observes dryly, "remained debarred from the experience even when they were physically admitted [to the newly opened museums]."[3] Since museum literacy—like library literacy and computer literacy— results from education and practice, mere physical access or superficial informational gestures fail to fulfill the museum's public mission.

It is difficult to decide if the long and honorable history of the call for museum literacy (in spirit if not by name) should be regarded as disquieting or legitimizing. Populists and elitists alike have voiced strong commitment to public museum literacy; then and now, it is clearly a valid and live issue in the literature.

George Brown Goode, the distinguished assistant secretary of the Smithsonian Institution, insisted vigorously in "The Museums of the Future" that the "public museum is, first of all, for the benefit of the public. . . . The museum cultivates the powers of observation, and the casual visitor even makes discoveries for himself." In his 1895 paper entitled "Principles of Museum Administration," Goode set down nuts-and-bolts advice for cultivating these "powers of observation" in the casual visitor; no factor escaped his attention—from a division of collections into exhibition and study series to the art of label writing—in his zeal to translate theory into practice. "The people's museum should be much more than a house full of specimens in glass cases," Goode proclaimed. "It should be a house full of ideas, arranged with the strictest attention to system . . . a series of objects selected with reference to their value to investigation, or their possibilities for public enlightenment."[4]

Benjamin Ives Gilman, generally held to be the archenemy of popular use of the museum, nonetheless echoed Goode in his solicitude for the visitor. Although Gilman argued for restricted public access, this authoritative administrator of the Boston Museum of Fine Arts also conducted and published research into museum fatigue, amusingly documented by illustrative photographs, revealing a deep-seated concern for the museum visitor's physical and psychological comfort.[5]

Contemporaneously, the equally formidable John Cotton Dana—the founder and director of the Newark Museum—was proselytizing for "the pleasure and profit of the common man" in "new museums." Dana declared that "common sense demands that a publicly supported institution do something for its supporters . . . adding to the pleasure, the general enlightenment, the physical well-being and the industrial power of the citizens."[6] In the more recent past, Francis Henry Taylor and Theodore Low reasserted Dana's advocacy of public accessibility in the name of cultural equity, whereas Paul Rea, Thomas R. Adam, and Karl Meyer reiterated Dana's championship of public accessibility in the name of economic equity.[7]

Regardless of their respective motivating imperatives, these students of the museum were proponents of museum literacy in all but name. The consensus may be best summed up in Paul Rea's description of the distinctive character of the public museum:

> The purpose is to enrich the life of the people generally. . . . The attitude is that of a public servant . . . constantly seeking to widen and deepen its influence. The methods are those of active interpretation. . . . When museums transferred their service from limited groups to the general public . . . they had necessarily to take upon themselves a new function of interpreting their subjects and collections and of arousing developing interest. In short, they became educational institutions.[8]

Public institutions and perforce educational institutions, museums owe the general public access to the knowledge, skills, and attitudes previously accessible to "limited groups." Moreover, the underlying principle of empowering the visitor dictates that delivering pertinent information is secondary to sparking intellectual participation. The museum, therefore, should undertake to offer the public something of the *caliber* of experience enjoyed by the expert.

One avenue worthy of further pursuit would attempt to merge two parallel lines of research—artifact study and audience surveys. Serious scholars like E. McClung Fleming and Erwin Panofsky have recounted their methods for encountering objects.[9] Their brilliant disquisitions attest to the potency of the object for the initiated. In contrast to such detailed accounts recorded by these and other practiced connoisseurs, however, information about the average visitor's encounter with objects remains sketchy. Scattered research efforts like those of Daryl Fischer at the Denver Art Museum or Mary Ellen Munley at the National Museum of American

History nonetheless contribute insight into the efficacy of the object for the uninitiated. Bringing these two bodies of information, with their startling discrepancies, into congruence offers a promising challenge to the concept of museum literacy.

Meeting the challenge of museum literacy, however, requires more than that museum educators act. The ramifications of a commitment to museum literacy permeates the budgetary and decision-making process for the entire institution, just as museum literacy has appeared as a *leitmotif* in the evolution of the public museum. This new coinage summarizes an old concept, both *denoting* learned visitor competence in the museum and *connoting* systematic museum efforts to foster full and genuine public access to museum holdings and services.

Notes

1. Pierre Bourdieu, "Outline of a Sociological Theory of Art Perception," *International Social Science Journal* 20, no. 4 (1968): 589–612.
2. Nelson Graburn, "Museum as a Social Instrument," paper presented at the annual meeting of the American Association of Museums, Philadelphia, June 1982, pp. 6–7.
3. Alma Wittlin, *Museums: In Search of a Usable Future* (Cambridge, Mass.: MIT Press, 1970), p. 119.
4. George Brown Goode, "The Museums of the Future," "Principles of Museum Administration," and "Museum-History and Museums of History," *Report of the U.S. National Museum for 1897*, pt. 2 (Washington, D.C.: Government Printing Office, 1901), pp. 248, 250, 199, 72–73.
5. Benjamin Ives Gilman, *Museum Ideals of Purpose and Method*, 2d ed. (Cambridge, Mass.: Harvard University Press, 1923).
6. John Cotton Dana, *The New Museum* (Woodstock, Vt.: Elm Tree Press, 1917), pp. 18–19; Dana, *A Plan for a New Museum: The Kind of a Museum It Will Profit a City to Maintain* (Woodstock, Vt.: Elm Tree Press, 1920), pp. 9, 13, 55.
7. Francis Henry Taylor, *Babel's Tower: The Dilemma of the Modern Museum* (New York: Columbia University Press, 1945); Theodore Low, *The Museum as a Social Instrument* (New York: Metropolitan Museum of Art, 1942); Paul Rea, *The Museum and the Community: A Study of Social Laws and Consequences* (Lancaster, Pa.: Science Press, 1932); Thomas R. Adam, *The Museum and Popular Culture* (New York: American Association for Adult Education, 1939); Karl Meyer, *The Art Museum: Power, Money, Ethics* (New York: Morrow, 1979).
8. Rea, *Museum and the Community*, pp. 16–17.
9. E. McClung Fleming, "Artifact Study: A Proposed Model," *Winterthur Portfolio* 9 (1974): 153–73; Erwin Panofsky, *Studies in Iconology: Humanistic Themes in the Art of the Renaissance* (New York: Harper and Row, 1939).

Afterword

The term and concept "museum literacy" seem to have been welcomed into the vocabulary of the profession. Theorists and practitioners refer to museum literacy as the framework that informs their stance on the optimal outcome for the visitor.[1] "Defining Museum Literacy" has been cited as an important contribution to the theory and practice of museum education.[2] The evidence thus supports the proposition that, while the term "museum literacy" may not have figured previously in the common professional parlance, the concept of museum literacy clearly struck a common professional chord.

Of course I find it immensely gratifying to come upon mention of museum literacy in articles or bibliographies. These occasions are nonetheless not without a degree of angst. I have discerned that I take a proprietary interest in ascertaining if the meaning I intended to convey by juxtaposing "museum" and "literacy" is indeed the meaning being conveyed. What lifts this interest beyond the merely proprietary, however, derives expressly from the ready acceptance of museum literacy by the field. Fellow theorists and practitioners have elected to clarify their position or bolster their argument by calling upon the ideology and methodology of museum literacy, much as I had turned to the writings of kindred spirits—from both the past and the present—to justify the notion of museum literacy.

And for the most past, those who refer to museum literacy get it mostly right. But the thrust of my manifesto—to replace object-centered learning with visitor-centered learning as the raison d'être of museum education—is not always fully grasped. When "Defining Museum Literacy" was evolving in my mind more than a decade ago, this line of thought was somewhat in eclipse among museum professionals. Part of the generative process for me included the fulsome documentation in "The 'Public' Museum" of audience advocacy as steeped in tradition and supported by scholarship.[3] Today it is evident that museum literacy's political and operational ramifications have lost much of their radical spin—witness the newly revised Code of Ethics for Museums; the recent report of the Task Force on Museum Education, *Excellence and Equity;* and the latest Museum Assessment Program, Public Dimension Assessment.

The fault nevertheless did not lie in the times or in the reader's deficiency of sympathy. Rather, the meaning I intended to convey by juxtaposing "museum" and "literacy" has been only partially understood because I obfuscated the term and concept with historical background and academic prose. At heart, museum literacy is so simple a philosophy—which in turn shapes so simple an approach—that I felt compelled to dress it up with a fine pedigree and fancy language to add to its credibility.

If I had it to write over, I would set down my thoughts more clearly, using the plainest words. For although museum literacy rests upon a simple premise, its implications are profound and its implementation anything but easy. Essentially, it is the contention that the full initiation of the public—visitors and nonvisitors— into the pleasures and challenges of the museum constitutes our charge as museum professionals. After all, what have we to offer but to share our own competence?

Regardless of the venue—formal classroom or museum gallery—the point of learning/experience is that the student or visitor is enhanced/advanced in attitude, knowledge, and/or skills. This sense of enhancement/advancement—if consciously recognized by the student or visitor—empowers him or her for the next encounter with learning/experience. The acquisition of a sense of competency in any and every domain requires a degree of self-consciousness, of reflection. Since the museum most assuredly is a distinctive domain, we would do well to provide not only direct access to learning/experience but also directed opportunities to take ownership of that learning/experience.

Indeed, the public should be able to draw upon all the resources of the museum purposefully and independently, from exhibitions, publications, and programming to library, study collections, and staff expertise. These usages represent specific examples of the basic obligation of the museum to the public—a pledge that our own sense of competency in the museum be widely exercised and enjoyed.

The proficiency we museum literates exercise and enjoy grew from an accumulation of learning/experience, acquired and assimilated in accord with the effectiveness of the source of the learning/experience and the richness of the repertory of our own resources. A commitment to museum literacy means that we will look to producing more effective sources of learning/experience in the museum *and* to awakening the broadest possible spectrum of the public to the richness of the repertory of its own resources.

Notes

1. Hope Jensen Leichter, Karen Hensel, and Eric Larsen, "Families and Museums: Issues and Perspectives," in *Museum Visits and Activities for Family Life Enrichment,* ed. Barbara H. Butler and Marvin B. Sussman (New York: Haworth Press, 1989), p. 27; Ross Loomis, *Museum Visitor Evaluation: New Tool for Management* (Nashville, Tenn.: American Association for State and Local History, 1987); Patterson B. Williams, "The Art Museum Experience," in *Museums as Learning Resources Seminar (International Research and Exchanges Board: United States/German Democratic Republic,* ed. Jane Glaser (Washington, D.C.: Smithsonian Institution Office of Museum Programs, 1988), unpaginated; Robert L. Wolf, "The Missing Link: A Look at the Role of Orientation in Enriching the Museum Experience," *Journal of Museum Education* 11, no. 1 (Winter 1986): 18.

2. Mary Bosdet and Gail Durbin, eds., *GEM Museum Education Bibliography, 1978–1988* (Aberdeen, Scotland: Group for Education in Museums [1988]), p. 8; Kenneth A. Yellis, "Museum Education," in *The Museum: A Reference Guide,* ed. Michael Steven Shapiro with Louis Ward Kemp (Westport, Conn.: Greenwood Press, 1990), p. 195.

3. Carol B. Stapp, "The 'Public' Museum: A Review of the Literature," *Journal of Museum Education* 15, no. 3 (Fall 1990): 4–11. The essay was written in 1980–81.

Object Contemplation: Theory into Practice

Patterson B. Williams

Some years ago, at a Smithsonian conference on children in museums, Peter Marzio—then director of the Corcoran Gallery of Art, now director of the Museum of Fine Arts, Houston—urged museum educators to develop "an intellectual framework" for museum education. I agree. In our daily lives museum teachers, docents, and museum education administrators desperately need to articulate the theoretical superstructure within which they operate. There are great teachers in museums—exhibition designers, curators, docents, and professional museum educators—who rely on unarticulated concepts of the way things ought to be done by visitors. But in these days of institutional goals, mission statements, and long-range plans, a clear, comprehensive written statement of theory is an indispensable tool. As a litmus test for proposed projects, a systematic statement of principles helps us both to make decisions efficiently and to build compelling cases for our decisions.

I would argue that the essence of a museum's public function is to enable the visitor to use museum objects to his or her own greatest advantage. To call for museum literacy, therefore, is to call for a theory of instruction focused on teaching visitors how to have personally significant experiences with objects. This prescription stems from the nature of museums and the definition of teaching: to teach is to show someone how to do something, and in museums that *something* is "having a personally significant experience with an object."

The instructional theory and methods for museum literacy that I am advocating are rooted in three beliefs:

■ Expertise in art objects can be taught and is not a God-given talent.

■ The most vital and interesting reason for a museum's existence is the potential that objects have for stimulating meaningful human experiences.

■ And, in the words of Max Friedlander, "Since art is a thing of the mind, any scientific study of art must always incorporate psychology."

It also seems to me that a theory of instruction designed to help museum visitors to have *personally significant experiences with museum objects* must take into account two givens. The first is that the goal must be an experience on the part of the visitor that *the visitor values;* therefore the significance, if any, of the encounter will be

Roundtable Reports 9, no. 1 (Winter 1984): 10–12.

determined by the visitor's value system, not by our own. The second given is that a museum object must be *central* to the experience.

To develop a method for such instruction we might begin by looking at the experience of people who are deeply involved with objects. What exactly do they *do* with objects? What do objects do for *them*? How do they get started with objects? How do they describe what they do? What does it look like when they do it? How long does it take? What stimulated them in their personal lives to get involved with objects? What "extras" do they need to make it easier to do what they do?

In the 1970s I was part of a group of museum teachers at the Philadelphia Museum of Art who looked at our own experience with objects as well as to the experiences of curatorial staff, art historians, critics, and artists to find answers to these questions. The theory and methods we developed over a 10-year period are still what I use today. In general terms, what all the museum or art experts whom we studied seemed to do with objects in museums was to contemplate them. To contemplate is, according to *Webster's* dictionary, "to look at or view with continued attention; to observe thoughtfully, to think studiously, meditate, consider deliberately." Consequently, contemplation became the skill we determined to teach museum audiences.

What constitutes the contemplation of an art object? In looking at all the various things people do that fall under the rubric of contemplation we found that there are four nearly separate kinds of mental activities that they perform on an art object. Plainly stated, they look at it, they react to it, they think about it in a variety of contexts, and they make judgments about it. And, much of the time, they do these things in that sequence.

To teach visitors to perform each of these activities is both complicated and simple. Each is a cluster of experiences. For instance, looking involves complex and often mysterious optical and mental processes—processes that are hard to understand, much less to teach. Similarly, making judgments is a matter of forming opinions by a disciplined process involving discerning and comparing after inquiry and deliberation. Yet, because visitors commonly perform these same acts in their everyday lives, it is also simple to teach museum visitors the skill of contemplation of an art object. Four examples will clarify how theory translates into practice.

Cluster I: Looking

Many introductory art museum tours for young people focus on subject matter of interest to children ("Animals in Art") or on basic art concepts ("The Elements of Art"). For adults the most familiar introductory tour is some sort of "Highlights of the Collection." A better basic tour would be one that induces self-consciousness about the way we perceive visually, a parallel to Jerome Bruner's "metacognition" or teaching students how to think about their own thinking. Experts know—but seldom teach—several very basic principles about visual perception: No two people "see" precisely the same thing; these differences are rooted in our differences as individual human beings. Seeing is a matter of focusing visual attention, or, as Ernst Gombrich says, "To see at all, we must isolate and select"; time, practice, and, most important, freedom to explore are needed for a fully rewarding visual experience.

"Perception Games," an introductory elementary school tour developed in the Philadelphia Museum of Art and now also offered in the Denver Art Museum, uses entertaining exercises to apply these theoretical principles, to teach visual perception. This fall in Denver we are introducing four lab sessions as an adjunct to a series of art history slide lectures for adult audiences, with similar intent. Each lab will teach one of the activities under discussion here, beginning with visual perception.

Cluster II: Reacting

One of the most generally accepted ideas about museum-quality art is that it has the power to move the viewer, to stimulate a response or reaction. The reactions of museum visitors, however, like the responses of art experts, are by no means uniform; they involve idiosyncratic feelings and thoughts, conscious and unconscious.

This evocative potency of art may create a painful dilemma for some art experts, when the public is moved for the "wrong" reason. A current example is the increasing popularity of "Western art." Images like those by Frederic Remington often stimulate a poignant memory of a lost life-style. Once when I was showing a slide of a Remington painting with a lone rider at sunset to a group of volunteers in Huntsville, Alabama, one woman responded with a detailed story of Saturday morning horseback rides with her family on a ranch in Wyoming. Her father led the ride and would usually stop and use his hat to dip drinking water from a stream for her to drink. She recalled the smell of the hat and the taste of the cold water. The dilemma for art experts is that subject matter alone—a cowboy on a horse—can stimulate a personal response regardless of how well or how poorly it is painted. But works of art are not, for the most part, collected (i.e., valued by experts) because of their subjects but because of the manner in which they are done. Should we museum professionals encourage a reaction like that of the woman in Alabama, or should we redirect it? Keeping in mind that one hallmark of the expert's reaction ought to be honesty, we risk depriving the visitor of what Sheldon Annis calls "dream space," in which visitors "distill meaning as an object jolts a memory, or provokes an internal dialogue of fantasy, wish or anxiety."

There is no dilemma for me in the Alabama volunteer's reaction to the Remington. Her reaction must not be redirected, for to do so would suggest that her *honest* feelings were to be shunned. Rather, we should make a subtle distinction between redirecting and augmenting, by adding to her reaction some knowledge or experience that might allow her to enrich her own reactions to the painting without any loss of the power of her personal associations.

Cluster III: Considering Cultural Context

The third activity we need to teach is thinking about art in cultural and historical context. Curators, art historians, critics, artists, and other art experts spend much time gathering and assimilating information about art—how it was made, the personality and life of the maker, the time and society in which it was made. They do so with a willingness that is rooted in personal interests, random—and sometimes even prurient—curiosity, or practical professional needs. Oddly, however, we often act as if information were not an essential ingredient for visitors also. The object alone is not enough.

To develop a visitor's willingness to absorb information is the essence of the arts of fine lecturing and superb label writing. All manner of subtleties must be employed to this end because absorbing complicated information is time and energy consuming and requires a willing audience. Denver's six ArtCarts, custom-designed cabinets on wheels, are didactic teaching tools designed for use in museum galleries. The Japanese Tea Ceremony ArtCart—with its tea ceremony implements that can be handled by visitors and its mounted photographs for showing tea gardens, teahouse interiors, and the tea ritual itself—functions effectively with adult and youth audiences not because the objects are touchable but because in the hands of a fine teacher it is a dramatic tool for giving complex information in an entertaining and magnetic way.

Cluster IV: Judging Art

Making judgments is in many ways the most important cluster of activities. It is also the one we ask visitors to perform least often. When pursued, making judgments provides experts and visitors with personal pleasure, refinement of their perceptions, and greater awareness of themselves and their own values. In isolated cases, art museums do ask visitors to make judgments by discerning and comparing after inquiry and deliberation. One fine example at the Philadelphia Museum of Art some years ago was a small didactic exhibition called *A Matter of Style* in which visitors were presented with several art historical problems related to identifying similarities in style.

At the Denver Art Museum the commitment to encouraging visitors to make their own judgments has affected label writing. A commonplace in writing about art is the statement of a personal value judgment in the third person, as though a subjective opinion were an objective fact. Typically these statements involve the word "beauty." Thomas Aquinas defines beauty as "that which gives us pleasure upon being beheld." Beauty is customarily held to be in the eye of the beholder, yet it would surprise none of us to read an art museum label declaring an object "one of the most beautiful examples of . . .". We are working in Denver to substitute for such *obiter dicta* more precise—and less intimidating—statements like "this is a typical . . ." or "a finely crafted example of . . ." or "Curator X considers this a beautiful example of . . .". Such efforts must be pursued consistently if we are to teach the visitor to make his or her own judgments rather than passively to accept an expert's judgments.

With these examples I have attempted to illustrate one approach to helping visitors develop museum literacy. Any method of instruction, or set of guidelines, that intends to accomplish something so broad and yet so subtle as helping visitors to have personally significant experiences with art objects must be grounded in carefully constructed theory and honed in encounters with real visitors and real art objects. Indeed, the experience of teaching in museum galleries is a fertile breeding ground for such theories. Perhaps the best environment in which valid methods of instruction supportive of museum literacy can be developed is one in which the entire museum staff—educators, curators, and administrators—involve themselves regularly and directly in aiding visitors to encounter their museum's collections. Unfortunately, one of the more distressing facts of museum life is the great distance between the visitor's experience—witnessed only by guards and sometimes volunteers—and the normal decision-making process by which mission statements, long-range priorities, and budget allocations are determined. As a result, the public is too often set adrift in galleries that satisfy only experts, that is, those already "literate."

An anecdote may suggest what I have in mind by "satisfaction." I sit with 15 other staff members on a committee to plan the next five years of temporary exhibitions at the Denver Art Museum. I was asked to distill into one succinct statement two rather lengthy objectives for the visitor's experience and proposed: We will plan exhibitions that satisfy audiences. This statement was met with overt uneasiness and some passive resistance from those I would categorize as object experts. But to the audience experts on the committee the statement seemed to make perfect sense. Such incidents pinpoint the marvelous, exciting essence of museums—institutions that encompass two wonderfully contradictory pursuits: that of collecting the rarest and most excellent objects and that of ensuring broad and genuine access to those objects. While the collecting of excellent objects has been addressed rather thoroughly in theory and practice, the ensuring of access to objects—museum literacy—has not been dealt with sufficiently in either theory or practice. Yet to do so will make museums more whole and, indeed, more wholesome for visitor and staff alike.

Responses to Schlereth, Stapp, and Williams

From What to Why
Joan C. Madden

It is very heartening that Tom Schlereth and Patterson Williams both aim at improving museum literacy by proposing to train museum visitors to understand objects preserved in museum collections. Williams states that a theory of museum instruction should focus on "teaching visitors how to have *personally significant experiences with museum objects*." In museum teaching, whether in an art gallery or a museum of history or science, the goal is to allow an observer to discover how to do something with the objects. The museum-literate visitor marshals an intellectual effort to transform the object from a meaningless artifact or specimen into an object that has particular meaning for him or her. How can this occur?

Both Schlereth and Williams see the answer to this question in latent capacities of museum visitors themselves. Can it be said that in every serious museum-goer lurks a hidden curator, designer, or interpreter? Museum educators have the task of releasing this potential by providing the visitor with some of the skills of museum professionals.

Art gallery visitors may, indeed, need assistance in learning to look at paintings, sculptures, and other art objects in order to see the qualities that are taken into account when a curator selects an object for inclusion in the collection. But this is not to say that the curator and the visitor will see exactly the same thing; each will be looking at, reacting to, and evaluating the object in relation to his or her own past experience. In art galleries in which Williams has practiced her technique of teaching, visitors have been led through games for enhancing perception and exercises in which the viewer is helped to recognize cultural relationships between the object and its creator.

This ability to find relationships is as important to understanding history and natural science objects or specimens as it is for understanding art, as Schlereth's remarks suggest. An object without any context—time, place, user, or finder—is often cast aside by a curator. Without documentation, the object loses much of its meaning and often its value for research. Although museum visitors will seldom

Roundtable Reports 9, no. 1 (Winter 1984): 12–14, 22.

know or want to know the kind of detailed documentation that is crucial for a curator, they do need to establish their own context. This can be accomplished in a number of ways, sometimes as simply as by juxtaposing two objects, one known and the other unfamiliar.

Williams describes several new strategies that are being employed at the Denver Art Museum to encourage visitors, both children and adults, to react to art and absorb information from the object itself. Visitors are also being shown how to make judgments about art objects and to feel that their value judgments have validity. This kind of instruction should go a long way toward assisting art museum visitors in finding that galleries are "user friendly."

Similarly, Schlereth describes methods to be learned by potential museum visitors for analyzing their own environments and the objects with which they are familiar. He suggests that open collections with computerized data or systematic study collections should be available to interested visitors. Workshops teaching the skills of research, such as seriation, analogy, and the recognition of "manifest and latent functions" could help develop the skills needed.

There is a science museum analog to these approaches: experience of precisely this kind is offered in the Naturalist Center of the National Museum of Natural History, where collections and the tools of research are available to the public. It should be noted, however, that in a museum which serves between 5 and 6 million people annually, only about 12,000 people take the time to find the Naturalist Center, and an even smaller number spend enough time and effort to learn about its collections. This fact is not noted to discourage similar efforts in other museums but to caution museum educators about expecting too much from "do-it-yourself" facilities. For visitors who do make use of the center, the experience appears to be extremely rewarding, if measured by the frequency of return visits, but hard-nosed museum administrators may not assign much weight to such considerations.

Schlereth has also suggested, provocatively, "sharing with visitors some of the theory and practice of exhibitions" by documenting the stages of exhibit preparation passed through by the curator, designer, and editor. Similarly, the professional aspects of collecting and collection-based research could be more readily understood through exhibits on research methods. Classes or workshops could offer the opportunity to practice these processes while deciding, for example, what objects from contemporary life should be collected to represent the last quarter of the 20th century.

In the past 20 or so years, museums have become more conscious of their responsibilities as educational institutions in the ordinary sense of the word. In the grand old Smithsonian, there were no education offices in any of the museums prior to 1968: "the diffusion of knowledge" meant scholarly publication. Other museums around the country were much more progressive; some had offices that provided educational services early in the century. But it is probably fair to argue that only in recent years has serious thought been given to how best to use museum collections to increase the public's understanding of art, history, science, and technology.

Early collections were usually presented only with identifying labels and, possibly, one major opening statement that attempted to provide a framework for the objects on view, but with little other help, reflecting an elitist bias toward their audience. Between the 1950s and the present, much experimentation in exhibit design has occurred. Studies of museum visitors have defined more clearly the skills and educational level of the "average" museum audience. Open exhibits, touchable objects, interactive exhibits, video and computer units, larger print, and more readable label script have all been tried with varying success.

While these exhibit design and interpretation changes were occurring, educators in museums were also experimenting. One of the results of this thoughtful wrestling with the problems of helping individuals get as much as possible from contact with museum collections has been the framing of new techniques for learning from objects. Patterson Williams's struggle to develop a theory and then a practice of doing something meaningful with art objects grows out of the evolution of museum education. Tom Schlereth's description—both of successful approaches he has seen and others he fantasizes—represents another part of the movement toward including the visitor actively, through his or her own experience, in a museum or gallery. In fact, Schlereth states that museums should invite the visitor to grapple with the fundamental and potentially embarrassing question of why an object or collection of objects is important enough to be in the museum. And, as Williams hints, museum people may not always be comforted by the public's conclusions on these questions or their newfound unwillingness to be awed by connoisseurs.

The mystique of museums may vanish—along with the obstacles to museum literacy. The skills needed for looking at and abstracting information from objects about their owner, their users, or creators *can* be learned. Once learned, these skills are cumulative, providing a richer background for understanding the reasons particular objects or artifacts are included in collections or exhibitions. These skills help the visitor see objects with the eyes of a curator, undoubtedly not at the same level of understanding but with improved perception. The skills needed to see relationships between past and present, to make comparisons in style, quality, function, and values, and to comprehend the connections between specimens and natural laws—all enhance the visitor's ability to read the importance of museum objects and artifacts. These skills allow the visitor to answer for himself or herself not only What? but Why?

Unhanding the Visitor
Ken Yellis

One of the problems with museum education over the years, it has occurred to me recently, is that very often we use different words to describe the same thing. This is not efficient, by any means, but it is much more productive than the reverse situation in which we would be using the same words to describe different things.

While that accusation, at least, we may be spared, we *have* been all too prone to evolve our own vocabularies to describe how we do what we do the way we do it. This apparently wasteful process is often called reinventing the wheel, but it is more like reinventing thought and may, in the long run, turn out to be more constructive than otherwise. In any case, it seems to be a fact of life in museum education, a field so diverse, scattered, personal, practically oriented, and poor as to be more of a preference than a profession or discipline.

I bring all this up because I have a sneaking suspicion that a phrase I have been working with for the last couple of years may be very close in intent and, perhaps, even closer in application to what is meant here by "museum literacy," as interpreted and used by Carol Stapp, Tom Schlereth, and Patterson Williams. The phrase: Hands-Off Museum Education.

Hands-off museum education means equipping visitors to establish their own relationships with objects, collections, and disciplines of the museum world. It means, among other things, museum educators' shifting their focus from what *they* should be *doing* to what they can do and, especially, what they *should not do* in order to free the visitor to do more. It is exciting that both Schlereth and Williams have stressed the role of the institution and the educator in that institution in creating a context, an intellectual framework in which the visitor becomes the active intelligence, the agent of his or her own education. There is an old Burt Lancaster movie called *His Majesty O'Keefe* in which Burt says something like, "Only sacred stone gathered in the old way has any value." The museum education equivalent—perhaps the Education equivalent—is that only something you teach yourself is truly learned. The educator, museum or otherwise, has the same task now as ever, since time out of mind: to put the learner in the position in which he or she can acquire his or her own mastery.

Most of us intuit this. I have noticed that museum educators almost invariably zero in on the salient feature of each other's programs, and this is, also almost invariably, some means we have contrived to "empower," to use Stapp's wonderful word, the learner. Williams's separation of theory and practice is, to some extent, artificial, like the eons-old critical controversy over form versus content. Much more to the point is her emphasis on articulating our theoretical principles as clearly and explicitly as we can.

But one might almost say that the problem is the reverse of turning theory into practice. We need to evolve out of our current practice, and the implicit principles and assumptions that activate it and guide our choices, a theoretical superstructure that can, in turn, support our future efforts. In fact, I am coming to see the concepts of museum and object literacy, and empowerment, as part of the foundation of that superstructure.

Schlereth's analogy to the artisan is useful here and dovetails nicely with Williams. Museum educators, I think, tend to work from the concrete toward the abstract, from the object to the concept, just as artisans working materials work from the physical reality toward the idea. But artisans also do the reverse: they impose some vision or purpose on the physical stuff of their craft.

Like them we should be working in both directions, shaping our thoughts to conform to the texture and possibilities of our materials, even as we try to craft our practice to follow the shape of our ideas. As Schlereth indicates, we are, in effect, abstracting from the artifact to our artifice: a construct or reconstruction of the past. By making clear to our audiences how we do this, what choices we make along the way, and what alternative constructs are available, and, most important, by providing the intellectual tools and raw materials for the visitor to erect his or her own construct, we will ultimately and inevitably strengthen ourselves as interpreters: our own view of reality, past and present, will be more dimensional and complex.

Indeed, our first audience is and ought to be ourselves; we ought to resist formulaic approaches to interpreting objects that deprive us of the fun of discovery and might prevent us from finding the best way of opening subjects up for others. Serendipity and surprise can be lost in our rush for our rigidity. They say down in Warm Springs, Georgia, that Franklin D. Roosevelt got interested in rural electrification when, as a result of his paralysis, he started going there for therapy and noticed that his electricity bills were four times what they were in Hyde Park. Out of this chance, the Tennessee Valley Authority and other wonders were born. No one can predict how or at what level he or she will best absorb new ideas or information; how dare we prescribe for others? And yet we do.

I have noticed in my work the alarming fact that very often the less I do, the more happens—and, as they say, vice versa: the harder I work in many cases, the less substantial the result. It is neither fair nor good for my ego, but I would have to be fairly obtuse not to notice it, and either stubborn or stupid not to want to exploit it. Since, particularly in my shop, what we are usually after is not the mere transfer of information but the transformation of the visitor's thought process—nothing less—it is, in fact, counterproductive for *us* to do the work. The best way to change someone's mind is to get him or her to change it for himself or herself: you cannot permanently change it for him or her, nor should you if you could. We must, therefore, somehow, minimize our own active role and maximize the individual visitor's in his or her own transformation. We must, in fact, enable him or her to transform himself or herself as we have ourselves been transformed. We must share the magic potion, we must do something very difficult: let go. We must unhand the visitor.

If hands-off museum education means anything, it means that seduction is better than assault. Assault may be a form of self-expression but it is certainly not education, which is an expression of love *for the other*. Seduction certainly takes longer, but it is the long term in which we should be interested. It certainly takes enormous preparation, planning, and thought to enable the active participation of both parties in the seductive process, and it may not always happen. But when it does, the results please both participants, precisely because no violence has been done. The welfare and dignity of each individual have been held paramount, not the assertion of will or force of one over the other.

Interpreting History through Objects

Barbara G. Carson

Tea tables, candlemolds, blanket chests, Terry clocks, and hand mills—these things speak for times past when they were made. Objects help us understand history. The displays and scene-settings of exhibitions and historic sites are built on that generally accepted but little understood premise. In trying to teach history with things, educational directors and their staff interpreters often end up teaching something else. Yet by paying attention to what history is and by following a few simple guidelines, they can come closer to their historical objective.

As a discipline, history concerns people, people from the past who behaved in various ways. History seeks to explain their thoughts and actions. In order to use objects in a historical context, we must first relate the objects to the men, women, and children who made, sold, bought, and used them. Second, we must relate the people and the objects to behavior patterns and then analyze the activities. The progression should move from things to people and their actions and then to an exploration of ideas about the behavior. From meat cleavers, bread peels, candlemolds, and a whole assortment of craft and domestic paraphernalia, we should try to envision butchers, bakers, candlestick makers, their kith and kin, and all the others up and down the social order. And once we have identified the people, we should try to identify the activities the people engaged in with the objects. Finally, we should ask. Why? What personal, economic, social, political, religious, and cultural assumptions motivated their actions?

This seems straightforward, and it can be. However, the fact is that most books, museum exhibitions, and historic sites that illustrate or display objects do not move from things to people, to activities, to ideas. They stop short of establishing these relationships; they fail to search for explanations. Let me take you to an unspecified but fashionable mid-19th-century historic house where the guide might say:

> This lovely bedroom is furnished in the Chippendale style. The tea table was a new form of furniture at that time. The curving legs and the carved border around the circular top mark it as the height of fashion. A mechanism under the pie crust surface allows it to

Journal of Museum Education 10, no. 3 (Summer 1985): 2, 4–5. This essay was adapted from a presentation at the annual meeting of the American Association of Museums, Washington, D.C., June 1984.

be turned up so the table could be placed against a wall when not in use. Isn't the hand-workmanship beautiful!

In 69 well-organized words visitors are introduced to a room full of objects that are identified by style, and the history of one item is selected for special mention. The history of things can be a useful first step in teaching history with artifacts, but these separate histories of dressing tables, looking glasses, and the fabrics that draped them fall short of, first, connecting the objects to people and activities and, second, looking for explanations for their behavior. Similarly, stories of technology that identify raw materials and the sequence of steps in production processes should not be confused with the discipline of history. They concentrate on the way things are made, not on the people who made them and the importance of production activity in their lives.

For most museums and historic houses the practical starting point has to be the structures and objects they have to display to visitors. In connecting people to the tangible survivals or to technological processes, I recommend that you ask a series of questions. They are based on the familiar ones: Who? What? When? Where? How? And Why? But they are adapted to interpretive purposes.

First, What is this object?

Second, What activity was it a part of? Was it used alone or as part of a larger functional system? Historical interpretations of objects become broader if you think systems rather than specific artifacts, and it is worth remembering that the original system may have included artifacts that have not survived. Think artificial illumination, not candles; think accounting and financial transactions or personal correspondence, not desks. One should begin with practical direct function and, if appropriate, move on to social and ideological aspects. A single candle may have lit the way to bed; seven created a "splendid" effect in Robert Carter's dining room in 1773.

Third, Who made, owned, maintained, or used the object? To explore the wide range of subjects a single artifact can open up, interpreters need to be aware of all people associated with every phase of the artifact's existence, although to keep the length of a specific interpretation manageable not all can be presented to the public.

Fourth, How did the people work together to make the activities happen or to achieve the desired result? Of course, people don't always share the same goals. Sometimes conflict replaces cooperation. As a reminder of the breadth of an adult individual's experience, I often think of six categories of human behavior anthropologists sometimes use to organize their fieldwork—making a home, earning a living, rearing and training the young, using leisure time, engaging in community activities, practicing religion. Everything people do can be placed in one of those six groups.

Fifth, How have things and people's circumstances and relationships with one another changed from one period to the next?

Sixth, Why? Or, as a consequence of what? The fifth and sixth questions address historians' interest in change over time; they help us explore why people and their actions differ from one decade to another.

A modern example may clarify the method. First, the object is a tin can containing 1 pound 5 ounces of cherry pie filling. Second, the obvious activities associated with it are cooking and eating. Cherries are made into pie, and, as a dessert, pie does more than provide basic sustenance. It suggests the pleasure of leisurely dining with family or friends. It also has ideological significance for Americans, thanks to Parson Weems and his story of little George and the hatchet.

Third, Who made, owned, or used the can of cherry pie filling? The list of people expands the range of activities associated with the object beyond cooking and eating—commercial growers, seasonal processors, metallurgists, miners, assembly-line makers of cans, color separation specialists and printers of labels, advertisers, food store stockholders, managers, and checkers, the home cook (the can is a domestic size), diners, garbagemen, and administrators of city waste.

Fourth, how did the people work together to make the activities happen? Many were hired, some were fired, others organized for better wages, and a few were invited to dinner. The activities may lead to harmonious or competitive relationships.

Fifth, How have things and people's circumstances and relationships with one another changed from one period to the next? Two hundred years ago rural farmers grew cherry trees, picked the fruit, and marketed it locally for housewives or servants to bake into pies. Today commercial agriculture, heavy industry, long-range transportation, and modern marketing have combined to reduce the seasonality of menus and to make meal preparation easier. Furthermore, family relationships have changed; the home cook may be the father.

Sixth, Why? Explanations are never simple. A full exploration of the significance of the can of cherry pie filling in modern society is certainly more complex than anyone of sound mind would introduce in a single museum interpretation. Although some answers are more plausible than others and museum interpretations should offer suggestions, people should be encouraged to form their own opinions about an answer to the open-ended question, Why?

This discussion of a can of cherry pie filling has shown how useful the six questions are in telling *history with things,* but it is far too long for a museum label or a historic site interpretation. I'd like to revise the earlier interpretation I offered for the tea table in the Chippendale bedroom. Based on the six questions, the content of the 76-word message centers on people and tries to indicate the role the tea table played in their lives. I would like to explain more, but since my visitors won't stand still, I only offer hints:

> A fashionable woman slept, dressed, and entertained in this bedroom. Her servants moved the chairs and the tea table away from the wall to a location near the fire in winter or near a breeze in summer. They adjusted the top to support the silver teapot, jug, sugar bowl, and spoons and china cups and saucers they carried from the kitchen, so their mistress and her visitors could leisurely gossip and laugh over a warm drink.

With practice any interpreter can learn to develop a coherent historical theme by using these six questions to move from objects to people and their behavior and to encourage visitors to search for their own reasons why people of earlier times might have behaved as they did.

Afterword

In the seven years since Renée Friedman, Margaret Piatt, and I prepared our session on interpretation for the 1984 annual meeting of the American Association of Museums, I have been emphasizing two messages: one is old, the other new—at least to me.

First, every professional interpreter of historic sites and objects needs to control messages more carefully for time, space, and socioeconomic status. Many exhibitions and historic sites now connect their objects and places with people. Often, however, interpreters do not fully identify them. Since people's experiences in the 1750s were no more like those of the 1820s than our lives are like those of our great-grandparents, interpreters should be sure visitors do not confuse or conflate one time period with another. Life in rural Virginia or Maine differed from life in New York, Cleveland, or New Orleans.

In addition to specifying time and place, interpreters must consider socioeconomic status. To make sense of the lives of people in the past, visitors need to be told whether the historical figures were slave or free, poor, of modest means, or wealthy. They should ask what it meant to be one or the other. Nearly all interpretations of objects and houses overestimate the richness of early material life and automatically raise the standards of living for everyone in the past. The impression created minimizes the significance of both the industrial revolution and the consumer revolution in transforming people's material lives, changing attitudes toward things and altering social relationships.

The second message I would like to communicate to interpreters builds on the idea that goods are imbedded in social process. They do not arise out of nowhere. People make objects because they use them to pursue social strategies, often to indicate their present status or to promote their bid for changing it. As agents of performances that succeed or fail, products are not neutral. Once brought into the arena of social activity, they help shape self and group identity. Having or not having access to a particular object or category of objects produces a different kind of person. For instance, people who own and drive cars and those who walk think differently about space and the limitations geography imposes on human relationships.

There is a simple and effective way to ensure that interpreters provide historical characters with spatial, temporal, and socioeconomic identities and that they convey to visitors the notion that people, consciously or unconsciously, used possessions to achieve certain objectives. Tom Woods of the Minnesota Historical Society calls it "perspectivistic interpretation." Others call it "third person with a first-person point of view." And still others use actors and first-person interpretations to achieve the same ends. Let me build on the examples I used in the original essay to show in 74 words how perspectivistic history can encourage visitors to use objects and houses to think about changing social relationships.

> At a rich man's city house on an evening in the early 19th century, a liveried slave opened the door to guests and later handed around trays with tea things. This African American might have hoped to be free and to manage his own catering business. However, he knew he would not have the opportunity to earn the wealth that bought the white man's house or the social position that led to fancy tea parties.

The Missing Link: The Role of Orientation in Enriching the Museum Experience

Robert L. Wolf

There is no simple way to describe the museum experience. My research efforts and those of others continuously underscore the fact that individual visitors perceive their experience in museums in uniquely different ways. Perhaps the most useful insight concerns the *engagement* between the visitor and the museum and how such engagement affects the quality of a person's experience. These engagements or interactions can be extremely varied but are always influenced not only by what the museum provides in the way of objects, context, and information, but also by what each visitor brings to the encounter in the way of personal interest, previous experience, frame of reference, and individual learning style.

Unpacking the Museum Experience

Some visitors have an enriched experience in a museum because they spend more time in a particular exhibition for one reason or another, including location, esthetic appeal, and hands-on opportunities. Others have meaningful experiences because certain objects appeal to their personal interest or because their interest is sparked by a label or film or interpretive event. Some visitors even come to the museum to learn something specific. Visitors engaged in learning activities ask questions, read labels, and even transfer information from one area to the next, thus enhancing their own enrichment as they move along in their experience.

The degree of engagement that results in favorable impact and increased learning is not the result of one single factor, nor is it easy to identify even a set of factors that contributes to the value of someone's museum experience. Ultimately what matters is how the visitor *uses* the environment—the information, the objects, the interpretations—to enrich his or her own experience. There has been an inordinate amount of discussion of late as to how visitors learn in museums. Why we even ask this question befuddles me. As a cognitive psychologist, I am convinced that people learn in museums in much the same way as they learn in other environments. Of course, museums might offer different opportunities for learning—through objects, labels, mediated presentations, interactions with other persons (visitors or museum staff), and the like, but beyond tactile, audio, visual, spatial, interactive, and verbal there really are not all that many unique modes of presentation that visitors cannot

Journal of Museum Education 11, no. 1 (Winter 1986): 17–21.

experience elsewhere. This should not suggest that museums are like other learning environments, for indeed they are special. But they are more special for what they *contain* than for how they *teach*.

To repeat, *the key in any meaningful learning experience is engagement.* What *is* unique about museums is that they have great potential to engage visitors in perceiving, questioning, comparing, and hypothesizing about their own experience in relationship to interesting objects, artifacts, and works of art, as well as representations of culture, history, natural history, science, and technology through the medium of the past, present, and future.

In a word, museums should be viewed more as places that can enrich visitors' lives—culturally, esthetically, and interpersonally, rather than as teaching institutions that can impart specific predefined content or knowledge. Rather than worry about how people learn—which represents only one aspect of their potential enrichment—museums should be devising ways to provoke, challenge, stimulate, energize, question, and absorb visitors in a life-enhancing opportunity. What people gain in information units is not nearly as important as what they gain emotionally—how connected they become to the object, the exhibit, or its interpretation.

The element that has been missing most in achieving that connection has been the kind of orientation visitors need to maximize their chances for self-enrichment. Museum professionals have been experimenting with every teaching fad and gimmick that have been developed by the educational research community but in the process have made little significant progress in creating constituents who possess "museum literacy" so that they can capitalize on being in the museum environment.

Museum literacy is just another way of describing museum orientation—that mechanism or support that visitors need in order to successfully process their (logistical and conceptual) experience. While many museums have developed effective logistical orientation strategies, few have helped visitors become literate on how to use the museum as a life-enriching opportunity. In providing visitors with orientation help, there are a number of psychological and pedagogical principles that should be kept in mind.

Psychological Orientation Principles
In a psychological sense, the term "orientation" represents a perceptual task involved in the processing of information to determine a course of action for coping with conventional demands.[1] In a museum setting visitors almost immediately attempt to orient themselves, even if that orientation behavior occurs on a subconscious level. The human tendency is to seek out sources of information that help make people comfortable with where they are and what they need to do. Such sources of information might include architectural cues, graphic print material, and direct contact with either human beings or some kind of self-initiated mediated format. From this array of available information museum visitors will try to find out where they are and begin to choose the next course of action.

In breaking the concept of orientation down to more specific terms, it is useful to consider a person's general response to the environment, how he or she creates mental images or maps about the environment's different properties, and what decision-making processes are needed. The key in planning a museum orientation is to provide the kinds and levels of stimuli necessary for visitors to adequately perform their critical perceptual tasks; namely, locating themselves and deciding their next step or steps. This kind of maintenance should be the primary goal of any orientation effort. If this perceptual maintenance is not achieved, disorientation occurs and with it come fatigue, loss of enjoyment in using the environment, frustration, irritability, and even panic. But most important, disorientation compromises the ultimate potential for quality experiences in the museum.

In attempting to avoid disorientation, museum professionals must be cognizant of certain psychological constructs that directly influence orientation behavior. Constructs such as concentration, arousal, information overload and stress, and social dynamics will each be briefly discussed below.

Concentration
All persons have certain innate abilities to concentrate on tasks that have value to them. Additionally, cognitive skills required for more intense kinds of concentration activities can be learned and mastered. These latter skills are mostly employed during formal or structured activities in which a person is aware of the importance of his or her concentration ability. Distractions such as unnecessary or unwarranted noise can often disrupt even the most serious effort at concentration and take attention away from the necessary tasks. On the other hand, concentration can be enhanced by any orientation aid that helps people attend to useful environmental stimuli. But for any aid to be useful, it must arouse a certain degree of interest or excitement in the visitor.

Arousal
Levels of tension or excitement that human beings experience have a direct effect on their ability to effectively process environmental information. Psychologists refer to this sense of excitement as "arousal," and it is applied to both emotional excitement and an increase in brain activity. States of arousal range from a low level near sleep or unconsciousness, often characterized by feelings of boredom, to highly excited feelings that could be associated with panic behavior. In general, very low (boring) or very high (panic) states of arousal are less pleasant to experience than are moderate levels. From the standpoint of orientation needs, what is most significant about psychological arousal is that information is processed most effectively at moderate or middle-range levels. If arousal is very high or very low, a person's attention to environmental cues is apt to be impaired. Orientation strategies should evoke these middle ranges using some complexity or novelty in their design and by avoiding schemes that are ambiguous or overly complicated or provide too much information.

Information Overload and Stress

Many museum environments notably provide more stimulation than most people can comfortably process or organize. This information overload can cause high levels of arousal and thus constitute a form of environmental stress. In a museum, a visitor's reaction to such overload is to channel or focus one's attention more narrowly, thus tuning out peripheral stimuli. Too many labels arranged in an incoherent fashion may be less instructive than too few, since visitors may totally ignore information that is presented in a crowded manner.

By the same token, settings may have insufficient stimulation or "information underload," resulting in low arousal, boredom, and fatigue. Such monotonous settings can also be stressful, and lowered levels of attention can make orientation cues less effective. Providing the right amount of information, on the other hand, and arranging it in a compelling but not overly demanding way will positively influence an orientation activity. Of course, information can be presented through social interaction and this latter strategy can also control for information overload.

Social Dynamics

It is certainly no surprise that people serve as sources of orientation information, and such socially based information can be direct or indirect.

In direct interaction, visitors might ask available museum staff for orientation help. Simply having staff present, however, does not necessarily guarantee that they will be used effectively. Some people will never initiate human contact with strangers or official personnel because of introverted personality characteristics—this is true in spite of their apparent disorientation. The key in providing direct social interaction as a way of facilitating orientation is to assist persons in overcoming their apprehension to seek help.

In addition to direct forms of human contact, it is also true that most persons will follow others who appear to know what they are doing. The close proximity of other visitors in a museum environment can serve as a guide to movement behavior. One way visitors can handle their orientation decisions is to follow the lead of other persons. Crowding, however, can be a source of disorientation. Other visitors can create distracting stimuli that continually evoke visitor attention and, thus, lead to information overload. In capitalizing on crowd behavior, orientation spaces should be created in such a way that the movement of visitors is dictated by the environmental design. In this manner, orientation aids can be built upon the social dynamics that visitors tend to display in public access spaces.

Pedagogical Orientation Principles

Over the past 20 years research on cognition and learning has shed significant light on how people acquire knowledge in nonformal educational settings. More recently, insights from this research have been applied to the kind of spontaneous learning that takes place in museums. In the context of visitor orientation such insight can help create mechanisms and formats that facilitate the orientation process. Specifically, concepts such as cognitive difference, multiple teaching opportunity, reinforcement theory, and conceptual focus contribute to the enrichment of the museum experience.

Cognitive Difference

Simply stated, it is a well-substantiated fact that individual people learn and think differently. These differences relate to being attracted to different objects or different types of information. And, once attracted, persons will employ different strategies in interacting with and processing the information about the stimulus in question. Because individuals possess different ways of thinking, they will put information together differently and use different interpretive modes. They will engage in different learning tasks by employing a variety of information-processing techniques. The most critical aspect of understanding the importance of different thinking strategies is to consider the range of interpretations the stimulus provokes. The design of the presentation must then merge the interpretive possibilities with the conceptual and esthetic goals of the exhibit. Variety of formats used to present information increases the probability that a wider range of individuals will benefit from the stimulus. It must also be recognized that in addition to cognitive variation, people bring to their museum experience a multiplicity of values, perceptions, and interests. Orientation success depends upon how astutely these factors are addressed.

Multiple Teaching Opportunity

Any good teacher uses redundancy to drive salient points home. Likewise, in a museum environment important messages must be repeated in different ways to ensure that the message is communicated to as large a number of persons as possible. Subtle messages tend to elude the visitor. If a major concept or point of information is to be conveyed, it must be done with clarity and succinctness. Thus, the skill in providing redundant information suggests that presentation formats and semantic constructions should vary so as to avoid boredom and at the same time be sufficiently similar to communicate critical aspects of the desired message.

Reinforcement Theory

It has long been established that human beings will seek out experiences that are rewarding to them and at the same time avoid experiences that are distasteful or unpleasant. This kind of conditioning has been employed by psychologists and educators in shaping behavior in most impressive ways. The effective use of behavioral reinforcement depends upon how well a person knows what is expected of him or her and the kind of guidance he or she receives along the way. As stated earlier, most museum visitors want to feel they have accomplished something during their experience. They want to feel that they haven't "wasted their time" and that the trip was "worth it." If people can be helped to understand what accomplishments are possible within the context of a museum and then are given appropriate reinforcement throughout their visit, this sense of achievement can be shaped rather effectively. To provide this information to the visitor requires that museum planners clearly identify the scope of possibilities throughout the context. This analysis can display the range and types of possibilities presently available and identify gaps or absence of reinforcing experiences.

Conceptual Focus

Within the museum field the concept of orientation is typically used to describe logistical and spatial considerations. In my research, however, it has been pointed out repeatedly that visitors experience disorientation when they are unable to understand what a museum is trying to convey through its exhibitions and its information presentations. In fact, visitors are often more frustrated about this latter kind of disorientation than they are about not finding their way around the space. Visitors benefit from the kind of guidance that lets them know what is expected of them if they wish to maximize their experience. What concepts, themes, or messages are being conveyed? What sense can they make from objects, exhibits, and labels? Museums can and should do a more effective job in presenting each piece of information so that it builds upon or relates to other information available. This process extends and enriches the kind of conceptual understanding that enables visitors to relate their experience to other aspects of their lives. Finally, a conceptual path must be established so that visitors have the opportunity to understand each concept in a sequential and interrelated manner. This approach by no means suggests that all presentations be linear and convergent. Nor does it suggest there is only one right way to experience the stimulus. It *does* suggest, however, that the presentation must be designed so that "room for error" is minimized. Orientation effectiveness will depend upon the ability of the museum to orchestrate spatial considerations with conceptual presentations and do so in a systematic and integrated manner.

The psychological and pedagogical factors taken together underscore the conclusion: people can only reap the full educational or esthetic benefit of a museum experience when the conceptual demands of that experience are made manifest. In this regard, museums need an area to which visitors come to find out what it will take to benefit from the time they have available for their visit. In this way, conceptual insight can be conveyed about what their options are, and then help can be provided as to how those options can be successfully achieved. Renewed thinking and creativity in the design of orientation areas is necessary to teach the public museum literacy, to assist visitors in their enjoyment, to bolster the impact of the museum itself. One clear challenge is to develop orientation so that visitors who rush into the museum environment will gradually be induced to consider orientation areas as a necessary beginning—for any museum context.

Framework for Orientation Design

Because the educational mission of museums is exceptionally broad, the orientation program should not attempt to do too much. Expectations about the role of the orientation must be kept reasonable. It cannot help each visitor understand all aspects of the museum, nor can it locate every object on display. What it can do, however, is give interested visitors a better sense of the place, and for many it can at least acquaint them with a range of options that perhaps they had never before considered much less experienced.

In designing the orientation space museum professionals should keep several important considerations in mind:

■ The area must be compact and straightforward. It should contain information about the function of visitor orientation, options for museum experience, and up-to-date announcements about events and exhibits.

■ The area must be comfortable and inviting. It should convey that no matter how crowded the museum is, it is still a place for reflection, contemplation, and cultural or esthetic appreciation.

■ The area should be attractive and thus contain representative objects from the collections. Each major collection or exhibition should be described and clear information available as to its location.

■ The area must be arranged for maximum flexibility, as the orientation purpose may change to accommodate future patterns of use.

■ The area must contain a variety of formats for presentation so as to account for visitor differences in perception, interest, ability, and prior experience.

■ The area must provide brochures and handouts that stimulate visitor curiosity and have the potential for suggesting new opportunities for how the museum can be used.

■ The area must be staffed with persons who understand the importance and value of orientation. Such persons must not only be familiar with the museum but must also be familiar with visitor needs, interests, and concerns. The overriding approach should be proactive, and staff should help open possibilities that visitors may not be aware of.

■ The area must not only be designed to avoid traffic flow problems but actually to facilitate movement through the arrangement of kiosks and wall graphics that create a logical conceptual path.

■ The area must provide multiple access to information as well as provide insight into questions visitors might have as they leave the museum.

Thus, the orientation component of the museum should be a center for the contemplation of the museum experience. It should help people enter that experience and exit it as well. It should avoid overload by keeping its messages simple and clear. Objects, posters, and wall graphics should enhance the visitor's interest in a compelling manner. The orientation component must inform but not intrude.

And at the very least, as visitors leave the orientation area they should have a better plan for their visit than they did before the orientation experience.

If museums further desire to present visitors with more advanced themes or concepts in the exhibits they offer, then additional assistance must be offered in each exhibition area. The following suggestions should help visitors derive a more detailed enrichment from their experience:

■ The purpose of any exhibit must be clearly stated to maximize its learning potential. Likewise, the purpose of each display area within the exhibit should also be made clear and the interrelationships among the display areas should be apparent to the average visitor.

■ Each major concept requiring emphasis must be strategically positioned by an artifact, specimen, object, or display area that has sufficient appeal (dramatic and/or esthetic) so as to attract visitor interest and attention.

■ Labels that convey important conceptual information must be stated succinctly to ensure that they will be read. Additionally, a smaller percentage of selected labels must present details that allow for more in-depth coverage of the messages being conveyed.

■ Conceptual labels must be cross-referenced with each other throughout the exhibit to help visitors comprehend conceptual relationships.

■ Highly detailed and technical information designed specifically for the exceptionally interested and/or sophisticated visitor should be presented through some kind of optional format (plexiglass placards, handouts, etc.). In other words, some visitors must have the opportunity to seek out greater degrees of specificity at the same time most visitors are not inundated with an overwhelming amount of printed text.

■ Mediated presentations within the exhibit deserve more careful consideration. On the one hand they work because they appeal to visitors' differential learning styles. For certain topics, there are clear advantages in a mediated format: scientific concepts that are dynamic in nature can be presented in a congruent format; historic or temporal progression can be conveyed within a brief time interval.

■ Technical components of the exhibit should be clarified so that the average visitor can readily comprehend them. Many persons express initial interest but show increasing disinterest (or at best, passing interest) because the technical depth of the information presented has not taken into account the individual who, in a typical visit, is required to stand and read or observe for several consecutive hours on a variety of topics that may or may not have any relationship with each other. This experience is akin to reading a portion from each of 26 volumes of an encyclopedia while walking or standing in place for several hours.

■ Illustrative examples that demonstrate conceptual relationships are critical.

■ The design of the exit area should be decidedly dramatic, as it leads the visitor to begin the museum experience.

Some Concluding Thoughts

The suggestions and considerations about orientation and exhibition design will assist visitors in gaining more effective and meaningful access to the vast resources of museums. This access will, in turn, help visitors take considerable advantage of the museum through exploration, participation, and personal expression. In providing visitors with extended opportunities to better grasp the magnitude of their experiences, museums can communicate and instruct in a manner that facilitates intellectual, esthetic, cultural, and educational satisfaction. Museums need to be less concerned about teaching specific facts and concentrate more on creating environments that enable individuals to gain more insight into the physical, cultural, and esthetic world that surrounds them. Museums can help visitors most by teaching them something about the museum and about the available possibilities that will make the visit a more meaningful one. Orientation efforts cannot be halfhearted. They require as much planning, conceptualization, and evaluation as the most lush and extensive exhibit. Orientation is a vital link in developing museum literacy. Done well, it has the potential for connecting the public to the museum, and, by virtue of this connection, to the pleasurable and valuable learning experience that will ultimately transpire. Accordingly, researchers should concentrate their energies on studying the hows and whys of visitor orientation, rather the merely the whats of learning.

Note

1. The discussion on psychological orientation principles is derived from the work of Ross Loomis, Colorado State University.

Afterword
Barbara L. Wolf

Perhaps most professionals would agree that when a "buzzword" enters the lexicon, we are somewhat wary of its validity and longevity. But the concept of visitor orientation and its accompanying principles have become embedded in our notions of the visitor experience as shown by the continuing research and literature on this topic. The principles that Robert Wolf described five years ago provided starting points for numerous avenues of research, but we have come to few *generalizable* conclusions or few *definitive* practices about orientation beyond those he originally presented. Paradoxically, in my view, I see this as an acceptable "state of the art" because museum professionals are vigorously and continuously asking questions about orientation and the engagement of the visitor as they plan exhibits and programs. This process of questioning has led to an expansion of the concept of orientation that has, in numerous instances, dramatically affected the museum and the way it views its mission.

Comparing the very questions that are asked about orientation portrays the expansion. In the conventional sense, we looked at orientation to include three dimensions. Our queries concerned:

■ the physical aspects of a museum and the consequent logistics of assisting the visitors as they navigated the space itself, including stairs and hallways

■ the location, selection, and scope of galleries within the museum in relation to the collection, the curatorial expertise, and the design presentation

■ the focus of exhibits and programs in relation to visitor learning and education.

In a growing number of institutions, museum professionals have now begun to view their entire museum as a catalyst for the community and its well-being. Increasingly, we ask new and different questions: What is it that our museum should say to its audiences by its presence (even its location) in the community? As a museum, what are we communicating to our publics by what we choose to acquire or how we allocate our funds? Among our audiences, what publics can and should be served by the choice and formats of our exhibits? How far do we go beyond what we know we do very well to contribute to museum and community outreach?

As these questions are posed, they will have an impact on the original questions once asked about orientation. The issues of orientation remain singular in the inquiry for enhancing the probability of engaging the greatest proportion possible of our visitors. The questions now being asked challenge the complexity of the original issues but hold significant promise for museum professionals who strive to connect their publics to their museums in ways that are meaningful for those who come to visit.

Vision and Culture: The Role of Museums in Visual Literacy

Danielle Rice

Much has been made in recent months of the importance of a disciplined and serious approach to the study of art. The implications of reports such as the Getty's *Beyond Creating* and the National Endowment for the Arts' *Toward Civilization*[1] is that visual literacy is an important issue high on the agenda of educational reformers. In this essay, I shall consider the problem of defining visual literacy and reflect on the museum's role in educating people to achieve it.

What is visual literacy? What type of information about art makes people "visually literate"? Is the control of a body of knowledge gleaned from the history of art and including a repertory of the world's greatest masterpieces sufficient? Or is visual literacy a set of critical and analytical skills for looking at art and at the world at large? Can one have the one without the other? Most art educators today would say no, but they disagree on the degree to which visual literacy requires both history and analysis.

The term "visual literacy" has been around for a little more than a decade, but it was used originally to refer to visual communication through film and the electronic media of television and computers.[2] Today the term is being adopted by educators and museum people to refer also to the ability to understand and use the fine arts. The definition of museum education developed at the Denver Meeting of Art Museum Educators in November 1987 states that the key aim of museum education "is to enhance the visitors' ability to understand and appreciate original works of art and to transfer these experiences into other aspects of the visitors' lives."[3] This, in effect, is what visual literacy is all about: making sense of art and being able to apply to daily life the learning and experiences derived from original objects in the museum setting. While this may be a fairly obvious goal, there are a number of reasons why achieving it is harder than it seems. In looking at the challenges involved in teaching visual literacy, we can begin to understand the complexity and value of the task.

Visual literacy is knowing what to do when you are confronted with an object that is made or displayed "just to be looked at," as is commonly done with art objects in this culture. But "just looking" is not a simple act. While people do not question the fact that art is meant to be looked at, those without any training in studio

Journal of Museum Education 13, no. 3 (Fall 1988): 13–17.

practice, art history, criticism, or esthetics generally have little sense of how to look at, or what to look for in, a work of art. Even well-educated people find themselves at a loss in the art museum if they have little or no background in art. A simple proof of this is the dependence that many museum-goers have on the structured, thematic environment of special exhibitions and on didactic materials, such as labels and tours.[4]

There are a number of reasons why "just looking," when applied to art, is not simple, obvious, and universal. In everyday life, we use our vision selectively and instrumentally to maneuver through the overabundance of sensory stimulation surrounding us. We learn to derive instant meaning from the objects we come into contact with. For example, we see a traffic sign and can interpret it immediately. Giant billboards are especially designed to convey their meaning in the few seconds that it takes motorists to drive past them. Furthermore, we learn to shut out a lot of visual information in order, quite literally, to survive. If we stop to admire the scenery while driving along a busy street or highway, we place ourselves and our passengers at risk. Thus, everyday experience generally trains people to look with very specific goals, such as navigating through traffic or finding a friend in a crowd. This directed looking that people practice outside the museum leaves them largely unprepared for the open-ended, contemplative looking necessary within its walls.

The tendency toward restricted, utilitarian seeing is perhaps one of the main reasons that many museum professionals feel so strongly that visual literacy is primarily a set of skills that can and should be taught in the museum setting. These skills include the ability to describe the formal elements of a work of art: its composition, design, and the use of line, shape, color, texture, space, and so forth. Identifying and analyzing such formal elements generally helps people to focus more attention on a work without their needing to know very much about it. Because all works of art have shape and form, these skills can be broadly applied in the museum setting.

The particular mission of opening people's eyes to the beauty of objects, teaching them how to attend to art and to look analytically, is certainly a high-minded goal. Learning the type of critical looking involved in analyzing a work of art adds a new dimension to the way people normally use their vision. Unfortunately, in the past, this goal has not, in itself, been sufficiently significant or deemed important enough to ensure the arts a solid place in basic education. In today's more conservative environment, the personal enrichment motive that is a major component of the goal of opening's people's eyes is even more suspect.

There is, however, a more urgent reason to encourage visual literacy. "Just looking" at art is actually a deeply complex, culturally loaded action requiring a specific framework. Visual literacy is, therefore, closely connected to cultural literacy and to literacy in general. As such, it is fully deserving of serious consideration in basic education.

Modern Western culture separates out and privileges the sense of sight. By contrast, in most non-Western and traditional cultures, artifacts are not just made to be looked at; they have an active function. Beautiful and expressive objects are crafted to be danced with, prayed with, healed with, used in everyday life. Outside of the European, post-Renaissance tradition, there is very little art that is functionless. Even in Western culture before the public museum age initiated in the late 18th century, many beautiful art objects were made to decorate luxurious palaces, to be treasured possessions, to be records of family members and badges of wealth and position. Their owners could admire them but did not have to do so exclusively, for they could also cherish and caress, buy or sell, hide or display them in a variety of contexts. Visitors to the museum, on the other hand, are only allowed to look.

It is not surprising that museums have to exhibit, along with the art, signs admonishing people not to touch. Touching as a way of making contact with the physical world is more basic than looking. Not touching is actually an unnatural thing to do. Children use the sense of touch almost exclusively in their early infancy to understand their surroundings. Analytical looking and understanding through seeing come much later, after much information about the nature of tangible reality has already been accumulated.

American museums display in fairly equal amounts art that was made in order to be owned and looked at, what André Malraux called "art by destination," and originally functional objects that are transformed into art by the museum context. Such objects, which include both Western decorative arts and objects made by non-Western cultures in which the concept of art did not exist, are considered by Malraux as "art by metamorphosis."[5] Most visitors with little arts background, in my experience, although they acknowledge painting and sculpture as art, generally feel more comfortable with objects belonging to the category of art by metamorphosis. In such objects the original function is either inferred or intuited and their design or ornamentation is appreciated in combination with an understanding of function. Furthermore, people have had more experience with similar types of objects— although not necessarily in as ornate or exotic a form. For example, few individuals own original paintings or sculptures, but almost all people own furniture and china. Although these pieces of furniture may not be the priceless antiques found in the institutional setting, almost everyone has had a chance to touch a chest of drawers and know how it works. Even sculpture, because it so often exists in the form of public monuments or architectural decoration, is more familiar and accessible than painting.

Painting is the most abstract of the art forms because it is two-dimensional and, when removed from its decorative or status-bearing function, serves no function outside of the visual one. It is the most difficult of the art forms for most lay people to understand and appreciate. Research indicates that associative experiences play a key role in the esthetic enjoyment of people with little background or previous exposure to art. In other words, such people tend to prefer some paintings over others primarily because they serve as reminders of pleasant events or places, such as a beautiful sunset or a lovely park. Or paintings are appreciated because they look hard to make, requiring a particular set of technical skills, or because they tell a particular story.[6] Paintings that tell an easily recognizable story do not seem as abstract because they appear to have a specific function. In other words, they are reminiscent of illustrations in a book or magazine. Since illustrations are basically functional and familiar, paintings, too, when they are likened to illustrations, seem easier to understand.

More than any other art form, painting requires familiarity with the vocabulary and history of art, oftentimes with religious and mythological subjects as well as with the particular skills involved in analyzing shape, color, line, and texture on a two-dimensional surface. In other words, just looking, when applied to painting, requires the broadest kind of cultural base. I do not mean to imply that people cannot have meaningful experiences without having taken courses in art history or studio practice. Indeed, novice museum visitors—those without specific training in the arts—treasure their time wandering through the museum. But it is important to note that most people with little background in art feel a little defensive about their reactions in the museum setting and express the desire to know more about art appreciation. Most of these visitors agree that additional knowledge about what they are seeing could significantly enhance their experiences with objects.[7]

There are also some rare individuals who start out with a keen visual sense and who feel completely comfortable in the museum setting. Many such individuals are moved by their initial experiences to undertake the rigorous training and sacrifices necessary to become artists or museum professionals. But such persons are the exception rather than the rule. For the most part, given the highly artificial position of art in our culture, esthetic delight in the museum setting comes naturally mainly to people who already have a great deal of familiarity with works of art. This kind of familiarity is generally achieved through repeated exposure to the art objects and to the theory and history of art.

Complete visual literacy is, therefore, not just a set of isolated skills, because the formal elements of art are actually part of a culturally bound system for understanding and exhibiting art. Giving people the analytical skills does not sufficiently answer the need that people have to make meaning of works of art. Meaning can only be derived if people have the necessary schema or knowledge base to understand both the diverse subject matter of art objects from a variety of different cultures and the abstracted function of museum art, to give visual delight and to open one's eyes.

In his best-selling book, *Cultural Literacy,* E. D. Hirsch makes a similar point about literacy. He establishes the connection between literacy, the ability to make meaning out of what one reads, and culture, a shared body of knowledge and assumptions. He faults the fragmentation of contemporary education with the production of individuals who, because they do not share the same background information, are not capable of communicating with one another and participating actively in the predominant culture. Hirsch is most convincing when he shows that literacy is not the mere skill of sounding out letters into words. Making meaning of language consists of being able to match words against a preexistent schema of knowledge. As he points out, "The explicit meanings of a piece of writing are the tip of an iceberg of meaning; the larger part lies below the surface of the text and is composed of the reader's own relevant knowledge."[8]

Hirsch lists some 5,000 terms representing the domain of the culturally literate.[9] Of these, fewer than 100 refer to art (see page 152), and there is little discussion in his book of the role of the visual arts in achieving cultural literacy. But while most of the terms on Hirsch's list do not apply specifically to art, I have already shown that making sense of art—being visually literate—presupposes a certain degree of cultural literacy. In fact, Hirsch's book, in its single-minded approach to literacy, fails to consider the important contribution that visual literacy can make to expanding literacy in general. Language plays an important part in structuring vision. An impoverished language often results in an impoverished art experience as well, and the opposite is also true.[10] In addition, a large number of nonart terms can be learned through art because the full appreciation of art requires a certain understanding of history, literature, religion, and mythology. Many an art history student learns mythological and biblical stories primarily through seeing them illustrated in paintings and sculptures, and making sense of non-Western art objects requires a knowledge of the religions and customs of other cultures. Furthermore, as Howard Gardner has shown, there are a great variety of intelligences, and for those people who are not verbally gifted, teaching literacy through visual learning may actually be more effective.[11]

Visual literacy and literacy are closely interconnected. The more literate a person is, the richer his or her personal schema and the greater the ability to have meaningful experiences with art objects. Thus, a visually literate person is generally also culturally literate. That is to say, someone who can make sense of art objects, both by knowing how they fit into a historical context and by having the skills to analyze objects visually, is usually fully literate and has a fairly broad understanding of culture. But the opposite is not necessarily true. It is significant that while a visually literate person is by definition also culturally literate, a culturally literate person is not visually literate simply by virtue of being culturally literate. An individual can have a great deal of knowledge about literature, history, science, and other areas and still not know how to look at art. As I pointed out earlier, looking at art does not come naturally to the vast majority of people. Instead, looking at art is informed by a particular stance, which takes as its starting point the primacy of vision in our culture and requires the ability to use one's eyes contemplatively and analytically rather than selectively and instrumentally. This use of vision is the result of a very specific set of analytical and critical skills derived from esthetics, art criticism, studio practice, and art history.

Because a visually literate person is also culturally literate but not the other way around, the importance of including visual literacy in the greater educational schema is obvious. In fact, the recent efforts of the Getty Center for Education in the Arts and the National Endowment for the Arts to define a discipline-based, structured approach to art education are oriented to providing visual literacy a solid and durable footing in basic education. Given this renewed emphasis on an integrated approach to arts education—one that combines analytical and historical approaches to the arts instead of just encouraging artistic creativity in the studio— what role is the art museum to play now? Since a disciplined approach to art will ideally prepare students to be visually literate, thereby enabling them to have more meaningful interaction with the art objects in the museum setting, does this mean that museum educators will no longer be necessary?

While having a population that is completely visually literate is a worthy goal that museum educators would endorse even at the risk of putting themselves out of business, for the time being that goal seems distant. In the interim, museum educators can play a significant role in teaching visual literacy by helping museum visitors learn the skills necessary to derive meaning from original art objects. These skills include the increased awareness that comes from directed observation, an expanded vocabulary adequate to talking about the formal elements of art and effective in communicating the feelings that one gets when looking at objects, and the ability to think critically about art. While these skills parallel quite well the skills taught through discipline-based art education, there is a difference in their use in the museum, where the emphasis is on deriving meaning, not on learning the particular language or vocabulary of a given discipline.

In fact, one of the greatest challenges to museum education is that visual literacy cannot be taught entirely in the museum setting. Because it is dependent both on a body of knowledge derived from the history of art and on a set of analytical skills derived from studio practice, esthetics, and art criticism, visual literacy requires more than a brief, occasional encounter with a skilled museum teacher and a beautiful work of art. And herein lies one of the great paradoxes of the museum education profession: we have to make every experience significant and meaningful without assuming prior knowledge and without placing the emphasis on factual information, such as dates and period names. We must give viewers a hint of how informed vision works, but we must do so without, on the one hand, making them feel ignorant and inadequate or, on the other hand, giving them a false sense that they have understood all there is to know in one short experience.

There are two common errors that stand in the way of museum educators' being completely effective contributors to increasing visual literacy. One mistake is the unquestioned assumption that the main content to be taught in the museum setting is the history of art; the other is the mindless emphasis on formal analysis removed from content and meaning. Although the knowledge of art history can inform and enrich the museum experience, it can also limit it to some degree. First, the information aspect of the history of art—the facts and dates about specific artists or artworks—are very poorly taught in the museum setting. Giving visitors facts takes time away from their opportunity to look at art and draw their own conclusions. Second, an undue emphasis on the facts of art history can also leave people with a sense that they cannot have meaningful experiences with objects without first learning a great deal. This increases their dependence on guided tours and interpretive materials.

In the museum, history is not learned for its own sake. Instead, it is used to answer a very important question: Why do these objects look the way they do? The history of art is thus subordinate to the process of analysis. Conjectures, based on research about an artist's intentions or a certain culture's patterns, allow us to differentiate between reactions grounded in our contemporary attitudes and concepts that may have shaped the world views of past artists.

But just as the history of art cannot be taught as a set of facts and figures in the museum setting, neither can the process of analysis be removed from the issue of meaning. In an attempt to give people skills for looking at art, museum educators have in the past stressed the formal elements of all objects—line, color, shape, texture—as recurring themes in all art objects. This emphasis has sometimes resulted in a very dry description of formal elements in relation to one another. It is only when these elements are considered in the context of the subject matter and the emotional effect they communicate that they are truly related to visual literacy. If diagonal lines communicate motion in a painting, it is important to know why and how that dynamism relates to the particular subject depicted, the personal style of the artist, as well as the style of the period or location. It is not enough merely to identify and notice them.

In conclusion, museums are in an excellent position to work in partnership with formal education in the teaching of visual literacy, and the time for such a partnership is ripe. Museums can reinforce the classroom-learned skills and information associated with a discipline-based art education, that is, one in which the emphasis is on analysis as well as practice. But there is a key difference between the museum and the classroom: in the museum setting, the emphasis is on deriving meaning, and this is a holistic process rather than one easily subdividable into specific discipline areas. Museum educators are constantly shifting gears, switching hats, being now an art historian, now a critic or a philosopher or an artist. They do this in order to respond actively to the perceptions, questions, and issues raised by their visitors. Museum education, at its best, is active and interactive, and master museum teachers have an excellent knack for mediating between objects and observers. When that mediation is successful, the numerous rewards and benefits of visual literacy are self-evident.

Notes

1. Getty Center for Education in the Arts, *Beyond Creating: The Place for Art in America's Schools* (Los Angeles, Calif.: J. Paul Getty Trust, 1985); National Endowment for the Arts, *Toward Civilization: A Report on Arts Education* (Washington, D.C.: NEA, 1988).

2. Deborah Curtiss, *Introduction to Visual Literacy: A Guide to the Visual Arts and Communication* (Englewood Cliffs, N.J.: Prentice Hall, 1987), p. 1. This college text on art appreciation offers little philosophy on the role of visual literacy in education.

3. "Museum Educators on Museum Education: Summary Report," submitted by Patterson Williams and Susan M. Mayer. Available from the Denver Art Museum, 100 West Fourteenth Avenue Parkway, Denver, Colo. 80204–2788.

4. See my article "Examining Exhibits," *Museum News* 68, no. 6 (November/December 1989): 47–50.

5. André Malraux, *The Voices of Silence* (Princeton, N.J.: Princeton University Press, 1978), pp. 131–273. See also Jacques Maquet, *The Aesthetic Experience* (New Haven, Conn.: Yale University Press, 1986), p. 18.

6. See Mihaly Csikszentmihalyi and Eugene Rochberg-Halton, *The Meaning of Things: Domestic Symbols and the Self* (Cambridge, Eng.: Cambridge University Press, 1981), esp. pp. 176–84; Melora McDermott, "Through Their Eyes: What Novices Value in Art Experiences," *Annual Meeting Program Sourcebook* (Washington, D.C.: American Association of Museums, 1988), pp. 133–62.

7. McDermott, "Through Their Eyes," p. 156.

8. E. D. Hirsch, Jr., *Cultural Literacy: What Every American Needs to Know* (New York: Vintage Books, 1988), p. 34.

9. Hirsch's main objective is to improve literacy through a return to a more standardized curriculum which would ensure that all students have at least a superficial knowledge of some of the terms that cultured people know. While I find many of Hirsch's arguments convincing, I take strong issue with a number of his points. It seems absurd to me to imply, as he does, that we cannot change the content of what the culturally literate know, which in its present form is racist, sexist, and limited to superficial, news-magazine–style information. He, himself, takes the liberty of adding more science terms. Why science and not art? Furthermore, I think settling for teaching students just a superficial grasp of a series of terms—something Hirsch does not actually advocate but his book implies is better than nothing—can lead to some very dangerous practices. There is no reason why we cannot have the highest expectations of our educational system and of our students, encouraging both control of the current body of cultural know-how and active manipulation of it to make it more truly representative of the diversity of ethnic and cultural backgrounds of Americans.

10. See, especially, Noam Chomsky, *Language and Mind* (New York: Harcourt Brace Jovanovich, 1968) and Benjamin Lee Whorf, *Language, Thought, and Reality* (Cambridge, Mass.: MIT Press, 1956).

11. Howard Gardner, *Frames of Mind* (New York: Basic Books, 1985).

E. D. Hirsch's Art Terms in *Cultural Literacy*

abstract art
abstract expressionism
aesthetics
art for art's sake
Art is long, life is short.
asymmetry
A thing of beauty is a joy
     forever.
baroque
basilica
bas-relief
Bauhaus movement
Blake, William
Birth of Venus (image)
Botticelli
Brueghel, Pieter (the
     elder)
Calder, Alexander
Cézanne, Paul
Chippendale
classicism
Constable, John
Corinthian
Dali, Salvador
David of Michelangelo,
     the (image)
Degas, Edgar
Doric
Dürer, Albrecht
fine arts
French Impressionism
fresco
functionalism
     (architecture)
Giotto
gothic

Goya, Francisco
Greco, El
Homer, Winslow
imagery
impressionism
Ionic (architecture)
kitsch
Laocoön
Leaning Tower of Pisa
Leonardo da Vinci
liberal arts
Manet, Édouard
Medici, the
Michelangelo
Mona Lisa (image)
Monet, Claude
Monticello
Morse, Samuel F. B.
mural
neoclassicism
Notre Dame Cathedral
objet d'art
oeuvre
op art
pagoda
Parthenon
perspective
Picasso, Pablo
Pietà (Michelangelo)
Pollock, Jackson
pop art
pre-Raphaelite
primitivism
Pyramids, the
Raphael
realism

relief (art)
Rembrandt van Rijn
Renaissance, the
Renoir, Pierre Auguste
Rockwell, Norman
rococo
Rodin, Auguste
romanticism
Rubens, Peter Paul
Saint Paul's Cathedral
Saint Peter's Church
Saint Sophia (basilica)
sphere
Sphinx, the
Stuart, Gilbert
surrealism
Taj Mahal
There's no disputing
     taste.
Thinker, the (image)
Tiffany glass
Tintoretto
Titian
Turner, J. M. W.
Van Gogh, Vincent
vanishing point
Venus de Milo (image)
Vermeer, Jan
Warhol, Andy
warp and woof
Washington Crossing the
     Delaware (image)
Wren, Sir Christopher
Wright, Frank Lloyd
Wyeth, Andrew

Source: E. D. Hirsch, Jr., *Cultural Literacy: What Every American Needs to Know* (New York: Vintage Books. 1988).

Museums and Knowledge: The Responsibility to Open Minds

Lisa Roberts

In what sense are museums "social instruments"? A number of disconnected, if colorful images come to mind: a traveling exhibit on AIDS; Chicago's Peace Museum; corporate-sponsored exhibits on everything from nuclear energy to healthy teeth; reports decrying the state of American public education; new critics espousing white, male, Eurocentrist views.

Perhaps one way to speak of the museum as a social instrument is to speak of the institution's role in giving voice to the collections with which society has entrusted it. How to represent to the public the artifacts of their heritage is a challenge compounded by the variety of stories these artifacts hold. It is a fact of the diversity of our world that social groups hold competing perspectives and interests. Whose views shall museums represent? Whose stories shall be told?

Museums have the authority to select, interpret, and present that which they decide has value or significance. Removed from their original contexts and functions, objects take on new meanings, meanings that are at times laden with unconscious interests. Sometimes museum professionals spend so much energy striving for objectivity that they lose sight of the fact that exhibition is by its very nature an interpretive act. The process of selecting and arranging objects into a display is at bottom a fabrication and, as such, a statement about what the fabricators suppose an object to say.

As educators we are charged with interpreting our collections through programs and exhibits. Decisions about what we want our objects to communicate rest in part on educational goals that museums have been struggling to define since their late 18th-century inception. At issue is not only the question, What is education? or more pointedly, What is education in museums? but, What shall we teach? and How shall we teach it? (or in the more recent vernacular, What shall visitors learn?).

Were one to chart the history of education in museums, one would discover the waxing and waning with almost clockwork regularity of a practice that is at one extreme scholarly, didactic, and elitist, and at the other sensational, shallow, and profoundly recreational. The dichotomy remains today as we struggle to reconcile our learning goals for our visitors with the desires of a media-saturated population that thrives on spectacle—discotheques, "Wheel of Fortune," theme parks.

Journal of Museum Education 14, no. 1 (Winter 1989): 9–12.

Condemning such low-brow enjoyment is hardly an answer (how many of us partake ourselves?), nor is coopting our institutional goals. The work of interpretation sits squarely on this dilemma: how to give our visitors experiences that are in some sense meaningful but that are consistent with the mission we strive to uphold—this stubborn thing called "education."

Although language about interpretation has pervaded the museum vernacular for some time, we still shy away from presenting interpretations that may appear too controversial or that may alienate segments of our audience. But it is useful to take a step back and look at how museums make decisions about what they address and how they interpret—controversial or not. The question is hardly a new one, but each generation treats it afresh in light of the conditions and events of the day. One contemporary debate in particular bears significantly on the dilemma of interpretation.

The Battle of the Books

A remarkable debate has been going on in Europe and America over the nature of knowledge—in particular, over what counts as knowledge and who says so. Two recent events have brought the debate to the fore and made "the Battle of the Books" the most heated controversy in the education field in years.

In 1987, a little-known but highly respected member of the Committee on Social Thought at the University of Chicago was thrust into the public eye with the publication of his book, *The Closing of the American Mind* (subtitled, "How Higher Education Has Failed Democracy and Impoverished the Souls of Today's Students"). Overnight, Allan Bloom became a celebrity among academics and laypeople alike. His attack on American higher education aroused both wrath and praise for its pointed criticisms and recommendations for reform. Among other things, Bloom claimed that the process of popularizing higher education in recent years had been achieved at the expense of the so-called Great Ideas and Great Books. Many American universities have been steadily drifting away from the study of the classics toward the popular forms of literature and culture like film, science fiction, and mass media. Bloom's book was in part a cry for the return to tradition.[1]

At about the same time, Stanford University was making its own national headlines over student demands for revisions of the standard Western civilization curriculum. Protesters wanted a more representative version of history that included the voices of blacks and other minority groups that had not been preserved in Western historical memory. Educators from all over the country, including then-Secretary of Education William Bennett, were swept into the debate.

Both events have raised serious questions about the traditional canon of knowledge: What counts as knowledge and what doesn't? The events are significant to educators insofar as they bear on the question, What shall we teach? Is knowledge absolute and eternal, or does it change across history and culture, according to the experiences and circumstances of the beholder?

As museum educators, many of us are already comfortable with the idea that learning and communication begin on the visitor's turf, with their interests and needs. From this perspective it is easy to be sympathetic with Stanford's students and with those who were outraged at Bloom's diatribe. Nevertheless, like Bloom and many other educators, we do not want to see the objects of our labor trivialized by the process of making them appealing. The dilemma is strikingly reminiscent of our own struggles to achieve a balance between making collections inviting and maintaining their integrity. The implications of the dilemma, however, cannot be fully understood apart from the history that led up to it.

The 1960s saw an enormous loosening of norms in almost every social arena. The catch phrase of the day was "Do your own thing," and nothing was exempt: fashion, living arrangements, work structures, sexual norms. In education, near-sacred structures like grades, curricular requirements, and mandatory attendance gave way to alternative arrangements that permitted highly flexible—and some would say overindulgent—methods of study. At the same time, the civil rights movement and the women's movement gave rise to new fields of scholarship that dealt with the history, philosophy, and politics of underrepresented groups. Literary movements like structuralism and deconstruction sought to articulate how knowledge comes to be created and how forces of interest, language, and value underlie what is said to be so.

Movements such as these carried in their wake a democratization of knowledge that left us floundering in contradiction. At one extreme is a totalitarian view that assigns knowledge a rank and value (this is so, this isn't), while at the other is the anarchic possibility that anything goes, everything is equal. The former insults our democratic sensibilities, while the latter leaves us groundless, with neither standards nor answers on which to take a stand. By what standard, then, are we to judge knowledge? To whose experience do we refer?

Questions like these have given way to an eminently interpretive theory of knowledge: What counts as knowledge does so with respect to its context. In the eyes of many theorists, knowledge has become a matter of interpretation, with reference to a whole constellation of values, tastes, and meanings. Thus the question that has dominated centuries of philosophical thought—What does a thing mean?—has become, What makes a thing meaningful? This shift gave credence to the practice of teaching popular forms of culture that are closer to the experience of today's students and, it can be said, more "meaningful." Opponents of these currents found their figurehead in Allan Bloom, whose book has since become one of the most acclaimed, denounced, and misrepresented publications of the decade.

Up to now, not surprisingly, the ramifications of these changes have been felt most acutely by members of the academic community, where the debate about knowledge rages the fiercest. Indeed, academics have an enormous investment in its outcome, because it relates not only to what should be taught but to what constitutes education, that enterprise which exists for the sake of teaching.

Museum educators, too, hold high stakes in this battle. We, too, are involved with the business of teaching and with decisions about what and how to interpret. Central to our work is communicating our interpretations. For museum educators, what is significant about the debate Bloom sparked is not whether there is one truth or many—even Bloom would not argue that—but whether there is one "Great Books" way of speaking about knowledge or many.

Museums traditionally have presented their collections in the mold Bloom prescribes. They possess Great Objects of Great Value that represent Great Traditions. Only through the painstaking efforts of museum educators have new ways of viewing these objects been incorporated into museum presentations. The idea of presenting exhibits in visitors' terms was born of the realization that the central fact of any museum visit is not what we do, what we want, or what we say, but what the visitor experiences. Museums are already filled with evidence of our attentiveness to this fact: "visitor-friendly" interpretive methods; fewer barriers between objects and viewers; new ways of experiencing objects; and, in some cases, the substitution of reproductions or teaching aids for the objects themselves. Some people believe these efforts trivialize unique objects. But in fact, they may be regarded as a shift in the language with which we talk about our collections. Changes such as these parallel the development of ideas about knowledge: in both cases, knowledge of an object exists in reference to the context of values, experiences, and language that gives it meaning.

Knowledge as Interpretation

If we are to take seriously the proposal that the enterprise of knowledge is fundamentally interpretive, that exhibits impart not facts but interpretations—and our activities suggest that we do—several implications follow that relate to how we think about and practice education in museums. Whether or not one agrees with Allan Bloom's position, he has sparked a debate about knowledge that has profoundly influenced the way educators are thinking about the nature of their profession. It is constructive, therefore, to consider some of its implications for museum education.

Teaching Skills of Perception

As museums have begun to shift to a more client-centered philosophy, we have seen a parallel shift to goals that increasingly call for teaching not facts but skills of perception. In light of the idea that museums deal largely with interpretations, this shift takes on new force. Making the visitor's own view available to him or her may be regarded as a form of empowerment, as museums help visitors learn to look, compare, and judge for themselves.

Teaching skills of perception is empowering in another sense as well. In today's society, visual literacy is becoming just as important as verbal literacy. For the last 20 years the nation has experienced a steady decline in literacy levels. At the same time, an explosion in electronic media, advertising, and high-tech entertainment has bombarded the public with images that speak a subliminal language of their own. Museums deal with objects, which are the raw stuff of images. By learning how to look at those objects, how to "read" their meanings, museum visitors also gain the skills to judge what any sort of image may say.

Legitimizing Other Views

Museums may be the guardians of society's material heritage, but they do not—and cannot—speak to every point of view. Yet we continue to present our collections authoritatively, as factual statements, because that is the habit and history of our institutions. If we understand interpretation to be a fundamental aspect not only of exhibition but of the enterprise of knowledge in general, we need to begin thinking of ways to reflect this understanding in museum exhibits and programs. Rather than try to obscure or correct the fact that museums can only interpret, why not make it more visible? The involvement of noncuratorial views in the interpretive process—teachers, advisory councils, minority groups—is one step in this direction. Presenting the act of interpretation is another. In 1987, for example, New York's Center for African Art interpreted an exhibit of African ritual objects through labels written by a variety of individuals. from within and outside of the museum profession. Each person wrote about the feelings and thoughts that some piece evoked in him or her. This manner of interpretation introduced visitors not only to the variety of experiences one might have with these objects but to the idea that the "knowledge" presented about them consisted of interpretations. As a result, the visitors' own interpretations were given legitimacy and value.

Making Knowledge Accessible

While we have seen a democratization of what counts as knowledge, we have not seen a democratization of the means by which it is pursued. The business of knowledge is still carried out in exclusive academies and journals by people in the know who hold specialized skills and languages. There is no reason that this should be so. Discussions about something as abstract as the nature of knowledge or something as concrete as the issues it treats—be they the importance of a painting, the fate of our natural resources, or the consequences of the AIDS virus—should be conducted by means and in language that are accessible to anyone who has an interest or is affected.

Supporting this argument is a more practical, economic one. In the face of serious competition for resources, we are increasingly forced to articulate and defend museums' contribution to society at large. At the 1988 annual meeting of the American Association of Museums, New York City commissioner of cultural affairs Mary Schmidt Campbell spoke pointedly: What kind of weight does the argument that "culture is good for you" hold for the untold numbers of people who are hungry, unemployed, and homeless? Why is it good? Perhaps it makes people better informed and better equipped to live in the world. A new exhibit at Chicago's Field Museum of Natural History, for example, presents the universal activity of parenting from a biological and cultural perspective, but in terms that are relevant and informative to today's viewer. Not only do we need to articulate our social role more clearly, but we need to practice it more effectively. In all our queries about the special nature of education in the museum, we must not forget the big picture: Why are we concerned about learning at all? What shall we achieve by it?

Only history will tell whether the so-called Battle of the Books is simply a way of rationalizing an undesirable situation—high illiteracy rates, declining educational standards, curriculums that are all flash and no substance—or whether we have indeed uncovered a serious flaw in our ideas about knowledge: that knowledge is a matter of the context of its producers, of their interests, values, and point of view.

It is not surprising, however, that the concerns of museum educators should parallel this academic debate so closely. The fact stands that our quest to provide visitors "meaningful" experiences with our collections is at bottom a matter of imparting relevance, making familiar what is strange. Balancing popularization and trivialization, attending to the perspectives of our visitors, incorporating broadened views and languages—concerns such as these suggest that whether we like it or not, museum educators are following a course that is not far from that defended by Allan Bloom's detractors.

Presenting our collections in terms relevant to our viewers need not mean trivializing them. It does mean shifting to a language that is inviting, not alienating. For museum educators, the significance of the Bloom debate has to do with whether there are one or many ways of speaking about What Matters. For museums to be effective they must communicate successfully, and successful communication often requires showing what a thing has to do with you, your life, your world. Museum educators know this; we have been trying to find ways of doing it for years. What museum educators may not know, however, is just how radical this suggestion is, for ultimately it has to do with the very nature of knowledge.

Note

1. The following reviews of Allan Bloom's *Closing of the American Mind* provide some insight into the controversy surrounding the nature of knowledge: Roger Kimball, *New York Times Book Review,* April 5, 1987, p. 7; Louis Menand, *New Republic* 196 (May 25, 1987): 38; Kenneth Minogue, *Times Literary Supplement,* July 24, 1987, p. 786; Martha Nussbaum, *New York Review of Books* 34 (November 5, 1987): 20; and *Time* (August 17, 1987): 56.

Further Reading

Atlas, James. "The Battle of the Books." *New York Times Magazine,* June 5, 1988, pp. 24–27, 72–75, 85, 94.

Bloom, Allan. *The Closing of the American Mind.* New York: Simon and Schuster, 1987.

Csikszentmihalyi, Mihaly, and Eugene Rochberg-Halton. *The Meaning of Things: Domestic Symbols and the Self.* Cambridge, Eng.: Cambridge University Press, 1981.

Hirsch, E. D. *Cultural Literacy: What Every American Needs to Know.* New York: Vintage Books, 1988.

Naive Notions and the Design of Science Museum Exhibits

Minda Borun

Visitors perceive science exhibits through a filter of naive notions that often distort or color their perceptions of an exhibit and its meaning. Exhibit planners must discover and explicitly address these naive notions in order to create exhibits that explain—not merely embody—science concepts.

Long before people are taught science, they develop their own ideas to explain how the world works. These "naive notions" are deeply rooted and widely shared. Studies of science students from elementary and middle school through high school and college indicate that students enter the classroom with preconceived notions about scientific phenomena. These notions tend to persist despite attempts to alter them through classroom instruction. What we assume to be science learning is often merely the memorization of verbal information. Even students who give correct answers to test questions often do not believe or apply what they learn to experiences outside the classroom.[1]

A common misconception about misconceptions is that they are held by children and replaced through formal instruction, but there are indications that naive notions are widespread among adults. Unless they have experiences that cause them to become aware of the flaws or limitations in their early explanations, people's naive notions persist.

Research on naive notions (also called alternative schema, misconceptions, or preconceptions) is changing our view of the process of formal science education. Only through understanding and addressing such misconceptions can we teach science. The task is not simply to provide students with correct concepts and information: educators must uncover preexisting misconceptions in order to get students to change their minds. These findings also have important implications for science in informal settings.

The museum environment has great potential for changing visitors' misconceptions. The combination of hands-on devices and explanatory text can

Journal of Museum Education 14, no. 2 (Spring/Summer 1989): 16–17. This article marked the debut of the series "What Research Says about Learning in Science Museums." The articles were published as a book under the same title by the Association of Science-Technology Centers in 1990.

produce the "aha" or breakthrough perception that opens people to new understandings.

The work of Elsa Feher at the Reuben H. Fleet Science Center in San Diego on children's concepts of light and vision indicates that the science museum can be used effectively to investigate how people learn and confirms that research into popular misconceptions can improve exhibits.[2]

Stephan Griggs and Paulette McManus, working with Roger Miles at the British Museum (Natural History) in London, have also conducted relevant research. Griggs coined the term "front-end evaluation" to describe the process of interviewing visitors before designing a new exhibit to find out what they know about the main concepts to be explained by the exhibit. While not explicitly citing the academic work on misconceptions, the interviews do, in fact, uncover naive notions that are then addressed in the exhibit's conceptual design. The positive results can be seen in the remarkable accessibility and clarity of the newer natural history exhibits at the British Museum (Natural History).[3]

William Walton, senior scientist at the Science Museum of Virginia, has developed an exhibit that addresses some of the naive notions people have about optics. The exhibit gets visitors to understand some basic principles of light and color, about which there is generally far more confusion than designers of standard lens and prism exhibits might suspect.

The Franklin Institute Science Museum is engaged in an 18-month study to discover visitors' naive notions about gravity and air pressure and to develop exhibits that help people to rethink these concepts.[4] Preliminary results indicate that very few of the 100 visitors interviewed at a Gravity Cone were able to explain the exhibit. The most common misconception about gravity is that it is or depends on air pressure. When asked whether a ball would fall in a vacuum, more than one-third of all visitors interviewed—regardless of age—predicted that the ball would float.

To test the idea that this naive conception could be corrected by means of a hands-on device, we attached a glass tube to an air pump. A ping-pong ball inside the tube falls from one end to the other as the tube is rotated by the visitor. Then the air is pumped out and the tube is rotated again; the ball does not float, it drops. The label explains that gravity has to do with the attraction of masses and that air is not necessary. Both the device and explanatory label went through a process of testing and modification (formative evaluation) until visitors were able to use the device correctly and understand the label.

Interviews with visitors indicate that a very high proportion of people who read the label and operate the device understand what it is supposed to show. Moreover, many people clearly state that this is not what they expected and that they now have a new understanding of gravity! This is a very important finding for science museums. It tells us that carefully constructed and labeled devices can really teach. It also tells us that this is most likely to happen if the device is developed through a process of front-end analysis and evaluation.

As science museum professionals, we believe in learning by doing. To understand naive notions about basic science concepts and how they interfere with science learning, you need to go out on the floor of your museum and station yourself at any device that deals with basic scientific principles. Ask 10 or so visitors (of various ages) to explain in their own words what they think the exhibit is about. It's a sobering experience! It will show you how quickly you can uncover important shared misconceptions and allow you to approach exhibit design empowered by this valuable insight.

Notes

1. Joseph Nussbaum, "Children's Conceptions of the Earth as a Cosmic Body: A Cross-Age Study," *Science Education* 63, no. 1 (1979): 83–93; L. A. Pines and J. D. Novak, "The Interaction of Audio-Tutorial Instruction with Student Prior Knowledge: A Proposed Qualitative Case Study Methodology," *Science Education* 69, no. 2 (1985): 213–28; John Clement, "Students' Preconceptions in Introductory Mechanics," *American Journal of Physics* 50, no. 1 (January 1982): 66–71; M. C. McClosky, "Naive Conceptions of Motion," paper presented at the annual meeting of the American Education Research Association, New York, March 1982.
2. Elsa Feher and Karen Rice, "Development of Scientific Concepts through the Use of Interactive Exhibits in a Museum," *Curator* 28 (1985): 35–46.
3. S. A. Griggs, "Front-end Evaluation: Three Case Studies" (London: Office of Museum Programs, Department of Public Services, British Museum [Natural History], 1982); R. S. Miles et al., *The Design of Educational Exhibits* (London: Allen and Unwin, 1982).
4. The Franklin Institute Science Museum study is supported by a grant from the National Science Foundation. This paper reflects the views of the author and not necessarily the position of the National Science Foundation.

Resource People

Minda Borun, Assistant Director of Programs, Franklin Institute Science Museum, Philadelphia, Pennsylvania
Elsa Feher, Director, Reuben H. Fleet Science Center, San Diego, California
Roger Miles, Director, British Museum (Natural History), London, England
William Walton, Senior Scientist, Science Museum of Virginia, Richmond, Virginia

Passionate and Purposeful: Adult Learning Communities

Luke Baldwin, Sharlene Cochrane, Constance Counts, Joan Dolamore, Martha McKenna, and Barbara Vacarr

A key concept in educating adults is the idea of a "learning community." Adults often learn most effectively in groups that they join by choice, groups characterized by discussion, interaction, and collaboration and in which participants both receive and provide academic and social support. Such groups value the individual; at the same time they require that the learner communicate and reflect within the group. These groups might be work partnerships, professional organizations, workshops, seminars, or internships. At Lesley College Graduate School a faculty group called the Collaborative on Adult Research and Practice is one such learning community. Our shared reflections and analyses of developmental theory and our own teaching have served as a model of the process through which adults learn effectively, and we have collaborated on this article.

The Nature of Adult Development

Adult learning is characterized by diversity. Adults bring a great variety of life experiences to learning communities, and their cultural backgrounds, interests, and passions generate the questions that help determine the shape and course of their learning. Adult development theorists concur that adulthood is marked by emerging challenges and opportunities for growth. Human development is a lifelong process that goes beyond the maturational competencies and understandings of adolescence. Views of self, relationships, and place in the world evolve into old age.

Contrary to earlier theories of human development that concentrated on childhood and adolescence, a life cycle perspective on development sees continued transitions and change as essential elements of adult growth as well. Recent research indicates that adults' lives are patterned in predictable sequences of growth, adaptation, and transformation.[1] The psychologist Daniel Levinson calls these predictable sequences "seasons."

> There is the idea of seasons: a series of periods or stages within the life cycle. The process is not simple, continuous, unchanging flow. There are qualitatively different seasons, each having its own distinctive character.[2]

Certain key issues and tasks are associated with each life stage. There is, however,

Journal of Museum Education 15, no. 1 (Winter 1990): 7–9.

a great deal of individual and contextual variation in how themes, stages, phases, or events characterize particular journeys through adulthood. Not all people deal with life events in the same way, and individuals vary considerably along the developmental continuum—even within the same relative positions.

The transitions of adulthood can be described as "decisive turning points" that carry the potential for "intrapersonal integration." In transition, adults rework prior learning, reformulate their identity, and reaffirm or renegotiate previous resolutions.[3] This period of vulnerability provides opportunities to challenge old assumptions, reach deeper understandings, seek new balances, and create new life meanings.

Earlier life experiences that were characterized by a need to work and produce in order to satisfy external authorities are transformed by adults' strong drive toward competence and achievement. The Harvard psychologist Robert Kegan describes the central transition in adult development as moving from an "interpersonal" stance to an "institutional" stance.[4] Adult learners make a transition to a culture of self-authorship as they become engaged in a learning community.

Many adults enter learning communities with the assumption that the ideas and opinions of others are what constitute knowledge, and learners tend to seek "truths" from those whom they perceive as experts. This tendency is exemplified in the following comments made by an adult who had recently returned to college to complete her undergraduate degree:

> The teacher asked the question: "What is the meaning of evil?" For the next three hours I had to sit and listen to all my classmates talk and waste time talking about what they thought evil was. It was so boring . . . but the worst part was that the teacher never gave us the answer.[5]

Development moves from a strict reliance on an absolute authority, through an understanding that truth is relative, to a conceptualization that knowledge is constructed. This movement is characteristic of the transition described by William Perry, in which exclusive reliance on external authority as the "source of truth" is rejected.[6] As adults enlarge their understandings of the world, they tend to move from a dualistic to a multiple, contextual view in which they may begin to see themselves as the creators of knowledge. The developmental position one inhabits affects the view of self in relation to the world.

Transitions that are marked by a process of questioning, evaluating, experiencing, and ultimately synthesizing diminish the importance of external authority, and through this process adults take ownership of their own learning. The comments of another returning adult student clarify this shift. She describes becoming an active participant in the process of her own growth:

> Things have opened up for me, and I'm much more sure about what I want to do. When I first came back to school I felt like it was just something I had to do, to finish. But now I really feel invested in what I'm doing, and I have so many things that I want to check out.[7]

This sense of direction is the beginning of self as knower, out of which grows an informed and more powerful personal voice.

Although this phase of development may be qualitatively different for men and women, when procedures for knowing are integrated with a more committed personal voice, adults are on the verge of constructing knowledge. Four psychologists explain the process:

> Once Knowers assume the general relativity of knowledge, that their frame of reference matters, and that they can construct frames of reference, they feel responsible for examining, questioning, and developing the systems they will use for constructing knowledge.[8]

At this point in the cycle of development adults have greater tolerance for ambiguity, and questions become more important than answers. They seek to determine criteria for learning, framed and tempered through an understanding that truth is contextually relative. Adults' capacity to construct knowledge is enhanced when communication with others facilitates a connection between the self and the wider community of learners.

The Process of Adult Development
Our understanding of adult development and our experience in successfully educating adult students have led us to understand our work as a three-step process: purposeful engagement in the content of the experience; reflection, evaluation, and analysis (as individuals and as a group); and the application of new learning to concrete situations. Slightly different versions of this construct have been suggested by John Dewey and David Kolb as models for solving problems or illustrating learning styles. Throughout these processes, adults are both passionate and purposeful. And that blend enlivens learning communities and contributes to the building of personal and intellectual support systems.

Diversity and Active Engagement
Although group participation and interaction are critical elements in our model, learning communities need to be flexible and multidimensional, encouraging and building on the diversity within the group. Differences in experience, culture, learning styles, and gender may serve to complement each other. Extremely diverse groups tend to generate many options for solving problems, examining content, or testing and applying theories. When adults share their strengths in those areas, the results can be both powerful and lasting. A dreamer and a mechanic make an impressive pair of inventors.

In addition, adults have a complex network of experiences through which they carry themes, questions, and interests that give their search for knowledge intensity and imagination. The community must allow the opportunity to engage material in different ways, nurturing different types of expression and activity that capitalize on a wide range of passions and styles of learning. Opportunities may include independent study and research, small groups for discussion or study, presentations for large groups, site visits, fieldwork, case study development or analysis, written or visual tasks, and movement between quiet reading and candid conversation. In guiding these types of activities, effective facilitators initiate dialogue among members of the learning community to identify shared and unique experiences, knowledge, expertise, and passions about the subject.

The educator may propose goals and activities for reaching them, but through this initial dialogue the learning community may respond to such plans and offer suggestions for making adjustments or modifications. The educator in such a setting is not the "expert dispensing truths" but the resource person and facilitator, adapting activities, helping to connect content with individual passions, and shaping experience that can provide meaningful learning within the set amount of time for the experience. This approach applies whether the learning situation is a semester course, a day-long workshop, or a two-hour museum visit. While the depth of learning may vary, learning communities are created whenever a group engages in a process of learning that interactively draws from the knowledge and experience of the participants.

The ways educators accomplish this learning again need to be varied, weaving individual interests into the exploration of content. Participants may prepare special projects or presentations, develop research teams, arrange debates, and so on. Invariably, by guiding individuals within the learning community in pursuing their own passions, important questions about the content emerge—in forms more meaningful and critical than educators often expect. This dynamic process of socially constructing new forms of knowledge through the learning community promotes both individual and collective growth and serves to empower adults as learners.

Reflection and Evaluation

A critical aspect of educational experiences for adults is the need for reflection and evaluation of new learning. Educators must provide time and space in every learning experience for participants to reflect on the experience and evaluate its meaning in their lives. In our experience as adult educators, we have found this stage to be the most creative of the learning experience and the one most likely to be overlooked without careful planning. Effective educators facilitate this stage within learning communities by encouraging participants to share their reflections and insights with their peers in every new learning activity.

This process requires learners to integrate new learning with past experiences, creating meaning for the present and looking toward expanding on the experience in the future. Participants should reflect critically on new experiences and have the opportunity to challenge information or beliefs set forth based on their own knowledge or experience in the field. The personal authority that adult learners bring to educational activities must be acknowledged and respected by educators.

Finally, as learners respond to each others' comments, comparing insights and possible meanings of the experience, collaboration is enhanced and learners have the opportunity to expand their range of possible meanings of the experience and learn to value various points of view. All participants should have the chance to express their ideas and listen to others as the learning community constructs its own meanings and values particular attributes of the learning activity.

Application and Further Inquiry
Without a context in which to test their new knowledge, adults run the risk of viewing learning as being separate from personal experience. Ideally, in order to ensure integration of knowledge, adults should have a forum for applying new insights and formulating new interactions. Such interactions offer adults opportunities not only to apply theory but to construct new theories based on subsequent experiences. This dynamic process of knowing and doing provides a vital connection in learning experiences.

Adult learning communities offer a variety of ways for adults to implement their new knowledge. Through practice, work experiences, and internships, adults act on what they have learned. Action projects provide a means for learners to try out their ideas through solving problems, collaborating with others to refine concepts, and reacting to changes. This kind of learning allows adults to modify ideas and assumptions by testing their validity or usefulness in the field. Theoretical concepts often represent ideals that do not fit everyday situations, and adults become constructors of knowledge by modifying and shaping theories to conform to their own experiences. In essence, the field becomes the laboratory. As adults continually apply and adapt what they have studied in learning communities, they become more aware of their own learning processes. This awareness ultimately results in a strong foundation from which adults build knowledge based on a broad range of interaction and integration.

A Final Note
The Collaborative on Adult Research and Practice formed at Lesley College to study adult development has experienced this shift between interaction and integration. Through collaborative efforts in small study groups, we compiled and assembled this article, and this task has served as an action project that has allowed us to reflect on our experiences in the group and to apply the knowledge we have gained. The final product also incorporates our hands-on learning as teachers.

The examination and articulation of our own learning processes and practices yielded new insights that enhanced our understanding of how adults develop and learn. It became clear that a view of development as a linear path in which adults grow to construct knowledge within a community of learners was not sufficient. Our experience informs our belief that entrance into a learning community becomes an integral part of the developmental process and facilitates growth to more complex and integrative epistemological positions. As our awareness of this phenomenon has continued to grow, our new knowledge has infused our teaching, leading to new interactions with our students, which we have then brought back and discussed with our collaborative group. That circle continues, inspiring our own research and practice and enlivening the academic experiences of our students.

Notes

1. Rita Weathersby, Rita Preszler, and Jill Matuck Tarule, *Adult Development: Implications for Higher Education,* American Association for Higher Education–ERIC/Higher Education Research Report 4 (Washington, D. C.: American Association for Higher Education, 1980), p. 2.
2. Daniel Levinson, *The Seasons of a Man's Life* (New York: Alfred A. Knopf, 1978), p. 6.
3. Weathersby, Preszler, and Tarule, *Adult Development,* p. 22.
4. Robert Kegan, *The Evolving Self* (Cambridge, Mass.: Harvard University Press, 1982).
5. Quoted in Barbara Vacarr, "Peer Mentoring and Epistemological Development of Adults," paper presented at the annual international meeting of the Mentoring Association, Kalamazoo, Mich., May 1989, p. 4.
6. William G. Perry, *Forms of Intellectual and Ethical Development in the College Years* (New York: Holt, Rinehart and Winston, 1970).
7. Quoted in Vacarr, "Peer Mentoring and Epistemological Development," p. 6.
8. M. F. Belenky, B. M. Clinchy, N. R. Goldberger, and J. M. Tarule, *Women's Ways of Knowing* (New York: Basic Books, 1986), pp. 138–39.

Further Reading

Adams, Frank. *Unearthing Seeds of Fire: The Idea of Highlander.* Winston-Salem, N.C.: Blair, 1975.
Brookfield, Stephen D. *Understanding and Facilitating Adult Learning.* San Francisco: Jossey-Bass, 1986.
Daloz, Laurent A. *Effective Teaching and Mentoring: Realizing the Transformational Power of Adult Learning.* San Francisco: Jossey-Bass, 1986.
Dewey, John. *Democracy and Education.* New York: Macmillan, 1916.
Freire, Paolo. *Education for Critical Consciousness.* New York: Seabury Press, 1973.
Kegan, Robert. *The Evolving Self.* Cambridge, Mass.: Harvard University Press, 1982.
Kolb, David. *Experiential Learning.* Englewood Cliffs, N.J.: Prentice Hall, 1984.

Museum Visitors and the Development of Understanding

Eleanor Duckworth

In setting out to say what I think is important for museum educators to have in mind about developmental theory, I want to use Jean Piaget's work on the development of understanding in infancy, where the roots of children's thinking lie—and our own as well. I hope this perspective will offer some useful insights into ways all of us can help learners approach new material.

The single most important aspect of Piaget's thought for museum educators is his emphasis on the centrality of actions to ways of knowing. Piaget traces all human knowledge to its roots in the activities of infants.[1] Transforming the knowledge gained through actions in infancy into conceptual, representational knowledge is a lifelong human endeavor. Childhood is an interesting middle ground. For the most part, we believe we understand children's experiences, and yet sometimes their perspectives can stun us. When this happens, it is usually because of the centrality of action as a means of understanding.

It is worthwhile to sketch out what Piaget means when he speaks of an infant's actions as the root of knowledge by looking at his presentation of the development of the notion of permanent objects during the first year of life. The general finding of his classic study *Construction of Reality in the Child* (1950) is well known. In their first few months, infants act as if an object has no continuing existence of its own. If an interesting plaything the infant is reaching for is covered with a cloth, he or she stops reaching for it. Or, even more significant, the infant will go back to look for it in a place he or she has found it before. To the infant the object does not seem to have an integrity, a location in space.

What is less well known is Piaget's interpretation of the infant's experience before he or she develops the notion of object permanence. To begin with, what we would call an object is for the child indissociable from his or her own action. Here is Piaget's description of a six-to-nine-month-old anticipating the reappearance of an object moving in the same direction it was going when it disappeared:

> The movement of the object is, for his awareness, one and the same as the kinesthetic or sensorimotor impressions that accompany his own eye, head, or body movements.

Journal of Museum Education 15, no. 1 (Winter 1990): 4–6. This essay is a revision of a paper originally presented at the annual meeting of the American Association of Museums, New Orleans, June 1989.

When the mobile disappears from sight, the only possible ways to find it are to keep on doing what he was already doing and to go back to how he was before. Nothing requires the infant to consider that the mobile itself has moved, independent of his own movements. All the infant has to go on is an immediate linking between his kinesthetic impressions and the reappearance of the mobile in his visual field—in short, a linking between a certain effort and a certain result.[2]

In the following example, we can also see the infant's focus on his or her own action in an attempt to understand the world:

Laurent . . . [at seven months, five days] loses a cigarette box that he had just been swinging around. He lets go of it involuntarily outside his visual field. He then immediately brings his hand back in front of his eyes and looks at it a long time, with an expression of surprise, disappointment. . . . He starts again to swing his hand around, even though there's nothing in it, after which he looks at it again. . . . It is impossible not to interpret this conduct as an attempt to make the object come back.[3]

Reaching for an object does not mean the infant understands the object is there; it reflects the infant's effort to continue the object's presence. It is the reaching for it or the looking at it that "generate" it, as it were.

Another fine example from the description of Laurent is the following: Providing he can see even the tiniest part of the nipple of his bottle he turns the bottle around to get the nipple into his mouth. If the nipple is completely hidden, though, he does not turn the bottle. Nonetheless he seeks to "generate" the nipple by sucking on the available end! Laurent considers the nipple as being "at the disposition" of his sucking action. "It is not the object that constitutes the permanent element . . . but the act itself."[4] The continuing existence of the nipple depends on the continuation of the child's own actions.

The primacy of the child's own actions can be seen in extraordinary ways. Israeli educator Malka Haas shows a two-year-old's drawing of a cake. It does not look like a cake. It is a thick set of swirls, which Haas explains as the traces of the gesture of mixing the batter. It is the gesture that is represented in the drawing.[5]

In another example a six-year-old has predicted that a rubber ball will sink. But it floats. So he pushes it down to the bottom of the pan and holds it there for a while before letting go to see whether this time it will stay there on its own. Here again it is a sense of the efficacy of his own actions, rather than the object's properties, that guide him.

This concentration on actions leads to a focus on success rather than on understanding, on attaining goals rather than attending to relationships. A four-year-old niece of mine watched her 10-year-old cousin climb a doorframe in the oppositional manner of a mountaineer climbing a rock chimney. With a hand and a foot pressing against each side of the frame, the 10-year-old lifted her own weight and reached the top of the doorway. The four-year-old set out to do the same, but she could not reach the sides of the doorframe well enough to press on them with her hands and feet. So, knowing that when you cannot reach something you get someone to lift you, she asked her father to lift her so she could reach the sides of the doorframe. She was disappointed and incomprehending that she still could not reach the edges. Her puzzlement is a commentary on her understanding not of what her cousin had done but of what goes on when someone lifts you up to reach better. She understood the action to have an almost magically efficacious result and had no grasp of the relationships involved. Lifting up helps you reach; the relationship between the direction you are lifted and the direction you want to reach is not noticed.

This example records an observation of someone else's action. In the child's own actions, too, there are a focus on outcome and a lack of understanding of what he or she is doing. One of Piaget's late books is called in English *The Grasp of Consciousness,* a bad translation of the French title, *La prise de conscience* (1974), which means "becoming aware." In this context Piaget is referring to becoming aware of the relationships between one's own actions and the world in which they are carried out. The book consists of studies of situations in which children are able to coordinate their own actions in order to accomplish a goal but do not know what they have done or what the objects have done in response. For example, they can perfectly well roll a ball so as to give another ball a slanting blow and direct it off to one side, thus avoiding hitting a little model person. But when asked how she did it, one six-year-old, for example, believed she had simply rolled the ball straight ahead. "The ball turned instead of going straight ahead," she said. "It pushed straight ahead and then when it got there it turned." Her drawing confirmed her perception: the trajectory of the first ball went straight to the second, and the second ball headed straight for the model person before turning away at the last moment. A 10-year-old, by contrast, while succeeding no better with the actual actions, knew what he had done: "Instead of aiming there [the middle of the second ball], I aim at the side."[6]

There is another way in which the child's focus on actions and practical success takes priority over understanding relationships. Barbel Inhelder and Piaget carried out an experiment in which rods of different material, length, thickness, and cross-sectional shape were provided along with different weights that could be placed on the ends of the rods.[7] The rods could be secured at the other end, thus extending horizontally. The object was to determine which factors—material, length, thickness, shape of rod, or amount of weight on end—made the rods bend more. Ideally, of course, in order to determine whether a square cross-section bends more or less than a round cross-section, we would compare two rods of identical length, thickness, and material and use the same amount of weight on each, varying only the shape of the cross-section. Young children tend to think, however, that the more they act and change things, the more they'll learn. So to see which factor might be responsible for a short thick round rod that is not bending a great deal, a nine-year-old would replace it, say, with a long thin rod. It is true that the more different actions you take simultaneously the more you are likely to effect some change; it is not true that the more different actions you take simultaneously the better you will understand.

One last aspect of Piaget's thought is important to mention. It is this rooting of understanding in actions that leads each child to have his or her own interpretation of a given situation. The history of his or her own actions determines the framework through which a child understands any new experience. This connection is exemplified in the following (true!) story.

The mother of a four-year-old friend of mine reported a visit to a large commercial egg farm, producing hundreds of thousands of eggs daily. The child was shown the hens being fed and watered, the hens laying, the eggs being washed, sorted, conveyed outside, packed, stacked for pickup, all of course with careful explanation by both her parents and the workers. Later in the day she told her uncle about this visit. She had been duly impressed by the magnitude of the operation—the number of hens and the number of eggs. And then she proceeded to explain how the eggs were the hens' food. Astonished, her mother asked where the eggs had come from. From the store, was the answer. There was no trace of the careful, thoroughly documented explanations that the child had spent the morning hearing and seeing.

There are two different ways I think an awareness of the centrality of actions in determining children's understanding can be of interest to museum educators.

One of them relates most closely to this last consequence. In reading an issue of this journal, I noticed a tension between the view that "people come first" and the importance of "the integrity of the object."[8] Thinking in terms of people's own ways of understanding seems to me to allow for a resolution of the tension between these perspectives. Objects are known to people only as taken in by them through the frameworks that they have developed and bring with them. The idea behind the development of a museum exhibit, then, would be to make a place for people's own ways of understanding and to work with them.

I had a conversation about this idea with an exhibit developer in a museum that set out to emphasize both science and the visual arts. We were agreeing that the museum needed to seek out phenomena that were multifaceted, which people could explore from the frameworks of understanding that they brought with them and without being expected to apprehend the phenomena in one given way. A few minutes later he referred to the phenomenon involved in an exhibit we had been discussing as "resonance"—an idea important to physicists. I did not understand at first, and then I did a double take. "Resonance" was not what I considered a phenomenon. For me, the phenomenon of that exhibit was "a great big heavy pendulum"! That is how I responded to the exhibit first and foremost.

I appreciate that it is difficult for a museum to present exhibits without wanting people to get a specific understanding from them. I also appreciate that part of this difficulty is that visitors would often feel cheated if they were not told what to understand from an exhibit. But the risk is that people's own ways of thinking about the material are not engaged—and therefore not affected.

There are fine precedents of exhibits that do not seek to convey a specific understanding. The most striking in my experience are historical reconstructions where, among other things, actors re-create persons from the period. No lesson is imposed. Visitors experience the phenomena.

Students of mine have started trying to work in open-ended ways in art museums. They ask visitors to say what they see in a painting. The longer the visitors stand and look at a single painting, telling each other what they see, the more ways each person has to see it. One's own view is both legitimized and enhanced.

In other kinds of museums I can imagine starting by acknowledging some idea: Many people who see this think of it this way. Why do you suppose they do? Can you see anything that doesn't work about that way of thinking of it? What else might people think? Why might they think that? And is there anything that doesn't work about that way? The way I think about it is this. What do you suppose some of my reasons are? What doesn't work about this way of thinking about it?

The second reason I wanted to focus on the centrality of actions in children's understanding is that they play an important part in our adult understanding as well. At first the focus is easier to see in children, but it is also possible to find it in ourselves. When I am trying to understand something that has gone wrong, for example, I often find myself tempted, just like the children with the rods, to change every variable at once in order to make a difference. No less frequently I find myself, like the child with the ball that did not sink, trying to impress my wishes through my own actions on some totally resistant object. David Hawkins has shown how few adults realize the relationships involved when they easily arrange themselves to look at someone else in a mirror[9]—just like the child rolling the ball or the child asking to be lifted in order to reach to the sides of the doorframe. I could go on and on.

As educators trying to anticipate or tune in to students' and museum visitors' ways of understanding, I find nothing more precious to keep than a connection with our own ways of seeing, our own confusions, our own conflicts between trying to succeed and trying to understand, our own surprises, our own feelings when we find out new things and have to let go of old ones. Capturing the moments when we can recognize the action-grounded roots of our own understanding is one of the most valuable exercises in moving outside our own later points of view and making connections with those who come to learn in our classes and our museums.

Notes

1. Jean Piaget, *Play, Dreams, and Imitation in Childhood,* trans. Caleb Gattegno and Frances Mary Hodgson (New York: Norton, 1962); Piaget, *The Origins of Intelligence in Children,* trans. Margaret Cook (New York: International Universities Press, 1966); Piaget, *The Construction of Reality in the Child,* trans. Margaret Cook (New York: Ballantine, 1986); Eleanor Duckworth, "Structures, Continuity and Other People's Minds," in Duckworth, *"The Having of Wonderful Ideas" and Other Essays on Teaching and Learning* (New York: Teachers College Press, 1987), pp. 98–112.

2. Jean Piaget, *La construction du réel* (Neuchatel: Delachaux et Niestle, 1950), p. 23, my translation. See also the English edition cited in n. 1, pp. 19–20.

3. Ibid., p. 25; English ed., p. 22.

4. Ibid., p. 29; English ed., p. 27.

5. Malka Haas, personal communication, 1978.

6. Jean Piaget, *La prise de conscience* (Paris: Presses Universitaires de France, 1974), pp. 118, 124, my translation. See also the English edition, *The Grasp of Consciousness,* trans. Susan Wedgewood (Cambridge, Mass.: Harvard University Press, 1974), pp. 155, 162.

7. Barbel Inhelder and Jean Piaget, *The Growth of Logical Thinking,* trans. Anne Parsons and Stanley Milgram (New York: Basic Books, 1958), pp. 46–66.

8. Sharon Blume, comments on Diane Brigham, "Preparation for Empowerment," *Journal of Museum Education* 13, no. 3 (1988): 11.

9. David Hawkins, "Critical Barriers to Science Learning," *Outlook* 29 (1978): 3–23.

Sending Them Home Alive

Anita Rui Olds

Ideally, a museum visit is a memorable experience that affects a person's life beyond the museum's walls. To be changed in this way, however, people must be fully *alive* where they are; free to drop their self-consciousness, their roles and facades, their fears of knowing too little, or of needing to judge and analyze; free to allow the objects and events to become part of themselves. Over and above the design requirements and neutral architectural backdrop of an exhibit, there is the opportunity and challenge to make each space a more successful place of learning and creativity, where people get more in touch with who they really are and what they might be. The following summary of ideas gathered from research in the field of environmental psychology suggests that achieving such "aliveness" depends on designing an ambience with sufficient environmental stimulation to keep the brain at optimal levels of alertness by meeting at least four basic needs: movement, comfort, competence, and control.

Movement
The freedom to move about in space, assume different body postures, create one's own boundaries, and enter diverse territories is a prime way in which people manifest health and power and fulfill their potential. Indoors, however, the presence of many bodies moving in unpredictable ways is often experienced as discomforting. And because motion is more apparent in small spaces and can make space feel more congested, it is not encouraged where square footage is limited or focused attention is required. In most museums and galleries, visitors are expected to be quiet, move carefully, and behave in a formal and subdued way. These restrictions tire the body and dull the mind.

People feel most alive, however, when they can move freely within a setting to explore its limits and facets, have access to needs (bathrooms, telephones, lockers, food), and can vary the pace of their activities over time. Thus museum visitors, especially children, may prefer to give an exhibit a "once over" at the outset to determine its physical and informational scope and then proceed to absorb its contents step by step. Some visitors are content to follow a given sequence, while for others the visit is enriched by a more random approach.

Journal of Museum Education 15, no. 1 (Winter 1990): 10–12.

It is particularly helpful, therefore, for aspects of an exhibit to allow for fine and gross motor interaction with the materials (pushing buttons, ringing bells, using body weight to unbalance or relocate objects) and encourage different types of movements and body postures: sitting (on chairs, floor, loft with feet dangling); standing; climbing (on stairs, ladders, inclines); lying (under or inside something); encircling something; bending or stooping (through lowered doorways); reaching; looking up, over, or under; moving (through wide and tight spaces, forward and backward, on level or inclined ground, with clear or minimal visibility, and with some or no light at the end of the tunnel). Where participants cannot be permitted to interact with the materials, demonstration by a craftsperson or operator can still have the powerful effect of introducing movement and change into the setting.

Just as a brisk walk may clear the mind, a period of standing or sitting to look at something, if followed by an active experience of walking a distance, changing levels, or using the body vigorously, helps wake up the brain. If this motion takes one to a space with an entirely different configuration and mood, so much the better. In homes, living rooms, kitchens, and bedrooms are distinct places involving different levels of activity, body postures, and degrees of privacy. Moving through such different rooms is often (as in the Pepsi ad) "the pause that refreshes." Similarly, moving through an exhibit in varied ways, through spaces with distinctly different moods and qualities, and using one's body (or someone else's) to make things happen in a display are all ways of creating movement, the sine qua non of life.

Comfort

In addition to bodily movement, the senses also must "move" and receive changing stimulation from the external environment. Our eyes see by scanning a visual field but are reduced to "nonsight" when forced to stare at a stationary image. Our ears hear when sound waves strike and vibrate the ear drum.

Dramatic fluctuations in stimulation level can be frightening and disorienting. But an environment that provides rhythmic patterns of predictable sameness combined with moderate diversity enables the senses to maintain optimal levels of responsivity and makes us feel "comfortable." Natural elements, such as blazing fires, babbling brooks, and gentle breezes exemplify this principle well. They are always moving in ways that are fairly predictable. Yet moderate variations—a flicker or flare, a new pitch, a cooler or warmer draft—prevent boredom or withdrawal by introducing a change that catches the attention and reawakens the nervous system.

The difference-within-sameness so exquisitely present in nature is difficult to create within the static built world. Clearly, in a museum one does not want the background to have such arousal levels that it detracts from the exhibit itself. Paradoxically, it is often the sensorial blandness of a museum's setting that makes it difficult for visitors to absorb the details of even a particularly wondrous exhibit. The old adage, "Variety is the spice of life," is the best guideline for generating an ambience that supports aliveness and learning.

This guideline means, first of all, that all the senses should be moderately stimulated. If an exhibit is largely visual, a quiet background of pleasantly varied sounds, odors, textures, and opportunities for movement will actually enhance the visual experience. Variety in physical parameters—scale, areas of light and shadow, floor levels and ceiling and partition heights, room size and number of occupants, degrees of intimacy, activities that are messy and clean—can also powerfully contribute to comfort and heightened awareness.

Attention to detail, especially to the finish materials used on floors, walls, ceilings, windows, and furniture, can have a more powerful impact on users and on the overall "feel" of a place than any other single factor. The textures, colors, and forms applied (or not applied) to interior surfaces are the environmental qualities with which occupants come most closely in contact. These are "read" continually as people experience any setting. Finishes and design details affect what is seen, heard, smelled, and touched, and therefore how people feel in a space.

To the extent that a comfortable environment is esthetically integrated and whole, it is also beautiful. Its physical wholeness and harmony transmit psychic wholeness and tranquillity, elevating the spirit and encouraging the senses to play with surrounding events and forms.

A powerful way to design for esthetic richness is to conceive of all elements of a room (floors, ceilings, walls, horizontal and vertical supports, objects, forms, and architectural details) as interactive surfaces that can be sculpted, painted, draped, and molded, much the way artists sculpt, paint, and mold wood, clay, canvas, fibers, colors, and forms. An environment is most comfortable when there are varied moods throughout the facility, created by interesting things to look at, unexpected surprises of light and shadow, sound, warmth, and color, nooks and crannies, and things that respond, smell, or feel inviting. Then the senses can play everywhere, not solely with the exhibits.

All environments affect people in at least two ways: they suggest a range of activities that can or cannot occur in a setting, and they evoke feelings. Thus environments are always both emotionally felt and mentally interpreted by each occupant. Exhibits tell people what they can do, whereas the beauty and esthetic qualities of a facility affect people's emotions and convey messages about their self-worth. A context of wholeness that unites body, mind, and spirit, thought and feeling, head and heart, invariably uplifts and transforms, helping people to learn and experience things they do not know and making them feel good about themselves and life. When the inner loveliness of the visitor meets the outer loveliness of an exhibit, then there is magic!

Competence

Aliveness also comes from being able to care for one's basic needs autonomously and from being successful at meaningful activities. Museum goers often experience a sense of inferiority and submissiveness since they come to encounter the unfamiliar.

They are unable to stake out territories over which they have jurisdiction or to control their activities and levels of social interaction in customary ways. To compensate for this loss of control and status, visitors should be helped to feel that they belong by being able to make their way easily through the facility and to participate in activities that grant them some control over territory, materials, and social encounters. An interpretable physical layout, reinforced by good signage and graphics in lobbies, corridors, elevators, exhibit areas, and at critical junctures, can help people get where they want to go. Facilities that enable them to fulfill basic personal needs without assistance—coat racks, coffee machines, water fountains, clocks, telephones, diaper-changing tables, conveniently located lavatories—honor independence and personal power.

Where people of a variety of ages and physical conditions are present, adaptive facilities, as well as those scaled to meet a range of developmental and educational levels and interests, further affirm the inherent learning capacities of each participant. Dioramas and full-scale mock-ups of a setting, which create an environment or contextual framework for an exhibit, help all visitors make inferences that bridge the gaps between the familiar and the unknown.

A sense of competence is also boosted by an ordered space whose parts are distinguishable from one another. Areas or zones within a room can be set apart by the amount of physical space between them, distinctive lighting and pools of light, boundaries and dividers, and the use of color—our most powerful visual organizer. With different colors on work surfaces and sitting surfaces at the visitor's eye level, even a visually chaotic environment becomes interpretable. Seeing a red, blue, or green space within a room communicates more powerfully than signage that where the colors begin and end, so do the activities.

There is another sense in which competence can be addressed. Studies of cognitive and personality styles suggest that people process information in different ways (left brain/right brain, screener/nonscreener, reflective/impulsive) and primarily along one of three dimensions: visual, auditory, or kinesthetic. A kinesthetic learner, for example, will have a hard time absorbing information from a purely visual display where there is nothing to touch or manipulate. To ensure that no one is "disabled," a successful exhibit presents the same information in at least these three modalities so everyone can approach and interpret the material in the way that suits him or her best.

Control

Because we do not have eyes in the backs of our heads and cannot protect ourselves from attack from the rear, control and physical security depend upon having something solid at our backs, with the ability to see and hear what approaches head-on. Thus people move across beaches, fields, and parks and stand still only when their backs are against a wall, a tree, or a bench. If protection at the rear is impossible, security may also be achieved by sitting or standing close to a wall, sitting or lying close to the ground, or attaining a position of height from which to survey the surrounding terrain. Most spaces have a zone (usually a corner) that is recognizably more protected than all other points in the room. It is there you will find the teacher's or doctor's desk, dad's favorite chair, and storage for precious items. People instinctively gravitate to a protected zone and like to stay there. Activities requiring a willingness to sit still and concentrate work best when placed in this location.

Physical security also depends upon being able to make predictions about territories and events beyond one's immediate spatial sphere. Broad vistas, rendered by an architecturally open plan, achieve this sense of security best. Interior windows or walls of glass, however, bold graphics, lighting that does not create mysterious shadows, and balanced acoustics can be intentionally employed in more enclosed settings to provide the "extension of the senses" that is required.

A Concluding Thought

Psychological and physiological harmony depend upon the balance maintained among movement, comfort, competence, and control. Whenever one factor is limited (when movement is restricted, for example, because an exhibit requires the visitor to sit), the value of the other factors must be increased (a more stimulating background ambience, more back protection, varied sensorial modes for approaching the information). Because museum environments often produce many limitations at once, including restricted movement, interaction with unfamiliar materials, and restricted territorial control, the comfort dimension is exceedingly important and requires far more attention than is often characteristic of exhibit design practice. But, when all four needs are met and balanced to complement the extremes of visitor and exhibit limitations and excesses, then the setting truly lives and people leave the museum renewed and more alive.

Further Reading

Alexander, Christopher. *The Timeless Way of Building.* New York: Oxford University Press, 1979.
———, et al. *A Pattern Language.* New York: Oxford University Press, 1977.
Bachelard, Gaston. *The Poetics of Space.* Boston: Beacon Press, 1969.
Fiske, D. W., and S. R. Maddi. *Functions of Varied Experience.* Homewood, Ill.: Dorsey, 1961.
Mehrabian, Albert. *Public Places and Private Spaces: The Psychology of Work, Play, and Living Environments.* New York: Basic Books, 1976.
Walter, Eugene Victor. *Placeways: A Theory of Human Environments.* Chapel Hill, N.C.: University of North Carolina Press, 1988.

Museum Multicultural Education for Young Learners

Joseph H. Suina

Multicultural education has been defined in numerous ways by various groups and individuals for the past 20 years.[1] Some definitions reflect the perspectives of specific disciplines such as psychology, anthropology, and sociology. Others represent the views of professional organizations and accrediting agencies that are concerned with what teachers need to teach and what students need to learn for effective participation in the multiple realities of life. An example is the statement on multicultural education issued by the American Association of Colleges for Teacher Education.[2] Still other definitions have been developed and adopted by educators within schools and school districts across the country.

Most teachers recognize the multiple realities that exist within the population of each school and, in many cases, within each classroom. They are also very aware of the demands that society places on them for preparing students for the world in immediate and long-range terms. These demands mean students must learn to communicate and interact with people from a wide range of cultural backgrounds. Thus multicultural education is first of all a process through which individuals develop ways of perceiving, evaluating, and behaving within cultural systems unlike their own.[3] Second, multicultural education requires a consideration of the forces that exert powerful influences within local, national, and global settings. These forces will affect priorities and direction in education at all dimensions.

In the final analysis multicultural education is education for all students in what is reality today—a multicultural society. What classroom teachers and museum educators ultimately do depends upon their point of view and their knowledge and ability to provide positive cross-cultural experiences and attitudes for their students.

Museums possess a tremendous potential for the development and encouragement of the goals of multicultural education. By their nature and function, museums confront the multiple dimensions of human cultures across time and space. For schools, museums serve as places where people collect, display, and share fragments of the world in which we live. Many focus on nonhuman topics, such as desert ecology, and many more focus on people from different cultures or at least on a part of their life. This slice of culture may be the world of work, or inventions over the years, or a famous artist. Museums are filled with a wealth of real things and

Journal of Museum Education 15, no. 1 (Winter 1990): 1–15.

replicas of people, places, processes, and events. Most important, museums are places for teaching and learning.

G. W. Maxim describes learning experiences for young students through three modes of contact with the material to be learned.[4] One is through the symbolic mode. The symbolic mode is by far the most prevalent in elementary schools, and it almost always takes the written form. Yet, while literacy is much valued in our society, experts tell us that the symbolic mode is highly abstract and too advanced for many elementary school–age pupils. Their concrete stage of cognitive development may not permit sufficient comprehension of the material even if the word symbols are recognized. The limited experience of most young children further limits the use of the symbolic mode.

The second type of contact is what Maxim refers to as the iconic mode. This mode involves "imagery" or the use of representations of the actual through physical models, films, and other means. Student-made dioramas or scenes from a unit of study are examples that can be found in classrooms. Pioneer life might be presented by means of a small-scale but lifelike model of a frontier town. Iconic material need not, however, be to scale; the important thing is that it illustrate in realistic form what is being taught. Students may have an opportunity to interact with iconic material through some kind of hands-on experience, but most often they experience it through the medium of film.

The enactive mode is the third form of learning experience. It is learning through the use of authentic items, events, ideas, and people. This form is only rarely used in classrooms, but it does occur when, for example, a community resource person is brought in to do a demonstration or students are taken on a field trip to observe a process. Because the enactive form requires planning, coordination, and possible fees, learners are not often exposed to the "real thing."

Yet the iconic and enactive modes are the most successful because younger learners learn best by doing and "just messing around" with materials and ideas, by experiencing through touching, hearing, seeing, smelling, and tasting. Firsthand interaction with learning materials tantalizes senses not usually exercised in symbolic school experiences. At best, textbooks provide facts and information about names, dates, places, and events, but models and authentic experiences "breathe life" into the print on the page.

At the same time, museums are incredibly rich with iconic and enactive learning opportunities. They furnish firsthand experiences and allow for learning by discovery. One museum, for example, offers a "Try-out Tools Kit" of materials from a prehistoric culture. Through their objects museums can provide the knowledge and stimulate the thinking skills, social and academic skills, and values and attitudes that can help achieve society's goals for multicultural living.

While all the kinds of learning that museums foster are important, their promotion of knowledge, values, and attitudes is most essential in the achievement of positive multiculturalism. Since museums frequently present different cultures at various points in time, their contribution to greater understanding and appreciation of different lifeways can be invaluable. Many museums state that their goal is to enhance the visitors' ability to understand, appreciate, and respect the cultures they feature. This goal can be accomplished through responsible and sensitive teaching practices in collecting, exhibiting, and explaining artifacts and ideas.

In museum education, as in any education, the educators are the critical variable. It is they who make the goals of acceptance, appreciation, and respect attainable. As teachers, they provide the inspiration for others to adopt pluralism as a positive goal to strive for.

The critical variable that begins with the teacher requires constant self-scrutiny.[5] Museum educators, like everyone else, have developed their share of biases and prejudices. Educators are often reluctant to admit that they harbor feelings and attitudes that relegate lesser status to certain groups. Like most people, they tend to think of prejudice and racism as blatant expressions of hatred toward those who are different. Since most educators do not perceive themselves as blatant discriminators, they might see themselves as free of prejudice. Yet their "color-blind" approach may be nothing more than a veneer of acceptance over true feelings, just below the surface, that remain unexamined and so ready to come into play. Dealing with these biases begins with awareness. Once the biases have been recognized, action can be taken to correct prejudices and to develop more suitable attitudes and behaviors.

It is important to recognize that the perception of the culturally different almost always involves some degree of ethnocentrism. The perceiver's own culture naturally tends to be the standard against which others are measured and is quite unconsciously accorded superior status.[6] The danger is that such measurement tends to obstruct understanding. Museum educators come into contact with school children who hold varying degrees of ethnocentrism, and the educators cannot be held responsible for that. They do have to assume responsibility, however, for the impression they leave with the school children.

It is extremely important that museum educators do not encourage the natural tendency toward ethnocentrism through insensitive dissemination of information. Instead, they should provide a context for the cultures they present, explaining the circumstances of time, place, and situation the people of the culture faced.

For many visitors both young and old, the museum may be the only "educational" contact they have had with another culture. The impression they get from the museum will persist in future encounters, be they casual conversation about the culture or face-to-face associations with the people and their descendants.

Proper presentation of a culture begins with a sound preparation for working with young people and a thorough knowledge about the culture to be shared. The knowledge should be accurate, up to date, and deep enough to cover what is significant for young learners. The presentation should allow the learners to understand people in terms of universal concerns as well as differing responses. Detailed information helps educators present individual artifacts in broad context.

Projectile points, for example, can be presented as important food-gathering tools as well as viable weapons for use against the enemy. Recognizing similar needs and cross-cultural concerns provides a framework within which young learners can achieve understanding and empathy.[7] It is also an effective means for combatting stereotypes, which develop by identifying those who are different through only a few isolated, salient features.

Knowledge also provides a basis with which to model respect for the culture. It is very important, for example, to know and respect a culture's prescribed practice for disposal of the dead. Some cultures believe that the spirit of the dead resides in the remains and will never be at rest until the remains are properly placed in the final resting site. Violating mores like these denigrates museums and those who run them. And insensitivity propagates insensitivity. On this issue of human remains, one Asian-American woman remarked, "Anglos have no sense of right and wrong, and that's just the way they are!" The victim culture will not be the only one to react with disdain on such matters. Many informed groups outside a culture have protested insensitive treatment of one group by another.

In situations where it is permissible to share skeletal remains, the sharing should always be with the utmost respect and dignity. An example of a serious breach of respect occurred in a display of the remains of a prehistoric woman at a much-visited museum. The museum staff renamed her Esther. No doubt the idea was that the name would affectionately personalize the woman, but in reality the name encouraged her to become the brunt of modern-day humor among the museum employees. This humor, thought to be clever, was shared, to the delight of museum visitors. One day Esther was adorned with a tourist hat and sunglasses and a cute notation at her side. After a while she became just a joke.

Callous, inhumane treatment of people and cultures should not be condoned, especially by those charged with the task of developing respect and appreciation for world cultures. Consider that none of us would want to have our remains or those of our loved ones on public display, much less be the brunt of jokes no matter how innocent the intent. Second, such treatment not only violates common decency across cultures but repulses many people. But most tragically, it sends a clear message to school children that it is perfectly acceptable to treat other human beings in this manner as long as they are not a member of one's immediate concern.

Religion is an area that is highly susceptible to misinterpretation and ridicule, particularly religions that are not Judeo-Christian. A religion that is not fully understood may appear to be "odd" or superstitious. That does not mean, however, that it cannot serve its people or that those who practice it are simpleminded pagans. When shamans are discussed, for example, they are often confused with witch doctors, magicians, and medicine men. Even when the term "medicine man" is correctly applied, it is often thought to suggest primitivism that closes off understanding. Yet the unexplained cannot be explained through scientific reasoning or modern-day religion. The truth of the matter is that many modern-day religions do not fare much better in their explanations of the metaphysical, resorting to faith as the catchall justification through which the unexplained becomes acceptable.

Some cultures have artifacts that are regarded as highly sensitive and even forbidden because of their deep religious significance. That is, the artifact and the meaning it holds are not to be shared with nonmembers of the culture. In some cases they are not to be shared with members who are not yet privileged: children who have not reached a predetermined stage of maturity or adults who have not been initiated.

While this meaning may seem like nothing more than information and so legitimate for sharing by the general public, museum educators need to take care that nonprivileged members of the culture are not exposed to the meaning. It is not always possible to honor a specific taboo, yet museum educators, particularly when they take a traveling display to a classroom, need to be alert to the composition of the student audience. One example of a forbidden artifact is the kachina doll or model of the Pueblo Indian spirit in the Southwest. Kachinas are considered highly sacred and should be respected accordingly. To the people of the Pueblo culture, museum displays or programs using kachinas violate the taboo that the dolls should not be seen in any form outside the ceremonial context. To them such a display or sharing is as sacrilegious as permitting children to play with a holy communion host would be to Roman Catholics. In both instances the artifacts were intended to be shared only under well-defined conditions. Some cultures represented in museums no longer exist, but there are others whose members maintain traditions, and issues regarding the display and treatment of their artifacts are increasingly sensitive.

There are other taboos of a less severe nature that still need to be acknowledged if not adhered to, especially if it is known that the cultural group will be affected in a personal way. Telling or reading stories designated for seasonal use are examples. One culture may have stories for winter use only. If possible, those should be read in winter only, and the seasonal associations should be explained. Such action is a lesson in respect for all cultures. In this way, children develop the caring and sensitivity that are essential to the values and attitudes of positive multicultural education.

In summary, museums offer young learners experiences that are highly desirable for their developmental level and have the potential to involve multiple senses in a discovery learning format. The content of this museum learning is often the culture of a people. Thus museum educators are in an excellent position to develop ideas and attitudes critical to the success of young learners in understanding and ultimately participating in our multicultural world.

Notes

1. C. E. Sleeter and C. A. Grant, "An Analysis of Multicultural Education in the United States," *Harvard Educational Review* 57, no. 4 (1987): 421–40; Hilda Hernandez, *Multicultural Education: A Teacher's Guide to Content and Process* (Columbus, Ohio: Merrill, 1989).

2. American Association of Colleges for Teacher Education, *AACTA Statement on Multicultural Education* (Washington, D.C.: AACTA, 1972–73).

3. P. G. Ramsey, "Multicultural Education in Early Childhood," *Young Children* 37, no. 2 (1982): 13–24.

4. G. W. Maxim, *Social Studies and the Elementary School Child* (Columbus, Ohio: Merrill, 1987), pp. 267–68.

5. M. J. Gold, C. A. Grant, and H. N. Rivlin, *In Praise of Diversity: A Resource Book for Multicultural Education* (Washington, D.C.: Teacher Corps, Association of Teacher Educators, 1977).

6. P. G. Ramsey, *Teaching and Learning in a Diverse World: Multicultural Education for Young Children* (New York: Teachers College Press, 1987).

7. J. E. Moyer and Guillermina Engelbrecht, "Multicultural Education: Where Do We Begin?" *Childhood Education* 53 (March 1977): 241–44.

CONSIDERING
THE MUSEUM EXPERIENCE

INTRODUCTION
New Directions for Research

Judy Diamond

The opportunity to study learning in a naturalistic setting spawned almost a century of research efforts in museums. Now, near the end of the century, we can look back and ask whether our understanding of informal learning has improved as a result. Have we gained insight into how people learn from their experiences with real objects? More important, do we know whether visitors' experiences with exhibits help them understand other events in their lives?

The early museum research described in Mary Ellen Munley's article in this section furnished a few generalizations about the behavior of people in museums. Arthur Melton, Edward Robinson, and other researchers of the 1920s and 1930s confirmed that visitors tend to turn right on entering galleries, that they show a predictable exit gradient, moving faster as they near the end of a hall, and that they remain longer at moving objects than at static exhibits. Significantly, these researchers also found extraordinary variety in the learning styles and attitudes of museum visitors.

More recent work on family behavior in museums, described by Lynn D. Dierking and by Marcia Brumit Kropf, also provides some general notions. There are, for example, striking and consistent sex differences among museum visitors. It is now well documented that families engage in much active interpretation of museum experiences, some of which appears to make the visit more meaningful by relating events to things already familiar. Other kinds of family interaction, however, can trivialize museum experiences, as when parents add their own prejudices and misconceptions to the events of a visit.

Has this research helped us design better museum learning environments for families? Maybe. Does it tell us how to design our halls so visitors will turn left, slow down, pay more attention to our graphics, become better teachers? Not necessarily. We need to know much more.

Research conducted in museums has drawn on a relatively diverse set of disciplines. Melton, Robinson, and John Balling, among others, used the methodologies and insights of psychology. The physicist Elsa Feher adapted the clinical interview methods of the developmental psychologist Jean Piaget. Sherman B. Rosenfeld, Mark St. John, and Samuel M. Taylor used naturalistic observation and interview techniques first derived from anthropology. John H. Falk's methods drew on various disciplines including ecology, while I utilized the observation techniques from ethology. Many others, including John J. Koran and Mary Lou Koran and Minda Borun and her colleagues, rely on methods drawn from educational research.[1] The fact that museum research need not be constrained by a single disciplinary approach is a strength of this area that should be further exploited.

Existing museum research efforts have raised important questions about informal learning that might usefully be pursued by examining and encouraging work in other contexts.[2] Three areas of research have relevance for museum researchers: developmental approaches to concept learning, the study of natural memory processes, and human factors research.

The field of developmental psychology has useful perspectives for understanding learning in museums. Ronald Vukelich provides striking examples of the influence of age and development on understanding time concepts in museums and recommends specific ways to word labels that will be meaningful to children of different ages.[3] Such developmental research can provide specific recommendations for designing multilevel exhibits that will reach diverse audiences by functioning in different ways for different age groups.

How memory functions in museums remains an intriguing and important issue. Most of us have encountered adults who have very specific childhood memories of museum exhibits. We have some evidence that short-term visitors to museums remember specific details of exhibits three months later.[4] In our study of teenagers who worked at the Exploratorium for several months, we found that subjects remembered details of exhibits as much as 15 years later. One example from the Exploratorium study suggests that such memories may be powerful learning aids:

> Some time after leaving the museum, a teenaged explainer saw a movie about a space battle, full of much battle fire and loud explosions. She immediately knew that the space battle could not be realistic, because she remembered an Exploratorium exhibit that demonstrates that sound is not conducted in a vacuum, like outer space.[5]

This example is evidence of significant learning in a museum: remembering the exhibit was used to make sense of new information.

The psychology of remembering in natural contexts is being actively explored by a number of researchers. Ulrich Neisser and his colleagues are now asking how people use their own past experiences in understanding the present and the future.[6] This research involves studying how memory functions under natural conditions, including the circumstances in which it occurs, the form it takes, the variables on which it depends, and the differences among individuals in their uses of the past. Such work conducted in museums would give us insight into how museum experiences can be applied to understanding events at home and in school.

Learning in interactive museums has much to do with learning tasks. Frank Oppenheimer pioneered the concept that exhibit design should be fully integrated with user feedback.[7] Patricia A. McNamara's description in this section of formative exhibit evaluation shows how this concept is being used in other museums.

These human elements of design have long been familiar to engineers and psychologists working in human factors research, and there is a well-established journal by that name. More recently, Donald A. Norman has emphasized the cognitive consequences of interacting with everyday objects and produced useful guidelines for anyone involved with three-dimensional design. Jill H. Larkin examines in fine detail the steps involved in completing everyday tasks such as making a cup of coffee.[8] Such cognitive research can help museums to understand how visitors—through design, graphics, and interpreters—can be led through a complex series of steps to learn a task or a concept.

Museums can easily become isolated from academic settings. The procedures and programs of museums often do not have well-established links to analogous work in universities. Whether research on informal learning makes significant progress in the future may well be determined by the ability of museums to attract people from academic research units who can help inject new theoretical concepts, research methodologies, and research standards into the field of informal learning.

Notes

1. Arthur Melton, *Problems of Installation in Museums of Art,* n.s. no. 14 (Washington, D.C.: American Association of Museums, 1935); Edward S. Robinson, *The Behavior of the Museum Visitor,* n.s. no. 5 (Washington, D.C.: American Association of Museums, 1928); John Balling, D. D. Hilke, Joan D. Liversidge, Elizabeth A. Cornell, and Nancy S. Perry, eds., *The Role of the Family in the Promotion of Science Literacy,* final report SED 81–12927 (Washington, D.C.: National Science Foundation, 1985); Elsa Feher, "Interactive Museum Exhibits as Tools for Learning: Explorations with Light," *International Journal for Science Education* 12, no. 1 (1990): 35–49; Sherman B. Rosenfeld, "Informal Learning in Zoos: Naturalistic Studies of Family Groups" (Ph.D. diss., University of California, Berkeley, 1980); Mark St. John, *First-Hand Learning: Teacher Education in Science Museums* (Washington, D.C.: Association of Science-Technology Centers, 1990); Samuel M. Taylor, "Understanding Processes of Informal Education: A Naturalistic Study of Visitors to a Public Aquarium" (Ph.D. diss., University of California, Berkeley, 1986); John H. Falk, "Time and Behavior as Predictors of Learning," *Science Education* 67 (1983): 267–76; Judy Diamond, "The Ethology of Teaching: A Perspective from the Observations of Families in Science Centers" (Ph.D. diss., University of California, Berkeley, 1980); John J. Koran and Mary Lou Koran, "The Relationship of Age, Sex, Attention, and Holding Power with Two Types of Science Exhibits," *Curator* 29, no. 3 (1986): 227–36; Minda Borun, Barbara K. Flexer, Alice F. Casey, and Lynn R. Baum, *Planets and Pulleys: Studies of Class Visits to Science Museums* (Philadelphia: Franklin Institute Science Museum, 1983).

2. Elsa Feher and Judy Diamond, "Science Centers as Research Laboratories," in *What Research Says about Learning in Science Museums,* ed. Beverly Serrell (Washington, D.C.: Association of Science-Technology Centers, 1990), pp. 26–28.

3. Feher, "Interactive Museum Exhibits"; Nina Jensen, "Children, Teenagers, and Adults in Museums: A Developmental Perspective," *Museum News* 60, no. 5 (May/June 1981): 25–36; Ronald Vukelich, "Time Language for Interpreting History Collections to Children," *Museum Studies Journal* 1, no. 4 (Fall 1984): 43–50.

4. Judy Diamond, "The Behavior of Family Groups in Science Museums," *Curator* 29, no. 2 (1986): 139–54.

5. Judy Diamond, Mark St. John, Beth Cleary, and Darlene Librero, "The Exploratorium's Explainer Program: The Long-Term Impacts on Teenagers of Teaching Science to the Public," *Science Education* 71, no. 5 (1987): 643–56.

6. Ulrich Neisser, *Memory Observed: Remembering in Natural Contexts* (San Francisco: W. H. Freeman, 1982).

7. Frank Oppenheimer, *Working Prototypes: Exhibit Design at the Exploratorium* (San Francisco: The Exploratorium, 1986).

8. Donald A. Norman, *The Design of Everyday Objects* (New York: Doubleday, 1990); Jill H. Larkin, "Display-Based Problem Solving," in *Twenty-First Carnegie Symposium on Cognition: Complex Information Processing, The Impact of Herbert S. Simon,* ed. D. Klahr and K. Kotovsky (Hillsdale, N.J.: L. Erlbaum and Assoc., 1989), pp. 319–41.

INTRODUCTION

Evaluating Visitors' Conversations with Exhibits

Mark St. John

Suppose that by some gross error in planning, all of the exhibits in a museum were sent out for repair and cleaning on the same day. And suppose that the staff of that museum, when they realized their error, decided to stand in for the exhibits themselves. Let us also suppose that they put the relevant phenomena or objects out on the floor and then, standing next to them, tried to have conversations with the visitors that would achieve the same goals they had sought to achieve when they designed the exhibits. What do you suppose we would see?

Would we see the staff saying the same things that the exhibit labels do? Would they try to engage the visitors with the phenomena? Would they lecture? Would they coach? Or would they be quiet? Would they answer the visitors' questions? Would they try to find out what those questions were? How would they know what the visitors already know? But would they seek to meet the visitors' interests, or would they pursue their own goals? Even more interesting would be the task of evaluating these exhibit stand-ins. How do we evaluate the quality or value of a conversation? Would we want to pretest and posttest visitors on their knowledge gains? Would we simply ask them if they enjoyed their interactions? Would we ask them to tell us about the most memorable or surprising conversations they had?

It is an interesting and, I think, relevant, exercise to consider how we might evaluate the success of a conversation. Looking at visitors interacting with exhibits as two-way conversations might lead us to ask the following questions:

■ How much and in what ways are the visitors engaged by the exhibits?

■ What are the conversations about? Who initiates them?

■ What do the visitors ask about? How do the exhibits answer these questions?

■ What do the exhibits ask about? How do the visitors respond to these questions?

■ Why do some conversations go well and others fail?

■ What do the conversations tell us about the images the staff have of the visitors? What do the visitors think the staff are trying to communicate? Are visitors and staff meeting, or are they "like ships passing in the night"?

■ What, then, does the conversation tell us about the nature of the relationship between the visitors and the staff with whom they are talking?

Studying the way that visitors and staff relate through the exhibits might tell us about the degree to which communication is happening. This focus, I argue, would allow us a new perspective on understanding the role and efficacy of our museums as measured in the currency of visitor experience.

In thinking about research and evaluation in the museum setting, it is important to examine the relation of the research effort to the enterprise being studied. In particular, it is important to ask if we have reached a point in the evolution and history of museums where there is great clarity and consensus about the mission and roles of museums. If there is strong consensus, then the function of evaluation and research would be to document outcomes and share the achievements within an agreed-upon framework. Research could then, in a technical way, help to fine-tune our efforts.

If, on the other hand, we have reached a period where there is debate and confusion about the role and associated design of museums, then research and evaluation need to play a very different and less technical role. They need to help the field understand itself, reflect on its mission, illuminate arguments, and ground itself in the reality of what happens in museums. Current debates about the most productive approaches to museum research and evaluation probably reflect the underlying ambiguities about the museum enterprise itself.

During the last two decades there has been a marked emphasis on an "educational" role for museums, particularly science museums. Museums are embracing the thinking (and funding) of the nation's educational reform efforts. Expanding beyond the curatorial role, museums now propose that they should primarily help people learn about the complex physical, technological, and social world in which they live.

As we all know, the assessment of what people learn in museums is not a trivial exercise. I would argue the first mistake we can make is to start from the assumption that a primary function of research and evaluation in museums is to measure what people learn. This approach is wrought with misconception and oversimplicity. While museums would love to prove that they are, in fact, succeeding at educating people, research efforts guided by this goal are, I believe, ultimately not productive. Rather, the function of research and evaluation should be broader and more introverted, leading to more insightful ways of conceptualizing and articulating the role of museums. Many of the articles in this section argue, although more obliquely, for the same shift in emphasis in our research and evaluation efforts.

Mary Ellen Munley makes an argument for a long-term and systematic approach to research in the museum setting. I agree with much of what she says. For example, many good ideas emerge from local research and evaluation studies that could be shared and pursued more broadly. She also notes that the museum is a natural setting for investigations of many different types. She calls for a movement to identify and support specific museum settings to serve as ongoing laboratories.

Munley points to another difficulty in establishing "learning" as the single focus of our studies. "Museums are about objects," she writes, "yet very few evaluations or research studies concentrate on how and what visitors learn from objects." Munley appropriately calls for more ethnographic research as a starting point. I agree with this approach, partly because it provides a platform for understanding what is actually happening in the museum but, more important, because it examines the world from the visitor's as well as the designer's point of view. Perhaps such research and evaluation will ultimately help us to identify more "appropriate outcome variables," but for the moment it is enough if it helps us understand the interactions (and conversations) happening in our museums.

Patricia A. McNamara describes an evaluation approach that, in contrast to a long-term research effort, is aimed at understanding the workings of specific exhibits. She argues that it is worthwhile to focus closely on what happens when visitors and exhibits interact and to watch the conversations that take place. By making incremental changes in our exhibits based on close observations and probing questions, we can not only make our exhibits better, but we can also perhaps glean more general lessons about what makes for successful (and unsuccessful) interactions between people and exhibits.

McNamara provides a good, if slightly vague, standard of when an exhibit is working—when the visitors "profit" from their interactions with the exhibit. She also argues that it is important to "document their confusion," find questions that illuminate the inner nature of their experience and thinking, and work with fewer visitors in greater depth.

Valorie Beer investigates the proposition that museums have "curriculum." Perhaps, she argues, by using the constructs of curriculum theorists (e.g., goals, teaching strategies, learning activities, and evaluation), we could better understand the museum experience. While I applaud the attempt, I confess I find the heuristic approach more dangerous than beneficial. The Latin root of the word "curriculum" means "the course to be run," and I worry that this metaphor is not the best one for framing the experience of a museum visitor. (Too often, I think, designers feel they must lead visitors through a preestablished course of ideas and concepts.)

Beer's analysis becomes more interesting when she asks, "What are the agreements and discrepancies between curriculum as planned by staff and as experienced by visitors?" Studies that examine the match of staff and visitor curriculums (like watching the nature of the conversation that happens) shed "light on the gulf that sometimes separates staff and visitors." I would agree with her when she goes on to suggest that the "primary target of museum curriculums may not be the visitor" (and certainly not the visitor's experience). Perhaps our research and evaluation studies could help illuminate the curricular gulf between designer and visitor and even help make explicit some of our own "hidden curriculums."

Lynn D. Dierking and Marcia Brumit Kropf summarize in their articles much of the research done to date about families in informal learning environments. While the focus on families is useful, I find most interesting the ideas that are general to all visitors. In particular, Dierking and Kropf point out that museum visitors come with their own agendas. One key part of this agenda is simply being together as a social unit. But the most important implication of this research is perhaps simple and obvious—that designers must know, acknowledge, and start from the interests and agendas of the visitors and focus on more than the "messages" that they feel are so important to get across.

Marlene Chambers works in an art museum, an environment not as heavily slanted toward "learning" as are science museums. It is not surprising, then, that she focuses more on experience than on learning. In particular, she is concerned with the nature of esthetic experiences and how visitors might be helped to achieve a kind of connoisseurship. As one who works primarily in science museums, I find her interest in "experience-driven" interpretive models very appealing. She regards museums primarily as places that allow for different (heightened) kinds of visitor experiences. She refers to Mihaly Csikszentmihalyi's concept of "flow" to make even more explicit the nature of experience that is valued.

In looking at science museums and the "aha" experience they offer visitors, Chambers points out the contradiction that exists when designers want to teach visitors the "proven" facts or principles of science and at the same time allow them the excitement of real exploration. She asks if we are to be "information-driven" or "experience-driven"—a dilemma for many museums and a question that evaluation and research can help illuminate more clearly by examining closely the match of exhibit design and visitor experience.

At some point it may even be possible to differentiate and understand our audiences in the same way that advertisers understand the public as a set of "publics." Barbara Birney and Carolyn Heinrich point out how we might use detailed knowledge about visitor demographics to inform interpretive design. They examine such issues as age and its correlation with attitudes toward wildlife, the preference of certain groups for certain kinds of exhibits, and, most important, the educational background of our visitors, which we know little about. Comparative studies, they point out, can help us find what is specific and what is generalizable in the wide range of visitors we attract. Most important, I feel, is the fact that in yet another way Birney and Heinrich reinforce the idea that we need to be able to "converse" with the visitors who come to us. When we reach the point that the exhibit and interpretive design processes truly do incorporate the authentic interests, questions, and concerns of visitors, then a finer-grained understanding of visitors is going to be very useful. While at the moment it is not clear (at least to me) exactly how we might "fine-tune" our exhibits based on these differences, I think we need to be addressing these questions and arguing for their importance.

One motif that runs throughout these articles is the implicit relationship between museum designers and museum visitors. If we look at our exhibits as surrogates for museum staff on the floor conversing with visitors, we can find a framework for future research and evaluation efforts. The knowledge we gain through such studies can tell us about the degree to which and the ways in which we are communicating with our visitors. We can study the relationship between designer and visitor in many different ways. But the important point is that by making "relationship" rather than "learning" the primary object of our study, our research efforts include ourselves for the first time. By examining our own intentions and actions, we may become wiser about ourselves and the enterprise we are engaged in.

Back to the Future: A Call for Coordinated Research Programs in Museums

Mary Ellen Munley

Research about learning in the museum has received little attention. By measure of activity alone the practice of museum evaluation has fared better. When asked if their museums conduct evaluations, nearly all museum professionals respond in the affirmative. It has become nearly axiomatic: Evaluation is central to sound management and decision making and has therefore become a part of responsible museum management.

Though these reports are encouraging, there is something unsettling about both the discussion and the practice of evaluation and audience research in museums. My discomfort begins with definitions. We are not all talking about the same thing when we use the terms "evaluation," "audience research," or "education research." For me, these terms represent three different types of activities, and as I listen to how museum professionals use the terms I find they carry even more meanings.

Evaluation as it is most commonly practiced refers to a process of self-analysis and review—an activity central to quality performance by professionals. Thus it is difficult to imagine a museum that does not engage in this type of evaluation of its programs and exhibits. The staff consider whether their offerings are good or bad, whether they need appropriate standards, and whether they are proud of their efforts.

By tradition evaluation has taken on another meaning in the museum setting. This second type of evaluation activity is less commonly practiced. Evaluation has come to describe all systematic efforts to examine the effectiveness of exhibits and programs from the perspective of the audience. Evaluators systematically track visitors' patterns through exhibits, determine which parts of an exhibit attract and hold interest, and interview visitors about their reactions to specific exhibits and programs. Such careful analysis of programs is commendable, but it is not research.

Similarities and differences between evaluation and research are worth remembering. Both evaluation and research attempt to describe the museum setting, trace sequences of behavior, and understand the relationships between visitors and museum offerings. Both use research methods to gather information, and each may even make use of experimental design in an effort to compare, for

Journal of Museum Education 11, no. 1 (Winter 1986): 3–6.

example, performance by comparable groups before and after viewing an exhibit or by groups exposed to different types of interpretive strategies.

Methods and subject matter do not distinguish evaluation and research. Evaluation and research differ in intent. Evaluation is intended to gather information that will be of immediate value. An evaluation can help a staff modify an interactive exhibit or can assess a program's success in meeting stated goals. Questions to be answered by an evaluation are based on the information needs of museum decision makers. Evaluators work in the actual setting of a program or exhibit; they deal directly with program planners and presenters and report their results to those same people in whatever form is most appropriate.

Research is quite different in intent. Research is driven by a generalized desire to know more. There may not be an immediate need for the findings, and research questions are more likely to come from the researcher or from a theoretical proposition intriguing enough to suggest testing and possible confirmation. Research requires methodological rigor. Research requirements influence decisions about sampling, location, and study procedures. Results tend to be widely disseminated through publications in an effort to contribute to theory development and a growing body of knowledge.

Probably the best examples of research studies in a museum setting were initiated in 1925, when a group of Yale professors, including the renowned psychologist Edward Thorndike, suggested a psychological study of the public museum. An initial grant to the American Association of Museums (AAM) by the Carnegie Corporation of New York allowed Edward S. Robinson of Yale University to conduct a 10-year program of research about visitor behavior in the museum.

Robinson and his associate, Arthur Melton, involved several notable museums in their research. In a speech at the 1926 annual meeting of the AAM in New York City, Robinson announced that "no real progress could be made in the understanding of the educational operations of the public museum until one or two institutions should be willing to modify their exhibits and labels for experimental purposes." His challenge was met by Chauncey J. Hamlin, president of the Buffalo (New York) Museum of Science, and Fiske Kimball, director of the Pennsylvania Museum of Art in Philadelphia. Further grants from Carnegie to the AAM (Arthur Melton was a staff research associate at the AAM during the early 1930s) and then to Yale University allowed for fairly elaborate experimental studies at the Buffalo Museum of Science, the Pennsylvania Museum of Art, the Peabody Museum of Natural History, the Newark Museum, and other museums.

In 1935, 10 years after they began, Robinson and Melton reported the results of their research in a monograph, *Problems of Installation in Museums of Art*. This monograph was one in a series of AAM publications edited by Robinson called the New Series.[1] The work of Robinson, Melton, and their associates abruptly stopped in 1936 with the publication of the New Series monograph number 15, *Experimental*

Studies of the Education of Children in a Museum of Science. A review of programs from AAM annual meetings show that the researchers gave their last presentation in 1935, and nothing from the group appears in *Museum News* or any other museum publication after 1936.

There has been no similar major, systematic effort to study the public museum since the work of Robinson and his associates. Instead, efforts have been scattered and emphasis has switched to evaluation and the more practical focus on program modification and assessment of program effectiveness. The result is a muddled view of both evaluation and research and little idea of what we do know about visitor behavior in the museum.

Fortunately, interest is turning once again to the museum's responsibility to its audiences and to the value of research. Although several decades have passed since the last coordinated research effort, the stage is set now to resume the kind of audience research pioneered by Robinson and his colleagues. Interest in visitors, their behavior, and learning in the museum is at an all-time high. People are beginning to see that museum education is not confined to special programs designed by the education department. The team approach to exhibit development suggests that a good exhibit is not only substantively strong, esthetically pleasing, and communicative but attentive to visitors' expectations and needs for learning. *Museums for a New Century* calls on museums to examine their potential as learning environments and to articulate their distinctive contribution in the realm of object-based, informal, voluntary, and lifelong learning. A commission recommendation explicitly calls for research about museum learning.[2]

In the commission report, leaders of the profession embrace learning as a defining element of the museum. The museum's responsibility to learning, like its responsibility to collections, requires commitment, resources, and constant attention. More and more curators, administrators, and exhibit designers seek information from audience studies that might inform their decisions. However, we have not yet developed adequate answers to the kinds of questions being asked about the museum as learning environment—and that is a shame.

We no longer need to convince people that learning is an important part of the museum experience. Our challenge is to organize a research program so that we can explore the questions already dominating professional conversations. We need a systematic effort to determine what is already known about learning in the museum and then to develop programs of research to further expand that knowledge. This is what must be done:

1. *Conduct a review of extant evaluation and visitor research findings.* Museum evaluation and visitor research is an applied science. Justification for the activity rests on its contribution to improved practice. Virtually hundreds of evaluations and scores of research studies have been conducted in museums, but the results are known to very few people. Information is embedded in hundreds of published

articles and perhaps thousands of occasional papers from conferences and in reports of studies whose results were prepared only for a particular museum.

Before we embark on new avenues of research—and to guard against conducting research to answer questions already sufficiently addressed—I propose that time and resources be devoted to finding out what we already know. A bibliography—even an annotated one—is not sufficient. Museum practitioners need critical reviews of existing literature. Studies vary in quality, sophistication, and applicability to the museum setting. The reports need to be reviewed for methodological rigor, and separate findings need to be synthesized. If evaluation and research are to be accepted as necessary to responsible program development, then practitioners must see their usefulness. Talking about the intrinsic value of research will not win the day. Presentation of evaluation and research results in a format that makes them interesting to exhibit designers, educators, and curators is what is needed.

2. *Establish a clearinghouse for evaluation and research.* The museum profession needs a central location where study reports can be gathered, abstracted, and cataloged. Through a clearinghouse professionals could gain access to studies and be kept informed of research and evaluation activities in museums across the country. Equally important, the clearinghouse could compile and disseminate information about evaluation procedures and research methods. The clearinghouse needs a location, a carefully designed computer system, and sufficient staff to assure that records of research activities are current.

3. *Develop a systematic program of research.* The evaluation literature is teeming with intriguing concepts and fascinating hypotheses just waiting for prolonged research. At the most, a typical evaluation is conducted over a six-month period in a museum. Issues for the investigation are tied to a specific exhibit or program, and evaluators are usually cautious about generalizing findings beyond the specific program or exhibit being evaluated. As a result, there is little carryover of concepts and research questions from study to study.

In my own work, evaluations have produced ideas worthy of further study. I have identified concepts and speculated about explanations for visitor behavior, but given the restriction of evaluation, it has been impossible to pursue investigation of these hypotheses in any depth. It would be interesting to know, for instance, if the hierarchy of information needs we found among visitors in an exhibit about 18th-century tools would be replicated in other settings.[3]

In that same study we found that attention to particular parts of an exhibit were gender-determined. Women, for instance, looked at cases of items used in an 18th-century kitchen, while men looked at cases of lighting fixtures and farm equipment. Furthermore, we observed that the groupings of objects in the exhibit seemed to encourage the tendency of the sexes to go separate ways. As the exhibit was designed, men rarely viewed artifacts traditionally used by women. The reverse was also true. While it is clear that the sexes had very distinct responsibilities in the 18th century, grouping objects by primary user is not the only option. Perhaps more visitors would attend to the objects if they were arranged using an organizing concept such as the time of day. This observation proved stimulating to the museum staff. But it also suggests a research program focused on experimenting with object groupings so that the museum might combat limited viewing by visitors that is unconsciously guided by social norms.

With a broader, more theoretical perspective regarding what happens in museums, several questions for research present themselves. What might museums contribute to knowledge about visual learning and visual literacy? What might behavior in the museum teach us about self-directed learning? And what would longitudinal studies tell us about developing esthetic sensibility and cultural sensitivity during a lifetime? The museum is a natural setting for such investigations.

4. *Identify museums willing to serve as laboratories for the study of museum learning specifically and informal learning generally.* Research about museum learning must be conducted in a museum setting. Museums will need the counsel of research methodologists as they begin their studies, but the research initiative and research activities need to come from museums. Currently there is no museum in this country with a program about visitor behavior and learning. Only a handful have committed resources to evaluation activities. Until a few institutions take the lead and begin to support and carry out audience research, we will see little progress.

5. *Create a place for social scientists on the museum staff and train people for the position.* A person responsible for directing evaluations or an audience research program must have formal training in a social science, including training in a research methodology. Traditionally, research and evaluation efforts in museums have been marred because the principal investigators were not properly trained. Many studies use sound methodology, but they fail because the focus of the study is inappropriate and lacks sensitivity to the special features of museums as learning environments. The emphasis in most evaluation studies on visitors' comprehension of label copy is a prime example of the limitation of studies designed by people familiar with more formal learning environments where mastery of words is important. Museums are about objects, yet very few evaluations or research studies concentrate on how and what visitors learn from objects.

Knowledge of research methods, principles of questionnaire construction, sampling, and statistics is necessary for any person directing a museum evaluation or research program. In addition, the evaluator or research director must be a highly skilled participant-observer and interviewer. Again, many existing study reports are of little value because the procedures used to gather information are so suspect that conclusions drawn from them lack validity.

In addition to methodological expertise, training in a social science provides theoretical foundations for thinking about visitors' museum experiences. Statements of hypotheses and analysis of research findings are influenced by the knowledge of the researcher. In my opinion, graduate training should include the study of perception, interpersonal communication, and ways of knowing. Understanding the content and relational parts of every message, individual differences in tolerance for ambiguity, and the influences of attitudes, beliefs, and values on perception are necessary for making sense of what is observed in a museum exhibit or program.

A new kind of expert is needed in the museum. Training programs should be established so that people with museum experience can learn about social science research and theory. Conversely, a program is needed to acquaint interested social scientists with the museum setting before they actually plan evaluations and design research studies.

A Modest Agenda for Research

Research efforts need a conceptual direction, and several research agendas suggest themselves. I am committed to two in particular:

Ethnographic Research

We still have simple questions to ask about visitor behavior. Until we have a more thorough understanding of the nature of visitors' experiences and expectations for museums, highly sophisticated hypothesizing and investigations strike me as premature. Again, I return to 1928 and Edward Robinson's thoughts on directions for museum research:

> When first the possibility suggested itself of a scientific study of the behavior of the museum visitor there was talk of refined physiological technique. There were thoughts of catching the visitor before and after his artistic or scientific excursion and of determining subtle differentials of blood pressure, pulse rate, respiration, and psychogalvanic reflex. Almost surely some facts could have been had in such manner— and almost surely nobody would have had the slightest idea what to do with them.[4]

Just as in the 1920s and 1930s, we still have much to learn by a careful study of museums modeled on the ethnographic work of anthropologists and sociologists. I suggest that our questions should stem from basic curiosities. For me, that means that I am still asking: What do people do when they come to the museum? How long do they stay? What do they look at? What do they pass by? What are they hoping to see? And what does looking at objects and artifacts mean to visitors?

Identification of Appropriate Outcome Variables

Determining the appropriate and measurable results of museum visits is not a new issue, but it is critical. Most studies take a limited view of visitors' museum experiences. Typically, evaluation studies measure effectiveness by tallying visitors' satisfaction ratings for a particular exhibit or program. Less frequently, but still quite common, are studies that determine effectiveness by measuring changes in levels of knowledge about an exhibit's topic. Usually these measures focus on acquisition of new information and facts. A few studies examine changes in visitors' attitudes while in the museum.

Longer-term effects of museum visits are virtually unexplored. Nearly all studies are designed to get information from visitors immediately after they experience a program or exhibit. And rarely do investigations systematically chart changes in curiosity, enthusiasm, or delight for something as a result of a museum experience. These are serious omissions.

Museum professionals and museum evaluators and researchers need to talk about what should be considered indicators of successful museum experiences. Anyone who works in a museum or has visited a museum knows that the experience is not adequately described by a report of new facts that were learned; the experience is more complex. Our evaluations and research need to reflect that complexity.

Conclusion

First priority must be given to finding out what we already know about visitors, visitor behavior, and the interaction between visitors and museum offerings. We need a critical review of existing literature and publications that can be available to museum educators, exhibit designers, administrators, and curators. Some museums must be willing to establish research programs and devote adequate resources to them. The profession must recognize the need for a new area of museum expertise and create museum research training programs for experienced museum professionals and social scientists. And as research and evaluation programs begin to develop and flourish, we must not lose sight of the aim of museum and audience research. We cannot let it become an esoteric field of inquiry. It must always help professionals to become thoughtful, well-versed students of the museum as an important educational institution for lifelong learning.

Notes

1. The AAM New Series included the following reports: Marguerite Bloomberg, *An Experiment in Museum Instruction,* no. 8 (1929); Arthur W. Melton, *Problems of Installation in Museums of Art,* no. 14 (1935); Mildred C. B. Porter, *Behavior of the Average Visitor in the Peabody Museum of Natural History, Yale University,* no. 16 (1938); Edward S. Robinson, *The Behavior of the Museum Visitor,* no. 5 (1928).

2. Commission on Museums for a New Century, *Museums for a New Century* (Washington, D.C.: American Association of Museums, 1984).

3. Mary Ellen Munley, *Telltale Tools: An Experimental Exhibit* (Washington, D.C.: Department of Social and Cultural History, National Museum of American History, Smithsonian Institution, 1982).

4. Robinson, *Behavior of the Museum Visitor,* p. 9.

Afterword

On rereading my call for coordinated research programs in museums I am in substantial agreement with the gist of the argument I made five years ago. Systematic efforts to advance our knowledge about learning in museums are still needed.

If I were writing this article today, however, I would give less emphasis to the nitty-gritty of what needs to be done to develop research programs about museum learning. Instead, I would emphasize the central goal of such programs and how that goal must necessarily shape them.

The ultimate goal of research about museum learning is the development and validation of conceptual frameworks that are useful for practitioners in museum settings. This goal suggests two things. First, because the world of practice is one of uncertainty, complexity, and politics, practitioners must often act without a research basis for their actions by identifying the most useful conceptual frameworks they can find and using them, even before they have been thoroughly researched. For example, I have found Carl Rogers's learning theory and his concepts of empathy, personal regard, congruence, and trust useful for thinking about how to develop the best learning environment in the New York State Museum's Discovery Place, although the effects of empathy in this context, for instance, still need to be researched. As a practitioner I will continue to use this conceptual framework as long as it is useful to me. In the meantime, I hope that Rogers's learning theory as it applies to museum learning will be studied so that its effects can be better understood. Philosophers of science speak of the "theory-then-research" approach to theory development, and it is this approach that the realities of practice dictate.

The second implication of the ultimate goal of museum research is that practitioners must take a more active and central role in the research process. Research questions should derive from the issues, concerns, and questions of practitioners and lead to conceptual frameworks that are useful for enhancing their understanding of the museum experience in all of its dimensions. The challenge for museum educators, I believe, is to refrain from too much focus on questions about specific techniques related to teaching and communication. If we are to help articulate questions to guide research, we need to spend more of our effort identifying conceptual frameworks as a foundation for goals, planning, practice, evaluation, and research.

Once research questions have been developed, the practitioner should be actively involved in creating programs and exhibits featuring concrete manifestations of the framework's abstract concepts. When research about empathy in a museum learning center is conducted, for example, the researcher should work closely with the museum practitioner to identify instances when empathy is and is not present.

The researcher reviewing the research literature in the library and the practitioner developing programs and exhibits in the museum's halls need each other. Practitioners lack the tools and training for research, and researchers lack practitioners' in-depth knowledge and experience of the museum setting and mission. The need for research programs aimed at developing conceptual frameworks to inform practice is great. Such programs will be more useful if museum practitioners assume a more central role in their creation and execution.

Visitor Participation in Formative Exhibit Evaluation

Patricia A. McNamara

At the Science Museum of Virginia, formative evaluation has become a routine and integral component of the planning process for most exhibits and programs. During the past five years we have developed a variety of exhibitions, ranging from collections of five or six small displays to major projects occupying several hundred square feet and including 60 or more individual components. The majority of these exhibitions made their first appearance in the Science Museum's public areas as prototypes, that is, as relatively rough and inexpensive approximations of their final, more permanent selves.

The Science Museum's size and character make it a good place to experiment with formative evaluation. Its public exhibition areas have been open only since 1977, and its early exhibits were inexpensive and quickly made adaptations of popular participatory exhibits. The museum's present exhibit areas remain a mix of small-scale, informal exhibits and much larger, formal, more permanent-looking structures. Prototype exhibits become a part of the diversity and seem to be easily assimilated by visitors.

While the museum staff would prefer that all exhibit components be prototyped, the comprehensiveness of prototyping efforts is usually dictated by an exhibition's size and development schedule. *Illusions, Magic, and Science,* a 2,000-square-foot exhibition developed over 18 months, is heavily participatory, and every component was tested during its development. On the other hand, time and resources permitted only about half of approximately 65 individual components of *Crystal World,* a 5,000-square-foot exhibition featuring the science of crystallography, to undergo formative testing.

A current [1987] exhibition project, *Seeing the Universe,* provides a good example of our present evaluation strategies. This relatively small and interactive exhibition emphasizes naked-eye astronomy and basic observational skills and will occupy approximately 1,500 square feet. Preliminary surveys indicated that only 15 percent of our audience own or have regular access to a telescope, so we chose to emphasize naked-eye viewing.

Visitor pretesting demonstrated the need for the sort of exhibit we had planned.

Journal of Museum Education 12, no. 1 (Winter 1987): 9–11.

Although the average visitor describes himself or herself as being fairly familiar with basic astronomy, relatively few possess any useful skills. For example:

■ Only three constellations were identified by more than 10 percent of the 40 visitors interviewed—Big Dipper, Orion, and Little Dipper.

■ Twenty-eight percent could not name any star, and only 10 percent could name three or more; 31 percent of the visitors named sky objects that are not individual stars (e.g., Andromeda, Capricorn).

■ Forty-one percent of the visitors interviewed incorrectly believed that the North Star is the brightest in the sky. Interestingly, even though almost 50 percent of the visitors interviewed could relate how one can use the Big Dipper to find the North Star, 27 percent added that one should just look for the brightest star (not helpful), and only 36 percent could properly locate the North Star if shown a picture of the northern sky.

Two questions frequently posed by museum staff about how to implement a project involving formative evaluation are: How do you decide when the exhibit is "good enough"? Should you try to make sure that the exhibit is effective for 80 percent of the visitors, or should you be happy with 75 percent? These questions seem prompted by a concern that an exhibit's effectiveness will be improved by just a few percentage points at a time. No prototype in our experience has actually followed that pattern. We are more often faced with exhibits that are initially effective for a small proportion of visitors and that are dramatically improved by the first few modifications we try. Sometimes drastic measures (such as starting over from scratch) are called for, but in other cases fairly simple changes can triple or quadruple the number of visitors who can profit from their interaction with an exhibit.

Feedback for Improvements

One component of *Seeing the Universe* shows visitors where the constellations and stars can be found in the sky overhead and how their positions can change in the course of an evening or a year. The exhibit consists of a plexiglass "bubble" mounted so that visitors can stand underneath it (with their "heads in the stars") and look up at stars and constellations marked on its surface. The sphere, mounted at a 40 degree angle to approximate an average North American latitude, can be rotated by the visitor standing inside it.

Although the staff was quite pleased with the initial version of this exhibit, it was very disappointing in its first trials. After observing 40 visitors interacting with this exhibit, we noted that:

■ Only 30 percent (12) put their heads into the globe.

■ Only 17 percent (7) actually looked at any stars from inside the globe.

■ Twenty-five percent (10) read the basic instructional or "To Do and Notice" label (while this was more easily readable from inside, visitors could also stand outside and read it).

■ While time spent by visitors is at best a crude indicator of an exhibit's effectiveness, the median time spent by visitors at this prototype was only 14 seconds and the longest time spent by any visitor was 1.5 minutes.

Given this pattern, it is not surprising that this exhibit had relatively little impact on those visitors who interacted with it. Adding directions to "step inside and star gaze" to the outside trim increased the proportion of visitors who read the "To Do and Notice" label but did not increase the proportion who put their heads in and looked around.

Before abandoning the concept altogether, we decided to change one feature of the prototype: we added a curtain suspended from the horizon line. The curtain left the top portion of the globe visible but hid everything from the horizon level to the floor. While we were not at all sure how visitors might react, an improvement was obvious immediately. Of the first 24 visitors observed, 75 percent (18) put their heads inside the globe, and 58 percent (13) spent some time actually looking at stars while standing with their heads in the sphere. Simply adding a cloth curtain more than tripled the proportion of visitors who used this exhibit in any appropriate fashion.

Unfortunately, this modification had virtually no effect on the time visitors were willing to spend with this exhibit or on the incidence of label reading. We suspect that the relatively small size of the dome creates an aversive environment and that although we had now persuaded visitors to put their heads inside it, they did not want to spend much time there. To justify the investment in a larger sphere, we attempted to increase the amount of time visitors were willing to spend interacting with this exhibit simply by asking them to use it and then speak with us afterwards. This procedure tested the educational potential of the prototype under conditions of high visitor motivation.[1] Given this pressure, visitors now spent considerably more time (median time increased from 14 seconds to four minutes), and all of these visitors looked at the stars from inside the globe and read the instruction label.

We were also encouraged by improvement in the exhibit's instructional effectiveness. Eighty-six percent (up from 53 percent in the pretest) could now locate at least one "northern sky" constellation. Seventy-one percent (up from 38 percent) could identify the Big Dipper. And 86 percent (up from 22 percent) identified the Little Dipper, although the identification of other sky objects remained at about pretest level. We are now building the next version of this exhibit, a sturdier prototype that features a four-foot diameter sphere and a new set of instructions.

Extending Visitor Involvement

Whenever one uses formative evaluation, the visitor, knowingly or not, contributes some time or effort to the exhibit's development. However, we may not always be using the visitor's time and energy as productively as we might. Most commonly, we observe self-directed visitors at an exhibit and then subject them to fairly brief interviews. While this technique usually provides helpful information, we have found that occasionally it can be more productive to control the visitors' interactions in such a way that they can provide more information than they might under usual circumstances.

On a museum-wide level, we often distribute questionnaires that visitors complete during the course of a visit. They are asked not only to supply the usual demographic and background information but also to record exhibits they enjoy or learn something from and exhibits that do not seem to be working properly. On an exhibit level, we may ask visitors to complete a set of questions during their exhibit interactions rather than during a postinteraction interview.

One prototype component of the astronomy exhibit, a model of the solar system, was designed to help visitors relate the position of the planets to their visibility and position in the evening sky. But the model presented a number of problems. It did not offer visitors obvious opportunities for interaction, and, as a result, visitors did not spend much time with it; median time spent by noncued visitors was 11 seconds. Question labels with answers hidden underneath were added to stimulate visitor interest. While these labels were commonly read by visitors, they did not increase the attention to the model itself.

Cued visitors spent considerably more time, but they seemed no better able to interpret the model than visitors who had remained for only seconds. Any information they were able to relate during the interview was drawn directly from the label text; they could not demonstrate how one could use the model to answer a particular question. Moreover, although visitors often described the model as confusing or complicated, no visitor could point to anything in particular that had posed problems. Several hours of visitor observations and interviews had left us with little information. It was obvious that to get more specific information on the model's shortcomings, we would have to find some way to increase the visitors' attention to it and make it easier for them to document their confusion.

We assembled a set of questions that visitors would be able to answer only by looking at the model; all accompanying labels were hidden. The questions included those designed to check whether visitors were really looking at the right thing (What color is the pin that represents the earth?), those directly related to the model's intended use (Are there any stars or constellations that you might look for to help you find Saturn?), and those that checked how visitors were actually interpreting specific parts of the model (How did you use the model to answer this question?). These visitors also answered questions that are included in any postexhibit interview (for example, What did you not like about this exhibit? What should we change?).

Because this activity occupied most visitors for a significant amount of time (from six to 20 minutes), our initial sample included only 10 visitors, yet this small sample provided us with far more information than all the previous testing. While some questions were easily answered by all visitors, a few key elements of the model were consistently misinterpreted. For example, four of the 10 visitors thought that the diagram fixed under the earth to indicate the midnight and noon sides of the earth was instead showing compass directions. These visitors also provided us with much more specific comments about their difficulties, such as, "I had trouble discerning the meaning of the division of the orbits."

This procedure pinpointed specific areas of confusion and prompted a new approach to the exhibit in general. This sample of visitors obviously spent much more time actually using the model, albeit somewhat reluctantly. More important, they behaved in ways that visitors had not before. They talked with each other about the model, pointed and gestured, and looked at the model from different positions and angles. This behavior suggested to us that this exhibit might benefit from the addition of a computer to respond to questions and give appropriate feedback. To this end, we are developing our program along lines suggested by Eve E. Van Rennes and are currently testing both the program and model modification with visitors.[2]

These examples from our current testing of *Seeing the Universe* demonstrate two important points about formative evaluation. First, dramatic changes in visitor behavior are more common than subtle changes as the result of exhibit modification. Second, visitors can be asked to do more during their visit than you think; they can be active partners in the exhibit-making process.

Notes

1. Chandler G. Screven, "Exhibit Evaluation: A Goal-Referenced Approach," *Curator* 19, no. 4 (1976): 271–90.
2. Eve E. Van Rennes, *Exhibits Enhanced by Stand-Alone Computers* (Bloomfield Hills, Mich.: Cranbrook Institute of Science, 1981). This study is available through the ERIC database, #ED–207523.

Do Museums Have "Curriculum"?

Valorie Beer

When we think and talk about "curriculum," we tend to associate the word only with formal educational institutions. But many institutions, including museums, have educational purposes and curriculums to achieve them. Notice that the question posed in the title of this article is not, Do museums have *a* curriculum? As John Balling once noted in the *Journal of Museum Education,* "The freedom from set curricula is one of the significant assets of the [museum] field and a source of enjoyment for audiences and professionals alike."[1] The problem for museum educators—and educators in other institutions that are not schools—lies in disentangling curriculum from its traditional context and giving it a unique meaning.

Definitions of "curriculum" usually specify that it is a plan for the learning that occurs in schools,[2] although a few definitions acknowledge that nonschool environments, too, may have curriculum.[3] Yet even recognizing the existence of nonschool curriculums often leads us to unproductive ends. Either we make unfavorable comparisons between those curriculums and school curriculums, or we remodel nonschool curriculums so that they look more like "the real thing"—the school curriculum. Thus we deny the educational legitimacy of nonschool institu-tions and suppress the unique and creative contributions they might make to curriculum theory and practice.

Broadening "curriculum" beyond its traditional definition does not, however, mean that we should ignore that definition and all the research on it. If we want to know the elements of museum curriculum, the elements of school curriculum at least provide a place to start, a list to be proved or disproved as applicable to curriculum in museums. (And for the moment, it is the only place to start, since descriptive studies and theories of nonschool curriculum that address its specific characteristics have not yet been devised.)

Discovering the Museum Curriculum

Curriculum theorists, regardless of their other major disagreements, often specify four of the same curriculum elements in their models: goals or objectives, teaching strategies, learning activities, and evaluation.[4] John I. Goodlad, Frances Klein, and Kenneth Tye expanded the list in their exhaustive description of school curriculum,

Journal of Museum Education 12, no. 3 (Fall 1987): 10–13.

A Study of Schooling. They added content, materials, grouping, time, and space as possible elements.[5]

A Study of Schooling's model has yet another aspect that could be useful in studies of museum curriculums. The model suggests that there are several perspectives from which we can look at curriculum, including a teacher's perspective and a student's perspective. In her discussion of the expectations of various museum stakeholders (for example, staff, patrons, and visitors) Marcia C. Linn has already anticipated that it is wise to take into account the various perspectives in the museum environment.[6] Her hypothesis can perhaps be extended to the museum curriculum.

With *A Study of Schooling*'s list of curriculum elements and perspectives as a starting point, I began in the summer of 1983 to investigate museum curriculum. My explicit intent was to modify or discard the list altogether, if necessary, to arrive at a description of curriculum in museums. Five questions guided the study:

1. What are the elements of the museum curriculum?
2. What are the relationships among these elements?
3. How do museum staff plan these elements?
4. How do museum visitors experience these elements?
5. What are the agreements and discrepancies between the curriculum as planned by staff and as experienced by visitors?

Implicit in the first question was an additional question: Can we get at the elements of museum curriculum by going through a model of school curriculum? Since there was no alternate route, I had to hope that *A Study of Schooling*'s list would at least point the way. As it turned out, the nine elements on the list can also be found in museum curriculums. Their strength, relationships, and very makeup are, however, quite different from those in school curriculums.

Table 1 lists the elements of the museum curriculum as I found them. I separated goals and objectives (*A Study of Schooling* combines them into one element) because I came across no museum staff or visitors who had specific learning outcomes (objectives) in mind. Since other students of the museum have either found such objectives or suggested that museums should have them,[7] objectives remain on the list, although this study did not validate their presence in the museum curriculum.

Agreements and Discrepancies

How do the elements of museum curriculum differ from their school counterparts, and how do they differ from the perspectives of the museum staff and the museum visitors? Museum visitors and staff have a variety of goals for the museum experience in addition to gaining knowledge. Visitors come to museums for a social experience, to get out of the weather, or just to have something to do. Museum staff want visitors to enjoy themselves and appreciate the collection—two goals that teachers and students probably do not hold for schools. Neither the museum visitors nor the staff in this study had specific objectives that they wanted to achieve in the museum.

Table 1
Elements of the Museum Curriculum

Element	Definition
Goals	General outcomes
Objectives	Specific learning outcomes
Materials	Manmade and natural objects in the exhibit environment
Content	Topic(s) of the materials
Activities	Experiences that result in knowledge gain
Presentation strategies	Selection and arrangement of the other elements that result in knowledge gain
Evaluation	Gathering and interpreting data to judge the effectiveness of the other elements
Grouping	Use of existing groups (such as school classes) or the formation of new groups
Time	Use of scheduled or unscheduled time in the exhibit environment
Space	Arrangement and use of the exhibit space

Content in most schools is divided among separate disciplines, with specific topics decided upon by textbook publishers and boards of education. Although museums are divided broadly by content—art, history, science—the division is flexible. I found historical artifacts and art objects in science museums and scientific equipment in historic houses. The museum staff indicated that they select much of the content according to their own interests, a luxury rarely afforded schoolteachers.

Objects are the salient materials in museums. My study confirmed that visitors respond more positively to exhibits that include objects and less positively to textual exhibits. The opposite situation prevails in schools, which rely predominantly on written materials. Because of this reliance on text, reading and other verbal tasks constitute most of the learning activities in school. In museums, however, visitors might read text, but only after engaging in other activities: touching, manipulating, watching, and listening. A science museums visitor, for example, often learns to operate a device by watching another visitor use it, not by reading the directions. In an art museum, a visitor might read a text panel only after looking at a painting and registering a response to its visual and emotional impact.

Teaching strategies, which *A Study of Schooling* calls "methods of instruction," are difficult to find in museums, for two reasons. First, the explanation and interpretation of each exhibit are usually not accomplished by direct, live instruction. Second, a major strategy in schools—organizing the materials, topics, and activities in some logical sequence—rarely works in museums. Visitors tend to experience exhibits in a random manner, even when a specific sequence is indicated.[8] Therefore,

I renamed this element "presentation strategies" in recognition of the fact that museum staff present materials for visitors to experience but do not endeavor to teach the content overtly.

Although evaluation studies are carried out in some museums, none of the museum staff in this study used formal testing devices to evaluate either the exhibits or the learning they might engender. And few of the visitors made specific evaluative comments about the exhibits. This situation is in marked contrast to the plethora of testing devices that characterize the school curriculum.

Grouping, too, is not a strong element in museum curriculums. Museum staff rarely group visitors who are not already part of organized tours or school classes. Visitors rarely interact with other groups or individuals, except those with whom they have come to the museum. Again, this situation contrasts with the age and ability grouping that is common in schools.

Time is perhaps the most contentious issue in museum curriculums. Museum staff consistently overestimate the time that visitors spend at exhibits. Although 36 percent of exhibits are seen by visitors for more than 30 seconds and 21 percent for less than 30 seconds, the striking finding is that *46 percent of museum exhibits are not seen at all by visitors.* If learning takes time, as school personnel believe, then the fleeting nature of most visitors' contact with museum exhibits surely cannot be conducive to learning. (On the other hand, perhaps museums present their content in such a way that learning takes less time.)

The space of the school is often arranged according to the demands of each discipline and the materials required for its study. Museum staff, too, organize space according to content and materials. However, visitors' use of that space cannot be consistently attributed to either content or materials or, for that matter, to how close the display is to the front door of the museum.

The separation of perspectives on museum curriculums sheds considerable light on the gulf that sometimes separates staff and visitors. Although there is agreement on some elements, such as the variety of goals or the relative unimportance of evaluation and grouping, there are significant areas in which visitors do not experience the museum curriculum as the staff have planned. Staff members usually do not expect their museums to be mere diversions, for example, yet one-quarter of visitors use the museum as a side trip or as an escape. And visitors do not attend exhibits for the amount of time that staff believe that they will.

The problem with this comparison between the staff's curriculum and the visitors' experiences is that the primary target of museum curriculums may not be the visitor. Museum curriculums are often planned to satisfy many different demands—to attract other museum educators, to serve the interests of specialists in artistic, historical, or scientific fields, or to impress funding agencies or private donors.[9] Museum staff members' first concern may be with the "fit" of the new materials into the museum, both spatially and thematically. The interests of visitors may not be the criteria for the selection of content and materials. Staff members' own specialties or interests may prevail, or exhibits may come prepackaged from another source. From the teacher's perspective, students are essential to the curriculum. The same cannot be said of museum visitors from the museum staff's perspective.

A Definition

So perhaps the "curriculum" in museums does not look like the curriculum we are accustomed to, and perhaps it is both difficult and inappropriate to look for "teachers" and "students" in this learning environment. Visitors come to a museum on their own volition. They cannot be compelled to learn, if indeed learning is even their goal. Visitors come with a variety of interests and learning styles, which makes it difficult to anticipate the strategies that might appeal to them.[10] Visitors often do not have much time to spend in a museum, yet they resist being guided through a strict sequence of exhibits, regardless of the time savings or learning efficiency involved.[11] Evaluation of the museum experience in terms of learning is also difficult. Chandler G. Screven has written that unlike schools, "museums are special and rather difficult places in which to seek a predictable educational impact."[12]

Yet the museum is an educational institution that displays many of the characteristics of a place that has curriculum. The museum does not need to look like the school to have a strong educational purpose. It is even unnecessary for education to be a museum's primary goal, since it is reasonable to assume that visitors can gain knowledge whether or not they or the museum have learning as a priority. We might define museum curriculum, then, as *the activities, objects, and organizational processes and arrangements used by museum staff and intended for or experienced by museum visitors for the purpose of fulfilling explicit or implicit educational goals.*

Why is it important to be able to answer yes to the question, Do museums have "curriculum"? Why should we be concerned with the pieces of that curriculum?

First, looking at museum curriculum as a collection of several elements allows us to take a rifle instead of a shotgun approach to the study of the curriculum. Instead of trying to tackle the problems of the whole, amorphous "museum curriculum" at once, we can, for example, focus on visitor behavior (activities), on the collection (materials and content), on the museum's educational direction (goals), or on progress toward those goals (evaluation). After we have looked at the pieces, we can then look at their relationships to each other and to the whole curriculum. Knowing the relationships, we can plan interventions and changes and anticipate their impact on a museum's entire curriculum.

Second, discovering the unique curriculum of museums and other educational institutions overcomes the unfortunate situation in which one type of curriculum is considered to be the negative or opposite of the other: school or nonschool curriculum, formal or informal curriculum. Such dichotomies ignore the diversity in types of curriculums and institutions of learning and overlook the potential for different types of learning to complement one another. Although this study, of necessity, started with a school-based model, the goal is to describe museum curriculum without having to make the obligatory reference to schools.

Finally, the unique feature of museum curriculums is that they are curriculums of direct experience, not of discourse. Such curriculums can encourage nonverbal learning and produce in visitors the ability to "read" and interpret objects. Museum curriculums go beyond the acquisition of facts, principles, and other cognitive gains to involve changes in attitudes and enhancement of feelings. Museums are well equipped to develop this type of curriculum and to alleviate a painful narrowness in modern educational experience—that "we live among miracles but tend to accept them without wonder or delight."[13]

Notes

1. John D. Balling, "Setting Standards for Museum Education: Throwing the Baby Out with the Bath?" *Journal of Museum Education* 10, no. 2 (Spring 1985): 3–5.

2. J. G. Saylor and W. M. Alexander, *Curriculum Planning for Modern Schools* (New York: Holt, Rinehart and Winston, 1966).

3. Elliot W. Eisner, *The Educational Imagination* (New York: Macmillan, 1977); J. B. MacDonald, B. J. Wolfson, and E. Zaret, *Reschooling Society: A Conceptual Model* (Washington, D.C.: Association for Supervision and Curriculum Development, 1973).

4. J. D. McNeil, *Curriculum* (Boston: Little, Brown, 1985); Saylor and Alexander, *Curriculum Planning for Modern Schools;* D. Tanner and L. N. Tanner, *Curriculum Development* (New York: Macmillan, 1980); Ralph W. Tyler, *Basic Principles of Curriculum and Instruction* (Chicago: University of Chicago Press, 1950).

5. John I. Goodlad, Frances Klein, and Kenneth Tye, *Curriculum Inquiry* (New York: McGraw-Hill, 1979).

6. Marcia C. Linn, "Evaluation in the Museum: Focus on Expectations," *Educational Evaluation and Policy Analysis* 5, no. 1 (1983): 119–27.

7. Chandler G. Screven, "Instructional Design," *Museum News* 52, no. 5 (January/February 1974): 67–75; Screven, *The Measurement and Facilitation of Learning in the Museum Environment: An Experimental Analysis* (Washington, D.C.: Smithsonian Institution Press, 1974); Screven, "Exhibit Evaluation: A Goal-Referenced Approach," *Curator* 19, no. 4 (1976): 271–90; Harris H. Shettel, "An Evaluation of Existing Criteria for Judging the Quality of Science Exhibits," *Curator* 11, no. 2 (1968): 137–53; Shettel, "Exhibits: Art Form or Educational Medium?" *Museum News* 52, no. 1 (September 1973): 32–41; S. B. Anderson, "Noseprints on the Glass, or How Do We Evaluate Museum Programs?" in *Museums and Education,* ed. Eric Larrabee (Washington, D.C.: Smithsonian Institution Press, 1968), pp. 115–26; B. Baker and J. Sellar, "Science Comes Alive in the Natural History Museum," *Curriculum Review* 22, no. 5 (1983): 71–74.

8. L. C. Nielson, "A Technique for Studying the Behavior of Museum Visitors," *Journal of Educational Psychology* 37 (1946): 103–10.

9. Marlene Chambers, "Is Anyone Out There?" *Museum News* 62, no. 5 (May/June 1984): 47–54.

10. Screven, "Exhibit Evaluation."

11. Barbara Y. Newsom and Adele Z. Silver, eds., *The Art Museum as Educator* (Berkeley: University of California Press, 1978).

12. Screven, "Exhibit Evaluation," p. 272.

13. M. Harrison, "Education in Museums," in *The Organization of Museums* (Paris: UNESCO, 1960), p. 92.

The Family Museum Experience: Implications from Research

Lynn D. Dierking

Almost every metropolitan area has a museum, zoo, or botanical garden, with family groups constituting a major portion of their visitors. M. B. Alt observed that 70 percent of the visitors to the British Museum (Natural History) who were not in school groups came in other social groups and that 60 percent of these groups were family groups. A similar pattern of visitation has been observed in the United States.[1]

Despite the fact that families constitute a major portion of visitors to free-choice, or informal, learning settings, very little educational research has focused on this important audience. Fortunately, research focuses are changing, and we are beginning to build a body of knowledge that describes why families are visiting museums and what they are doing while they are there. In reviewing this research, I will explore the following broad areas: (1) characteristics of families that influence their informal learning setting visits, (2) behaviors of families in informal learning settings, and (3) implications that these findings have for museum educators. In the first two sections I will raise questions that will be answered in the final section.

Characteristics of Families

Families can be described as social groups made up of at least one adult and one child. As we know too well, the nuclear family is becoming less and less common. In 1960, 60 percent of families could be described as nuclear, that is, a family with two parents living under the same roof. In 1985 only 6 percent of families had this configuration.[2] Families in the last decades of the 20th century come in all shapes and sizes, including single-parent families, blended families, extended families, and co-parented families. The main point for us to remember as museum educators is that families are a multigenerational social unit.

Its diversity makes the family a challenge to serve. The family unit is made up of individuals of different ages, varying intellectual abilities and attentional capacities, different physical limitations, and a continuum of experiences. What can we do to meet the needs of such diverse groups?

More important, the family unit is also a social unit. Family members have chosen to visit our institution for a variety of reasons: to kill time, to entertain "Aunt

Journal of Museum Education 14, no. 2 (Spring/Summer 1989): 9–11.

Mildred," to help the children "learn" something. They have elected to visit as a social group, and that is extremely important for us to remember.

This multigenerational social unit has also come with an agenda, one that may or may not be in agreement with our institution's idealized agenda for visitors. First, the family has decided to visit our institution and gone to the trouble to get to us—in some cases a great deal of trouble! Families have traveled at least 30 minutes, more likely an hour. If small children are along, the adults have worried about the availability of rest rooms, food, and rest areas. They may plan to stay at our institution only an hour. Will they be able to figure out a meaningful way to spend that hour? They also view the gift shop as an important part of their visit; in fact, they often want to purchase a souvenir to remember this visit or to share the experience of it with a friend. These are just a few of the concerns that families have before they even think about viewing our collections.

But the family has also come to "do the museum," and research suggests that family members do want to read some labels, participate in some activities if available, and "learn" something new. Research data indicate that family groups are attempting to do these things, but they are also at times disoriented, overwhelmed by the quantity and level of material, and desperately trying to personalize the information they are processing. How can we better accommodate their agendas but also accomplish our goal of educating these visitors?

Behaviors of Families

Marcia Brumit Kropf has described the behaviors that families engage in while visiting informal learning settings (see her article in this section). Furthermore, I am aware of at least six dissertations currently being written on some aspect of family behavior. Here I would like to suggest that families view museums as (1) social settings, (2) behavior settings, and (3) learning settings.

Museums as Social Settings

As indicated above, families are first and foremost social groups. Thus our free-choice learning setting provides a backdrop for their social interactions. Our museum provides them an opportunity to do something together as a family in a unique and interesting place.

If one spends any time watching families in free-choice learning settings (an exercise I highly recommend for those designing special programs and exhibits for families), one becomes acutely aware of the social nature of the museum experience. Families joke together, talk about where they are going to eat lunch, and relate objects to their own concrete experiences: "Gee, remember when we were camping last summer, we saw a bird that looked like that!" One also observes a great deal of social management; discipline and checking to see if children are hungry or need to use rest rooms are examples.

A considerable amount of research has focused on the differences between ways mothers and fathers interact socially with children in informal learning settings. Judy Diamond and Sherman B. Rosenfeld conclude that males tend to assume a more dominant role in the family, often choosing which exhibits to view and engaging sons in exhibit-related conversations, while females tend to deal with social management issues.[3] My research, which analyzed mother-daughter, mother-son, father-daughter, and father-son interactions, suggests that fathers tend to interact similarly with sons and daughters while mothers vary their behavior, tending to be more exhibit focused with sons than with daughters.[4] In order to be very meaningful, these results need to be replicated, but they do suggest that the relationship between different sex parents and children is perhaps less straightforward than originally thought.

Rosenfeld also observed that parents seemed to use their children as "tickets" to visit informal learning settings. The children's presence somehow sanctions the trip, although it is often evident that the parent is the one really enjoying this special "social" outing.[5]

Museums as Behavior Settings
A behavior setting is a social-physical setting in which an individual's behavior is predictable and defined by contextually defined social norms and expectations.[6] What this means in terms of family visitors to museums is that they have a sense of what they are supposed to do in the behavior setting called "museum." Research suggests that families act in fairly predictable ways once they enter the doors of the museum.[7] In two separate but related studies, one conducted at the Florida State Museum in Gainesville and the other at the Smithsonian's National Museum of Natural History, researchers were able to replicate results in two very different museums and to describe four phases that seem to encompass the "typical" museum visit:

1. an orientation phase, lasting 3–10 minutes, when visitors begin their tour and become familiar with the surroundings

2. intense exhibit viewing, lasting 25–30 minutes, when visitors concentrate attention on exhibits, reading labels and interacting in an exhibit-directed fashion

3. exhibit skimming, lasting 30–40 minutes, when visitors scan exhibits quickly, infrequently reading labels

4. preparation for departure, lasting 5–10 minutes, when visitors prepare to exit the museum.[8]

Of course, families will vary slightly in how well they "fit" this time-allocation model, often according to how much museum "savvy" they have. Frequent family visitors know where they are; their orientation period may be much shorter. They may also have strategies for dealing with "museum fatigue," and, consequently, their visit may last longer. Infrequent visitors or visitors coming to an institution for the first time may require a longer orientation phase and may need to watch other people to see "what they are supposed to be doing." Taking into account these slight variations, this time-allocation model still proves quite useful in understanding how museums act as behavior settings for visitors.

Museums as Learning Settings

There is no question that families visiting museums engage in "learning behaviors." Families read some labels together; family members discuss what they are looking at and ask each other questions. Whether these behaviors result in learning is less clear, however. My sense is that families learn a great deal, much of it very different from what was intended. John Falk discusses the "museum gestalt" learning experience, which may involve recall of some exhibits but also includes the "feel" of the architecture and other more affective aspects of the visit.[9]

One aspect of my research indicates that families exhibit two different learning styles, which I visualize as on different ends of a continuum. On one end are families that arrive together and stay together, for the most part, throughout their visit. Often the parent or parents direct the visit, asking questions of children and selecting what exhibits are viewed. I call these "guided learning" families or "collaborative learning" families. On the other end of the continuum are "independent learning" families, who tend to split up, even when the children are young, and not to interact as much. These families view exhibits separately, checking back occasionally with each other to share what they have seen. During data collection, because I was counting frequencies of "learning behaviors," I naively assumed that parents in guided learning families were the "best" teachers. When I began analyzing the data, however, I realized that the interactions of parents in independent learning families, though less frequent, were learning behaviors also. Both types of families were learning. In guided learning families, children were learning not only the content of the museum but also that museums are fun places for families to learn in together. In independent learning families, children were learning not only about the exhibits but also that museums are great places to visit, that we can all learn different things, and that parents like to learn, too![10]

Implications for Museum Educators

What do these findings mean to us as museum educators? How do we meet the needs of such a diverse group of visitors as the family? I think we need to keep in mind five important points as we design our exhibit spaces and our family programs.

1. *A family comes to the museum with its own agenda, and, rather than fighting it (a battle we are likely to lose anyway), we must try to accommodate it.* We need to do everything we can to orient visitors to our institutions, including not only exhibit spaces but rest rooms, restaurants, and gift shops. Visitors will be happier and more likely to want to deal with "our" agenda if we accommodate theirs.

2. *The family visit is a social event, so we need to develop creative ways for families to be social together.* Discovery rooms, participatory exhibits, and special programs that allow families to do things together are examples. We must also keep in mind

that independent learning families like to do some things separately, so options in both exhibits and programs should be provided.

3. *Most visitors, including families, deal with exhibits in a very concrete fashion.* As we assist in exhibit design, we need to be audience advocates. Label copy must be clear, and concepts that make sense to laypeople should be emphasized.

4. *Even though it may not always be obvious, visitors do come to our institutions to "look" at exhibits.* Sometimes museum staff are distressed if family guides are not used or families do not get excited about a lecture in the museum classroom. We need to remember that families may perceive such programs as diverting them from their primary goal of "doing" the museum.

5. *Because of the diverse nature of families, we must provide a variety of options in exhibits and programs to accommodate varying learning styles, different knowledge levels, and uneven attentional levels.* Some families will want a family guide that directs their visit; others will find a guide confining. Some will want to participate in a family workshop; others will prefer to be left alone to enjoy the exhibits.

If your institution is interested in providing special family exhibits or programs, or wants to improve existing ones, the best place to start is with the families themselves. Spend time in your galleries watching families interact. Talk with family members. Conduct a simple survey. Invite families to be part of a focus group. Time and effort spent on the front end of exhibit and program planning will save countless hours later and help ensure that exhibits and programs truly meet the needs of their audiences.

Notes

1. M. B. Alt, "Four Years of Visitor Surveys at the British Museum (Natural History), 1976–1979," *Museum Journal* 80 (1980): 10–19; John D. Balling, D. D. Hilke, Joan D. Liversidge, Elizabeth Cornell, and Nancy Perry, "The Role of the Family in the Promotion of Science Literacy," Final Report SED 81–12927 (Washington, D.C.: National Science Foundation, 1985); Minda Borun, *Measuring the Immeasurable: A Pilot Study of Museum Effectiveness* (Washington, D.C.: Association of Science-Technology Centers, 1977); N. H. Cheek, D. R. Field, and R. J. Burdge, *Leisure and Recreation Places* (Ann Arbor, Mich.: Ann Arbor Science Publications, 1976); S. H. Ham, "The Significance of the Family as a Unit of Analysis in Interpretive Research," *Proceedings of the 53rd Annual Conference of the Association of Interpretive Naturalists* 9 (1979): 56–72; Watson M. Laetsch, Judy Diamond, J. L. Gottfried, and Sherman B. Rosenfeld, "Children and Family Groups in Science Centers," *Science and Children* 15 (1980): 14–17.

2. Lynn D. Dierking and John H. Falk, *The Museum Experience* (Washington, D.C.: Whalesback Books, 1991).

3. Judy Diamond, "The Ethology of Teaching: A Perspective from the Observations of Families in Science Centers" (Ph.D. diss., University of California, Berkeley, 1980); Sherman B. Rosenfeld, "Informal Learning in Zoos: Naturalistic Studies of Family Groups" (Ph.D. diss., University of California, Berkeley, 1980). These studies compare mother-daughter interactions with father-son interactions.

4. Lynn D. Dierking, "Parent-Child Interactions in a Free Choice Learning Setting: An Examination of Attention-Directing Behaviors" (Ph.D. diss., University of Florida, 1987); Lynn D. Dierking, John J. Koran, Jr., James Algina, Mary Lou Koran, and John H. Falk,

"Parent-Child Interactions in a Free Choice Learning Setting: An Examination of Attention-Directing Behaviors," *Curator,* in press; Lynn D. Dierking, J. J. Koran, Jr., M. L. Koran, and John H. Falk, "Family Behavior in Free Choice Learning Settings: A Review of the Research," *Science Education,* in press.

5. Sherman B. Rosenfeld, "The Context of Informal Learning in Zoos," *Roundtable Reports* 4 (1979): 3–5.

6. R. G. Barker and H. F. Wright, *Midwest and Its Children* (New York: Harper and Row, 1955).

7. John H. Falk, John J. Koran, Jr., Lynn D. Dierking, and Lewis Dreblow, "Predicting Visitor Behavior," *Curator* 28, no. 4 (1985): 249–57.

8. John H. Falk, "Analysis of the Behavior of Family Visitors in Natural History Museums," *Curator* 34, no. 1 (1991): 44–52.

9. Dierking and Falk, *Museum Experience.*

10. Dierking, "Parent-Child Interactions." Helen Santini at the Phillips Collection, Washington, D.C., has observed similar patterns independently while working with families during parent-child workshops. Some families like to work collaboratively on one project; others prefer working independently, each person creating his or her own product.

Afterword

Families continue to represent a major audience for museums, and professionals in the field have made great progress in understanding the ways that families use and make meaning of the objects, programs, and exhibitions offered them. Useful constructs such as agendas and the importance of social interaction for families have become a part of the museum professional's knowledge base and are used in the development of exhibits and programs for families. Whereas 10 years ago there were relatively few systematic studies of family behavior in museums, in the past five years a number of excellent studies have been conducted.

Despite the great progress museum professionals have made, I continue to struggle with my own understanding of the family museum experience. As the complexity of that experience has emerged, it has been humbling even to begin to suggest how one could understand and "measure" such a phenomenon. The issue of whether families learn in museums and, if so, how, adds another layer of complexity to a system that is already exceedingly complex.

As an approach to tackling this problem, John Falk and I have developed a concept of the museum experience—and hence museum learning—as an interactive experience that includes a range of outcomes such as increased knowledge but that also can include changed attitudes or enhanced social skills. At the heart of this model, which we call the Interactive Experience Model, is a visitor-centered perspective and the notion that all learning and experience are contextual. We suggest that the very nature of the interactive experience is dictated by four interacting contexts:

1. the personal context that the visitor brings to the visit, including prior knowledge, experience, attitudes, motivation, and interests

2. the physical context that the visitor encounters, including the objects and artifacts as well as the architecture and ambience of the building

3. the social context of the experience, including those individuals with whom the visitor attends as well as those he or she encounters during the visit, such as museum staff and other visitors

4. the immediate experience context, that is, what the visitor is doing at any particular moment during the visit.

Our model can be visualized as a three-dimensional set of four interacting spheres, with each sphere representing one of the four contexts. The museum experience occurs within the physical context called "museum" and includes not just objects and artifacts but physical structures. Within this museum is the visitor, who perceives the world through his or her own personal context. Sharing this experience are other people, in the case of the family visitor an extremely important influence on the visit. Finally, at any given moment the visitor is focused on a particular object, individual, or thought, or more likely on several of these simultaneously. This focus represents the immediate experience context. The visitor's experience can be thought of as a continually shifting interchange among personal, physical, social, and immediate experience contexts. By analyzing the nature and extent of these four contextual influences we suggest that the visitor's museum experience can begin to be understood—and ideally, if understood, enhanced.

We have found this model useful in providing an initial understanding of the museum experience, but it now needs to be tested to validate its assumptions, particularly those pertaining to learning. The Interactive Experience Model has the potential to provide a framework for understanding the totality of museum learning—a socially, cognitively, kinesthetically, and esthetically rich experience.

The Family Museum Experience: A Review of the Literature

Marcia Brumit Kropf

In the last decade, a number of researchers have begun to examine the experiences family visitor groups have in museums. This focus on families is part of an effort to gain a clearer understanding of these experiences and of the learning that takes place. Researchers have found that learning is not the primary reason families visit museums. Nevertheless, they have consistently observed the teaching and learning behaviors of family members. These behaviors focus on three sources of information and ideas: the exhibits, the labels and educational materials accompanying the exhibits, and other people.

This article will examine the relationship of family visitors to each of these sources of information as described by recent research.

■ Deborah P. Benton studied the interactions of family group members with each other and the exhibits by conducting unobtrusive observations of a minimum of 25 adult-child visitor groups at specific exhibit areas at four museums in the New York City area: the American Museum of Natural History, the Bronx Zoo, the Brooklyn Children's Museum, and the Metropolitan Museum of Art.

■ Robert L. Wolf and Barbara L. Tymitz studied visitors' perceptions by conducting several hundred hours of unobtrusive observations and interviewing 300 visitors at the National Zoological Park in Washington, D.C.

■ Sherman B. Rosenfeld studied family visits in order to develop strategies for enhancing learning at zoos. He interviewed 80 family groups at the San Francisco Zoo, unobtrusively observed and then interviewed 25 family groups for the duration of their visits, recorded and transcribed the conversations of 65 groups at specific exhibits, unobtrusively observed questions visitors asked at specific exhibits, and interviewed the eight student docents being questioned. He also designed an experimental mini-zoo, unobtrusively observed 23 groups visiting the mini-zoo, and interviewed 16 groups.

■ Judy Diamond studied how teaching occurs in spontaneous family interactions by observing 28 family groups totaling 81 people at both the Lawrence Hall of Science in Berkeley and the Exploratorium in San Francisco for the duration of their visits. This sample was compared for accuracy to a sample of 828 visitors at the two

Journal of Museum Education 14, no. 2 (Spring/Summer 1989): 5–8.

institutions. The families gave her permission to observe, so she was able to be close to the group and note subtle behaviors and verbal information.

■ D. D. Hilke and John D. Balling studied the learning agenda of family visitors, the strategies used to meet it, and the roles of family members in relation to it. They observed, with permission, 42 family groups at a traditional exhibit hall and a participatory exhibit hall at a large museum of natural history in an urban area.

■ Samuel M. Taylor studied the behavior and interests of visitors to the Steinhart Aquarium in San Francisco by observing, with permission, the entire visits of 25 family groups, collecting 418 visitor questions regarding specific displays, and conducting many unobtrusive observations and informal interviews.

Exhibits

Researchers found that observation of exhibits was the most prevalent learning behavior for family visitors. Not surprisingly, this behavior was dramatically affected by the exhibit type, the museum environment, and the family's orientation to the museum. Museum staff can influence family learning behavior when designing exhibits, determining exhibit location, and planning the museum environment.

How Long Did Families Spend at Exhibits?

The length of time spent at an exhibit provides some indication of the learning that may take place. For example, Rosenfeld found that the exhibits where children spent the most time were the exhibits they recalled the best. Typically, however, family visitors were observed walking past exhibits and looking at them without breaking stride. Researchers give this behavior various names: exploratory behavior (Rosenfeld), shopping around (Diamond), and move-on looking (Hilke and Balling). In these studies, family visitors viewed most exhibits for less than 45 seconds and only a small number of exhibits for three minutes or more.

Visitors spent longer periods viewing exhibits at the beginning of their visit, Taylor observed, and much less time at individual exhibits as the visit progressed and museum fatigue developed. Rosenfeld found that some families returned to an exhibit during the course of the museum visit, and the second visit was significantly longer than the first.

What Type of Exhibits Sustained the Interest of Families?

In these studies, the type of exhibit appeared to influence the time families spent observing it. Families spent several minutes at exhibits that were participatory, allowed touching, or involved physical activities such as crawling and climbing. They showed less move-on looking behavior at participatory exhibits. When a staff member or docent was available to answer questions informally, the time spent at an exhibit increased to as much as 22 minutes. Researchers consistently found that families spent more time at the exhibits that involved interaction between visitors and the exhibit, between visitors and docents, or—in zoos—between animals or between zookeepers and animals. In addition, novel or unusual exhibit content attracted families for longer periods, in spite of a pattern of decreasing viewing times due to museum fatigue.

How Does the Museum Environment Influence a Family's Response to an Exhibit?
A number of environmental factors influenced the amount of time families spent at an exhibit. Benton found that they spent less time at exhibits with dim lighting and exhibits that were visually inaccessible for children either because of the exhibit's height or because of the presence of physical barriers. These results led Benton to the conclusion that museums predetermine visitor attention to an exhibit when making decisions about the design, location, and lighting.

This conclusion is reiterated in Taylor's work, which confirms earlier studies of visitor traffic patterns and the existence of two dominant patterns. He found that right-hand turns were predominant and that, as the visits progressed, visitors spent decreasing times at each display. Taylor concluded that the museum layout did determine visitors' traffic patterns and, therefore, the exhibits they visited.

Benton found that the museum environment also influenced both the appropriateness of the children's behavior and the need for adults to restrict that behavior. As a result, the environment also influenced the group's attention to an exhibit. Children tended to walk with the adults in quiet indoor settings where guards were present. They tended to behave more exuberantly in outdoor settings where adults did not restrict their behavior.

Activities other than exhibits also attracted families. Rosenfeld found that families spent about one-third of their time in the zoo watching animals. They spent the rest of the time walking, using the playground, eating, and riding on the zoo train. He noted that most families spent more time at the food concessions than at any exhibit.

The presence of other museum visitors influenced a family's attention to an exhibit. Families in Benton's study tended to walk past exhibits when other visitors were blocking their view. If an exhibit included a lot of viewing space, the family stopped to view it only when they found an empty space. Taylor found that in a museum layout with a determined traffic pattern, a new family group arriving at an exhibit would "bump" the family on to a new exhibit, limiting their time at the display. In fact, Wolf and Tymitz found that visitors planned their visits to avoid crowds.

How Do Other Exhibits Influence a Family's Response to a Specific Exhibit?
Some exhibits, because of their size or attractiveness, can distract the family from viewing exhibits nearby. Visitors were attracted to interactive exhibits, for example, while they neglected the noninteractive ones. Wolf and Tymitz found that visitors compared specific exhibits with other exhibits in the zoo and with other zoo trips. Visitors tried to draw associations, transferring information learned at one exhibit

to another. This behavior led Wolf and Tymitz to recommend that the museum facilitate the transfer of learning and help the visitor integrate observations. Taylor also made this recommendation, noting that in museums where the layout causes visitors to travel in one direction, museum educators have an opportunity to use sequential displays for more in-depth interpretation.

How Does the Length of the Museum Visit Influence a Family's Response to an Exhibit?

Rosenfeld found that most families viewed less than half the zoo's exhibits. He also found a direct relationship between the time spent watching animals and the number of exhibits viewed for at least two minutes. Diamond observed that the amount of reading and the amount of describing decreased as the visit progressed. She also found that aggressive behaviors increased during the second quarter of the visit and that interactions with people outside the family group increased during the third quarter of the visit.

How Does a Family's Familiarity with the Museum Influence the Response to an Exhibit?

Orientation to the museum's floor plan seemed to be a problem for many families in these studies. Taylor found that many groups missed exhibits because, in an effort to avoid backtracking, they tended to leave the aquarium when they came to an exit.

What Questions Do Families Have about the Exhibits?

Researchers commonly found that visitors were interested in concrete information about what they were seeing. Wolf and Tymitz observed that visitors asked about the animal, the species, and zoo care. Rosenfeld also found that most questions concerned a specific animal. In addition, he discovered that children asked most questions and that these commonly concerned the animal's name and their personal interactions with the animal. Hilke and Balling concluded that the majority of behaviors involving the acquisition and exchange of information dealt with simple facts. And in Taylor's study, the most frequently asked questions concerned concrete, visually verifiable aspects of the fish exhibits.

Labels

Research shows that family visitors read labels and signage infrequently. They do not use exhibit labels accurately or to their fullest potential, an indication that museum staff could use labels more effectively to influence the information families share.

What Family Members Read the Labels?

Benton found that 5 to 10 percent of the adults read the labels and that this group was largely composed of men who read silently, sharing the information only when asked. Rosenfeld also found that reading labels and signs was infrequent, occurring at only 8 percent of the exhibits, and that the immediate sharing of information read was rare. In Hilke and Balling's study, less than 18 percent of the learning strategies recorded involved reading labels and diagrams; most family members focused on acquiring firsthand information from the exhibit. Taylor frequently observed the scanning behavior of the adult men in the family group, who scanned the labels as they walked, stopping to look at an exhibit when a name or a picture captured their attention.

Do Labels Provide the Information Family Visitors Seek?

Taylor found little relationship between the information visitors sought and the information the labels provided. The visitors were interested in concrete information about the aspects of the display that immediately caught their attention, but the labels were often focused on more abstract concepts. Taylor suggested that museums design labels that provide information of immediate relevance to visitors and capitalize on this information to introduce important concepts.

People

Taylor points out that "in terms of sheer quantity of information, nothing comes close to that exchanged between members of a group of visitors." There is some evidence across these studies, however, that the information exchanged is inaccurate or misunderstood. This exchange of misconceptions can undermine the learning that might take place and is of critical concern for museum staff, who can address misconceptions through exhibit design, label design and content, and staff training.

How Do Individual Family Members Influence the Family's Response to the Exhibit?

Adults tended to pace the visit, select exhibits to view, and determine the time spent at specific exhibits either by calling and sustaining the children's attention to an exhibit or by motivating the children to move on. Although children might be allowed to select an exhibit, they rarely led the group away from the exhibit. In small, enclosed settings, however, children did lead the groups.

Adults were often required to carry or lift small children to enable them to view an exhibit, fatiguing the parents and contributing to a shorter museum visit. Taylor found that "scouts" (usually young boys) would investigate exhibits ahead of the family group, encourage the family to visit the next exhibit, and quickly move on. This behavior seemed to limit the time the whole family spent at exhibits. Children also tended to motivate activities that were not exhibit related, such as eating.

Benton found that the leadership style of the family tended to influence the time spent at exhibits. Families in which children had some leadership spent less time with disciplinary issues and more time in exhibit-directed behavior. Those that were led by the adults tended to spend a short time at each exhibit.

What Roles Do Individuals Take in the Family?

Adults tended to interact more often with children than with other adults, and children tended to interact more often with adults than with other children. Parents took on the role of showing their children what to do in a museum: how to behave, how to use labels, what to look at. In groups that included adult males, the male was the dominant leader. At interactive exhibits, children tended to be the ones who interacted with the exhibits, while the adults watched and read instructions.

Rosenfeld found that families came to the zoo with a range of social agendas, such as spending time together, that were as important or more so than viewing the exhibits. Taylor reiterated the importance of these social factors in influencing the family's experiences in museums.

What Do Families Talk About and How?

In the Wolf and Tymitz study, the most common form of conversation was descriptions of observed animal behavior; the second most common was questions about the animal, species, or zoo care. In Rosenfeld's study, the major conversational themes included naming the animal, pointing out an animal's behavior or a physical attribute, instigating animal behavior, and reflecting on related issues.

In Taylor's study, families talked about what they knew from previous experiences, discussing the exhibits in terms of these experiences and memories. As Taylor observed, these discussions provide parents with opportunities to reinforce past experiences and family history and to develop a shared understanding among the family members. In fact, Taylor writes that "the use of the aquarium as an environment for reinforcement of previously held knowledge or experience is far more frequent than is using the aquarium for the acquisition of new knowledge."

How Do Family Members Provide Information?

Wolf and Tymitz found that individuals tended to share their interpretations of what they observed with other members of the group. In their study, these interpretations—which were described in general terms—concerned animal habitat, structural characteristics, and activity. Wolf and Tymitz noted many examples of misconceptions, especially in relation to animal activity where visitor comments were anthropomorphic, assigning human reactions and emotions to animals. Rosenfeld and Taylor also observed that comments and questions were anthropomorphic in nature.

Wolf and Tymitz found many examples of direct teaching on the part of individuals in the group, including children. When parents took on the role of teacher, there appeared to be two patterns. Mothers with young children tended to teach about animal activity and the discussions were overwhelmingly anthropomorphic. Fathers tended to take on the direct teaching role and to focus on animal characteristics and specific behavior, relying on outside information that was correct and incorrect.

Diamond found that teaching was a reciprocal activity, but that "different family members teach in different contexts and for different reasons." Children tended to share information about the operation of the exhibit and the phenomena being observed. Adults tended to share symbolic information gained from reading the labels and from their previous experience. Hilke and Balling also found that children and parents shared control of the family's learning processes.

Taylor observed visitors reading labels and then sharing the information they acquired. In some cases, visitors shared inaccurate information, both from misinterpretation of the labels and from passing on their own incorrect knowledge. In the case of parents of young children, the labels were read aloud, but difficult words were simultaneously translated to simpler words.

What Information Do People Outside the Group Provide?

Benton found that guards primarily provided directions and guidance as to appropriate behavior, but they did not encourage any interaction with exhibits. She found, however, that staff at the children's museum in her study encouraged interaction with exhibits.

Wolf and Tymitz observed that visitors initiated informal conversations with zoo personnel in order to acquire information about the animals. These conversations were repeated to family members who had not heard the discussion, and, following the conversation, children continued to question their parents. Wolf and Tymitz recommended the increased use of well-trained roving guides, especially to address the misinformation visitors share. In the Rosenfeld study, however, families did not listen to the commentary by the trained guides on the zoo train, nor did they ask questions. Taylor found that volunteer interpreters frequently did not have enough training or knowledge to respond to visitor questions and saw their role as policing rather than explaining.

Recent research has provided a clearer picture of the experiences family groups have in museums and contributed to our understanding of the informal learning that takes place. Museum educators can use this new understanding to improve learning by family visitors through the design and placement of exhibits, the use of labels, and the training of museum staff. The research described here was conducted for the most part in zoos, aquariums, natural history museums, and science museums. The experiences families have in these types of museums may be quite different from the experiences they have in art museums. Further research incorporating a wider range of museums would be of great value to museum educators as they shape their vision of how families learn together and what museums can offer family visitors.

References

Benton, Deborah P. "Intergenerational Interaction in Museums." Ed.D. diss., Columbia University Teacher's College, 1979.

Diamond, Judy. "The Ethology of Teaching: A Perspective from the Observations of Families in Science Centers." Ph.D. diss., University of California, Berkeley, 1980.

Hilke, D. D., and John D. Balling. "The Family as a Learning System: An Observational Study of Families in Museums." Washington, D.C.: Smithsonian Institution Press, 1985.

Rosenfeld, Sherman B. "Informal Learning in Zoos: Naturalistic Studies of Family Groups." Ph.D. diss., University of California, Berkeley, 1980.

Taylor, Samuel M. "Understanding Processes of Informal Education: A Naturalistic Study of Visitors to a Public Aquarium." Ph.D. diss., University of California, Berkeley, 1986.

Wolf, Robert L., and Barbara L. Tymitz. "Do Giraffes Ever Sit? A Study of Visitor Perceptions at the National Zoological Park." Washington, D.C.: Smithsonian Institution, 1979.

Beyond "Aha!": Motivating Museum Visitors

Marlene Chambers

The "aha!" experiences many science museums now offer visitors resemble traditional science education demonstrations that are driven by the information they purport to teach rather than by the visitor's motivational needs. Research that has led to a new experience-driven interpretive model for art museums may also have something fruitful to say to science museums.

In 1986, Melora McDermott undertook research at the Denver Art Museum to identify the nature of art novices' esthetic experiences so we could understand how these resembled and differed from those of experts.[1] By analyzing novices' perceptions of their art experiences, we identified skills and attitudes they need to develop if their experiences with art objects are to be enriched. McDermott's study has allowed us to take novices' preconceptions and preferences about art into account as we develop experience-driven interpretive materials.[2]

Our understanding of the kind of experience we want to promote and the conditions necessary to promote it has also been guided by the esthetic theories of philosopher Monroe C. Beardsley[3] and by an intrinsic-motivation model based on the research of behavioral psychologist Mihaly Csikszentmihalyi. Looking for the roots of motivation, Csikszentmihalyi examined the way experts in intrinsically rewarding activities like rock climbing and chess describe their experiences.[4] He found that the experience of "flow"—a term these experts frequently use to describe "the deep involvement and effortless progression" they feel when an activity goes well—is what motivates them to spend time doing something that has no reward other than the act itself.

Csikszentmihalyi singles out three conditions critical to flow: (1) the tasks must be equal to one's present ability to perform, (2) attention must be centered on a limited stimulus field, and (3) usually, the experience must contain "coherent, noncontradictory demands for action and provide clear, unambiguous feedback." Among the rewards of a flow experience are a sense of being freed from normal cares, a sense of being competent and in control of the situation, a sense of discovery, and a sense of personal enrichment.

Journal of Museum Education 14, no. 3 (Fall 1989): 14–15. This article was part of the series "What Research Says about Learning in Science Museums." The articles were published as a book under the same title by the Association of Science-Technology Centers in 1990.

Obviously, museum-going is a freely chosen activity, with no other reward than the activity itself. If we regard experiences in museums as *varieties of flow experience*, we gain a key to creating conditions that make them more rewarding.[5] By offering challenges equal to the novice's current skills, we can facilitate discoveries that share in the nature of the expert's flow experience.[6]

What kind of experience is uniquely available in science museums that parallels the esthetic experience art museums offer? As a science amateur, I think this must be the experience of the process of science. Yet, by rigidly controlling the outcome of its "discovery" activities, the science museum really offers visitors demonstrations calculated to "prove" established facts or principles—illustrated examples of what one should *know* rather than opportunities to explore what science is or how it works.[7] As long as science museums continue to tie their "aha!" experiences directly to teaching specific facts or principles, their exhibits will remain information driven, not experience driven.

An inherent, indispensable component of the process of science is the "clinker" fact, information that cannot be explained by hypothesis based on current accepted theory. Thomas Kuhn's view of scientific revolutions emphasizes the role of such anomalies—"violations of expectations"—in creating crises that lead to new perspectives.[8] Failures of expectation, with the opportunities they present for new conjecture and refutation, seem to be central to the kind of experience a science museum could offer its visitors. To set up an "aha!" experience in which there is only one right answer is to betray the process of science. Surely visitors to a science museum deserve to confront exhibits that help them actually experience the force of one of Stephen Jay Gould's recurring themes: "Science is a method for testing claims about the natural world, not an immutable compendium of absolute truths."[9]

If science museums were to define the goal of their exhibits and interpretive devices as facilitating a specifically "how science works" discovery as a variety of the science expert's flow experience, the selection of informational content would be at once easier and more rigorous. Information offered in a science exhibit would have to pass the test of contributing to the visitor's experience of the way science works. Such information could be used to suggest problems or offer clues to their resolution. It could be the "clinker" that demands a reexamination of conclusions or theories. But, above all, it would not itself be the goal of that experience.

One of the dangers I have found in setting up esthetic discovery experiences in an art museum is the tendency to want to control the specific content of the discovery visitors make—a quite normal desire for anyone in a teaching role. It is difficult to point the way to a challenge open-ended enough to be met by a wide range of skill levels—one that allows for a variety of discoveries. But it is even more difficult to remember that the ultimate goal of providing a discovery opportunity is to give the visitor a flow experience: a sense of being competent and in control and a chance to find new, personally significant insights in the activity. After all, these feelings of satisfaction—not the information learned—motivate repeat experience and continued learning.

Resource People
Marlene Chambers and Melora McDermott, Denver Art Museum, Denver, Colorado

Notes
1. Melora McDermott, "Through Their Eyes: What Novices Value in Art Experiences," in *Annual Meeting Program Sourcebook* (Washington, D.C.: American Association of Museums, 1988), pp. 133–62.
2. Marlene Chambers, "Improving the Esthetic Experience for Art Novices: A New Paradigm for Interpretive Labels," in ibid., pp. 213–26; Chambers, "To Create Discovery," *Museum News* 68, no. 3 (May/June 1989): 41–44.
3. Monroe C. Beardsley, *The Esthetic Point of View,* ed. Michael J. Wreen and Donald M. Callen (Ithaca, N.Y.: Cornell University Press, 1982).
4. Mihaly Csikszentmihalyi, *Beyond Boredom and Anxiety: The Experience of Play in Work and Games* (San Francisco: Jossey-Bass, 1975).
5. Mihaly Csikszentmihalyi, Rich E. Robinson, et al., "The Art of Seeing: Toward an Interpretive Psychology of the Visual Experience," unpublished research report, J. Paul Getty Foundation, July 1986; Chambers, "To Create Discovery."
6. Chambers, "Improving the Esthetic Experience."
7. Mihaly Csikszentmihalyi, "Human Behavior and the Science Center," in *Science Learning in the Informal Setting,* ed. Paul G. Heltne and Linda A. Marquardt (Chicago: Chicago Academy of Sciences, 1988), pp. 79–87.
8. Thomas S. Kuhn, *The Structure of Scientific Revolutions,* 2d ed. (Chicago: University of Chicago Press, 1970).
9. Stephen Jay Gould, "An Essay on a Pig Roast," *Natural History* 98 (January 1989): 60.

Understanding Demographic Data on Zoo Visitors

Barbara A. Birney and Carolyn Heinrich

At first, the review of demographic data from a variety of zoos and aquariums may seem a futile exercise. Most reports offer little more than a list of basic frequency counts and percentages. Questionnaire items are often incompatible, making comparisons difficult. It is not uncommon to discover that important demographic information has been omitted altogether or summed up in one vague phrase. One compelling argument suggests that since each institution is different in nature and located in a different area, demographic comparisons are meaningless.

These observations are valid and certainly daunting. At the other extreme, researchers have attempted to identify the "average" zoo-goer. Such attempts tend to homogenize data, making the information less applicable for decision making about programs, exhibits, or services for visitors.[1] While data specific to zoos are scant, it is still possible to approach them meaningfully. One way to think about the audiences of these institutions is to group them by profiles.

This article attempts to provide one context for examining demographic data. We recognize that demographic data presented in isolation hold little meaning for any institution. We are interested in them because of their relationship to other concerns that all zoos and aquariums share.

All zoos and aquariums are interested in the public's attitudes toward wildlife. This first concern enables zoos to think about the challenges they face in developing programs to educate the public in accordance with their missions. In addition, all zoos and aquariums are concerned about visitors' effective use of learning opportunities during their visits. While zoos and aquariums cannot control visitors' prior knowledge or attitudes, they can seek to increase their level of scientific knowledge and concern for the natural world. This second concern directly reflects the institution's ability to carry out its mission.

Between the extremes, one can search for some trends among visitor groups. Treating each survey as an isolated piece of information is as useless as a homogenization of data. To learn what was available from zoo and aquarium settings, we reviewed more than 75 articles about studies conducted in these settings. Available research from other kinds of museums was not used for this article. Since we were interested in presenting demographic factors in a larger context, two factors related to the

Journal of Museum Education 16, no. 2 (Spring/Summer 1991): 19–22.

public's attitudes toward animals and use of interpretive media in zoos are discussed first. We then examine the demographics of some zoos and aquariums for their implications in this context. Age, sex, and educational background are three of the most important demographic factors to consider in examining the public's attitude toward animals. Most studies of children's orientation to animals are confined to one age group.[2] A few studies compare differences among age groups.

Age and Sex: An Overview

M. O. Westervelt conducted interviews with 267 children aged six to 18 years. Overall, the most common attitude toward animals found in the sample was a humanistic one. Younger children, however, consistently placed the needs of people over animals and expressed minimal concern for the rights and protection of animals. Attitudes that reflected a utilitarian or dominating outlook toward animals decreased with an increase in age. Older children showed a greater tendency to express attitudes that showed an awareness of animals as part of a larger ecological system. Older children also showed more of a moralistic orientation to animals.[3]

In a study intended to examine whether the changes that have been observed in individuals' reasoning about human moral dilemmas could be applied to moral dilemmas involving animals, J. Dunlap looked at how eighth-grade boys and 12th-grade boys responded to moral dilemmas involving animals and found that 12th-graders used more advanced moral reasoning than eighth-graders, suggesting that these abilities continue to increase during adolescence.[4]

Stephen Kellert's national survey of 3,107 American adults offers insight into the importance of age to wildlife issues. Respondents least likely to support species protection were those over age 55. Those most likely to support the protection of endangered species were under age 35. Respondents under age 25 were most willing to shoulder a variety of socioeconomic burdens for the sake of protecting endangered or threatened wildlife.

Kellert's study also examined adults' orientation to animals. Adults under age 25 appeared more appreciative and affectionate toward animals and were more concerned about their protection and less utilitarian in their attitudes. Adults under age 25 attained the highest scores for a humane orientation compared to all other age groups, while those over age 76 scored the lowest in this category.[5]

Sex is another factor that influences the public's attitudes toward animals. The findings with respect to sex differences show strong agreement. First, females appear to be more oriented to animals than males.[6] Second, both female children and female adults have a more humane orientation to animals than do males.[7] Males were more likely to have a detached and pragmatic view of animals. Third, the sexes respond differently to different species. Females respond more negatively to animals that are traditionally known as "noxious species," such as snakes or invertebrates.[8] Furthermore, males were consistently found to be drawn to predatory and dangerous animals such as the hawk, tiger, or wolf.[9] Finally, one of the few behavioral studies comparing sex differences in a zoo reptile house is consistent with these general findings; males reportedly viewed venomous snakes longer than females.[10]

A separate study raises yet another issue, however. No sex differences were found when a Scale of Attitudes toward the Treatment of Animals (SATA) was administered to 187 active Christian churchgoers.[11] The intent of the study was to compare three Christian groups. Could the degree or type of religious participation of both males and females be a confounding factor in the study of their attitudes toward animals?

The importance of sex and age to the public's orientation to animals is clear and must be of interest to all zoos and aquariums. It suggests some of the challenges these institutions face with respect to their visiting public. In response, exhibits have been developed with these factors in mind, and the impact of public interpretation efforts has been assessed. Perhaps the major shortcoming of the studies available in this area is that so few of them report demographic differences, instead referring to visitors in general terms. Still, some common findings emerge.

The findings suggest that the key to understanding age differences in visitors' response to public interpretation is the degree to which both the interpretation and the audience are mixed. In studies of live exhibits combined with graphics, no differences for adult visitor age groups were found.[12] When adults and children are compared, children are less likely to read signs than adults.[13] Complex mixes of public interpretation include live exhibits, graphics, hands-on exhibits, and interactive exhibits. In these settings adults spend more time than children observing live exhibits, while children spend more time manipulating exhibits.[14] Groups spend more time in multimedia exhibits than in live exhibits.

A paucity of information is available on sex differences with respect to using exhibits. While no sex differences were found when considering visitors' overall use of interactive exhibits in Brookfield Zoo's Bird Discovery Point, there were sex differences for specific exhibit components.[15] Both T. J. Brennan and Beverly Serrell recorded no sex differences for adults who read graphics near Brookfield Zoo's live exhibits.[16]

The age and sex of visitors to our cultural institutions are indeed important. Institutions vary, however, and our understanding of our visitors is not advanced by attempts to describe the average zoo visitor. Indeed, it may be misleading to suggest that the average visitor has a higher level of education,[17] or travels in groups of three to four people[18] when a review of the demographic data suggests distinctions among the groups. Without providing specific data, E. Kelsey suggests that the visitor profile at the Vancouver Aquarium in Vancouver, British Columbia, is similar to the average visitor profiled by M. Greene. Barbara Birney's study of visitors to the Brookfield Zoo shows a very different portrait.[19]

Reports on the sex of zoo and aquarium visitors vary with the institution. Comparisons are difficult, since many reports fail to indicate how the respondents were interviewed. At least most samples are large. At San Diego, where the head of household was chosen as a respondent, the ratio of males to females was 50:50. At the Arizona–Sonora Desert Museum in Tucson, Arizona, 48 percent of the sample was female. Both institutions draw tourist populations that probably have a high socioeconomic background.[20]

Other studies, which do not state whether the subjects were self-selected within groups, report that at the National Aquarium in Baltimore, the Metro Washington Park Zoo in Portland, Oregon, the Denver Zoo, and the Philadelphia Zoo females constituted from 53 percent to 56 percent of each sample.[21]

In conflict with Kellert and J. Dunlap's findings on visitors to the Sedgwick Zoo, Wichita, Kansas, the Research Center found that females constituted 66 percent of the sample in a comprehensive study of the same zoo. There were 1,430 subjects in the Research Center's sample, more than 10 times the size of Kellert and Dunlap's sample, which may explain the discrepancy.[22] Almost two-thirds of the visitors to the Santa Barbara Zoo and 64 percent of those to the Brookfield Zoo were female.[23]

Is there a way to make sense of the findings? The explanation may lie less in the socioeconomic background of the individual and more in the way the public uses the institutions. In the communities surrounding the Santa Barbara, Brookfield, and Sedgwick zoos, which have low tourist populations and high zoo use, females may make frequent visits as part of a caretaking tradition.

It is frustrating to get comparable data from reports that simply state the mean number of visitors, indicate that most visitors are in nuclear groups, or simply omit the data.[24] Nonetheless, it appears that further research should concentrate not on whether zoos draw nuclear groups but on which institutions are characterized by high numbers of visitors coming in pairs and which ones draw extended family groups of five or more persons. These categories enable one to distinguish among institutions. While the San Diego Zoo reports that only 2 percent of its visitors attend in extended groups, 31 percent of Brookfield Zoo's visitors and 20 percent of Santa Barbara's visitors were in extended groups.[25] Extended groups respond to exhibit areas differently from the way pairs respond.

Data on visitor age groups are more complete. While 60 percent of the adults visiting the San Diego Zoo were 18–39 years old, 52 percent of those visiting the Arizona–Sonora Desert Museum were 17–45 years old. In contrast, 70 percent of the adult visitors to the National Aquarium in Baltimore were under 45 years of age. Seventy-five percent of adult visitors to the San Antonio Zoo were under age 45, and 82 percent of Brookfield Zoo visitors were 18–39, while 83 percent and 80 percent of the adult visitors to the Philadelphia and Sedgwick zoos, respectively, were between 17 and 45 years of age. In sum, institutions may be distinguished by whether they attract pairs or extended family groups and by whether they have proportionately more visitors from older age groups.[26]

Surprisingly, studies may not indicate the number of children that constitute the zoo audience. Kellert's national sample indicated that 38 percent of all zoo visitors were children. At the Brookfield Zoo and the Reid Park Zoo in Tucson, Arizona, 45 percent of each sample was composed of children.[27]

Educational Background: An Overview

The omission of information on visitors' educational background in zoo studies is stunning. Of the 75 studies reviewed for this article, only three contain this information. Educational background has been associated with visitors' satisfaction rating of their experience at the zoo, membership status, the ability to use interpretive guides successfully, attitudes toward conservation management issues, the desirability of purchasing interpretive media in merchandising areas, and visitors' cognitive gains associated with using interactive exhibits.[28]

Greene's assessment that most visitors are highly educated cannot be supported from existing reports. At the Sedgwick Zoo, 78 percent of the adult visitors sampled had completed high school only, and 62 percent of those at Brookfield had this level of education. The shift occurred with respect to the number of college graduates, since both institutions have few visitors with graduate degrees (10 percent and 11 percent, respectively). At the San Diego and Philadelphia zoos and the Arizona–Sonora Desert Museum, approximately 40 to 43 percent of the respondents had completed high school only. However, half of San Diego's sample and 44 percent of Philadelphia's sample had completed college. The Arizona–Sonora Desert Museum had proportionately fewer college graduates, but only because 25 percent of the sample had attained a graduate degree.[29]

We began this article with some observations about the importance of demographics to understanding the public's prior attitudes toward wildlife and the differential use of exhibits by individuals. There is a critical need for information about the educational background of our visitors. Kellert found that of all the demographic variables, education was the most sensitive indicator of concern, knowledge, and respect for animals. A more complete understanding of visitor demographics is necessary if zoos and aquariums are to seriously address their missions.

Notes

1. M. Greene, "Stalking the Average North American Zoogoer," *Museum News* 67, no. 1 (September/October 1988): 50–51.

2. B. A. Birney, "A Comparative Study of Children's Perceptions and Knowledge of Wildlife and Conservation as They Relate to Field Trip Experiences at the Los Angeles Museum of Natural History and the Los Angeles Zoo" (Ph. D. diss., University of California, Los Angeles, 1986); J. Lien, S. Staniforth, and L. Fawcett, "Teaching Fishermen about Whales: The Role of Education in a Fisheries Management and Conservation Problem," in *Marine Parks and Conservation: Challenge and Promise,* ed. J. Lien and R. Graham, vol. 1 (Ontario: National and Provincial Parks Association of Canada, 1985).

3. M. O. Westervelt, "A Provocative Look at Young People's Perceptions of Animals," *Children's Environments Quarterly* 1, no. 3 (1984): 4–7.

4. J. Dunlap, "Moral Reasoning about Animal Treatment," *Anthrozoos* 2, no. 4 (Spring 1989): 245–58.

5. S. R. Kellert, *Public Attitudes toward Critical Wildlife and Natural Habitat Issues,* phase 1 (Washington, D.C.: U.S. Fish and Wildlife Service, 1979).

6. C. Hill, "An Analysis of the Zoo Visitor," *International Zoo Yearbook* 29 (1989): 158–65.

7. Hill, 1989; Westervelt, 1984; S. R. Kellert, *Activities of the American Public Relating to Animals*, phase 2 (Washington, D.C.: U.S. Fish and Wildlife Service, 1980).

8. M. Surinova, "An Analysis of the Popularity of Animals," *International Zoo Yearbook* 11 (1971): 165–67; S. R. Kellert and J. K. Berry, *Attitudes, Knowledge, and Behaviors toward Wildlife as Affected by Gender* (New Haven: Yale University, School of Forestry and Environmental Studies, 1989); R. A. Bevins and S. Bitgood, "Developing a Device to Assess Attitudes toward Snakes," in *Visitor Studies: Theory, Research, and Practice,* ed. S. Bitgood (Jacksonville, Ala.: Center for Social Design, 1989), 2:123–30.

9. Hill, 1989; Kellert and Berry, 1989; Surinova, 1971; Westervelt, 1984.

10. D. L. Marcellini and T. A. Jensen, "Visitor Behavior in the National Zoo's Reptile House: A Preliminary Report," unpublished report (Washington, D.C.: National Zoological Park, 1986).

11. A. D. Bowd and A. C. Bowd, "Attitudes toward the Treatment of Animals: A Study of Christian Groups in Australia," *Anthrozoos* 3, no. 1 (Summer 1989): 20–24.

12. B. Serrell, "Zoo Label Study at Brookfield Zoo," *International Zoo Yearbook* 21 (1981): 54–61; J. S. Foster, J. J. Koran, M. L. Koran, S. Stark, A. Blackwood, and H. Landers, "The Effect of Multispecies Exhibits on Visitor Attention at the Jacksonville Zoological Park," in *Visitor Studies–1988: Theory, Research, and Practice,* ed. S. Bitgood, J. T. Roper, and A. Benefield (Jacksonville, Ala.: Center for Social Design, 1988), 1:113–19.

13. S. B. Rosenfeld, "Informal Learning in Zoos: Naturalistic Studies of Family Groups" (Ph.D. diss., University of California, Berkeley, 1980); C. Derwin, "An Evaluation of the Interpretive Elements of the Kopje Exhibit at the San Diego Zoo," unpublished report (San Diego, Calif.: San Diego Zoological Society, 1987); C. Deans, J. Martin, K. Noon, B. Nuesa, and J. O'Reilly, *A Zoo for Who? A Pilot Study in Zoo Design for Children,* technical report no. 87–10 (Jacksonville, Ala.: Center for Social Design, 1987).

14. B. A. Birney, "A Study of Visitor Behavior on Interactive Exhibits in Bird Discovery Point, Aquatic Bird House," unpublished report (Brookfield, Ill.: Chicago Zoological Society, 1990); Rosenfeld, 1980; Derwin, 1987; M. S. Korenic and A. M. Young, "Summative Evaluation of the Milwaukee Public Museum Biology Hall, 'Rain Forest: Exploring Life on Earth,'" unpublished report (Milwaukee, Wis.: Milwaukee Public Museum, 1989); Marcellini and Jensen, 1986.

15. Birney, "Study of Visitor Behavior," 1990.

16. T. J. Brennan, "Elements of Social Group Behavior in a Natural Setting" (Master's thesis, Texas A & M University, 1977); Serrell, 1981.

17. Greene, 1988.

18. B. Serrell, "Looking at Zoo and Aquarium Visitors," *Museum News* 58, no. 2 (November/ December 1980): 37–41.

19. E. Kelsey, "Parameters for Consideration in the Planning and Design of a New Exhibit–Arctic Canada," in *Visitor Studies,* 2:140–48; B. A. Birney, "Characteristics of Brookfield Zoo Visitors: Five Analyses of Our Audience," unpublished report (Brookfield, Ill.: Chicago Zoological Society, 1990).

20. Hill, 1989; S. R. Kellert and J. Dunlap, "Informal Learning at the Zoo: A Study of Attitude and Knowledge Impacts," unpublished report (Philadelphia: Zoological Society of Philadelphia, 1989).

21. Unpublished data, National Aquarium in Baltimore; Intercept Research Corp., "A Gate Survey of Washington Park Zoo," unpublished report (Portland, Oreg.: Metro Washington Park Zoo, 1990); Ciruli Associates, "Denver Zoo Visitor Survey and Economic Impact Study," unpublished report (Denver, Colo.: Denver Zoological Foundation, 1989); Kellert and Dunlap, 1989.

22. Kellert and Dunlap, 1989; Research Center, "1988 Economic Impact Study of the Sedgwick County Zoo and Botanical Gardens," unpublished report (Wichita, Kans.: Sedgwick County Zoo, 1988).

23. A. Bunn, "A Focused Investigation of Key Demographic Characteristics and the Importance of Museum Type on Who Visits," in *Museum Audiences Today: Building Constituencies for the Future*, ed. L. Draper (Los Angeles: Museum Educators of Southern California, 1987), pp. 33–51; Birney, "Characteristics of Brookfield Zoo Visitors," 1990.

24. Serrell, 1980; Rosenfeld, 1980; Derwin, 1987; Ciruli Associates, 1989.

25. Hill, 1989; Birney, "Characteristics of Brookfield Zoo Visitors," 1990; Bunn, 1987.

26. Hill, 1989; Kellert and Dunlap, 1989; unpublished data, National Aquarium in Baltimore; Gossen and Associates, "San Antonio Zoo: A Quantitative and Qualitative Research Report," unpublished report (San Antonio, Tex.: San Antonio Zoological Society, 1989); Birney, "Characteristics of Brookfield Zoo Visitors," 1990; Kellert and Dunlap, 1989; Research Center, 1988.

27. Kellert, 1980; Birney, "Characteristics of Brookfield Zoo Visitors," 1990; Deans et al., 1987.

28. B. A. Birney, "African Scenes Interpretation: Visitors' Knowledge of Concepts Related to Kopje and Waterhole Ecosystems and Wildlife," unpublished report (Brookfield, Ill.: Chicago Zoological Society, 1989); Birney, "Characteristics of Brookfield Zoo Visitors," 1990; Birney, "Using Rotating Guides to Interpret Immersion Exhibits: A Solution to Public Display Problems in Brookfield Zoo's Tropic World," unpublished report (Brookfield, Ill.: Chicago Zoological Society, 1989); Birney, "A Survey of Visitors' Attitudes towards Conservation Issues Related to Birds," unpublished report (Brookfield, Ill.: Chicago Zoological Society, 1988).

29. Greene, 1988; Research Center, 1988; Birney, "Characteristics of Brookfield Zoo Visitors," 1990; Derwin, 1987; Kellert and Dunlap, 1989.

PUTTING PLANS
INTO PRACTICE

Ideas on Informal Learning and Teaching

Susan M. Mayer

For me, the articles in this section reinforce a favorite theory, namely that it's difficult to be a generalist in an age of specialization. Why? Because appreciation for the generalist went out with the family physician. Everyone wants to be a specialist. But museum education (and education in general) is a generalist's domain. Read the ads for museum educator positions in any professional journal or newsletter and you will find a long and varied list of qualifications. The museum educator is expected to know much—and do more.

Museum education is a complex field abounding in outside forces and inside conventions, but it is also an area in education in which experimentation is still encouraged and rewarded. We make room for people with multiple backgrounds and viewpoints. Thank heavens our audiences don't have to pass tests or prove competency and our practitioners don't have to be certified by some bureaucracy. Museum education can be fun and profound at the same time. I like to think of those of us in museum education as pioneers in the field of education, and this section certainly supports that viewpoint.

We operate in a conservative environment, but it is important that we don't let that situation inhibit us. I have heard museum educators lament that they cannot make changes—but I wonder if they have really tried. Only you can answer that. Just don't give up too soon.

My experience has been one of witness to change. I came into this field at about the time that *Arts Awareness* was introduced at the Metropolitan Museum of Art.[1] The impact on the field was staggering, and most of the changes were good. I remembered that as a child I didn't like museums. I found them quiet, dull, and restrictive. When I was introduced to the theatrics and the participation of the *Arts Awareness* ideas, I was excited. The challenge of how to make museums come alive for the young visitor has intrigued me ever since.

A recent television program entitled "The Truth about Teachers" showed some outstanding teachers in their classrooms across the country, amid much speculation about the reasons for their success. Both teachers and students were of all ages and backgrounds. The teachers had just one thing in common: they all used theater and drama techniques of some kind. To my amazement this commonality was never mentioned. I suspect the fact that these teachers were "artists" was not even recognized as contributing to their success.

On the subject of individual differences, consider the visitors to our museums. Whether you were influenced by Viktor Lowenfeld and his haptic/visual learners, Betty Edwards's right brain-left brain theories, or more recently Howard Gardner's multiple intelligences, you must have realized by now that there are many ways that people see and learn.[2] David Keirsey and Marilyn Bates's research shows that although teachers in schools fall into two basic learning style groups, the majority of the children they teach fall into two quite opposite groups. These types "hunger for action" and "need physical involvement" in their learning. They "need a hands-on experience" and "enjoy performing."[3] Participation seems to be the operative concept. Only 4 percent of teachers in schools—one in 25!—are in this learning group.

In the museum education correspondence course that I coauthored, we seriously consider the "educational exhibition."[4] I have had directors and curators look at me blankly when I bring up the concept. Why is it so difficult to explain? (Remember the old line, "All exhibitions are educational. You only need to turn on the lights"?) Once again we thought about the common denominator of exhibitions whose purpose we consider distinctly educational (as opposed to, for example, retrospective or survey or theme shows) and found it to be "interactive" or "participatory." (These words can also describe emerging technology in museums, such as interactive video and participatory computer programs, as research is beginning to demonstrate.)

A museum exhibition that asks the visitor to think, compare, choose, or evaluate—not just to look—fits easily into this category. This mental activity must take place in the museum while viewing the exhibition, not at home curled up with the catalog. I recently visited the *High and Low* exhibition organized by the Museum of Modern Art and found that it fits my definition exactly. Participation also applies to didactic labels better known as "wall chat." When they pose a question or ask the viewer to make a comparison, they are most effective. Remember John Walsh's *Dutch Couples* exhibition at the Met? And what about my all-time favorite: Sherman Lee's idea of planting a copyist in the Cleveland Museum of Art in front of a generally overlooked painting to attract attention and entice the viewer to make comparisons without even realizing it?[5]

The operative idea is participation. The message here is to avoid anything passive—and this is especially true for children. Recent research shows that museum learning has a longitudinal impact as well.[6] This research can be extremely useful when defending budgets and programs or writing grants. When you can show statistics, corporate ears perk up.

I write from the perspective of a teacher of future museum educators, so I must consider some other issues. I believe that more research must be done in learning theory. Our early research on the use of varying educational techniques showed us that the method was not as important as the teacher.[7] And so the ultimate question is how to teach teachers. Teaching is one of the finest of arts. All the mystery, beauty, and individuality of art must go into it.

A word of warning: Be careful that you don't give up the "E" word too easily. I have noticed some drift toward renaming the Education Office the Department of Public Programs. We must consider the implications of that change very carefully. Are these programs tied to the collections and exhibitions? Is programming about body count? Are programs building visual literacy or merely entertaining? Do we really want to be called "programmers"? Are you satisfied that a series of lectures is really education? Do you want to turn your museum into a community center? Perhaps you will answer yes to some of these questions. I feel, however, that we must not only educate the public about collections but also educate the museum staff about what constitutes real education.

Finally, consider the word "education" itself—much abused, but a beautiful word whose original meaning is "to educe, to lead forth, to draw out as something latent." These ideas are freeing in that they don't restrict learning to stuffing in facts or to entertainment. In this definition it is the *response* that counts, not just the information. This is where real teaching comes in. This is where the artistry is. When a teacher catches this distinction, teaching is no longer a job but a calling.

Notes

1. Bernard Friedberg, *Arts Awareness* (New York: Metropolitan Museum of Art, n.d.).
2. Viktor Lowenfeld and W. Lambert Brittain, *Creative and Mental Growth*, 7th ed. (New York: Macmillan, 1982); Betty Edwards, *Drawing on the Right Side of the Brain* (New York: St. Martin's Press, 1979); Howard Gardner, *Frames of Mind: The Theory of Multiple Intelligences* (New York: Basic Books, 1983).
3. David Keirsey and Marilyn Bates, *Please Understand Me: Character and Temperament Types* (Del Mar, Calif.: Prometheus Nemesis Books, 1984), p. 122.
4. Susan M. Mayer and Becky Duval Reese, *An Introduction to Museum Education* (Austin, Tex.: University of Texas ExtensionService and Texas Association of Museums, 1980).
5. Barbara Y. Newsom and Adele Z. Silver, eds., *The Art Museum as Educator* (Berkeley: University of California Press, 1978), pp. 575–76.
6. Melinda M. Mayer, "The Real Object versus the Art Reproduction," *Texas Trends in Art Education* 4, no. 1 (Fall 1986): 20–23; Donna Love Vliet, *An Evaluation of the Extended Benefits of a Museum/School Art Study Program* (Master's thesis, University of Texas at Austin, 1987).
7. Susan M. Mayer, "Alternatives in Me-You-Zeums," *Journal of Art Education* 31, no. 3 (March 1978): 18–22.

INTRODUCTION
Inviting the Public to Learn in Art Museums

Vasundhara Prabhu

The beginning of every decade provides an opportunity to review the past and anticipate the future. For better or for worse, the 1990s are upon us. What changes will this decade bring to art museums and to art museum education? The pendulum of change has swung slowly from museum educators serving as primary advocates for the public to educators, curators, and administrators planning as a team to best serve the art and the museum's audience. Museums are now beginning to understand that they need a cohesive and explicit mission concerning art and the public. This mission must be easily understandable, for when people can see clearly the intent behind an institution or a program, they will feel more receptive to the museum and more comfortable in seeking it out.

In the 1990s, the programs museums develop to carry out their missions seem to be shifting from those targeted for a particular audience and based on specific funding to those designed for the general visitor. Who is this elusive, mythical visitor? Museum staff and trustees often have different or even conflicting ideas about how the "general public" is defined, especially in relation to traditional versus nontraditional visitors. Traditional visitors are usually defined as those who already visit the museum, while nontraditional visitors are those who live in the communities surrounding the museum but whose presence is not reflected in the museum attendance profile. While museums are expending much effort to analyze their visitor profile, one thing is clear: museums depend on the income from both types of visitors. A creative and attuned museum will encourage both groups to return again and again. What exemplifies such a museum, and, more specifically, what does the general visitor want or need from a museum in order to keep returning?

Assuming that a museum "delivers"—that is, it consistently offers exhibitions that reflect a variety of art forms, diverse artists, and a variety of cultures—visitors need to feel that there is no gap between what they expect and what they experience. They need to feel happy about getting to and arriving at the institution. Amenities should abound. The importance of simple yet comprehensive public relations is paramount. Directions should be concise, parking easy and affordable. Inside, plenty of comfortable seating should be available. A café is essential. The information visitors receive about the museum should be clear and informative. They should be able to visualize the exhibit they want to attend. Signage should be informative, direct, and plentiful. The exhibit installation should allow people to feel comfortable and happy in the space. Museum staff must be approachable, affable, and available.

Beyond the amenities, visitors will want to tune in to the museum environment. They need a way to retrieve information about artists, art, and cultural context quickly, through a variety of means. Wall text is usually one of the first means by which a visitor engages with a particular work of art. It is crucial, therefore, that the labels—as well as quotations from artists, time lines, and other text—be clear, concise, and short. Owing in part to American commercialism and television viewing patterns, the attention span of visitors is often very limited. Time is also of the essence for museum visitors. The text must be selective so that the visitor is not distracted from the art or overwhelmed by lengthy art jargon. Clarity and brevity are crucial as well to publications such as gallery guides and family guides. When appropriate, publications should be available in various languages.

Another information avenue open to the visitor is technology. We live in an audio, video, and computer world. Museums need to make better use of techniques that are integral to visitors' life experiences. Videotapes and audiotapes have been used for quite some time in the museum setting, but they need to be updated and streamlined. Videotapes must make information available quickly. A series of three- to five-minute videos can substitute for a 30-minute film. Audiotapes, too, should be concise, precise, and vibrant. Professional readers presenting interesting points of view help sustain a visitor's attention while illuminating the art on view. Interactive video is a new and exciting tool that has tremendous possibilities in an art museum setting. Children and adults alike enjoy this responsive medium.

Diverse programming is a necessary component in attracting and holding the general visitor. It also adds depth to the context of an exhibit. Timely lectures, symposiums, workshops, and demonstrations provide different perspectives on exhibitions. Tours and visits to artists' studios introduce visitors to the everyday world of art. With this greater accessibility comes greater understanding of and interest in the art, the artist, and the museum.

Museums are social places, and programming also attracts visitors who are interested in making new social contacts. While one museum's recent ad—"a great place to Meat," referring to a work by Roy Lichtenstein—may be an overstatement, it does strike a chord of truth. Visitors sometimes attend for purely social reasons. But if the programming is educational and entertaining, they often return for more art, regardless of social outcome. Interesting, pertinent speakers who present diverse points of view in well-organized, simply structured lectures, workshops, and demonstrations stimulate the visitor to spend time in the museum environment. Ultimately, the visitor will view the museum as an invaluable resource and communicate his or her enthusiasm to family and friends.

All of these strategies are visitor-centered in that the visitor selects and gains access to both the format and the content of the information that he or she needs in order to appreciate the art on view. What these strategies suggest, then, is a change in the way museums perceive the business of presenting and interpreting art to their public. The challenge for museum educators is to provide cohesive leadership toward a museum-wide focus on reaching the general visitor and getting him or her to return. All of the research, writing, and program development that curatorial and education staff currently perform should be redirected to meet the needs of the general visitor. Ultimately, the crucial point museums need to grapple with is that no matter how great the art or the exhibition, without creative education programs, high-quality publications, inviting spaces, and sufficient visitor amenities, the general public will not feel inspired to think about the art or return to the museum.

A Personal Viewpoint

Zora Felton

More than two decades ago when I entered the museum field—a naive but enthusiastic novice—I knew a lot about education in a settlement house but virtually nothing about education in a museum. I often smiled uncomfortably about "stumbling and bumbling" my way about, working 60- and 70-hour weeks with the rest of the small staff at the Smithsonian's Anacostia Neighborhood Museum (now the Anacostia Museum) as we tried to ferret out and define our roles and determine what worked best in our museum.

Our most frequent visitors were the folks who stopped to visit on their way to the supermarket or the drugstore or while they waited for the bus in front of our door. Others were the precocious teenagers who lived within hailing distance of the museum, the ever-present two- and three-feet tall little people who came to "see about the animals," the tour groups, and the men who hung out on the corner.

Then there were no guards, no mandatory I.D. badges, no sign-in books, and staff members ran a vacuum cleaner as often as they ran the old, hand-cranked mimeograph machine. And we prided ourselves on the lack of vandalism and theft. When I asked a child why she thought no one ever stole anything from our museum, she answered, wide-eyed, "Because there's nothing to steal!" (So much for the artifacts, art and crafts materials, objects in the mini-touchable areas, and animals in the small zoo!)

The exhibitions and the informal educational programs that grew out of them were driven by those who chose the make the museum their special possession. Hence, more than two decades ago we role-played and created flannelboards that invited preschool and primary-grade children to help museum educators tell stories about their African heritage. Our museum held seminars, workshops, symposiums, and neighborhood meetings on everything from housing needs to the arts. Entire bands practiced over the dinner hour, and karate, acrobatic, and dance and drama classes called the museum home.

And in between, we churned butter, pulled taffy, made lye soap, and offered groups of 30 adults or children opportunities to make ice cream for less than $1.

The ensuing years have brought many expected and unexpected changes. A rapidly developing, sophisticated exhibitions schedule led to the loss of program space—including the Children's Room where we created and fine-tuned many of our programs. We no longer offer the "old Anacostia" demonstrations. Instead, our programs are keyed more specifically to current exhibitions, times of the year, or seasonal holidays such as Kwanzaa or Juneteenth. We might provide a printmaking or a "So You Want to Be an Inventor" workshop for children or for adults and children, or a summer science camp in collaboration with the National Air and Space Museum, or a teacher workshop in African-American art.

The most significant change is that we no longer are located on the busy, arterial thoroughfare of Martin Luther King, Jr., Avenue. We moved about four years ago to a quiet, pastoral setting nestled in the nearby Anacostia hills. We were sorry to leave behind most of our foot traffic but glad to say goodbye to an antiquated building and the ubiquitous young drug dealers who had invaded our block.

We are gradually learning to use our new resources. Even now, we are developing a Dr. George Washington Carver Nature Trail that will focus on urban ecology. Here visitors will also be able to take a simulated journey on Harriet Tubman's Underground Railroad. Travelers will not only learn about the natural sciences but come face to face with the manner in which escaped slaves used the natural environment to help facilitate their flight to freedom.

We are still a community-based museum, but we now include communities outside of metropolitan Washington, D.C., in our expanded target area. And we continue to use our resources to cast penetrating lights on urban issues that afflict the African-American community. AIDS is but one example of an urban blight in a community such as ours.

When I reflect on our keys to whatever programmatic successes we may continue to have, some need to be added to the more obvious knowledge of subject matter, mastery of a process, and so forth:

■ a warm, enveloping setting that does not intimidate (sometimes being small is not all bad)

■ an expectation that all visitors will learn

■ an ability to communicate with diverse groups

■ the absence of fear in the face of those who are "different"

■ the presence of people in significant capacities who look like most of our visitors.

Visitors still comment on "how nice the people are here." This suggests to us that not all of their previous museum encounters have been positive. Therein lies a lesson for all of us. As to the programs described in this section, all are exemplary in their own right. Who can quarrel with success? Given additional resources, these programs would introduce even larger numbers of diverse audiences to the wonder and awe of our museums so that those who come to admire will return to learn.

Decentralizing Interpretation: Developing Museum Education Materials with and for Schools

Peter S. O'Connell

In developing educational programs for museums, the educator's first task is to organize the basic framework of exhibits, tours, staff training, promotional announcements, and logistical procedures. Once these are in place, museum educators are only too painfully aware of the limitations of a one-shot experience; we seek immediately to expand the museum walls by reaching into the classroom through previsit orientation materials (usually free), teacher workshops, staff visits to the classroom, and educational materials such as loan kits, primary source packets, and audiovisual materials. Ultimately, our objective is to help the teacher become an adjunct to the museum education staff—and vice versa. An important and often undervalued benefit to the museum is the constructive and friendly criticism of its programs by teachers who use them. Many become museum members and in turn promote the museum's programs to parents, friends, and colleagues.

Several museums and historical societies began developing curriculum materials during the 1970s, often through grants from the National Endowment for the Humanities, state arts and humanities councils, and other public and private funding agencies. Old Sturbridge Village, for example, began developing educational materials in 1971, first in mimeograph form using museum funds. With grants from the National Endowment for the Humanities, the National Endowment for the Arts, the Massachusetts State Department of Education, and private foundations, the materials were upgraded and diversified, resulting in packets of primary sources, audiovisual materials, teacher background papers, curriculum guides (such as day-by-day teaching plans), local history sourcebooks, and student hands-on activity packets. These materials have proven invaluable in raising the quality of programs through teacher workshops, and they formed the basis of our collaboration with schools.

The Old Sturbridge Village marketing strategy for these materials has paralleled their development. Initially the materials were promoted through regular program announcements and through workshops. Later a catalog was developed and mailed to a regional audience. This two-color publication was replaced by a four-color catalog, and most recently [1984], after more than 12 years in the works, the

Roundtable Reports 9, no. 1 (Winter 1984): 17–22.

museum is negotiating with Longman, Inc., to promote and distribute materials to a national market.

Educational materials development is a relatively complex task, however, and comparatively few museums or historical organizations have done much in this area. The museums that have assembled educational resources have found the process difficult for a variety of reasons. The National Endowment for the Humanities Division of Education, which had previously supported many museum-related educational materials projects, has now changed its priorities to focus on teacher training institutes. Evaluation led NEH staff to question whether such materials were sufficiently well integrated into the school curriculum to justify their relatively high development cost.

Surprisingly little has been written about this very important part of museum education programming, and what has been written or presented at conferences has emphasized the content or the products of the packet or kit. We have not shared either the problems we have encountered or the questions left unanswered. I have found similar kinds of questions and problems faced by museum educators, who dealt with them in isolation and ignorance of one another's experience. Thus, similar procedural errors may have limited the success of projects and resulted in the judgment that these kinds of projects cannot be successful. The baby has been thrown out with the bath water.

As museum professionals we know that our resources are important if teachers are to teach the arts and the humanities effectively. Without educational materials and teacher workshops as linking elements, the museum's programs will be isolated satellites in orbit around the school systems we wish to serve; in turn, classrooms will continue to suffer from the use of general texts and to experience poor teaching techniques. Given the recent critical reports of schooling, the opportunity for museums to work with schools and the need for such collaboration have never been stronger.

Our task, then, is to share our experiences in developing educational materials with and for schools, analyze those experiences, and arrive at some guidelines to use in structuring our work and anticipating problems. Based on our experience at Old Sturbridge Village and on several discussions with other museum educators, I'd like to propose some basic guidelines derived from successful case studies or in reaction to common problems. My hope is that these guidelines will not only be useful to others but will also initiate a dialogue that will result in more comprehensive guidelines.

The development of successful educational materials depends on four factors:

1. a well-thought-out educational philosophy of how children learn, what is important for them to learn generally, and the role our educational institutions can and should play in the child's education

2. an experimental approach to teaching and learning in which theory is put into practice in classroom and museum situations, evaluated, and revised before final

publication of materials

3. a good organizational planning model involving collaboration with schools from the beginning of a project, clear role definitions, deadlines, and a budget adequate for the scope of the project

4. a long-term financial and marketing plan for the materials.

If one of these elements is weak, problems can and will limit the project's success.

How Do Children Learn?

With the mere mention of course titles like Educational Philosophy, History of Education, and Theory of Curriculum Development in Schools of Education, I can hear your groans. These are infamous courses universally condemned as boring, unhelpful, and generally useless by everyone in education, except perhaps by the state certification boards that continue to require them and the professors of education who continue to teach them. This reputation is deserved since the courses are usually taught before teachers have sufficient teaching experience to be interested in the questions and without reference to the educational experience of the people in the course; they all too often violate the very educational principle they seek to teach. "Do as I say, not as I do," becomes the slogan and the practice.

Nevertheless, without a clear sense of how children learn in the museum—a general philosophy of teaching and learning, shared by museum staff and teachers alike—any materials development project and probably the education program itself is in trouble. In my experience, particularly in programs for grades 3–8, our major museum education audience, two different educational philosophies are at work, though perhaps not consciously.

Nelson Graburn, drawing on the work of Claude Levi-Strauss, suggests that museums make sense of the world through rational, cognitive, and scientific approaches in which facts are organized into ideas, analyzed into principles and theories, and then presented to the public as exhibits and programs designed to help the visitor understand how the world has changed and how it works. But as Graburn points out, most visitors (including children) tend not to think scientifically unless they have been trained in the discipline of the museum they are visiting. Rather, they experience the encounter with objects "mythically," that is, the new experience in all its details is absorbed into their previous experiences and then a new synthesis of experience is formed. By contrast, "the cognitive, scientific mode, then, strips objects and events of their associations and contingencies, the very things that relate them to life," in Graburn's view.[1]

John Dewey uses different terms to describe the potential gap between a child's approach to learning and the assumption underlying a scientifically organized curriculum:

> The child lives in a somewhat narrow world of personal contacts. Things hardly come within his experience unless they touch, intimately and obviously, his own well-being, or that of his family and friends. His world is a world of persons with their personal

interests, rather than a realm of facts and laws. It has the unity and completeness of his own life. He goes to school, and various studies divide and fractionalize the world for him. Geography selects, it abstracts and analyzes one set of facts, and from one particular point of view. Arithmetic is another division, grammar another department, and so on indefinitely. . . . Facts are torn away from their original place in experience and rearranged with reference to some general principle.[2]

Dewey goes on to note that proponents of scientific approaches to curriculum view each child as simply an "immature being who is to be deepened: his is the narrow experience to be widened." Dewey opposed to this approach the child-centered school, declaring, "The source of whatever is dead, mechanical, and formal in schools is found precisely in the subordination of the life and experience of the child to the curriculum. It is because of this that 'study' has become a synonym for what is irksome, and a lesson identical with task."[3]

This debate has waxed and waned in American education for more than a hundred years, with a current emphasis on basic skills separated from both content and experience. But rather than seeing these as competing ideologies, Dewey suggested a synthesis in which (museum) teachers see within the child's experience elements (facts and principles) of formal study, attitudes and interests that can be directed to a more complete and more abstract understanding of a topic. From the side of the content specialist, he observed, "It is a question of interpreting them [formal studies] as outgrowths of forces operating in the child's life, and of discovering the steps that intervene between the child's present experience and their richer maturity."[4]

In practice, many of our educational materials projects develop from previously developed exhibits and museum research. The intellectual structure is in place, and our tendency is to develop learning activities to teach these facts, ideas, and conclusions to children through vocabulary, thinking processes, and resources selected because we are very familiar and comfortable with them. But we may not consider what form the ideas may have already assumed in the child's experience or how we can create more complete experiences in substantial detail (feeling, senses, action) that might guide the child toward the abstract ideas that result in higher level thinking and feelings. We must consider whether our vocabulary needs to replace the student's or whether terms can complement one another, our names for things growing out of a new experience for the child.

Each of these differing educational approaches—one content-centered, emphasizing facts and principles, the other child-centered, emphasizing experience—is incomplete without the other. Unless they are synthesized in an atmosphere of mutual respect, several problems result:

■ The museum staff tend to regard teachers as ignorant and immature, needing to be educated but unwilling to recognize the need. The teacher becomes an obstacle to be worked around. The museum tends to develop "teacher-proof" materials and prefers to send its own staff into the classroom to prepare students.

■ Teachers regard the museum staff as content specialists ignorant of how kids learn. They tolerate museum staff in order to get into the museum and have their kids see the objects firsthand, creating their own preparation and follow-up.

■ The child's experience tends to be the lowest common denominator of content and experience. Some activities are strong in content and weak in experience or vice versa, but in either case the integration of the museum experience into the child's school curriculum tends to be weak. We run the risk of potentially exciting lessons becoming mere drudgery, or we leave lessons at the level of experience without drawing them into a complete understanding for and with these students.

To forestall these disappointments and broken promises in developing materials, museum staff need an educational background in curriculum theory and practice or need to hire someone on the team with formal training in that area. In addition, we need to involve teachers early and often and adopt an experimental approach in applying theory to practice.

From Experience to Reflection, From Theory to Experience
Our objective is to create learning experiences for children that promote meaningful interactions with objects, buildings, people, processes, documents, visuals, or other sources of data. As teachers we hope to help students draw meaning out of these experiences and to stimulate further interest. In general, museum-based materials projects are successful in selecting stimulating and significant learning resources, putting information-rich slide-tapes together, and identifying key questions for discussion. The difficulty comes in identifying teaching strategies that will begin the learning sequence at the level of the child's experience with the organizing concepts involved in the unit, suggest a direction of inquiry, and create a sense of curiosity.

It is a tall order but a necessary one. Museum staff often structure the work so that this task is assigned to teachers, and rightly so. Good teachers are curriculum designers and activity inventors *par excellence*. However, classroom teachers are inexperienced with museum sources and need help brainstorming possible activities. And as museum staff become more skilled in designing and sequencing activities, they discover that their skill influences the resources they seek and choose, the training of docents, and the implementation of teacher workshops.

At Old Sturbridge Village several types of learning strategies have proven successful with students and teachers; "model" teaching, in which museum staff demonstrate a technique, is both instructive and fun.

Begin with the Children's Experience
Use concrete observations and experiences in a contemporary context. Students keep diaries, make visual collages of family space on floor plans, and construct a class census. Out of these experiences are drawn ideas of family roles, functions, room use, interaction, or customs that become the basis of comparison with the early 19th century. These concepts have meaning because of their concrete associations, but

they come to have more abstract power as students apply them in an investigation of a new culture. The initial activities are fun and result in classroom exhibits.

Establish a Beginning Point of Reference

Give the students a point of reference for the museum experience that has implied in it a dynamic direction. Usually this is accomplished at Old Sturbridge Village by assigning students an identity as a 19th-century family or community member, which in turn creates a need to know personal information. A direction is implied, and previous classroom activities suggest relevant exhibits to visit and questions to ask. Skills and ideas previously introduced are applied and practiced, much as the content specialist does in his or her own research.

Create an Organizing Activity

A problem, task, or question provides some focus but requires initiative and thought by the children. They can be asked to prepare a story, draw a picture or map of "their" house (1830), or create a short role-play situation in which their characters have a problem. These tasks give meaningful shape to an exploration, suggest the kinds of information needed, and strengthen the children's roles as active learners. Most such "organizing" activities need to be completed back in the classroom, which ensures an integral and continuing relationship between museum and classroom.

Emphasize Sensory Learning

The more senses a child uses, the more fully he or she explores a topic and the more likely he or she is to remember the experience. The more the student can become part of the museum experience and be an active thinker and imaginative doer within the limits of evidence, the more likely he or she will move on to higher levels of thinking. When the data are in the form of a formal exhibit, a primary source, a lecture, or a slide-tape, it is important for the student to have a point of view, an interesting task beyond the data, and an active imagination.

Use Hands-On Activities

Participatory activities can be used to balance information-centered activities. All of us do this in our museums, but it is helpful for development teams to identify crafts and art projects, games, creative language arts activities, and experiments for the classroom. When possible, these materials need to be spelled out in step-by-step instructions with laminated diagrams given to the students for use in small groups. Teachers survive on activities that involve kids—especially on Friday afternoons! If the hands-on activities are there in easy-to-use form, an uninitiated teacher is more likely to buy and use the materials. We make a mistake by not developing our "Suggested Activities for Using These Materials" section into actual activity formats: teachers simply do not have the time to gather the resources, organize the questions, and structure the logistics for more than two to four activities in a unit.

Organize the Teaching Activities into a Sequence

Museum educators are reluctant to overstructure the teaching either because of a fear of preempting the teacher's prerogatives or their own lack of classroom experience. But in practice, busy teachers appreciate knowing what the materials are intended to do; the activity sequence presents a clear and understandable road map. Teachers rarely feel compelled to follow any set plan; they pick and choose, recombine activities, or plug in previously successful ones of their own. An initial sequence is easily adaptable, more likely to lead to abstract thinking by students, and more likely to be useful to a teacher as well.

Each museum is, of course, a unique learning environment with its own content strengths and appeals for students. These strategies may or may not lend themselves to generalization in other museums. In either case, however, the most important task for the materials development team is to begin with the experiences of learners and with the integrity of the content in order to develop a clear sense of a teaching sequence centered on the museum visit.

Project Structure

The structure of a project follows logically from its rationale. Staff members represent particular points of view: the content (historian in a history museum, scientist in a science museum, etc.); the student in the classroom (curriculum specialist, teachers); the student in the museum (museum educator); the attractiveness of the materials (designer); and the logistics of the work (administrator). Working together, these role players represent needs and propose solutions to potential conflicts.

It is easy to see how difficulties would arise if one or another of these roles were missing or inadequately represented. The content is in error or weakly conceptualized if the researcher or curator is missing. If teachers are not represented from the beginning (the most common error made by museums developing educational materials), several problems can result, all of them disastrous. The materials may be at too high a reading level for students, the activities insufficiently developed or unworkable, the sequence inappropriate for the logistics and timetable of the school, the topic inappropriate to the grade level, the materials too expensive, and so on.

Moreover, museums also often harbor the bias that teachers have to be trained in content before they can effectively prepare students. In fact, we find that teachers do need more content training, and many are interested in acquiring it if they feel the resulting program will lead to good learning for kids. The teachers bring classroom teaching expertise to the museum and, in turn, expect to learn content and museum teaching techniques. If the museum conveys the impression that teachers' involvement is unnecessary or the last step in the process, teachers will be less likely to use the materials or seek the content training necessary to do so effectively. Museums have trained teachers to expect a museum experience to be heavily factual and not very much fun for kids aged 10–16. If we expect to break this deadlock, we must be prepared to reach out to teachers with both realism and optimism.

By the same token, the lack of a designer or too much designer input can be a problem. Materials printed on colored paper or on sizes larger than 8 1/2 by 11 inches are inconvenient to photocopy. Too much glossy design or too many photographs make the materials overly expensive. An experienced educational designer can help a team produce attractive, inexpensive materials, can speak a printer's language, and can educate the whole team in the mysterious arts of color screens, photo reductions, type size and style, and layout techniques. The designer must function as part of a team, however; if the designer zips in and out, has insufficient contact with teachers or museum staff, is inexperienced in educational materials development, or is under pressure of deadlines, the resulting materials may not turn out well. The designer works for the team; if push comes to shove, design decisions are made by team leaders.

Materials development projects inevitably experience planning and logistical problems. At the outset, everything is possible—the tasks generally defined and the team members all lined up to do what they promised. By the end of the project, everyone is pressed for time, the budget is either overexpended or the funding period will end before the money is spent, team members may not be speaking to one another, and everyone is exhausted. Apart from the principles outlined above, some of these problems can be avoided if the project director–administrator defines deadlines early on for project conceptualization, teacher workshops, piloting of materials, printing, and final reports. Such planning will allow people to schedule their time far enough in advance to ensure that commitments are firm and the project director can hold everyone accountable. The project director must have institutional support from the museum and from a counterpart in the school structure if the project is to meet deadlines. The project director and the team members must be prepared to compromise their dreams by eliminating some project activities and scaling down others as a result of insufficient time or money. Clear checkpoints ensure that decision making occurs early enough in the process so that compromises, substitutions, and personal adjustments are not traumatic.

Of course, some of the roles can be combined, or consultants can be hired to perform certain roles, but both these approaches can cause problems. In one project, an education curator, traditionally low on the museum status pole, wrote a grant and became project director. Her authority on paper did not necessarily correspond with her traditional relationships, so she had difficulty in getting tasks accomplished. A new consultant needs time to learn the museum or a new content area and cannot begin to contribute as quickly as a grant timeline might call for. In fact, if there is one fault common to materials development projects, it is insufficient time allowed to accomplish the tasks. At Old Sturbridge Village, we generally presume that a project will last about two years before publication is complete. A one-year project involving field testing of materials puts a great deal of pressure on all concerned, even if staff are on the project full time.

Financial Strategy

Museums are relatively inexperienced in developing financial plans and marketing strategies for their educational materials. We tend to concentrate first on the development of high-quality materials and only later to consider marketing questions. However, unless we consider these questions early in the development process, we may produce a highly designed, complicated kit that when replicated will be too expensive for purchase by most schools.

In developing educational materials we become publishers. Our materials compete with those already being offered to schools by sales representatives of large publishers and promoted through four-color brochures or elaborate catalogs of supplementary media. Museum materials have an initial marketing advantage in that teachers realize that we have the primary sources that interest students and that we are the keepers of historical, scientific, and artistic "truth." However, our materials must also be attractive, easily used, reasonably priced, and effectively promoted.

If we are to function successfully in the educational materials business, even in a small way, we need to think seriously about our potential market, the demand for particular products we are uniquely able to supply, the price range appropriate to the market and the product, and a method of promoting the materials we produce. Analysis of these factors will establish some parameters, which in turn may determine how many items are in our initial production run, whether reproduction artifacts can be included, whether materials will be sold or rented, and a host of other decisions that directly affect the educational quality of our materials.

I hear your inward groans at the business jargon, but it's not that bad; we simply need to give some thought to how we will replace our initial materials once they have been used up or sold. Will we have generated enough income from sales to be able to reprint them? If not, through inadequate financial planning, we will have allowed an important educational link to the schools to lapse. Museum administrators, faced with increasingly tight budgets, are asking all departments to project what the return (educational and financial) will be for a given investment of staff time and money. Unless we can provide this data in a convincing way, we may not get permission to initiate the first materials project; if the first project does not meet expectations, permission and funding for the second project will be even more difficult to secure.

All of us know our market in general terms. Most of our visitors are students and teachers in grades 3–8. Teachers in the middle grades take more field trips, utilize more experience-based teaching techniques, and are more likely to purchase the so-called enrichment or supplementary materials we produce than are their secondary colleagues. We are already mailing our regular program announcements to this audience and can expect a reasonable response to an inexpensive promotional mailing announcing a new educational resource. Many museums have found that professional teacher organizations (reading and social studies) will include flyers in their regular mailings to members and include museum workshops at their annual meetings. Some museums have collaborated to purchase exhibit space at these teacher meetings. Some state departments of education have assisted in the promotion of museum materials.

The demand for and response to our resources depends upon audience size, method of promotion, and price range. Consequently, it is difficult to predict. If the materials were free, we could give away thousands, while in a year we might be lucky to sell a dozen large curriculum kits containing artifacts, source material, and a color videotape. It is reasonable to expect to sell 50 to 150 copies annually of items in the $5 to $15 range. Remember that your materials will take two to three years to become known; you'll need to continue promoting them. Remember also that teachers will be buying materials only once or twice a year, either when they are focusing on a topic relevant to your materials or when money has to be spent from the budget. Talk with teachers about the best time to mail your promotions.

Museum educators are often uncertain about the proper price for educational materials; we tend to sell our materials too cheaply because we want schools to be able to afford them. In doing so, we do ourselves a disservice because we earn insufficient return to continue to produce materials. A more reliable procedure is to compile an accurate assessment of the actual costs of producing the initial run of a resource: staff time, printing, typing, promotion, mailing, design, and all other costs. Double these costs and divide by the number of items produced on the first run to arrive at a selling price. This procedure is more likely to assure that you will recover your costs in the first run, enable you to reprint, and provide enough funds to start another materials project.

You may decide that you need to spread the costs over two production runs in order to keep the price low enough for the market; you may choose not to include some expenses because of the training experience it provided, because the museum received substantial free publicity, or because of some other benefit. These are options, but it is important to think about selling price early in the project as you make decisions about the make-up of the kits, resource packets, and slide-tapes. A quick check of commercial education resources will provide a sense of the going price ranges.

Conclusion

The process of developing resources for schools may seem formidable. But in fact, most museums already sell educational materials to the general public. We need only walk through our own museum gift shops with a group of classroom teachers to see these materials. Sometimes we are a bit shocked at the inaccuracy or low quality of some of the commercially available materials sold in our shops. But since there is a demand, and since we have not produced anything of higher quality, this is what will be sold.

However, many of the commercially produced materials can be combined with resources we develop, supplemented by background books, and turned into a respectable and thoroughly helpful set of education resources for classroom teachers. A promotional mailing can be developed to feature these materials, generating income to allow the development of new resource materials. Gradually, the museum can expand its resources using grant funds when available, and in the process it can increase its reputation among teachers.

Without the links to school classrooms that our museums' educational resources and workshops supply, museum education programs will be limited in their impact on the minds of children. Well-conceived projects can succeed in developing and marketing museum materials. I encourage you to share your experiences and your resources with fellow museum educators.

Notes

1. Nelson Graburn, "The Museum and the Visitor Experience," in *Museum Education Anthology,* ed. Susan K. Nichols (Washington, D.C.: Museum Education Roundtable, 1984), p. 179.
2. John Dewey, *The Child and the Curriculum* (1902; reprint, Chicago: University of Chicago Press, 1956).
3. Ibid.
4. Ibid.

Education Programs for Older Adults

Elizabeth M. Sharpe

America's older adults, numbering more than 25 million, are too diverse to fit any single mold. They are perhaps best described as millions of different individuals, each with his or her own unique combination of past and present interests, life-styles, personality traits, and occupations. In addition, they experience a great variety of changing physical, sensory, emotional, and mental capabilities.

How, then, do museum educators develop programs that will pique the interests and satisfy the needs of all the individuals in this diverse group? Quite literally, it is impossible, but well-planned programs, appropriately presented, can involve many older adults.

One experience to draw on is the Senior Series program that was sponsored by the National Museum of American History. It combined artifacts, illustrated lectures, demonstrations, discussions, and historic activities to fulfill several objectives:

■ to extend museum services to those Washington, D.C., older adults who could not travel to the Smithsonian

■ to promote an understanding of the change in American culture and technology and its effect on American life

■ to enrich the lives of elderly participants by providing opportunities to relate personal experiences to changes in technology and society and to share the experiences with others.

The Older Adult Audience

As of 1980, one in nine Americans (11.3 percent) was age 65 and older, according to the U.S. census. This percentage varied by sex, race, and ethnic group. The ratio of women to men, on the average, was nearly three to two. About 12 percent of whites were 65 and over, compared to 8 percent of blacks, 6 percent of Asian and Pacific Islanders, and 5 percent each of Native Americans and Hispanics.[1]

Most older people are functioning and healthy. More than 90 percent of all persons age 65 and over require no help in daily living.[2] Similarly, most are mentally alert. Only 5 to 6 percent of older adults ever in their lives develop senile dementia, or "senility" as it is popularly called.[3]

In 1980, most older adults lived in family settings. One-third of all older persons

Roundtable Reports 9, no. 4 (Fall 1984): 3–5.

lived alone or with nonrelatives. Only 5 percent lived in an institution such as a nursing home.[4] While many older adults were well off in 1979, nearly one in four was in poverty or near-poverty. More blacks and Hispanics were poor compared with whites.[5]

Many older adults come to museums individually or with friends and family to take advantage of programs billed for adults or the general public. However, if programs are offered, greater numbers of older adults will come in groups of their peers. These groups typically are organized by health and social service agencies, religious groups, and social clubs and associations. There are an estimated 83,000 such groups nationwide, including more than 29,000 board and care facilities, 23,000 nursing homes, about 13,000 nutrition programs providing hot meals, 10,000 senior citizen centers, almost 7,000 retirement communities and housing sites, and nearly 1,000 adult day care centers. These figures do not reflect the tens of thousands of older adult clubs that gather on a regular basis for religious, social, or leisure interests.[6]

There are more than 700 such groups in the Washington, D.C., metropolitan area alone. All share one need—providing education and recreation for their members. Here, the museum can respond with intellectually challenging, stimulating, and enjoyable programming.

Program Development

The subject matter is the most important part of the program. There is no evidence to suggest that the aging process diminishes cognitive capacity. Learning can occur if the older adult is willing, if the information has relevance, and if it is presented properly.[7]

Nevertheless, formal schooling varies greatly among older adults. While the average older adult has completed 10.2 years of school, about four in ten (41 percent) have completed high school, and about one in ten (9 percent) has had four or more years of college.[8]

Compounding the differences in education level is heterogeneity: individuals "may be at different ages at the same time in terms of mental capacity, physical health, endurance, creativity."[9] To respond to the needs of this varied audience, a program must offer something for everyone. Presenting in a multisensory mode makes it possible to include everyone in the program. The Senior Series staff found that informal lecture discussions combined with object handling, demonstrations, activities, and personal chats were essential to the learning experience. The older adults could gain information through their sharpest senses.

Another important program ingredient is the incorporation of older adults' experiences. In an education program for adults of any age, the students' experiences should be drawn on as a teaching tool. According to educator Malcolm Knowles, "Experience is a resource for learning and when experience is ignored, the adult perceives it as a rejection of him or herself as a person."[10]

Experience is even more important to older adults because the recollection of past experiences—reminiscing—is an integral part of the aging process. According to Robert Butler, as death nears, an older person's concern turns from the future to the past in a process called "life review."[11] The team of psychologist Harriet Wrye and educational therapist Jacqueline Churilla detailed the benefits that elderly people derive from reminiscing:

> Simply summing up one's life can enhance pride and self-esteem; elderly people who are not active in the present often gain pleasure in recalling what they have achieved in the past. The life review may serve to restore a sense of ethnic identity, since individuals sometimes lose sight of their cultural and ethnic heritage in the press of daily life. Reminiscence can reweave those lost threads of the past.[12]

By encouraging older adults to share their experiences and to reminisce, one ensures their involvement and participation. Even the less informed older participants will have something to offer. In addition, with a varied program format, many activities, including taking part in a demonstration, handling an object, or offering a point in discussion, constitutes participation.

Program Presentation

After subject matter and format, presentation style is the most important program component. Although each older adult is different from all the others, each forms groups with other persons who have similar abilities and needs. This means that education program design must be flexible enough to be presented in a number of ways.

For the purposes of presentation, the Senior Series staff presenters were able to identify three loose categories of older adult audiences. The first group is composed of people who live alone or with their families, are in good physical and mental health, and belong to senior citizen clubs, nutrition programs, or senior centers or live in residences for older adults. This group tends to be the most healthy, mobile, and active. Most members of this group would be able to attend programs in the museum.

In the second group, members may also live with their families but require some nursing care during the day and therefore attend adult day care programs. While most are well, many have limited mobility and will need some help in passing objects to one another. Perhaps not all, but most, would enjoy attending a program in the museum.

The third group, nursing home residents, are generally more frail and infirm. The majority in this group has limited mobility and will need assistance in passing objects and in doing activities. But for the most part their minds are sharp, and they are eager to participate in an educational program. A small number of nursing home residents would be able to travel to the museum.

These three categories should be used only as a general guideline. For more specific information, the museum staff should discuss the group's characteristics with the activity director before the program and spend some time at the beginning of the program meeting the group members to determine their interests and abilities. (For more specific suggestions, see below.) Remember that physical disability is not an indicator of mental disability. During the Senior Series one nursing home participant, a former professor of philosophy, was brought in his wheelchair to every program. He could not sit up well, never participated, and appeared to be uninterested. At the conclusion of the series, he called a presenter aside to tell her how much he appreciated the intellectual content of the program.

Conclusion

America is growing older daily. Between 1900 and 1980, the percentage of the U.S. population aged 65 and over nearly tripled, while the number of older Americans increased about eight times. The older adult population is expanding so rapidly that it will more than double within the next 50 years.[13]

Museums must prepare for this population shift. In the past, museum educators have spent much of their time and energy with school children. In the future, they will be challenged to reassess who their priority audiences are, thus considering the needs of older adults, the fastest-growing age group. Perhaps then, museum educators will have the skills and experience to replace age-specific programming with programming that addresses lifelong learning.

Notes

1. U.S. Department of Health and Human Services, *Facts about Older Americans, 1980–81* (Washington, D.C.: U.S. Department of Health and Human Services, 1981), p. 1.
2. Office of Museum Programs, Smithsonian Institution, *Older Adults and the Museum World: An Emerging Partnership,* conference proceedings (Washington, D.C.: Smithsonian Institution, 1982), p. 14.
3. National Institute of Mental Health, " Senile Dementia (Alzheimer's Disease)," fact sheet, p. 1.
4. U.S. Department of Health and Human Services, *Facts about Older Americans, 1980–81,* p. 8.
5. Ibid., p. 10.
6. Richard Ohlhausen, "Data on the Elderly," internal document, Department of Public Programs, National Museum of American History, Smithsonian Institution, July 20, 1983.
7. Office of Museum Programs, *Older Adults and the Museum World,* pp. 27–28.
8. U.S. Department of Health and Human Services, *Facts about Older Americans, 1980–81,* p. 7.
9. Robert N. Butler, quoted in Frank Trippett, "Taking a Look at Ageism," *Time,* March 24, 1980, p. 88.
10. Malcolm Knowles, *The Adult Learner: A Neglected Species* (Houston, Tex.: Gulf Publishing Co., 1973), pp. 45–48, quoted in Center for Museum Education, *Lifelong Learning/Adult Audiences* (Washington, D.C.: George Washington University, 1978), p. 38.
11. Robert N. Butler, *Why Survive? Being Old in America* (New York: Harper & Row, 1975), quoted in Berit Ingersoll and Lili Goodman, "History Comes Alive: Facilitating Reminiscence in a

Group of Institutionalized Elderly," *Journal of Gerontological Social Work* 2, no. 4 (Summer 1980): 306.

12. Harriet Wrye and Jacqueline Churilla, "Looking Inward, Looking Backward: Reminiscence and the Life Review," *Frontiers* 2, no. 2 (summer 1977): 99.

13. U.S. Department of Health and Human Services, *Facts about Older Americans, 1980–81*, p. 1.

Presentation Techniques: Programs for Older Adults

1. When conducting an outreach program, arrive at the site at least 15 minutes before the program is to begin in order to set up, talk with the activity director, and greet participants, who frequently arrive early for programs. Leave time after programs to chat with participants who may not have been able or inclined to speak up during the program.

2. Room set-up is very important, especially if the participants have limited mobility. For object-oriented discussion programs, a semicircle is best. For groups in which most members have difficulty passing objects to one another, the participants can be seated around a table so that they can slide the objects from one to the next.

3. Greet participants personally. Introduce yourself, ask their names, shake hands. Use their names in discussion.

4. Speak to the group as though speaking to any adult group. Elderly people are very sensitive to people talking down to them or speaking in a sing-song fashion as if addressing a group of school children.

5. Speak loudly and clearly without shouting. Do not talk when facing away from the group. Some sites may provide a microphone to be used in the presentation to amplify the presenter's voice.

6. Make the presentation versatile enough to be appropriate for all education levels. State both simple and complex information using nontechnical language.

7. Remember that too many stimuli at one time can be confusing. Keep the presentation simple and direct.

8. Allow for a slow reaction time. When asking a question, give enough time for the group to think before responding.

9. If it is difficult to understand a participant's comment, ask him or her to repeat it. If necessary, move closer to the speaker. If the comment is still not understandable, repeat what may be the gist of the comment, phrasing it as a question, so the speaker can answer yes or no. Never ignore a participant who has difficulty communicating.

10. If objects are used, make certain that the participants can see them while they are being discussed. Simply holding the object up high will not enable the participants to see it adequately. Carry the object around in front of the group while describing it, or ask one person to examine it and describe it to the group. Once everyone has seen it briefly, ask the participants to pass it around among themselves, allowing each person to take a closer look at it. An activity director may have to assist in passing objects.

Afterword

When I wrote this article in 1984 I honestly believed that the prediction I made in the conclusion would come true. It hasn't. Citing museums' preoccupation with school children, I anticipated that, in light of the aging of America, museums would "reassess who their priority audiences are" and begin to consider "the needs of older adults." I expected that every museum, including my own, would have many opportunities for older adults to expand their horizons, put their life experiences in perspective, and make new friends. In short, the older adult audience would become another major constituency of the museum.

With a few notable exceptions, this has not happened. It certainly has not happened in my museum. The Senior Series, the program featured here, existed until 1983 when its funding ran out. Despite many attempts to raise funds both within and outside the Smithsonian, we came up empty-handed and were forced to cancel the program. (I was still optimistic at the time I wrote the article.) The problem was not that potential funders thought it was an unsatisfactory program. Quite the contrary, they believed that it was much needed and of genuine benefit to both the museum and the participants. In hindsight, I think this program fell victim to a changing social climate. While potential funders applauded our goals and results, our program smacked of do-good social work, which was no longer in vogue in the early 1980s. There was no pay-off for the investment of resources—no promise of increased test scores or an invigorated curriculum, just more enriched and happier older adults. In short, the program had no public relations value. Moreover, in the museum community, where new audiences move in and out of fashion in predictable cycles, there was the sense that we had already "done" senior citizens. Ironically, in the 1980s older adults flooded to museums to volunteer and participate in adult education courses.

The worst result of ending the program was the great disappointment we caused in the older adult community in Washington, D.C. We reached out to them in 1979 when we began the program, and they met us with open arms. They gave us honest feedback, shared their meager resources, and helped train our staff. Four years later we closed the door, and we have not been back. But the older adult community has not forgotten us, and they continue to call on us for services that we no longer provide.

I encourage those planning a program for older adults to take a long, hard look at all of their museum's offerings to determine how new programs for older adults fit in with the overall educational goals of the institution and how they will be supported in the long term. I hope that other museums won't "love 'em and leave 'em" as we did.

Case Studies: Museum Programs for Older Adults

EldeReach at the New England Aquarium

Rita gently reaches out one finger to touch the animal. "That's a starfish, isn't it? Ooh, it's wet. We used to find these at the beach when I was a girl." Rita is 83 years old with thinning gray hair and a wrinkled maze of lines across her face. But as she strokes the rough, wet skin of the starfish her eyes sparkle and the corners of her mouth lift into a smile, making her seem younger.

Rita is a participant in EldeReach, a program developed by the Education Department of the New England Aquarium in Boston, Massachusetts, and funded by the Lowell Institute. EldeReach is offered to senior citizen clubs, housing centers, day care programs, nursing homes, and other organizations serving older adults. The two-part EldeReach program includes an outreach session at the seniors' site and a field trip to the New England Aquarium.

The outreach session is a crucial starting point for EldeReach, especially since many of the elders have not visited the aquarium before. This first meeting generates interest in the program, establishes rapport between the instructor and participants, and allows this initial contact to take place in a comfortable and familiar setting. During the outreach session an aquarium teacher introduces the program and the New England Aquarium with a slide show highlighting the many sea creatures exhibited. This introduction is followed by a live animal presentation. The seniors are encouraged to handle live sea stars, sea urchins, snails, mussels, crabs, and lobsters, which are brought to the site in a large picnic cooler filled with salt water. Program developer and instructor Cindy Richardson explains, "I am always amazed by the enthusiasm generated by the live animals. Everyone wants to touch the sea stars and crabs, and it is the rare individual who doesn't have a story to tell."

Handling the live animals and dipping their hands into cold salt water is a dynamic sensory experience that often inspires the program participants to recall and share stories of their experience with the sea. These recollections range from memories of days at the beach to tales of successful fishing trips or even the memory of a good fish dinner. "Most of the people who participate in EldeReach have grown up in New England and have spent most of their life close to the sea," Richardson

Roundtable Reports 9, no. 4 (Fall 1984): 9–13.

says. "We've met retired fishermen, beachcombers, shell collectors, fish hobbyists, and many others who share a fascination of the ocean world. The aquarium's EldeReach program is designed to build on this familiarity and fascination."

But even the most exciting outreach program cannot take the place of a visit to the New England Aquarium, with its collection of exotic fish, penguins, and marine mammals. For many EldeReach participants this visit is their first to the aquarium and one of the few times they venture beyond their housing center or nursing home. The visits are scheduled for weekday afternoons, a quiet time at the aquarium, and take place one week after the outreach session. The group is met by the instructor from the outreach session, who then leads them through their visit. The reminiscing and sensory experiences that began in that first session continue in the aquarium's exhibit halls, where the elders watch beautiful tropical fish swim by just inches from their faces, handle artifacts such as shark jaws and pieces of coral, and then attend a dolphin and sea lion performance.

EldeReach's combination of teaching new information and recalling past experiences has helped to make the program a success, so much so that EldeReach has tripled in size since its initiation three years ago [1981]. "EldeReach is definitely growing," Richardson says. "Many groups request the program year after year, and they have spread the word to other organizations. Although we distribute flyers describing the program, word of mouth has been our best publicity." She adds, "One of the most exciting yet unexpected outcomes of EldeReach is how much the aquarium staff has learned from the seniors. The participants come to the program with rich and diverse backgrounds, and when they share their experiences and memories with us they add a new dimension to the program and to our understanding of the marine world."

National Council on the Aging's "Self-Discovery through the Humanities"

The National Council on the Aging's humanities program for older adults has involved more than 75,000 adults in discussion programs nationwide during the past seven years. Entitled "Self-Discovery through the Humanities," it is based on a series of study units that serve as basic texts for the group discussion. Each unit is based on a general theme and includes selections from literature, history, philosophy, folklore, autobiography, and visual arts. The ready-made program units, many of them in large print and with taped audio components, explore such themes as local history, the American family as reflected in literature and history, the remembered past, work and life, the heritage of the future, the search for meaning, and issues in contemporary values. Since its inception, the program has been funded by the National Endowment for the Humanities.

The program rests on the dual premise that the humanities have special relevance for older adults and, conversely, that older adults can make a special contribution to the humanities. Engaged more or less consciously in the process of interpreting and evaluating one's life and lifetime, the older person participating in one of the program's 1,200 local sites often finds that humanities works provide the focus and opportunity for sharing and comparing life experiences. By becoming an active interpreter of the past, the older person encounters new learning by reflecting on knowledge and experience gained throughout a lifetime—on the job, in family activities, through ethnic and religious tradition, with volunteer community service, and through travel.

"Remembering Your Town" at the Lyceum

"You made me think of things I hadn't thought about in years," is a typical response to the program, "Remembering Your Town" offered by the Lyceum in Alexandria, Virginia. The program is designed to teach Alexandria's history—and, indirectly, the country's history—by encouraging older adults to share life experiences. The idea for the program came from past staff experience working with senior citizens through the National Museum of American History and its outreach program, the Senior Series. Lyceum staff members were able to adapt some of the Senior Series ideas to a program with a local history focus.

"Remembering Your Town" uses a two-part format to encourage continuity and participation: an outreach slide program and an in-museum lesson and discussion on "reading" historical objects. The program is limited to more mobile elderly groups, such as church, community, and lunch clubs, which are able to visit the museum for the second part of the program. In some instances, a slide presentation is given to a large group at its facility with only those group members able to travel attending the in-museum part of the program.

In the outreach program, slides of Alexandria and northern Virginia are shown to provide a context for history from the late 19th century to the present, focusing on changes in transportation, communication, everyday life, and entertainment. The program presenter encourages participants to share their memories. One individual's experience often sparks recollections from others, fostering a genuine sharing of information. This program, while dealing with local history, is general enough to involve people who grew up in other areas of the country.

An interpretive object-based discussion amid an exhibition of hand tools is the focus of the program's second part. Many of the participants grew up in rural areas and frequently make comparisons between country and urban living in the early 20th century. During the session ice cream is made the old-fashioned, hand-cranked way, and artifacts are handled and discussed, bringing back vivid memories. At the end of the session, participants enjoy the ice cream. Before they leave, group members are invited to participate in other public programs and to spend time visiting the rest of the museum.

The Lyceum is a small museum with limited funds and staff. Costs for this program, therefore, had to be kept to a minimum. The slides were selected from local libraries and museums and inexpensively reproduced. The artifacts used for the in-museum program were acquired from yard sales at little cost. In addition, each group supplies the ice cream ingredients.

The Lyceum has benefited from the program in a number of ways. The tremendous response has widened the museum's audience and enabled the museum to identify participants for an oral history project and as potential donors to the museum's collection.

Evolution of a Collaborative Outreach Program at the National Museum of Natural History

In 1977, the Office of Education of the National Museum of Natural History sponsored an outreach program for Title 1 schools in the District of Columbia. At the end of the year, responses solicited from teachers, docents, and the museum staff revealed that we had not met our goals of attracting city classes to the museum, satisfying teachers, and converting docents to the joys of outreach. Yet we knew that a large segment of the population could not enjoy the museum, for one reason or another. We went back to the planning stage to determine which audience most needed and could be most realistically served by outreach programs. We discovered that three of the most appropriate audiences were the elderly, disabled, and incarcerated.

With the help of a sizable grant, we inaugurated an outreach program aimed at these audiences. We offered six different programs related to natural history and cultural anthropology. In general, the programs provided the audience with the opportunities to handle and discuss a collection of related objects that illustrated one or two themes. The programs were titled "Washington Animals: Night and Day," "Washington Rock Scene" (geology of the District), "Indians of Long-Ago Washington," "The Ashanti of Ghana," "Sharks," and "Fossils." Using a mailing list obtained from community organizations, we advertised the programs and were promptly deluged with requests. Our presenters were graduate students recruited from local universities and paid for not more than 12 hours weekly. Evaluation of the program indicated a high level of audience satisfaction. As a result, other museums within the Smithsonian voiced an interest in collaborating for the next year.

In 1980–81 and part of 1982–83, we established a collaborative outreach program with the National Zoological Park and the National Museum of African Art. Each museum offered several programs with trained presenters who were paid by the hour and reimbursed for travel. The requests for programs came to a central scheduler who also trained the presenters.

In each successive year, we tried different methods of improving our services, meeting the expressed needs of the audiences, reducing the cost per person, and improving the programs. Combining programs from the three museums allowed groups to have multiple visits from the museums if they wished to plan them. In the final full year of the collaborative program, 387 individual programs served 10,282 persons. Of these, 7,614 were elderly individuals in day care centers, nursing homes, or church-affiliated centers. The other 2,668 persons were school-aged, disabled, or incarcerated.

At the end of three and one-half years of this outreach program, and despite the fact that each year the cost per person had decreased, the program was discontinued for lack of funding. Our audience was very disappointed, and so were we.

In 1984 we made one final effort. The three museums, again collaborating, have packaged two programs each with self-help guides, background information, and questions to start discussions. Two workshops introduced recreation supervisors to the program kits, each of which included 10 to 12 objects. Individuals who attended the workshops were then encouraged to borrow the kits for a week and give presentations to their audiences of older adults. Our testing period has been completed, and evaluation reveals that the kits can stand up on their own, recreation supervisors can do the presentations, and the convenience of having the kit for a week allows it to be used several times within one establishment.

One further segment of the program remains to be tested and distributed: program booklets providing resource lists, ideas, background information, and discussion guides for natural history and cultural anthropology programs. The recreation supervisor or community volunteer is asked to collect materials listed but not included in the kit. These written programs will be tested by some of our past consumers. When we have had some response from them and have made revisions based on their comments, we will make the program booklets available nationally.

What have we learned in the seven years of outreach efforts to older and disabled audiences? First, we have learned that an enormous need exists in most communities for programs delivered to audiences that cannot come to places where programs are provided. Second, we learned that outreach programs are very expensive unless delivered by volunteers or the resident staff of facilities to which the programs are available. Some economies can be made by collaborative efforts, chiefly through combining support and scheduling services, minimizing transportation costs, and sharing ideas in the development of materials and programs. Finally, outreach programs for older audiences can and should evolve, changing and improving as the provider gains experience and expertise.

"Parallels" at the Cloisters Children's Museum

Bringing together older adults from nursing centers and school children with learning disabilities, a special program at the Cloisters Children's Museum of Baltimore enhanced the lives of its elderly and young participants by creating an environment in which they worked together to explore and express their feelings, experiences, and expectations through art and poetry. "Parallels: A Program of Art and Poetry with Special Populations" operated during the fall of 1983 under the cosponsorship of the Cloisters and the Maryland State Arts Council's Poet-in-the-Schools program.

The six-part program was held in the historic setting of the Cloisters. The groups consisted of six older adults paired with six children. Three program instructors, assisted by school and nursing personnel, supervised the programs. Each week the program centered on a theme such as feelings, senses, weather, gifts, and even ice cream making.

In the art projects, the children and the older adults worked together in teams: tracing each other's hands, making collages to depict their feelings, and designing flags that symbolized thunder, sunshine, and other weather conditions. When hands are busy, the generations come together in lively conversation.

In the poetry workshops, the children became the hands and eyes of the older adults, writing down poems they had created together. The adults helped with sentence structure and spelling, sometimes advising on which direction a "B" or a "D" should face. Ethel, an older adult, and Monica, age nine, wrote the following poem after examining an object from the museum collection:

The Candle Maker
I like the candle maker
because it gives light.
It makes me want to sing.
It is like columns.
If this candle maker was mine
I would put it out
so others could enjoy it.

A party for families, friends, and other interested people concluded the six-week program and featured poetry readings by participants, an art exhibit, and a performance.

The response to the program has been very favorable. One school principal wrote of her students "who learn better through nontraditional approaches" that their "motivation for learning has greatly increased" as a result of this program. Older adults noted that it "brings back memories," that it is "rewarding to be among children," and that "I never thought I was creative."

Materials, administrative support, and instructor's fees for this year's program were provided by Rite Aid Corporation; the Cloisters Children's Museum, which is a project of the Mayor's Advisory Committee on Art and Culture; and the Maryland State Arts Council's Poet-in-the-Schools program.

Artful Grandparenting at the Baltimore Museum of Art

The special relationship between children and their grandparents is the magic ingredient in a program created by the Education Department of the Baltimore

Museum of Art during the summer of 1983. Because each brings a unique set of experiences, adults and children "doing art together" add an extra dimension to the museum visit. The staff has fashioned a series of workshops that combine gallery visits with related creative activities in print making, portraiture, drawing, and even stitchery.

Skilled and experienced art educators lead the workshops, which are limited to 10 to 12 "couples" (one child and one real or surrogate grandparent). Younger participants range in age from five to 11. Each "couple" attends three or four two-hour sessions. A $12 fee for three sessions ($15 for four sessions) covers the cost of materials and museum admission. Additional costs, including contracts for the studio art teachers, are paid by the Education Department budget.

The success of the program has encouraged the Education Department to plan sessions for vacation periods during 1984 and 1985. The staff offers two suggestions to those planning to develop similar programs:

1. Presentation is very important, and not all educators are skilled at teaching children and older adults simultaneously.

2. The "couples" should complete a project during each workshop, and at the end of the series all of the individual projects should comprise a larger product.

Elderhostel at Old Sturbridge Village

Elderhostel, which began in 1975, is a network of several hundred colleges, universities, independent schools, environmental parks, and museums throughout the United States, Canada, and Europe that offer low-cost, week-long, residential academic programs for adults at least 60 years old. It provides an exciting opportunity for the elderly participants to experience new intellectual stimulation and physical adventure as well as to make new friends. In response to a suggestion from an Elderhostel representative, Old Sturbridge Village became an active participant in the program in 1981.

We designed a program in which the entire "living history" museum at Old Sturbridge Village became a classroom for the 36 Elderhostelers. Rather than use the typical three-course format adopted by most colleges, we selected several interpretation, curatorial, and research department staff members to present one and one-half hour sessions on various aspects of life in rural New England during the period from 1790 to 1840. Topics ranged from "19th-Century Economics" to "From Farm to Factory: A Factory Operative's (Worker's) View." Behind-the-scenes tours to the archeology lab, curatorial collections, and research library helped the students understand how we develop our historical interpretation. To round out the program, we used the Museum Education Building facilities for hands-on activities such as cooking, spinning, weaving, and woodworking.

Each year, we increased the number of one-week programs offered. We began with two programs and now offer six. We chose the winter months to take advantage of the lowest local food and lodging costs, which account for 80 percent of the budget for the week-long programs.

The programs have required a great amount of museum staff time to coordinate, although Elderhostel's main office handles all advertising and registrations. Financially, the sessions are a break-even proposition. What are the benefits to Old Sturbridge Village of all of these efforts? Certainly, for an outdoor museum open year-round, the cash flow generated during slow visitation time helps, but more important, our evaluations of the programs are as enthusiastic as those of the Elderhostel participants.

Learning about Reptiles and Amphibians: A Family Experience

Judith White, Dale Marcellini, and Sharon Barry

In the center of the Reptile House at the National Zoological Park in Washington, D.C., is a family classroom where zoo-goers can learn about herpetology, the study of reptiles and amphibians. This classroom, called HERPlab, was developed by the zoo's Office of Education and Department of Herpetology through a grant from the National Science Foundation. The purpose of the HERPlab project was to create a core of interactive educational materials that would enable families to learn about zoology when they visit a zoo. Although the materials focus on reptiles and amphibians, the concepts around which they are designed are general ones—such as anatomy, behavior, and communication—and apply to other animals as well. The HERPlab materials are aimed at the variety of ages you might expect in a family group. Activities range from simple sorting games and puzzles to more complicated and conceptual exercises. Children's books and advanced reference texts supplement the HERPlab materials.

The lab is about the size of a small classroom and holds 20 to 25 people comfortably. To avoid crowding, a free-ticket system regulates visitors on busy days. The lab is a pleasant environment, furnished with tables and chairs, and along its walls are a few exhibits. The majority of the materials, however, are contained in activity boxes located behind a check-out counter. When visitors enter the lab they receive a list of these activities and select what interests them. They may take an activity box to a table and explore its contents during their visit. The lab is staffed by one or two volunteers who work as facilitators, helping visitors use the materials and find answers to their questions.

There are currently [1986] 14 activity boxes, with a few additional ones being developed. Most are based around games or objects like bones or eggs. Four, however, focus on living animals: snakes, frogs, lizards, and turtles. "Snake," for example, lets visitors look closely at and learn about a live corn snake. The animal is housed in a clear plastic box that is secured on a special plastic stand with a mirror on the bottom. This arrangement allows the visitor to view the snake from all sides without moving the box and possibly causing stress to the animal. Accompanying the boxed animal is a packet of observation cards that encourage visitors to look

Journal of Museum Education 11, no. 2 (Spring 1986): 3–4.

closely at and think about the animals. Short answers in fairly simple language are provided for parents to read to children. Information in smaller print provides more details for those with more interest.

Other activity boxes include a range of materials, topics, and approaches. "Territory" is a board game with the board printed to resemble the woodland home of an anolis lizard. Each player takes the role of a lizard: one is the resident defending its territory, and the other is the intruder. "Turtle Bones" is an anatomy puzzle built around a skeleton. "Communications" includes the sounds of frogs and lizards. "Eggs" offers shells, tadpoles, and a guided quiz to explore the topic of reproduction. Additional boxes include "Venomous Snakes," "Reptile or Amphibian?" "Endangered Herps," "Reptile Keepers" (husbandry), "Skullduggery" (teeth and eating), and "Herp Sorting Cards."

In addition to the activity boxes, there are some interactive exhibits and film loops; the latter are 8mm films showing common behaviors that visitors may not have been able to observe in the Reptile House. Four loops were produced for this project: "Eating," "Snake Feeding," "Locomotion," and "Lizard Aggressive Behavior." A written guide accompanying each loop highlights important points.

One of the interactive exhibits is called "Lizard World." It includes three tanks, each containing a pair of anolis lizards, and visitors can participate in an ongoing experiment about lizard color change. Another display, "Reptile Keepers," contains information on husbandry and keepers' tools such as snake hooks, triple beam balance, and boots.

The team approach was the key to the success of the HERPlab project. We found that developing the materials required a combination of talents and experiences that few single individuals possess. Our team consisted of the curator of herpetology, the chief of the Office of Education, and two people hired specifically for the project, one skilled in communication techniques and the other familiar with the design and production of educational materials.

We also had an unusual fifth member of the team: the family audience for whom HERPlab was developed. We consulted family visitors continually during the 18 months in which we were developing our materials. In the early stages of devising the activity boxes we frequently asked visitors to help us by looking at the animals or objects and telling us what they noticed or wondered about. Later on, when we were actually designing the activity boxes, we went to the public to try out the activities or other parts of units. After we assembled the parts into prototype activity boxes, the next step was to find out how they worked.

We set up prototype boxes in a partially completed HERPlab and invited visitors to try them out and let us know their reactions. We soon found out what worked and what did not. These tryouts led to many fine-tunings, changes that made the boxes clearer and easier to use. In addition, the tryouts showed us what our visitors liked and what was fun for them.

We also consulted the visitors a final time, after the revised boxes were completed and HERPlab was officially open to the public. At that point, we conducted a three-month formal evaluation of HERPlab. To help ensure that the materials could have general applicability, two other zoos joined the project as field test sites: the John Ball Zoo in Grand Rapids, Michigan, and the Philadelphia (Pennsylvania) Zoo. Both sites received copies of the HERPlab education materials and set up areas to try them out with zoo-goers as part of the final evaluation. More than 1,000 questionnaires were completed, and 200 interviews were conducted at the three sites.

This evaluation helped us understand what visitors got out of a HERPlab visit as a whole and provided insight into the kinds of experiences families value. Visitors said they enjoyed the chance to participate: "If you do things, you remember more than if you just look. If you saw this on TV, you couldn't remember as much as if you had come here." Visitors especially valued the chance to deal with real objects: "It's clear, first-hand. You feel like a scientist." They also valued the shared family experience: "It gives parents more of an opportunity to interact in a meaningful way with their kids," said one. "It's a family experience," said another. "We can do it together."

What we heard most often was visitors speaking enthusiastically about having learned something new: "I learned snakes have no ear opening and that they have one long lung," or "I learned the difference between reptiles and amphibians. I've been mixed up in that since I was a kid." And, most important, visitors said that the experience in HERPlab helped them gain appreciation for the animals. In the words of one sixth-grade child, "This is like opening a big door. There is a lot more to reptiles than we know."

While we were pleased to hear these enthusiastic comments, we were not really too surprised. After all, we had been listening to visitors for months already, and they had helped us design the kinds of things they liked to do. In an important sense, HERPlab was as much theirs as ours.

A book describing the development of the HERPlab project, *Families, Frogs, and Fun,* by Judith White and Sharon Barry, can be sent to museum colleagues involved in developing interactive materials.

Student Interpreters: Narrowing the Gap between Visitor and Exhibit

Karen A. Hensel with Merryl Kafka

Museums and the collections housed within them have a multitude of stories to tell. As museum educators, one of our most challenging tasks is to help determine which part of and how much of a story to tell about a given object or exhibition. Who among us has not at some time been frustrated by the inability to tell it all in limited label formats? Given the diversity and magnitude of museum audiences and exhibitions, communicating with this audience is an area of ongoing concern for the educator.

Curiosity about the visitor's experience in the galleries of the New York Aquarium (NYA) in Brooklyn, New York, led us to use techniques borrowed from ethnography. Through the use of videotape analysis, participant observation, and interview, we became acutely aware of the gap between what we are able to present via the label format and the incredibly broad variety of conversations and unanswered questions visitors generated in front of our exhibits.

Since 1970, our solution to narrowing this gap has been to use adolescent student interpreters, or junior docents. Selected and trained to be specialists in one exhibit area, junior docents relate the behavior, biology, ecology, and conservation of the animal and its habitat to the visitors. Using mini-talks developed by the staff, lectures, and artifacts, junior docents deliver presentations that they tailor to suit their individual personalities and styles of presentation. The docents work primarily during the summer or peak visitor season, and they function as conversation facilitators for the aquarium as well as "living graphics."

Their presentations vary depending upon visitor density, from brief formal lectures to one-on-one conversations. The use of junior docents enables diverse audiences to have esoteric information simplified and made relevant to their lives.

Background

In 1970 the burgeoning interest in marine science curriculum on state and national level spearheaded by the NYA compelled us to recognize the importance of cooperation between museums and schools. By working as a partner with educators creating marine science programs, the aquarium developed a large pool of students

Journal of Museum Education 11, no. 3 (Summer 1986): 8–11.

from which to draw junior docents. The program was initially limited to students in nearby schools offering marine science, but we subsequently opened it to highly motivated students from schools throughout the city.

Student volunteers were originally employed in activities ranging from animal care to office work. However, the most apparent and pressing need of the museum soon surfaced. Since our labeling system was undergoing a major renovation, we experimented with students serving as interpreters. After an evaluation, the junior docent program appeared to have such potential and serve so many needs that an institutional commitment was made to greatly expand it.

Recruitment

Recruitment is ongoing throughout the year. In the early years of the program, NYA instructors went "on the road" to promote the program, visiting guidance counselors, principals, classroom teachers, district supervisors, and students with workshop presentations, posters, and slide shows. Since the program is now well established, calls and letters each year remind science coordinators and teachers to publicize and recruit for the Junior Docent Program.

The program's best advertisement is often transmitted by word of mouth. Sometimes students see their peers in action and apply to the program. Students fill out applications throughout the year and are interviewed several months prior to the beginning of the training.

Selection

Unlike schools, the Junior Docent Program does not place a strong emphasis on high academic performance, and each new training class usually represents the entire spectrum of academic achievement. We seek and select highly motivated students. Ideally, they possess the following qualities:

- good oral communication skills
- a background in the sciences as well as basic knowledge of our subject matter
- enthusiasm for learning and sharing information
- poise and social skills
- a career-related interest in an associated discipline.

The personal interest of each participant in the program is a large factor in its success and in the rewards afforded the student in return. Former docent Merryl Kafka says:

> I lived near the aquarium all my life, occasionally visiting it—but like so many institutions, it was an impersonal housing for a collection and had no special relevance to me. Becoming a docent changed my entire perspective and interest level. It was here, through this program, that this marine biologist was spawned!

Training

Training junior docents is in some ways similar to training adults, with curriculums consisting of lectures by museum staff, tours, audiovisual presentations, artifact handling, and required reading. At the end of the training program an ungraded quiz is given and used as a diagnostic tool.

In spite of some similarities to adults, adolescents clearly have different emotional, behavioral, and developmental needs that the institution must meet. Perhaps one of the most critical elements of the training is building confidence. Teenagers are sometimes shy, awkward, and lacking in confidence. The week-long training helps them develop the skills and competencies needed for teaching and dealing with the public.

Four strategies have been developed over the years. During the training, students are taught to observe and listen to both visitor interactions with exhibits and with each other in order to become sensitized to visitor behavior, questions, interests, misconceptions, and communication strategies. Based on their newly developed understanding of visitor behavior and with our supervision, the students develop their own delivery styles as well as a sense of timing for approaching groups or entering into conversations. Kafka remembers:

> I was nervous. I was preparing for "high-falutin" scientific questions. Suddenly, in a tiny voice, a question came from the crowd: "Do da belugas wear pajamaz?" I realized then, and I tell the docents now, that humor is an important element.

An ethnically mixed junior docent class allows the students to develop a sensitivity to the multiethnic nature of the aquarium's audience. Not only does this class makeup allow us to utilize bilingualism and other special abilities of the students, but it also sensitizes the junior docents to the diverse mores, cultures, and attitudes of our visitors, an invaluable part of any people-to-people program.

Another key strategy is peer review. Students present, evaluate, and critique each other and help one another develop an individualized style for working with the public.

Specialization of subject matter during training is the fourth key element in the program. The current [1986] training class lasts five intensive days. In the first two days a thorough orientation is given, including a meeting with the staff, behind-the-scenes and gallery tours, and a thorough introduction to every facet of the aquarium and adjacent laboratories. On the second day, students are asked to select their first and second choice of specialization (whales, sharks, birds, invertebrates, etc.)

Since most of our students come with a firm foundation in the sciences, each junior docent is given a lengthy and scholarly bibliography in his or her chosen specialty and is expected to complete the reading before working with the public. Throughout the training program, staff, resource people, and literature are made available to the students. Junior docents attend lectures that have been approved by all department heads in the aquarium.

Junior docents are allowed considerable latitude in selecting methods for delivering information, ranging from lecturelike presentations for large groups using a microphone to one-on-one informal conversations with individuals or families. Information is delivered in the style most appropriate to the occasion. Junior docents are required to restrict the information given to approved lectures. Additional information that the docent may wish to present must be submitted in writing to the education department for approval. In this way we are reasonably confident that we will not be embarrassed or surprised by misinformation presented by the junior docents. Upon obtaining approval, students can weave special knowledge or their particular interests into their presentations.

Except for the exceptionally popular or large exhibits, junior docents staff exhibits alone. As aquarium "diplomats" they are the "front-line" educators representing the institution. We stress that they have a responsibility to be constantly aware of their role and its importance.

Because adolescents need firm parameters it is important that they know and understand that they will be observed on a daily basis. The junior docents need to know that we are concerned with attendance and performance and also with them as individuals.

We are aware that as museum staff members we are role models for these students. Participants rarely request identifiable career counseling sessions, but by example, casual conversation, and exposure, some students may be formulating career decisions. Kafka says:

> The name of the curator of the education department became an almost household word because of the deep impression she left upon me. Recognizing the importance of staff as role models, I actively encourage staff-docent interaction.

At some point during each day, a staff member circulates throughout the museum to check on junior docents' progress, solve problems, give information, provide relief, and, if necessary, dismiss those who are not following rules or guidelines.

As a result of our research on how multigenerational groups of visitors relate and respond to our docents, the program has been restructured over the years. Types of uniforms, training assignment models, and types of students utilized have been modified to reflect changing educational and social mores as well as the needs of our public.

For example, in the past all junior docents learned an extensive and comprehensive marine biology curriculum syllabus that included all aquarium exhibits. In this way, docents were interchangeable. However, we found that it was unrealistic to ask the junior volunteers to retain that much information given the short amount of time that they participated in the program. The training time for our program was inordinately long, and the students could not develop the depth of information required to handle visitors' questions adequately or make themselves feel confident. Now students specialize in areas they select themselves.

Developing a Junior Docent Program

Those wishing to create a Junior Docent Program may find the following recommendations developed during the past 16 years useful.

Rewards for the Junior Docent

Career counseling and job experience, letters of recommendation, letter grades, and a unique educational experience are much sought after by both students and parents. The academic connection is an extremely important facet of the program for students. Over the years a variety of credit-awarding systems have been developed with participating schools, ranging from grades to letters of recommendation.

Students are always anxious to become "insiders" within the institution: meeting staff, witnessing and assisting at special events and observing and learning about daily activities that the general public never sees.

We also recognize the importance of the social aspect of this program. It provides like-minded teenagers with an opportunity to meet, interact, and socialize. We have found that over the years some junior docents remain fast friends. In fact, we recently celebrated the marriage of two former docents!

Recruitment

Advertise. Contact school and district coordinators, chairpersons, and librarians. Send announcements in the form of posters, flyers, and letters into the educational community. If you develop relationships with educators who teach your discipline, use them to recruit and select students for your program, and arrange for and handle school credit where appropriate.

Interviewing

Selecting junior docents who will prove to be successful is a difficult and unpredictable job. However, the following guidelines may prove useful:

■ During a brief interview (10 minutes) the docent coordinator must make important decisions for the institution. First impressions count—trust your instincts.

■ Look for the following: basic knowledge of subject matter, poise, enthusiasm, maturity, a cooperative attitude, good communication skills, and the ability to maintain eye contact. Factor into your decision that this may be the student's first interview experience and he or she may be terrified. Be compassionate.

■ During the interview be sure the reason for participation in the program is primarily student motivated and is not solely a result of parental expectations. Neither the student nor the museum will benefit from an obvious mismatch. Try not to be pressured by parents, teachers, or others if you genuinely feel a student will not work out in the program. The student might be better suited working in another capacity within the museum.

■ Make sure the prospective junior docent is fully informed of the parameters of the position. Expectations and an overview of responsibilities and accessibility must be carefully explained and defined. Now is the time to tell the student that dolphin-petting and valuable storage areas are off-limits.

Uniforms

We feel a readily identifiable uniform is a must. It helps overcome the visitor's reluctance to talk with strangers. Think carefully of the institutional image you wish the docent to project and also of the sociological aspects of visitor behavior and interactions with strangers. At the same time, junior docents should feel comfortable and proud to wear whatever uniform has been approved. Kafka says:

> My T-shirt was my passport into the aquarium. It made me feel important and part of the staff. Recently, I wondered why I saved that faded T-shirt with the letters falling off. I managed to throw away my docent ID card after 15 years, but clearly the T-shirt was a cherished symbol of what hooked me into the aquarium and this career pathway.

Our initial attempt at a uniform (white pants, blue T-shirt, name tag) met with failure during two years of use. Research showed that, given New Yorkers' reluctance to talk to strangers, a more obvious uniform was necessary. After several years of testing uniform types and audience reaction, we developed a format that meshed with visitor, docent, and museum needs. T-shirts advertising the docent specialty (e.g., Sharks?/Ask Me!/New York Aquarium) serve as billboards on the junior docents, immediately highlighting their functions and availability to the visitor.

Docent Stations

Carefully evaluate your audience's needs and patterns. Also consider your own notions about which exhibits may require interpreters. Surveys, questionnaires, visitor observation, and interviews will give you a good sense of which exhibits require, demand, or suggest an expansion of information.

Carefully evaluate the carrying capacity of the exhibit you wish to interpret. Size and shape of the area, crowd dynamics, peak visitor attendance times, and manner of docent presentation (lectures, question-and-answer, artifact handling, or use of microphones) are factors you should consider.

Don't overstaff an exhibit unless it is extremely popular and busy. Two or more docents may spend more time talking to each other than to the visitors.

The Benefits of Junior Docents

For career, financial, social, or educational reasons, student interpreters will be with you for a relatively short time compared to adult volunteers. Is a junior docent program worth the investment for the institution? Absolutely!

Students are generally intellectually highly charged, enthusiastic about learning, discovery, growing, and sharing new information. We have found adolescents to be eager and ready for a great deal of mental stimulation. Already geared for learning, they are quick to absorb information, and research and reading assignments come easily.

As museum educators, we are all aware that the success of public programs can only be determined with great difficulty. Over the years, visitor surveys, letters, and interviews have attested to overwhelming visitor receptivity to the Junior Docent Program at the New York Aquarium. In addition, our program boasts not only longevity but has resulted in more than 20 professionals now working in the field, ranging from dolphin trainers to marine biology instructors.

Some of the most rewarding times for us have been when our junior docents return to volunteer their professional skills, such as when a former docent turned medical student spent his summer recess programming a robot to train our marine mammals.

Former docent Kafka sums up the close ties that will always exist between these students and the New York Aquarium:

> Like so many docents, I feel like I grew up at the aquarium. It became a part of my extended family, caring, nurturing, guiding, directing, and teaching me. Homecomings have always included a visit to the aquarium.

The Junior Docent Program benefits the institution, the visitor, and the docent enormously. Not only does the museum visitor learn about the collection, but the junior docent also learns biology and gains confidence and career preparation. The museum as educator is nowhere more evident than in this type of program.

The University Gallery as a Field Setting for Teacher Education

Marian L. Martinello and Mauricio Gonzalez

When we watch busloads of children swarm into a museum, we find it difficult to be enthusiastic about the learning experiences they will have there. Seeing the children's cursory attention to artifacts and artworks in the gallery reinforces our chagrin. Despite the presence of skilled docents in many museums and the good intentions of many teachers who bring their students to the museum, this instructional resource is, more often than not, poorly used.

Whatever their discipline or size, museums are indeed treasure troves for teaching and learning. Especially today, with decreasing funds for classroom activities, a museum's collections can contribute substantially to school instruction—if teachers know how to use them. But museum educators express concern that classroom teachers do not always know how, and teachers admit feeling inadequately prepared to teach in galleries. Museums offer opportunities for lifelong learning, but only to visually literate visitors who have learned how to inquire into artworks and artifacts. Most people do not become visually literate unless they are taught, and teachers cannot develop that learning in their students unless they themselves know how to both learn and teach in museum settings. Judith Hodgson offers a solution in a 1986 *Museum News* article—teach practicing teachers how to engage their students with the contents of museum exhibits.[1] We believe in starting even earlier by building museum practice into preservice teacher education programs.

In these days of educational reform, teacher education programs that do not prepare teachers to use the museum's resources for children's instruction are remiss in their obligation to build collaborative networks for education among schools, museums, and universities. Universities must initiate the effort by building requirements for museum learning and teaching into their degree and certification programs. The University of Texas at San Antonio may emerge as a leader in this reform; its elementary teacher education programs include required field experiences in the San Antonio community's museum settings, including the gallery at the University of Texas at San Antonio.

A University Gallery's Educational Mission

In the four years since its beginning, the main concern of the University of Texas

Journal of Museum Education 12, no. 3 (Fall 1987): 16–19.

at San Antonio Teaching Art Gallery has been education, with a focus on developing an ongoing educational program that serves both academic and civic audiences. During the first fiscal year, to create a place for the gallery in San Antonio's art community, the emphasis was energetic, well-exhibited artwork. Although educational programs were second to exhibits, such exhibit elements as traffic flow, placement of artwork, color, lighting, and labels were considered part of the gallery's attempt to make an educational impact on its audience. In fact, the gallery depended on the various elements of its exhibits to achieve its general educational purpose: what Chandler Screven has described as changing attitudes, perceptions, knowledge, and sensitivities about art.[2]

Visitor interest has been a strong force in the development of new exhibit elements and educational programs at the gallery. In response to visitors' requests for information about the artists whose work was exhibited, for example, panels were installed containing photos of the artists with brief descriptions of their views on art. Printed critiques of artists' work have also been given to visitors in an effort to inform. In the fall of 1983, the evening gallery talk series was initiated, again in response to requests from visitors for opportunities to ask questions that were not answered by the printed information. Now the gallery offers less formal noontime talks, which have encouraged dialogue among visitors and the exhibited artists. These interactions help make art accessible and comprehensible to visitors, especially those who have no background or training in art. But only a small proportion of gallery visitors attend the talks. To reach a larger audience, the evening talks are videotaped and shown in the gallery through the duration of the exhibition. The tapes are also being shown on a local cable arts channel operated by the Arts Council of San Antonio.

In 1985 the gallery extended its outreach efforts to begin to address the needs of the local schools. At first, junior high and high school art teachers were simply invited to bring their classes to the exhibitions. But we received only four responses to the 40 letters of invitation we sent to the schools. In our second letter to art and classroom teachers, we said that a gallery staff member would be available to accompany the school group through the exhibit, and the response was more encouraging. Students from 10 schools were given tours by two well-qualified art professionals.

Although the art teachers' responses after the tour indicated their interest in more frequent tours, we noted an obvious discomfort among the classroom teachers who participated. One of the reasons they are uneasy in art galleries is that they have had so little training and experience in art and in the use of the museum as a teaching and learning resource.

The Gallery in Teacher Education

The UTSA Gallery is a unique field setting for the preparation of elementary teachers because it is on campus. This eliminates the logistical problems—caused by travel limitations and schedule conflicts—that can be obstacles to field assignments in off-campus museums. We have begun to involve students in the elementary teacher education and certification program with the art gallery during the term when they take the required course "The Expressive Modes of Children in the Elementary School." Designed to be an alternative to conventional art education courses, this one develops the visual thinking abilities of preservice teachers and increases their knowledge of how to engage children with images, develop children's imagery, and help them acquire an active interest in the arts. Knowing how to look at art is important to the program of studies, but the focus of the course is on the pedagogy of helping children see and understand the visual elements and design principles that define works of art. Students are expected to learn professional skills—teaching children how to look and see, how to observe, interpret, and derive meaning from images. An assumption undergirding the use of a university art gallery in teacher education is that those skills should be developed outside the classroom, in places where art is seen most often and by most people. If the goal of building an audience for art from the earliest days of schooling is achievable, it must be pursued where art is displayed for the general public: in the museum gallery. The UTSA Gallery offers a convenient place to begin, so it has become a resource for our course as well as a laboratory for studying the museum as a field setting for teacher education.

Reported here is a pilot study of one question we have asked: How will fieldwork in a museum gallery during a course in the regular preservice teacher education program affect prospective teachers' perceptions of the museum in children's instruction?

The term's work in "The Expressive Modes of Children in the Elementary School" includes several class sessions in the gallery to guide the students' viewing of artworks on display there. The emphasis is on ways of asking questions to promote children's awareness of how artists use visual elements such as line, shape, light, color, and texture to communicate and to achieve principles of design. But perhaps the most significant use of the gallery in this course is associated with two assignments.

First, the teacher education students viewed and attended gallery talks on two exhibits during the semester. Then they wrote reports describing their interpretations of the exhibited art, explaining what they learned from the gallery talk, and suggesting ideas for using the art with children on a tour of the exhibit and in follow-up classroom experiences. They responded to several questions:

■ What are the characteristics of the art in the exhibit? Describe them in terms of the visual elements and principles of design.

■ How would you guide elementary school children in looking at this art? Describe your instructional approach using at least two artworks from the show as examples.

■ What did you learn about visual thinking and visual expression during the gallery talk, the lecture, or the exhibit itself that helps you better understand class readings and lectures?

■ What might be a metaphor for the exhibit?

The students' second assignment was a written tour plan for each exhibit, prepared in the form of a script for the teacher to use when guiding children through the exhibit. The script includes information to be supplied to the viewer along with sequences of questions that will encourage the children's interaction with each artwork on the tour.

Subjective evaluation of these assignments clearly shows the students' strengths and weaknesses in "reading" visuals and especially in creating questions that promote the viewers' interaction with artworks. Further study will assess how these skills develop. Our first effort at evaluating the assignments and the use of the gallery for preparing teachers to help children become engaged with art focused on student perceptions of those experiences and their anticipated use of museums in their work as classroom teachers.

Survey Findings

Immediately after the fall 1985 semester, the first time gallery experiences were included in the course, we sent a questionnaire to each of the 18 students containing seven items for rating on a five-point Likert scale. Respondents were asked to express their degree of agreement or disagreement with statements about course assignments and course experiences in the university gallery, as well as about the value of those experiences for developing teaching skills (see table 1). In addition to a rating response, comments were requested.

Eleven students returned completed, anonymous questionnaires. The small number of respondents—just more than half—demands a cautious interpretation of the findings. Furthermore, because all the students expressed positive points of view, the distinction between "agree" and "strongly agree" ratings bears inspection. The comments are also meaningful.

According to table 1, it appears that all respondents felt the course assignments helped them learn how to view artworks. But they did not express as much confidence that those experiences had helped them develop their skills in teaching children to do so. One respondent commented that she didn't yet feel sure of herself in helping children see art because the course represented her first encounter with such teaching. Another thought that she needed more training and experience before she will teach with confidence in an art gallery. Interestingly, one respondent, who strongly agreed with the statement that course experiences helped students develop their ability to teach children how to view artworks, said that her work with docents in a museum of the San Antonio Museum Association during the term had helped her develop the relevant teaching skills.

Seven respondents strongly agreed with the statement that experiences in the gallery increased the likelihood that they would take their classes to art galleries and

Table 1
Student Opinions on Gallery Experiences for Teacher Education

Questionnaire Items	Number of Student Responses (n=11)				
	Strongly Disagree	Disagree	Undecided	Agree	Strongly Agree
1. Course assignments that required viewing and reporting on exhibits in the UTSA Teaching Art Gallery developed my abilities to view artworks.	—	—	—	2	9
2. Course assignments that required viewing and reporting on exhibits in the UTSA Teaching Art Gallery developed my skills to teach children how to view artworks.	—	—	—	5	6
3. Course assignments that required me to view and report on special exhibits for class (e.g., photographs) developed my knowledge of ways to help children view artworks.	—	—	1	6	4
4. As a result of my experiences in the UTSA Teaching Art Gallery, I am more likely to take the classes I teach to art galleries and museums.	—	—	1	3	7
5. As a result of my experiences in the UTSA Teaching Art Gallery, I am more likely to conduct my own tours of artworks in galleries and museums for the children I teach than rely on docents to do it for me.	—	—	1	6	4
6. Experiences in the UTSA Teaching Art Gallery should be included in the Teacher Education Program to develop teaching skills.	—	—	—	2	9
7. The Teacher Education Program should prepare teachers to use museum exhibits for work with children.	—	—	—	2	9

museums; three others agreed, and one was undecided. On the issue of the likelihood that they would conduct their own tours rather than ask a docent to do so, the emphasis shifted: more students agreed than strongly agreed. This item tended to elicit more comments than the others. Even when students gave the item a rating of "4" rather than "5," their comments suggest that they would seriously consider conducting their own tours. For instance, three who strongly agreed with this item wrote:

■ "Most definitely, I know my objectives better than a docent (and my students too!). Why let the docents have all the fun?"

■ "I think that with the knowledge I obtained, and preplanning, I would be more able to know the capabilities and interests of my class."

■ "As a teacher you know what the class has been studying and will be studying and can use the museum experience to its fullest."

Those who rated the item as "4" (agree) expressed some concern about having enough background knowledge but said they would conduct a tour.

■ "Yes! If I'm familiar enough with the exhibit or if I'm able to get information on it. I feel knowledgeable docents do their job well. But I wouldn't mind conducting a tour to help children see specific things in art that I would like to see."

■ "I am more likely to add to the docents. I am *definitely* more aware of how important it is to prepare myself and the children for what we will be viewing—to really talk about what will happen."

Even the student who was "undecided" and rated this statement as "3" commented: "I do not have a confident feeling about viewing artworks with children. It might be beneficial to students to have a professional guide them. However, if one isn't available, it will not stop me from taking them."

On the last two items, dealing with the use of the gallery in the teacher education program and the desirability of preparing teachers to use museum exhibits, nine of the 11 respondents were in strong agreement and the remaining two were in agreement. One student claimed the work in the gallery helped her develop her questioning skills; another commented that it caused her to see interdisciplinary connections in the elementary school curriculum. In response to the statement that experiences in the gallery should be included in the teacher education program, a third gave an unequivocal "Absolutely."

Among the comments associated with the last question were several that focused on central issues in museum education. One referred to the continuing problem of misuse of museum visits: "Many classes visit museum exhibits during the school year. I think teachers need to know how to prepare and guide students to view exhibits. I have often seen children visit a museum with no purpose." Two students commented on the importance of museums for fostering interdisciplinary education. One said it this way: "Museums are an extremely good way to instruct students in *all* subjects, but teachers need to be instructed on how to use them as such." Two others addressed the school curriculum directly. One said: "Too often in elementary schools art is thought of as: 'Oh, it's just art—do anything—make something out of a paper plate.' Art is so much more and should not be allowed to be trivialized."

Practicing Pedagogy in Museums

What makes some teachers better able to use the museum as an instructional resource with their students? There are many influential variables, including knowledge of exhibit content; experience with museums; perceptions of the museum's role, purposes, accessibility, and potential for education; and knowledge of how to teach with exhibits. The results of our pilot survey of teacher education students' opinions about their gallery experiences hold some clues to understanding teachers' need for museum education.

We cannot say why seven students did not respond to our survey, but we can look probingly at the responses of the 11 who did. There are hints of tentativeness in their positive responses to questions about teaching in museum settings. It appears that the students saw course assignments in the gallery as more effective in helping *them* learn how to view artworks than in helping them teach *children* how to view artworks. This is especially evident in the shift from strong agreement on item 1 to agreement on item 2 and in the reversed ratings for items 4 and 5. Despite assignments that were focused on teaching, not on learning about the artworks displayed, the students were not convinced that they had learned how to teach in the gallery.

The pedagogy of museum education is very much at issue here. The students claimed to have gained background knowledge of art. They were seniors in the teacher education program and had had some classroom field experience. Their responses make us suspect that knowledge of exhibit content and classroom teaching experience are not enough for successful teaching in museum settings. We believe that the development of museum teaching skills is intimately linked with the acquisition of visual learning concepts. Effective teaching in museum settings may require the asking of questions that promote careful observation and inferential thinking based on what can be observed. The questions should also seek to connect the observations in analytical and detailed as well as holistic and intuitive ways. The practice of teaching in museum settings may also demand skills that guide students in making metaphorical connections between what they see and what they know. Teaching for the development of thinking skills may be of far greater importance in museum settings than is teaching for content alone.[3] If so, the types of questioning sequences teachers use in the gallery are critical catalysts for children's learning.

Directions for Research

The issues related to the study of teaching in museums and the use of galleries as field settings for teacher education seem unlimited.[4] Work is needed to determine the distinguishing characteristics of teachers who promote children's thinking in museum settings. What skills and talents differentiate museum teaching from classroom teaching? Which are the same in both settings? How is the practice of teaching in museums associated with visual literacy and sensory learning among children?

Studies of the effectiveness of museum settings for instructional practicums are critical to understanding the museum as a field setting for teacher education. What types of experiences can we offer prospective teachers so they can learn how to teach in museum settings? What can they learn about teaching in museum settings that is different from what they learn about teaching in classrooms? And how does museum fieldwork by preservice teachers ultimately affect their use of museums in their teaching experience?

At UTSA we are investigating these questions through fieldwork at the San Antonio Museum Association and the Institute of Texan Cultures that is integrated with classroom practice in selected elementary schools. This collaborative effort of museum educators, curators, teacher educators, and classroom teachers is central to our model school project and should yield important findings for museum and teacher education.

The museum is still an underused and unexplored field setting for preservice teacher education. Inquiry into its promise may help us better understand the unique capabilities as well as the limitations of teaching practice within its galleries.

Notes

1. Judith Hodgson, "Teaching Teachers: Museums Team Up with Schools and Universities," *Museum News* 64, no. 5 (June 1986): 28–35.
2. Chandler G. Screven, "Instructional Design," *Museum News* 52, no. 5 (January/February 1974): 67.
3. Deanna Kuhn, "Education for Thinking," *Teachers College Record* 87, no. 4 (1986): 495–512.
4. "Issues in Research: Language and Methodology," *Journal of Museum Education* 7, no. 4 (Fall 1982): entire issue.

Master Teaching in an Art Museum

Philip Yenawine

All great teaching demonstrates an intimate knowledge and appreciation of the subject, an ability to communicate, passion (whether for subject, students, or communication itself), and unwavering commitment to teaching and to the ability of students to learn.

Effective pedagogical communication is usually highly personal in style. For example, some teachers do not concern themselves unduly about the needs or abilities of their pupils but are vitally interested in communicating their enthusiasm, command of material, insights, and imagination, whether or not they elicit or attend to responses from their listeners. Others are highly attuned to their audiences, often providing a role model for how something is to be done, known, or experienced. Still others inspire students to exceed their own expectations, dragging from them resources they did not know they had, forcing them to grow by an insistence upon and confidence in their intelligence and imagination. There are others who nurture and encourage, creating an environment so supportive that the self-motivated push to learn is hardly noticed. Each style has an audience and a setting in which it works best. Perhaps the greatest of teachers will combine these styles, but palpable excellence at producing the desired result—learning—can and does come from a number of possible approaches. In the museum setting, great teaching occurs in diverse ways. Consider the variety of techniques in the following examples:

■ *In the study center of a major art museum,* a curator presents a series of prints to graduate students from a nearby university. They use magnifying glasses to study minute details of plate impressions, examining nuances of different states, considering the artist's changes, and discussing how the totality of technique and materials reveals the decision-making process and allows interpretation and intimate understanding. The curator's trained eye, sharp intelligence, and command of information provide both a model and a challenge for the apprentice art historians.

■ *In a gallery of that same museum,* a very different but no less skilled teacher is conducting a lively conversation with a class of teenagers, many of whom struggle with English. The teacher alternately lectures and asks questions, laughs with funny responses, and encourages probing and deeper thinking. The teacher finds appropriate

Journal of Museum Education 13, no. 3 (Fall 1988): 17–21.

amounts of understandable language to provide helpful background and some information about the artist, "humanizing" the work and setting it into meaningful context. The young people are encouraged to notice and discuss colors, lines, techniques, and materials and to consider how such elements communicate meaning.

■ *In a quiet studio setting,* a teacher tells stories, conjures up images, and gives five-year-olds some art materials and a set of instructions. Once engaged, the teacher moves the group into the galleries, where they see work by artists, making connections between these objects and what they heard, talked about, and made. The teacher asks stimulating questions, follows up on the answers, brings out every child, and then takes the children back to their classroom for another activity that effectively synthesizes the experience.

■ *In a sculpture gallery,* another "special" teacher leads a group of blind visitors on a "touch tour," helping to evoke esthetic enjoyment among people who have lost or never had vision.

Despite their diversity, these teaching styles have a great deal in common. Circumstances vary, as do methods, types, and amounts of information, but each involves a process, structured by the teacher, in which information and experience are provided in a manner designed to be both comprehensible to and retainable by the learner.

While "experience" may in fact be life's best teacher, there are a number of reasons for structuring experience to make the learning process more efficient. These functions may be described as:

■ supplying information and focusing attention, thereby reducing the time it takes to "get" something

■ presenting background data in a way that allows a subject to be seen in relationship to its past and present contexts as well as to the learner's own experience

■ helping develop systems for recalling and using new data

■ creating an environment that arouses curiosity and increases openness and willingness to probe for subtleties, to study and to think

■ making it clear that the process of learning is available to any and all—and worth the effort.

These functions are all applicable to art museum teaching, and they are essential given the fact that most visitors have little knowledge of art and, at the same time, expect museums to be sites for learning. The paltry art education students receive in school is a factor art museum teachers have to deal with. Moreover, outside of school, there are few opportunities for people to see and learn about art—both historical and contemporary—except in museums.

Containing, as they do, the primary documents of world cultures, past and present, museums remain the most effective site for bringing aspects of culture to light. Museums provide the concrete data upon which to base open-ended thinking about our dynamic and complex civilization and the basis for studying both tradition and change. The challenge for museum professionals is to provide easy access to this material culture and to do so in ways useful to a variety of people not as inspirational accessories but as essential mechanisms for understanding new realities and new opportunities. Regrettably, there is no consistent belief among museum professionals that art museums must, by definition, assume an active instructional posture in order to do this. Despite the assertion underlying this essay that teaching in museums is essential, there are within institutions professionals who still feel strongly that art "speaks for itself," who thus ignore their own hard-earned expertise. Fortunately, their influence is waning, and the debate these days is less about whether or not to teach and more about what to teach and to whom efforts should be directed.

Yet, while museums are great places to teach, encounters with art are still highly personal acts. Many people require information-giving programs in order to enjoy art more fully, but these programs should not take precedence over the capacity of the museum to provide the peaceful environment that also nourishes the creative, individual response to works of art. Teaching of art must allow for a great deal of quiet, unstructured time. Moments of contemplation are necessary for the esthetic experience—especially given the hectic pace at which most people operate today.

It seems, then, that the four major variables of a successful learning experience are:

- teaching style
- knowledge of the audience and its needs
- an appropriate site for the learning to take place
- the content of the teaching itself—the information and skills imparted.

For museums as teaching institutions, the greatest assets are, quite obviously, the galleries. There, face to face with art works, people can learn and relearn the languages and forms of art. For novices and connoisseurs alike, excitement and real learning stem from the experience with original art. Most visitors are not experts, and given the relatively informal nature, short duration, and infrequency of typical museum visits, galleries should not be the setting for extended lectures on art history, nor can those aspects of connoisseurship that involve minute examination be taught in a 45-minute tour. Neither can involved studio activities take place next to masterpieces regardless of how useful any of these activities might be to a comprehensive understanding of art. While art history, studio experiences, and the like can be offered in appropriate spaces and greatly enrich education in art museums, most teaching programs should take place in galleries. In this setting, teaching should also take into account the visitor's physical endurance, the installation or gallery ambience, and the existence of other instructional devices that do not involve a "live" expert—labels, printed catalogs or guides, audio tours, audiovisual orientations, interactive information systems, and others.

There is a developing consensus among museum educators that the proper subject for museum teaching is "visual literacy." Visual literacy focuses on the cultural developmental levels that characterize our audiences and define their relationships to art. The goal of these programs is to create audiences that can approach art easily and pleasurably on a variety of terms. It can be accomplished within the setting and time frame of museum visit patterns; skills, behavior, and attitudes can be affected during brief encounters that accumulate and permanently color experience. Furthermore, visual literacy, unlike reading, is most fruitfully learned from studying masterpieces—the best and most complex works available. While to learn to read it may be essential to begin with Dick and Jane and work up to Shakespeare, learning to "read" art is greatly enhanced by the richness of the best art, even for the beginner.

Lessons in visual literacy center on art objects. They also involve the presentation of carefully chosen pertinent information by way of a strategy (lecturing, questioning, activities) designed to affect a specific audience whose needs, abilities, interests, and intents are accommodated by the teacher. In terms of content, lessons in visual literacy will:

■ introduce a subject, topic, or theme and suggest why it is significant in terms of the art and culture to be discussed

■ define essential vocabulary

■ direct the viewer's attention to certain of the physical and illusionistic properties in the work, including subject matter (however representational, abstract, or conceptual), formal elements (color, line), principles (space, light, motion, balance), and materials or media and related technical issues

■ analyze the functions and relationships of the properties listed above

■ provide other pertinent background (history, biography) in appropriate amounts and at various times to illuminate the subject and define its relationship to a variety of contexts, past and present

■ provide suggestions that encourage thought and perhaps generate discussion about how all of these factors contribute to meaning

■ demonstrate the possible variety of meanings, including insight from artists themselves and from other experts and, most important, acknowledging the right of the individual to shape his or her own conclusions

■ summarize the presentation in order to emphasize both the process and the outcome of the discussion.

The methods for presenting these elements may vary as widely as the number of teachers. Whether asking questions or engaging the audience through a lecture, the expert teacher's style will ultimately reflect how he or she has learned. Given a basic instinct, a good teacher usually improves with guidance from a knowledgeable observer, and team teaching can sometimes result in growth through transference of skills. Great teaching is itself not easily taught, however; it can only be sought and nurtured. Nevertheless this skill must be valued as highly as expert curatorial ability. It must be compensated and rewarded so that the best practitioners remain attracted to it. Great teaching should be (and to date is not) a professional career track in museums, as it is in the best colleges and universities.

The principles involved in teaching visual literacy can be and— particularly in this era of electronic media and curricular change in schools—should be applied to programs outside the museum. Visual literacy should be taught in classrooms and for all ages of people. It should be taught through films, television programs, and interactive computer technologies. The emphasis of visual literacy is redirecting and honing skills that most people use every day. Vision and thought are accessible, known activities. The best of museum teaching enhances and extends their use and thus frees people to explore and understand the world in enriched ways.

Addressing Community Needs: The Pontiac Art Center

Ann Treadwell

The year 1984 was the end of one era in Pontiac and the beginning of another. This Michigan rust-belt city of 80,000 was crippled by changes in the automobile industry. By 1988, no Pontiacs would roll off assembly lines in the town with the same name as the car. Our schools, under court-ordered busing for desegregation, lost their substantial tax base and their quality reputation. "White flight" gave us a new minority majority that would soon be firmly in place in all economic levels. Bilingual programming was introduced to accommodate some of these changes. More than 200 churches, a synagogue, and a United Way with 35 local agencies affirmed Pontiac's commitment to human and social services. But what of the arts?

The Pontiac Art Center, the only community arts facility in north Oakland County, had to decide whether to preserve its fine arts past or address the community's present needs. Our membership base was dwindling, and our patron support was aging or moving from the area. We were not receiving community support and, in fact, had developed a reputation of elitism, fringed with racism. Conflicts at the board of directors' level spread to staff and volunteers. Our board was desegregated, but our staff was not representative of minorities or Pontiac residents. The traditional museum volunteer system had deteriorated.

In 1968, our founder, Dr. Harold Furlong, had made a radical proposal. He suggested that the art center face its potential lack of resources by not collecting artworks. He pointed to substantial collecting institutions within a comfortable driving distance—the Detroit Institute of Arts, the Flint Institute of Arts, and the Cranbrook Museums. Nor was the Pontiac Art Center committed to collecting by donation agreements.

Furlong's foresight became one of the cornerstones in determining our new vision. Not collecting gave us the freedom to use our resources to explore programs that would serve the community. In 1986, after the directors reviewed the minutes from the art center's foundation period, the works we owned by previous donation were deaccessioned. Art was removed from our assets.

To implement our new vision, we first had to determine who our community was. It was no longer the predominantly white, financially stable, automobile-driving community of the early 1960s. A trip to city hall, the census bureau, the

Journal of Museum Education 14, no. 1 (Winter 1989): 16–18.

division of planning, the board of education, and United Way agencies presented a landscape of Pontiac today: who we *really* are versus who we thought we were. We are approximately 46 percent African American, 7.5 percent Hispanic and growing, 3 percent Asian (mostly Hmong), and 3 percent Native American. The 1990 census will confirm what is now speculation. The majority of us are renters, and our average family income is $19,000. Fifty percent of our adults have less than a high school education.

Next we needed to determine how we could serve this community. At first we believed that building on community spirit was sufficient. As we examined our in-house structures to ensure that they spoke to the community in the way we intended, however, we realized that we thought we had an educational philosophy but in fact had the structures for service—exhibitions, classrooms, community arts activities, a docent-style or art-school format of teaching—without ever having articulated their purposes. We needed a working philosophy to delineate our various responsibilities, and we anticipated that in examining the purposes of our structures, new structures might emerge as more useful.

Determining that our task was to build a community by creating forms of meaning within the greater community's environment, we gathered artists, art center faculty, and concerned volunteers to work with a board member in developing a working philosophy. The following statements are the result:

1. Art is composing and creating using verbal, visual, musical, or movement forms.

2. Art is created in all cultures.

3. The social nature of art also means that whenever a student is involved in arts education, he or she is presented the opportunity to say something to others.

4. Art creates forms of knowing the world as it provides forms for thought.

5. Making art always has the potential of being an empowering activity that can renew and revitalize both individual and community vision.

How has setting the stage and determining the concepts for community service enabled us to achieve our goals? Let me elaborate on several program areas and explain how the Pontiac Art Center has implemented its educational philosophy by addressing the community's diversity and the various concerns. Programming in all areas includes art history, criticism, esthetics, and art making, though not necessarily in equal amounts.

Children at Risk

Like most communities, Pontiac has recognized the impact that abuse and neglect are having on our children. To help counteract that impact, the Pontiac Art Center has teamed up with two separate organizations in the development of direct and indirect programming. One of the organizations is Help against Violent Encounters Now (HAVEN), Oakland County's shelter for victims of domestic violence and sexual abuse. The shelter, located in Pontiac, has resident and day clients. Art center and HAVEN staff have implemented a program, now in its third year, in which an artist works with children once a week. Self-esteem and communication skills are emphasized in two-hour sessions with the children, and occasionally with their mothers, to help them develop a dialogue with the world about their hopes, fears, and concerns. Drawing, painting, and storytelling (with the children encouraged to write the story) are among the most successful media. As the population at the shelter is transient, each week's unit has to be complete in itself. For safety reasons, all programs take place at the shelter. Our most recent project involved foam core, collage elements, and markers. The children drew, pasted, and constructed storyboard panels to describe "My Favorite Things." The components are now installed in the art center's Community Gallery, but they will be permanently housed in the resident area of the shelter.

Another partnership has been developed with the Child Abuse and Neglect Council of Oakland County. The theme of what has become an annual drawing contest for fifth graders remains "Peace Begins at Home," and last year, when entries were received, art center staff realized that several of them needed review by local social workers. A continuing relationship was established with the county council, and, during Child Abuse Prevention Month in April, the art center will display the work of the children. In March an artist will address child abuse themes in the Community Gallery.

The Disabled

Individuals recovering from mental, emotional, or physical disabilities are served by the Pontiac Art Center's Challenge Program, which works with organizations that do not have the ability or stability to provide arts education to their clients on a regular basis. Partnerships with schools, United Way agencies, mental halfway houses, and state facilities have helped disabled individuals socialize with the greater community.

For example, in 1988 the art center sponsored an artist-in-residence program at Vocare, a public school for disabled students. Four visiting artists, working in four different media, each worked at the school for a month. In addition, an artist was in residence at the school for a three-month period and worked with students throughout the school day. For the Special 26ers, an organization for mentally impaired adults over age 26, the art center hosts weekly classes in the visual arts from January to May. Recently Vocare and the Special 26ers applied for funding for a special summer arts camp to be held at the center.

One of our goals has been to develop a regional coalition of organizations and resources in support of the disabled, and a recent partnership with the Jay Shop, which provides employment and training for the disabled, will help achieve that goal. Together we hope to develop an introductory arts program and eventually a cottage industry crafts program.

Minority Populations

Minority populations in the Pontiac community include African Americans, Hispanics, Asians, and Native Americans. We have sought to develop programs for all these groups and to showcase their specific contributions as well as universal concerns. We invite representatives of these groups to assist in the planning and implementation of all programs and discontinue programs that do not attract representatives.

Programming for African Americans involves traditions from Africa, the Caribbean, and America. Activities include three art center exhibitions a year, three presentations celebrating African-American achievements, and a developing relationship with the Urban League and other support organizations.

Hispanics in Pontiac come largely from Mexico and Puerto Rico. There are also some people from Central and South America and from the Caribbean. Among programs for Hispanics is one that trains senior volunteers to teach traditional crafts to children. The art center has also established a heritage program with La Amistad Senior Center in order to preserve cultural traditions. Annually the art center presents three major Hispanic performances and at least two exhibitions that are either historical or contemporary in nature. The art center also observes Cinco de Mayo, a Mexican freedom celebration.

The art center is actively pursuing a relationship with the Hmong community, relatively new immigrants whose desire for assimilation is extremely high. Last summer, at Confetti Camp, described below, 60 percent of the participants were Hmong children. The art center has exhibited the needlework of local Hmong women and is working to develop a cottage industry program for the Hmong community to preserve their rich heritage.

For Native-American populations, we have organized an exhibition of contemporary works using traditional symbolism. We are also researching ways to expand our programming for this component of our community by building a relationship with the Genesee Valley Indian Center's curator in Flint.

Every summer for three weeks Confetti Camp brings together bilingual Asian, Hispanic, and Native-American children ages seven to 14. The camp's program promotes art history, communication skills, and self-esteem through drama, creative writing, and the visual arts. Each year the camp completes a project that is presented to the community. Confetti Camp's four successful summers are currently being expanded through the establishment of an after-school program.

We have also learned that scheduling activities by ethnic group and by month—by celebrating Black History Month in February, for example—is only a first step toward full representation of the community in our programs. We now seek to maintain a commitment to "equal representation" throughout the year, and all our programs and calendars are fully "desegregated."

School-Children

Pontiac has not had mandatory arts education at the elementary level for more than 15 years. Working with school administrators, teachers, and Parent-Teachers Association representatives, art center staff have devised unique methods of raising funds to provide arts education to Pontiac's 17 elementary schools and 8,400 elementary school children. A coalition of these groups is developing an arts curriculum that will include field trips at each grade level, and the PTA and schools are hoping to purchase curriculums from the art center, through corporate and private support, to be presented by artists hired from the art center. We are also developing a structure for the presentation of elective arts classes for secondary students.

Community Artists

Our Community Gallery is the voice of the community. It is a showcase for local amateur artists, who design, install, and label their works in monthly exhibitions. Proposals for exhibitions are reviewed by volunteers and staff. Past exhibitions have included the works of recovering alcoholics, the city's homeless, clients from HAVEN and the runaway shelter, local Chinese brush painters, and art center students.

The art center also promotes the work of more than 100 studio artists in the Pontiac area by contracting with local businesses and industries to offer quarterly rotating exhibitions in their public spaces. The art center's exhibition committee, consisting of two Pontiac studio artists, two local university faculty, and a gallery marketing person, reviews proposals for exhibitions and presents them to the executive director for approval. The companies pay the art center to install the exhibits by the linear foot of exhibition space. Annually the art center hosts the Pontiac Studio Artists Juried Exhibit in its main gallery and awards a $1,000 Best-of-Show.

Area artists were also integral to last summer's Moving Mural project, which involved area merchants and residents as well. The artists set up temporary studios at popular locations throughout the city: the local ice cream stand, the dry cleaners, the police station, the Hispanic senior center, and local playgrounds. The theme was self-portraiture, and passers-by were asked to paint their self-portraits on a small sheet of plywood. Artists had resources on hand, such as art supplies, mirrors, and samples of completed boards. The people of Pontiac, ranging in age from 10 months to 85 years, completed 900 panels that have been assembled into several large quilts now on display at the Pontiac Public Library. Participants have come with their families and friends to admire their work and to talk to each other about the faces of Pontiac. The project helped build the self-esteem of the entire community.

Art Center Volunteers

As the Pontiac community changed, the traditional volunteer program at the art center deteriorated. Single-parent families, working women, and the pressing needs of emergency service organizations had cut into the base of traditional museum volunteers. A new volunteer program had to be developed, one tailored to meet the needs and interests of the new volunteer base.

Our new program provides a training format for potential members of such art center committees as special events, community arts program, lunch with art, and off-site facility development. Our program also stresses issue-based and bartered services. Groups and individuals are invited to use the art center as a resource to advance their causes. For example, the local semiprofessional African-American theater company wished to present its 15th anniversary production of James Baldwin's *Amen Corner* at the art center. Rehearsals were scheduled within our normal operating hours. In lieu of rental fees ($30 per hour for nonprofits), the company is presenting workshops on African-American theater at two public elementary schools. In this way theater history and dramatics are part of the art center's in-school program at no cost to the art center. Local service clubs also host exhibition receptions in exchange for the right to nominate a student to the art center's scholarship program.

The transition to our new vision and programming has not been easy. In the early stages the Pontiac Art Center lost supporters, made major staff and structural changes, increased its operating budget by 50 percent, and discovered new limitations along with new goals. But we kept going in the belief that museums are places for assuming social responsibilities and for making commitments to the community. Since 1984, we have increased the numbers of those we serve from 6,200 to more than 60,000. In Pontiac, we are making a difference.

Afterword

In late 1989, the Pontiac Art Center completed a strategic plan and changed its name to the Creative ARTS Center. We also surveyed the community and revised our mission. The center's purpose became the creation of arts education, with the community, to build community. Armed with this mission, we set out to revise our education and exhibition programming.

An example of reconstructed programming is the Jump Ahead project, which involved 12 low-income youth, aged 14–16, who were considered at risk of substance abuse, criminal activity, gang violence, and teen parenthood. Working with artists and the curator of education, these youths participated in an intensive 12-week arts education and child development training program. Most had never experienced a museum or arts education setting. As paid assistants to the artists-in-residence for the center's summer programming, the participants designed activities for arts-related summer youth programs. They also used their newly acquired skills to write an "arts first" curriculum for 14–19 year olds as a way of speaking to their peers about substance abuse. This pilot program was funded through a Community Development Block Grant and our local United Way.

Exhibitions have also taken a new approach. In April 1991, the fruits of our work were evident in an exhibition called *Unemployed Autoworker.* This exhibition reflected the center's philosophy of quality, dealt with issues of diversity, and had a strong educational component. Its three parts were all attentive to community priorities. The first part, by Carlos Diaz, was composed of videotaped oral histories and photographs of seven local unemployed autoworkers. These men and women spoke of how they might do their jobs better, what expectations they had of their employers, and how their lives had been changed by unemployment. The second part of the exhibition consisted of photographs from the archives of six local labor unions. This segment celebrated the importance of family in the 1940s and 1950s, the political influence of Michigan labor in presidential elections, and the pride of union employees in their workmanship. The final component of the exhibition was two series of historical photographs. The first series highlighted the esthetics of the automobile plant through Charles Sheeler's 1922 photographs of the Rouge River Ford assembly line. Many Pontiac autoworkers started their work lives at the Rouge plant, which was the largest manufacturing plant in the world during its time. The second series documented changes in the assembly line since 1912. Both series of photographs were made available by Henry Ford Museum and Greenfield Village.

Unemployed Autoworker was significant for the diversity of the audience it attracted. Artists came to see Diaz's work, historians came to see the assembly line documentation, and labor union members came to celebrate their history. Yet in almost every case people crossed into the other parts of the exhibit. The labor history of Pontiac is very inclusive of people of color. For example, photographer and installation artist Carlos Diaz comes from a Mexican-American family that has been involved in automaking for generations.

The education components at the center have also changed. We now design our labels to engage visitors in conversations. In addition to the necessary identification (artist, title, medium, and date), we ask questions such as: How do the changes on the assembly line affect you and your family? Why was it important for then-Senator John F. Kennedy to solicit union support in Pontiac? Why did the artist choose to create a living room in which to view the videos? How do the larger than life black-and-white portraits of the autoworkers make you feel?

The center's dedication to listening to community issues and social concerns continues to be the key to the growth in audience. In 1990, we served 84,000 people. We are securing an additional 6,000 square feet of donated space for classroom activities and additional property for parking. Private contributions remain difficult to obtain due to the still-troubled nature of the automotive economy. However, as we grow from a city museum into a county-wide facility, we are finding increased demand for our services. Our earned income increased more than 88 percent in less than 12 months. Our commitment to quality was acknowledged by accreditation by the American Association of Museums.

We will continue to dedicate ourselves to the issues and concerns of Pontiac. We have come to realize that a group of people working together to achieve a common goal can help others learn to "see" and create community.

Role-Playing in Children's Museums

Jim LaVilla-Havelin

> By trading another's sorrow for our own; another's
> Impossibilities, still unbelieved in, for our own . . .
> "I am myself still"?
> For a little while, forget:
> The world's selves cure that short disease, myself,
> And we see bending to us, dewy-eyed, the great
> CHANGE, dear to all things not themselves endeared.
> —Randall Jarrell, "Children Selecting Books in a Library"

Childhood is a masquerade, a journey through ever-changing roles, expectations, and appearances on the way toward selfhood. If museums, with their new contexts, whole new worlds, and resonating objects, are places not only for understanding "other" but for learning about oneself as well, then children's museums, confronted with seekers still forming that self, have a special function to perform on the way toward self-discovery.

On the child's journey, children's museums offer a treasure chest of roles, masks, and possibilities to try on and explore. They are an opportunity for play, especially physically engaging play. In a world increasingly dominated by "spectator play," role-playing that engages all the senses is crucial. The child must experience the texture, time, sound, voice, and feel of another role.

Some pictures:

■ *A shy child is suddenly transformed* when he is able to hide behind the structure of a puppet stage. With body concealed and a new voice for presenting the moving hand puppet, a character emerges—voice, gesture, movement, and story. The child, not afraid of being found out or seen, is able to move, talk, act, and react as the character.

■ *A little leaguer comes to bat.* She goes through the same elaborate ritual that a major leaguer, one she's watched repeatedly on television, would. She spits tobacco juice, taps dirt from her cleats with her bat, checks for the sign, and calls for time. It's all an act, a replication of what she knows someone in the role must do even though she has no tobacco to spit, no cleats to tap, no sign to check for. It is an act

Journal of Museum Education 15, no. 2 (Spring/Summer 1990): 12–13.

that fits its frame, a role that, in its completeness and believability, helps all the players around the young batter to play their roles better.

Children in a children's museum are presented with a double message. On the one hand they are encouraged to become themselves. The experiences they engage in are meant to help them grow, develop, learn, and be enriched. In achieving selfhood, children stretch what they can do, who they can be, what they think, and how they see.

At the same time, in the museum setting this personal growth takes place with other children and families. Other people's approaches, skills, and points of view are present from the outset. In addition the exhibits give children opportunities to understand another culture, to see the world through other people's eyes, to know what they're thinking, how they live, and what they believe in and desire. In this understanding of others, children come to understand themselves as well. The selves they form are a patchwork of the roles, attempts, worlds, changes, and others they've experienced.

The role-playing children's museums encourage includes:

- role-playing with props and objects that define the role and interaction
- role-playing within settings and environments that define the role
- role-playing in familiar situations, sometimes involving intergenerational role reversals
- role-playing designed to develop empathy with a specific culture
- role-playing that is pure fantasy.

Props and Objects

Historically toys have taught children lessons and prepared them for life as adults. Whether the lessons are symbolic or didactic, the toys—objects—are crucial to the experience. Patricia P. Minuchin has observed that "children's play was often a rehearsal for the roles and skills that awaited them."[1] We understand doll as object with which to rehearse nurturing activities, microscope as object with which to rehearse discovery activities. Philippe Aries, looking more closely at objects and roles, has written: "Some toys originated in that spirit of emulation which induces children to imitate adult processes, while reducing them to their own scale. This is the case of the hobby horse, at a time when the horse was the principal means of transport and traction."[2]

In a children's museum a fire truck—or an ambulance, a mail truck, telephone repair truck, or lunar module—is a "prop" of a job (a role), and with it the children are able to become fire fighters. They bring to the role what they already know of the job, television's version of it, suggestions from parents and the museum's staff, ideas from peers, and imagination. They come to understand the role through the bell, siren, tools, hose, and boots that serve as the basis for their activities. If the job, in its particulars, is unknown or "underknown" or the props are nonspecific, the children are unable to complete the transformation.

Scale and its impact on role-playing interactions would be well worth future study. The real "props" of a fire fighter's work are too big for children. Is the message that the adult world is too big for kids? Or does fantasy take over? Margaret Crocker of the Discovery Center of the Southern Tier in Binghamton, New York, acknowledges that children exploring the center's fire truck are taken with "the idea of being a hero."[3] Their role-playing, grounded in real objects and the power of "real things," encompasses also the extraordinariness, the heroism, of the role.

Serious consideration of the role of props and objects in role-playing must be informed by Mihaly Csikszentmihalyi's studies on the meaning of things, especially on the varied uses of objects in the shaping of self and meaning. Csikszentmihalyi contends that people define themselves by their objects. Keepsakes are touchstones (the elements of these words speak for themselves) that evoke other times, places, and selves. In some people's lives objects or their presentation are an ordering device.[4]

A child wears a paper crown and is suddenly a monarch, the ruler of the kingdom. The object transforms the child. The child, in turn, within the role, transforms the object. Role-playing with objects is metaphoric thought.

Settings and Environments

Settings may be nothing more than an extended set of props. Children's museums rely heavily on environmental settings to create places where children will know what to do and will understand the roles and choices available to them. One strategy for developing such settings is to prepare a concrete journey or story line for children to follow, complete with choices of paths based on the role the child has assumed (a model that sounds surprisingly close to a number of video games!).

In an exhibit called *Tales in Tall Trees* at the Staten Island Children's Museum, children and their families enter a forest. Each tree has a component of a story (character, plot, setting), and the sequence of activities the visitor chooses constitutes his or her story. Some activities involve role-playing, including puppetry, storytelling, television performance, and beasts from a variety of stories. The differences between role-playing activities and other kinds of interactions are worthy of further study.

Environments can, in themselves, stimulate role-playing. *Tales in Tall Trees* is a forest with which museum visitors are comfortable and a place to which they return. For environments to stimulate role-playing, the transformation of the space must be complete and believable, the role must be clear and understandable, and other interactions or distractions held to a minimum.

Familiar Situations and Role Reversals

Power in a child's world is dearly held. Children cherish opportunities to make the rules, to do the selecting, to assert their will, to be arbitrary and able to answer a "Why?" with a "Because I say so." Grocery stores in children's museums offer the child a chance to play the parent's role. The child replicates the parent's choices and decisions. Because the parent's choices in a real grocery store have a direct impact on the child's life—what he or she eats—this role reversal is especially meaningful. The transactions within the role are filled with insights into math, nutrition, supply and demand, packaging, and money. In a subtler way, editing activities in an exhibit at the Staten Island Children's Museum called *It's News to Me* allow the child to pick what will and will not be news.

Children's museums also offer parents the chance to reverse roles, to be learners while the children "teach." To the extent that both parents and children are comfortable with this role reversal and aware of its framework, parents can gain an enriched appreciation of the skills, interests, and learning styles of their children. Parents may also gain insights into how they are perceived by their children—as rule givers? as facilitators?

Other Cultures

For children, approaches to other cultures are best made through things they know or care about, things that, however transformed in another culture, are still related to their own world. Food, other children, school, games, clothing, homes, especially the child's own room, are good cultural bridges. They help to emphasize common connections among cultures, not differences, and so reduce the dangers of stereotyping.

In the Dutch schoolroom of old New York at the Staten Island Children's Museum children play the role of students (an easy but telling transformation) and the role of teachers (another intergenerational role reversal). With extended props and settings, they experience a living and interactive social studies lesson. They try on the roles of people of another country, experience a different world view, and participate in the folkways of another culture.

In *To Walk in Two Worlds* the Children's Museum of Manhattan presents a powerful experience of a culture in transition. With props, games, activities, and interactions related to contemporary Native-American life, the exhibit demonstrates the dilemma of a people caught between their own traditions and the life-style of another people. The exhibit broadens experience and develops empathy—a willingness and ability to see the world from the point of view of another people, another culture. And empathy is an essential element in the child's development toward selfhood.

Fantasy Play

In Maurice Sendak's beloved children's story *Where the Wild Things Are* (1963), Max, crowned king of the wild things, swings through the trees. He does many things he's been told not to do, but he does them without defiance and receives neither harm nor punishment.

Some role-playing is sheer fantasy. Consider the child driving a toy car. Does he take cues from his parents' driving or from the high-speed chases he sees on television? Which is the most fun? The answers are obvious.

In *Bugs and Other Insects* at the Staten Island Children's Museum children crawl into a giant ant home. They are not asked to become ants but to pay ants a visit—and to suspend their disbelief. Rocketships and space gear, lunar modules and simulators are fine teachers of science, but when it comes to role-playing, the science fiction models may be more interesting.

Inevitably, as the child grows, a shift takes place. Young players begin to see themselves as young entomologists and young astronomers. Through role-playing, children's museums foster these transformations and enrich them.

Role-playing in a children's museum offers children opportunities and raises questions about museum learning as well. How can museums help a child to play various roles? Are cues, props, or time limits important? How can museums presenting role-playing opportunities classify roles? or avoid stereotyping? Can we correlate kinds of role-playing activities to a matrix like Howard Gardner's multiple intelligences?[5] Is role-playing an individual or a social activity?

On the way to selfhood, children's museum visitors need roles they can enter, believe, perform, succeed at, replay, grow into, and interpret. They need those roles and the objectives of those role-playing opportunities to be clear and direct, even when the changing selves that take them on are a source of uncertainty. At the heart of these activities is the individual's and the object's and the museum's ability to transform.

Notes

The quotation in the epigraph is from Randall Jarrell, *The Complete Poems* (New York: Farrar, Straus and Giroux, 1969), p. 107.

1. Patricia P. Minuchin, *The Middle Years of Childhood* (Belmont, Calif.: Wadsworth Publishing Company, 1977), p. 71.

2. Philippe Aries, *Centuries of Childhood: A Social History of Family Life,* trans. Robert Baldick (New York: Vintage/Random House, 1962), p. 68.

3. Margaret Crocker, executive director of the Discovery Center of the Southern Tier, Binghamton, New York, telephone interview, October 11, 1989.

4. Mihaly Csikszentmihalyi and Eugene Rochberg-Halton, *The Meaning of Things: Domestic Symbols and the Self* (Cambridge, Eng.: Cambridge University Press, 1981).

5. Howard Gardner, *Frames of Mind: The Theory of Multiple Intelligences* (New York: Basic Books, 1983).

Theater Techniques in an Aquarium or a Natural History Museum

Patricia Rutowski

Educational techniques using costumes and theatrical skits to portray animals other than *Homo sapiens* hold many rewards for aquariums and natural history museums and their audiences. But they also present practical and logistical problems and raise philosophical questions that should be worked through before they are undertaken. At the Monterey Bay Aquarium in Monterey, California, we have used theatrical methods since 1985. Even as our program evolves we continue to refine both our techniques and our thinking about the purposes and uses of theater for museum education. The issues we face fall into three areas of concern: issues about educational approaches for different audiences; issues about logistics and the mission of the aquarium; and issues about representing animals through theater.

Educational Approaches and Dramatic Techniques
The theater pieces we have developed use a variety of theatrical techniques and different plot lines to suit the needs of various audiences. Outreach Education, the program within the Education Department that uses theater, offers classroom programs for preschool groups and school children from kindergarten through grade 12 and assembly programs for elementary school students. During the school year, 95 percent of Outreach's programs are presented for elementary school audiences. We also perform at public weekend events, such as festivals or conferences, and at aquarium events. We have found that different types of theatrical activities work well for different age groups.

Children in preschool and primary school age groups live in a world of imagination. They want to touch, and they want to move. They are receptive to believing in puppets and to pantomiming the behaviors of animals, and these kinds of dramatic activities successfully involve them in learning about the way animals behave.

Older elementary school students, aware of peer judgments, are unwilling to pantomime animals and unlikely to still be captivated by the wonder of puppetry. Yet they are often not only willing but eager to be dressed up as an animal in the classroom or on an auditorium stage. At this age level the students can respond to questions about which body parts allow an animal to survive certain environmental

Journal of Museum Education 15, no. 2 (Spring/Summer 1990): 5–7.

conditions. Behind a crab mask, they spontaneously scuttle across the floor and imitate other arthropod gesticulations with abandon.

High school students are, for the most part, not so willing to dress up like an animal, but they enjoy seeing their teacher turned into an anglerfish or otter. Some teachers have had high school students write plays about marine animals and perform for younger students. A colleague in Florida visited classrooms and directed students in performing a simple play about the water cycle during an hour-long class period. We have yet to explore the full use of theater in upper grade levels.

Theater techniques offer excellent ways to involve students who do not learn visually or aurally. Pantomiming or dressing up allows kinesthetic learners to move like an animal or feel the animal's body parts in the costume around them.

Assembly programs for elementary students represent animals in their natural context and present natural history and habitat information. They generally last 30 minutes for primary students and 45 minutes for upper elementary students. Employing a more conservative strategy than public event pieces, they present animals interacting with a human who asks them about their life histories. In "An Otter Adventure" a young otter searches for her lost mother. On the way she learns what she needs to know to survive and recognizes how she is different from other ocean animals. Primary school audiences mime swimming along with the young otter and chant rhymes that briefly summarize what she learns in each of her encounters with other animals, including a shark:

You're no otter nosirree
You have big sharp teeth
And want to eat me!

Public event skits have to attract and hold audiences as they wander by the stage, and the approach clearly differs from that used in classroom and assembly settings. These skits have attention-getting introductions requiring audience participation, and the plots make use of popular culture. "Squids in Space" opens with the musical theme from *Star Wars*, and the narrator sets the scene with these words: "Mysteriously drawn back to the waters of his birth, our hero, Luke Squidwalker, feels he must return to Monterey Bay." "Deep Side Story" uses the plot of *Romeo and Juliet* to teach about deep sea lantern fish and species recognition. Public event skits last only 15 to 20 minutes—just long enough to hold an audience in a festival setting. To keep the audience interested, there are quick appearances by animal characters, and volunteers from the audience dress up like animals. In "Squids in Space," for example, "betentacled" youngsters help Luke fight the evil Shark Vader.

The big question we continue to have as we reflect on our presentations for all these audiences is, Are we entertainment or education? The intent of our theatrical pieces is to make the audience excited about the information we present. In most school and library settings, the theater pieces set the scene for a face-to-face interview with live animals—the truly educational experience.

Logistical Concerns

Being theatrical presents practical and logistical problems that begin with the staff itself. The aquarium's Education Department hires marine biologists who are trained to interpret natural phenomena for children and the public generally. Adding theater requires that these people be actors as well as good public speakers. While we do on occasion enlist the aid of theater professionals in training and direction, we recognize that our programs do not always have the polish that trained actors and actresses could bring to a stage.

We have chosen not to create elaborate sets, props, or costumes and have refrained from adding lighting and music. We have even cut back on the use of slides. Outreach Education staff go out to schools three and four times a week, 10 months of the year. Staff members haul carts of live animals in tubs and a variety of instructional props. If they had to haul tape decks, lights, and elaborate stages as well, this complex job would become even more stressful. Moreover, as available stage area differs from school to school, the addition of props would make presentations even more complicated.

Making the decision to staff a theater program with content specialists and not with actors and to use a bare minimum of theatrical stage sets and props meant, for the Monterey Bay Aquarium, clearly defining the place and purpose of theater within the institution's educational mission.

Representing Animals through Theater

Logistical concerns seem relatively minor when compared to the philosophical questions raised by using theater to represent animals for educational purposes. Aquariums and natural history museums make hard choices when they decide to write a script to teach visitors about animals. Some naturalists and educators believe that animals are exciting enough to serve as their own attraction and that the best way to teach about an animal is to stand up in front of a group with the animal, or with pictures of it, and discuss its characteristics. These people maintain that any hoopla other than just the straight facts upstages the creature itself, possibly distracting from the lesson in biology.

Storytellers and some other educators believe that a plot emphasizing some of the real-life problems an animal faces builds empathy in the listeners. Theater helps people relate to the animal, and they can more easily absorb information about its habits. Theatrical techniques have the added advantage of offering a way to present animals that cannot be handled or used for demonstration.

At the Monterey Bay Aquarium we have opted for this second approach. The students who see "An Otter Adventure" are invited to put themselves in the place of the young otter, and they empathize with her dilemma. In "Sea Stars on Vacation," written for young readers at libraries, a child brings a sea star (played by a human) home from the beach. The child and the sea star compare their strategies for filling basic needs for food, water, and shelter. Students learn that not all animals eat pizza or put their food into their mouths. Instead, sea stars stick their stomachs out of their mouths to slurp up and digest such delectables as gooey clams and sea snails. In contrasting another animal's way of filling basic needs with their own, students relate information about sea stars to their own experience.

At the same time, however, the plot of "Sea Stars on Vacation" involves a child's bringing a sea creature home from the beach. After debating whether we should depict this action on stage, we decided to go ahead with it only by emphasizing throughout the skit that sea creatures should be left where they are found. At the end of each program instructors ask the children what they would do if they found a sea star at the beach, and while young audiences seem to have gotten the message about not taking sea creatures home, we discovered that other confusions arose. After one performance, when we brought out live animals for the students to touch, a little girl looked up at me to exclaim, "My sea star won't talk!" We sometimes wonder if our theatrical pieces actually confuse young people still trying to develop the ability to tell the "imaginary" from the "real."

Moreover, in the effort to make an animal as understandable as possible, it is always tempting to make it as human as possible. The balance between empathy and biological accuracy is often difficult to achieve. While the audience may be invited to empathize with the animal character, the "human" character given to the animal must not overshadow the animal itself.

In one of our older pieces, "Billy the Squid: A Calamari Western," we may not have achieved the balance. We wanted to teach visitors that squid return to Monterey Bay in the late spring to mate, lay their eggs, and die. Our hero followed his life history accurately, but he wore cowboy boots, toted a holster filled with cephalopodan ink, and sought revenge for all the squids who never returned to the open ocean from Monterey Bay. In the bay's shallow waters, he confronted a shark in a pace-off and inky duel. Did the skit cause misconceptions? Did visitors leave with the impression, even subconscious, that squid have human motivations like seeking revenge? Did they think of sharks as "bad guys" even though the plot had stressed that sharks actually eat very few squid in Monterey Bay?

These are hard questions for us to answer. It's clear that educational and dramatic impulses can sometimes be at cross-purposes. It's also clear that our staff can never be completely certain about what visitors actually learn from theater pieces. Research in science education has just begun to focus on misconceptions that people acquire in school, in museums, and from television programs. We can only hope to ferret out what we are really conveying about our animal stars and to avoid potential sources of misconceptions in our programs.

Theater and the Museum's Mission

Theater serves a definite purpose in the educational program at the Monterey Bay Aquarium. The skits presented as public events allow us to reach people in "noneducational" settings with an educational message. The aquarium's public relations staff sees Outreach Education as creating a positive and "fun" community image for the aquarium as well. In the schools, the use of dramatic techniques involves students in plot lines and with animal stars in ways that they remember for years.

The evolution of our program has been guided by our institution's mission. Before initiating theater in an aquarium or natural history museum, we believe it is important for staff to consider these questions:

■ *What is the institution's mission?* Does it emphasize education, or entertainment, or both? How would theater be viewed by those who work in the institution? In what arena or department could dramatic techniques be best used? What audiences would be best served by the use of theater?

■ *What style should be selected to represent information about animals?* Should animals be represented as anthropomorphic characters? Does the institution hold to a style of presenting natural history information that would prevent the artistic liberties sometimes necessary in dramatics?

■ *How much support for theater is the institution willing to provide?* There is a great difference between providing costumes for animal dress-ups and staging full productions. Who will write the scripts? Who will direct and perform skits and productions? Will these people also serve as naturalists on the staff? Are there local people with the talents needed?

At Monterey Bay we continue to frame and answer hard questions about the use of theater for education. Our audiences and our own satisfaction testify to the worth of the endeavor.

Current Approaches to Interpretation in Zoos

edited by Janet S. Jackson-Gould

From New York to San Francisco, zoos are seeking the most effective approaches to communicating with visitors. These seven essays address issues in the interpretation of zoo exhibits and describe the methods several zoos have chosen to convey their important messages.

Designed to Be Interpreted
Sharon Kramer and John Gwynne

Imagine that you have reached the steep grasslands of Ethiopia's high plateau. You have come here in search of the gelada baboon, unique in its physiognomy, diet, social relationships, and vocalizations. Because this remarkable primate is found only in a few areas of this geologically remote Afro-Alpine life zone, few Americans have ever seen it in its natural habitat.

As you cross a dry stream bed, the overarching tall grasses rustle slightly. Acacia-like shrubs grow on the eroded banks. The hillsides are wreathed in silver-gray plants. You walk further down the cracked mud path, and the sound of rushing water grows stronger. A crude wooden bridge spans a narrow, swift stream. You look up and are rewarded by your first glimpse of the grass-eating geladas. The large male, surrounded by his harem, gazes into the distance; the pinkish skin on his chest turns a vivid red as he flashes his eyelids and flips his lip at an unseen adversary.

But you are not in Ethiopia. You are in the Bronx Zoo's Ethiopian Baboon Reserve, which was carefully designed to educate the public about this threatened habitat. As an organization dedicated to sustaining biological diversity, teaching ecology, and inspiring care, the New York Zoological Society made a purposeful decision to try to re-create the sort of wilderness experience that most of us will never have in our increasingly urbanized world. The multifaceted project was an intense collaboration that joined design consultants and fabricators with the zoological society's zoologists, field scientists, exhibit designers, educators, landscape architects, horticulturists, graphic designers, sculptors, and artists. The challenge was to incorporate both affective and cognitive interpretation methods in the exhibit design.

Journal of Museum Education 16, no. 2 (Spring/Summer 1991): 8–13.

On an affective level, the Baboon Reserve shows nature in harmony by including two other species: Nubian ibex, which are closely related to the endangered Walia ibex of Ethiopia's high plateau, and rock hyrax, which are endemic to much of Africa. Visitors delight in watching the animals relate. The ideal affective method would have been to enable visitors to walk among the baboons, but concern for the well-being of both primate species in an exhibit designed for an annual visitation of one million people made such a firsthand view impossible. The exhibit planners did, however, assure that visitors do not dominate the baboons' environment but feel like guests there. Several viewing areas were carved into the reserve, using moats and the thinnest acceptable glass as barriers. Care was taken to plant authentic Afro-Alpine or analogous plants in both the animals' and the visitors' spaces to equate the two areas as one habitat. All the construction—from the viewing blinds to the small bridges over the stream to the posts that support the graphics—was executed in a rustic way to allow the affective message an uninterrupted flow.

This atmosphere sets the tone for the cognitive aspect of the experience. The best scenario would involve an excellent guide—the zoo director, a field biologist, a curator or keeper—who would interpret what the visitor sees, enhance it with natural history, spice it with anecdotes, and make it come alive in an unforgettable way. The rare visitor is privileged to have such an experience. For the average zoo visitor, the cognitive messages must come from the graphics. The design challenge of the Baboon Reserve was to convey these messages in fresh, unexpected ways and to make them as interesting as a guide's narrative. The graphics are placed in an Ethiopian-style painted wood setting, with vertical signs supported by rustic posts and angled graphics placed on worn, softly painted planks. Silkscreened panels incorporate sketches made in the field depicting behavior and ecology, which attempt to engage the visitor in learning about geladas.

But even the most sensitive, culturally appropriate graphics do not reach every visitor. Two-dimensional design has limitations in a visually complex environment. To counter this problem and to make the learning experience more individual, the exhibit planners incorporated interactive interpretive methods in the Baboon Reserve. Many of the signs pose questions that encourage visitors to discover the answers on the reverse side. Telescopes in one of the viewing blinds afford visitors an even closer view of the geladas and their world.

A "Fossil Dig" adjacent to the Baboon Reserve introduces the fourth dimension—time—by examining our three-million-year-old coexistence with gelada baboons. Cast skulls of ancestral geladas, modern geladas, hominids, and humans enliven this dig for visitors. A cast of the bones of our *Australopithecus afarensis* ancestor "Lucy," herself no larger than a contemporary gelada, adds a human element to the conservation message. The poignant story of the massacre of the giant gelada species by early *Homo sapiens* provides additional food for thought. Interpreting the passage of time in another way is a "Search for the Signs" graphic that encourages visitors to find and understand field marks left by animals such as hyenas, ratels, leopards, and vultures, which in nature would share the geladas' habitat but could not be included in the zoo exhibit.

The Bronx Zoo's Ethiopian Baboon Reserve was conceived as an experiment. Visitors are encouraged to linger and be rewarded by close-up views of fascinating social primates behaving exactly as they do in the wild. On a cognitive level, graphics, footprints, burrows, and even defecation locations transmit the message of how nature works and stimulate the desire to learn more. On an affective level, the visitors' immersion into a total environment in harmony may enable the zoo to plant the seeds of caring for earth's wild places.

An Integrative Process for Exhibit Design
Jon Charles Coe

To most curators, integration means taxonomy, displaying like with like. But are the display items related? Do they share maintenance needs? Does the display appeal to several age groups and types of visitors? Is it energy efficient, does it improve air quality, and does it smell good? Can it accommodate special evening events, offer photo opportunities for visitors, and provide a backdrop for the local TV station's weather report? Will car dealers promote it and bring their families? Will restaurants feature it on their placemats? That's multilayered integration: a zoo exhibit that is a community resource.

Multilayered integration is, first of all, an attitude. It happens because the people in charge are joiners, not splitters, and because it is good business. Zoos and aquariums can no longer afford single-shot approaches. Money is too scarce and time too short. An integrative approach also leads to a richer experience for zoo visitors. Zoos and museums always present objects and information in context, whether intentionally or not. But the context often negates the experience, as when a beautiful tiger is shown in a rusty cage or a delicate mollusk shell is displayed in a crowded hallway. A highly memorable setting incorporating sight, sound, smell, touch, and mood strongly affects visitors' perception of the subject. There is a growing awareness of the value of supportive, integrative context, evidenced in the popularity of contextual displays and walk-through dioramas in museums and landscape immersion displays in zoos.

How is multilayered integration achieved? Here are some pointers:

1. During the planning process, bring all points of view to the table. Each participant must be well grounded in his or her area of expertise, but each should also be quick to recognize mutual benefits or new possibilities.

2. Give everyone a voice. Use a structured brainstorming approach with a strong facilitator so that no one person or group dominates. Create an atmosphere in which it is all right to suggest a crazy idea or a nontraditional point of view.

3. Involve one or more participants who are natural synthesizers and can create

alternative visions from a stream of apparently random suggestions. These participants should also know something about all of the fields represented.

4. Make sure someone with authority participates. Dozens, if not scores, of wonderful brainstorming sessions have gone for naught because participants failed to develop a constituency among decision makers.

5. Begin by asking what message you want to communicate. Rather than considering whether to use flat graphics, dioramas, or computer interactives, ask what you would like visitors to remember or feel about their encounter with the exhibit a month or 10 years later. Will the experience be worth remembering? Will they come back for more? Then consider the best means of delivering the experience that supports the desired message. You may find success has more to do with clean, uncrowded rest rooms than with interactive computers.

6. Create firsthand experiences for visitors. A hands-on approach makes believers and changes attitudes. When visitors have a supportive or at least an open attitude toward the display, they will pay attention to information.

7. Create delight. People visit zoos, aquariums, botanical gardens, and museums for recreation and inspiration. Few come for education. Delight can open minds. Inspiration can touch heartstrings. Then new possibilities open, and information finds a place to perch.

8. Add layers of function and meaning. Can the context that led to heightened awareness of the primary exhibit communicate with different age and education levels? Can it complement an eating or resting experience? Can it encourage sales of appropriate merchandise, providing revenue to support institutional goals? Can it provide a memorable setting for an evening cocktail party or afternoon corporate picnic that showcases your work to a new audience? Can parts of the display or support items enrich local school curriculums, tour sponsoring supermarkets, or nurture zoo programs in third world nations?

We live in the Age of Ecology; we are, after all, "one house." Zoos and aquariums should use this extraordinary realization to reconsider their messages, recalculate their costs and benefits, and restructure their exhibit design processes. Integration at all levels will help them get more from their resources and provide more for their visitors and their communities.

High-Tech Interactive Exhibits
Howard Litwak

In many zoos, interpretation once meant identification signs for the animals on display. Better interpretation meant producing nicer identification signs. In recent years, however, zoos have been seeking ways to communicate more effectively with the public. Encouraged by a variety of factors—including the growing urgency of their conservation message, the greater professionalism of their education departments, the popular success of science centers, and the increased sophistication of their visitors—zoos have begun to integrate interpretive techniques that are commonly used in museums. Among the variety of interpretive elements are high-tech approaches once thought more appropriate to a science center or history museum setting.

Recent advances in zoo interpretation were prefigured by William Conway, general director of the New York Zoological Society, in his 1968 article "How to Exhibit a Bullfrog,"[1] which proposed a richness of techniques that no real zoo exhibit has yet matched. Nonetheless, in the past five to seven years many new zoo exhibits—including the St. Louis Zoo's Living World, the Bronx Zoo's Keith W. Johnson Zoo Center, the Cincinnati Zoo's Cat House, the San Francisco Zoo's Primate Discovery Center, and the Los Angeles Zoo's new children's zoo—have employed diverse interpretive elements, many of them high-tech interactive exhibits.

A high-tech interactive device is any exhibit information delivery technique beyond the most straightforward graphic or lift-and-drop method. Examples are computers and audiovisual systems, including interactive video; hands-on devices intended to replicate an animal behavior or sense; and enhanced sound systems that respond in real time to a visitor's presence. In a science center, such approaches are generally consistent with the information being presented; there is no conflict between form and content. In a zoo exhibit, however, a fundamental conflict exists: high-tech elements are not found in natural settings. As a result, many zoo professionals question their appropriateness, regardless of the potential for enhancing visitor experience. When using high-tech devices, exhibit planners must take care that they do not intrude on the natural landscape or on the visitor. Some zoo exhibits place interactive devices in galleries where they do not compete with animal viewing.

Why are zoos using high-tech interactive devices? One fundamental reason is that hands-on activities facilitate learning, a point repeatedly verified in museums. In addition, exhibit planners are aware that even the most naturalistic immersion-oriented habitat provides only a snapshot of an animal's life, not a full picture of the ecological role and behavioral varieties of the animal in the wild. Interactive exhibits can expand the picture; those that use computers and interactive video can provide information at a variety of depths and interest levels. Finally, zoos increasingly recognize that they are in part in the entertainment business. They must give their visitors a multifaceted experience that will result in a pleasant afternoon, a repeat visit, or a change in awareness, behavior, or position on an important issue.

Lessons science centers have learned about interactive devices are gradually being understood in the zoo world. For example, the sheer cost and complexity of these devices often come as a surprise to zoo staff intrigued by their possibilities. Successful interactive exhibits are, of course, neither inexpensive nor easy to design; prototyping has begun to be recognized as integral to the process. Maintenance costs and the related matter of down time must be accounted for. In the first flush of enthusiasm, many zoos optimistically overlook these considerations. But as zoo staff gain experience in the integration of high-tech elements into exhibits, they will recognize the special issues related to them and consider these issues in the planning and budgeting process.

Note
1. William Conway, "How to Exhibit a Bullfrog," *Curator* 11, no. 4 (December 1968): 310.

Low-Tech Interactive Exhibits
James F. Peterson
Interpretation in zoos and aquariums supplies basic information and fosters an attitude of care and appreciation. One interpretive method is low-tech interactive exhibits, devices that enable visitors to use the senses or engage in physical activity. Interactive devices produce positive visitor response, increase exhibit use, and promote retention of information. In zoo exhibits, low-tech interactive methods are preferable to electronic or laser-powered devices. They blend into natural settings, do not require power, and are safe to use outdoors, unattended, or in areas of risk. They can relate well to the animal displays; interpretive text in zoos must often be short and direct, and supportive interactive exhibits share this quality.

The design of interactive exhibits requires the integration of information about the exhibit users with the selection of materials, mechanisms, location, and other design details. Subjective data about visitors—their behavior, values, and attitudes—should be combined with data about the physical attributes of the exhibit user groups to arrive at a profile of the typical user. Then the materials and methods can be chosen. An interactive exhibit should act as designed, when asked, forever. The materials and methods should be appropriate to the task, engineered for reliable operation, and well tested. A rule of thumb is to use the least complex mechanism and assembly that will do the job. Simple three-dimensional objects to discover and handle, items that reverse or flip over, slide doors, and other simple devices are always better than electronic or laser-powered arrangements.

A successful interactive exhibit is easy to operate and forgiving of error. It works every time, and the reward is information or insight. An exhibit that is awkward or annoying to operate or hard to understand will fail to communicate with the visitor. The exhibit dollar is well spent if the exhibit can quickly deliver a short message quickly to many visitors rather than requiring a long time to convey a short message to one visitor. Devices involving lift doors or slides, for example, are quick to use and, if the text is well written, quick to deliver the message. At the opposite extreme are computer keyboards and interactive video systems, which require a substantial investment of time and money for each message delivery.

Zoo exhibits have incorporated low-tech interactive devices with varying degrees of success but with great imagination. Shells, nests, tracks, and other animal evidence are displayed to expand interpretation. Giant webs, nests, shells, burrows, and caves invite participation and role playing. Tools, harnesses, and equipment reveal the relationships between ourselves and domesticated animal species. Horticultural plantings can contain familiar plants or favorite animal food items. All these approaches share the characteristics of simplicity, directness, and appropriateness to the task. An interactive exhibit has succeeded when the message shines through without undue attention to the materials or the medium of presentation.

The Use of Humor in Zoological Interpretation
Linda Taylor

Graphic designers faced with interpreting complex scientific information might consider tattooing one guiding rule on each hand: (1) No matter what, keep it brief; (2) Try your best to warm it up. It is my absolute and unshakable belief that information—no matter how important or worthwhile—will be actively ignored if presented in a dry, traditionally "curatorial" mode.

This is not to suggest that we should try to make jokes of serious subjects. Humor often implies a depreciation of fact, and we should never use it to diminish or compromise the importance of science. But if we can use it to achieve a measure of lightness—a gentle seduction—our visitors' interest, concentration, and receptivity to our messages will be greatly enhanced. At the San Francisco Zoo, we have enjoyed record-breaking readership of our graphics due largely, I believe, to our commitment to this premise.

On page 324 are examples of graphic titles and subheads in which we have attempted to animate difficult concepts with lively language and a spirit of fun.

While the use of humor is personal, subjective, and difficult—maybe impossible—to codify, a few guidelines might be helpful:

■ Never assume that graphics should be more clever, interesting, or beautiful than the subject you've been assigned to interpret. The painting, artifact, rhino, or whale is infinitely more interesting. Your wit and whimsy should be used to direct attention *to* the subject, not *away* from it. Keep this principle in mind during both the design and the installation stages. Don't create drop-dead gorgeous interpretive graphics that block the view of what the visitor is there to admire.

■ Consider local attitudes toward humor. Humor has an undeniably regional aspect: a deliciously witty headline in San Francisco may land on its head in Miami or, worse yet, offend a donor in Topeka. Writers and designers in museums, zoos, and aquariums must bear in mind a sensitivity to the people and politics of their communities—not as a restraining order but as a guiding conscience.

■ Stay alert to the "weights and measures" of humor. In most cases a light touch of whimsy works better than a heavy-handed ladleful of laughs, unabashedly impregnating every line of copy. Use humor as an artist would use a dash of vibrant color—sparingly, wisely, always with balance, style, and good taste.

A paper I presented to the American Association of Zoological Parks and Aquariums in 1982 entitled "Gorilla Gorilla Giraphics" ended with a poem I wrote that still communicates what I believe to be a worthy goal in reaching visitors:

If they looked, but didn't stop	If they looked, but didn't see,
Perhaps they didn't care.	We can't help them—not a one.
If they stopped, but didn't look,	But if they stopped—and looked—and saw
What they hoped for wasn't there.	The job was truly done.

Koalas

- Panel on plate tectonics, continental drift, and the impact of geographic isolation on evolution:

  ### A Lucky Break for Marsupials
  Breaking up is hard to do and took millions of years, but set Australia apart from the rest of the world . . . an island in time where marsupials could flourish.

- Panel on marsupial development and differences between marsupials and placental mammals:

  ### Womb with a View

- Panel on the koala's two-thumbed adaptation to arboreal life:

  ### A Firm Grip on Life
  When you sleep in windy trees, two thumbs are better than one.

- Panel on the difficulty of getting to the pouch:

  ### Fantastic Journey
  The koala's journey to the pouch is only 2 inches. But getting there is no easy task. It would be like a 5 foot 8 inch blindfolded person with back feet tied together and hands deep in boxing gloves having only 5 minutes to crawl 15½ feet with mites the size of small lobsters all around.

Giant Pandas

Born to Chew
Crush, crunch, munch. . . . The giant panda is a bamboo-eating machine.

Sex & the Single Panda
Rarely do they get the urge to merge . . . and that makes them rare!

It's All in the Wrist
Evolution's solution to holding bamboo

Asian Elephants

Of Tummies, Trunks, Tusks & Toes
How Much Lunch Can an Elephant Munch?
Eating to Live, Living to Eat
These Feet Were Made for Walking

- Panel on conservation:

  ### A Ponderous Predicament for Pachyderms
  (This panel includes a section entitled "Conservation Conversations" to answer difficult questions about the management of Asian elephants in zoos and in the wild.)

Entertainment and Education: Antonyms or Allies?

Catherine Tompson

The last decade has witnessed a strong and growing interest in live animal shows as an educational tool in zoos. Much time and energy—perhaps too much—has been spent debating the use of "show" versus "presentation/demonstration" and "education" versus that remarkable buzzword, "entertainment."

Among zoo staff, the terms "entertainment" and "education" are often considered to be antonyms, but in fact the entertainment industry helps shape many attitudes about wildlife. From the portrayal of Disney's *Charlie the Lonesome Cougar* we learn, for example, that cougar cubs make adorable if somewhat mischievous pets. (They don't.) Such misinformation fuels the educator's belief that zoos must "combat" entertainment with education. The real point, however, is that the filmmakers presented misinformation in such a way that it was readily assimilated. Perhaps zoos could achieve better results by presenting their "good" information in as entertaining a format as possible.

What makes a show entertaining? The entertainment industry offers some lessons. Most good movies put the viewer through the gambit of emotions. They sequence light and intense mood segments carefully and attempt to end on an emotional "bang." In an animal show, strong conceptual development plus good dramatic pacing plus audience participation equal an audience that is with you long enough to enable you to drive home your parting message. Audience participation is an important part of pacing. It can take a variety of forms, from silently answering rhetorical questions to visualization, movement, making or listening to sounds, or, in the extreme, touching an animal or artifact. The techniques of involving the audience should be varied and must weigh heavily in the show's pacing plan. Education steers the course, but entertainment drives the program. Zoos compete with everything from shopping malls to Nintendo for the public's free time. If zoos want their audiences to learn to love, then they must present a message that the public will love to learn.

Theater in a Zoo?

Rosemary Harms

The average visitor to a museum or a zoo probably does not expect to encounter actors. Across North America, however, museums of all types are showing an increasing interest in the idea that theater can be used as a technique to interpret exhibits. This approach has captured the attention of the public, too. Evaluation study reports presented at the 1991 museum theater workshop at the Science Museum of Minnesota confirm that visitors like it when an institution uses theater to help them better understand an exhibit. Theater as an interpretive technique offers a fresh approach to communicating ideas; showing is better than telling. When a collection of objects or animals is treated dramatically, its educational potential is increased. Theater encourages visitors to use all their senses and get emotionally involved in what they are observing.

As the following examples illustrate, the scope of educational theater in zoos is broad. In exhibit settings, theater need not be limited to the production of a scripted play. The traditional museum demonstration or animal show can be enhanced by the use of theater. Participatory games, songs, stories, the improvisation techniques of street theater and the circus, puppetry, and characterization are all very much the methods of museum-zoo theater.

At the Philadelphia Zoo, the Treehouse is the main stage. Play becomes learning as visitors explore six larger-than-life simulated habitats. Using all their senses and their imagination to appreciate and understand the animals' natural surroundings as well as their own, visitors are immersed in a fantasy world that delivers a real message about the world of nature. The Treehouse troupe of five performers creates and performs daily a repertoire of plays, 10–20 minutes in length, on subjects ranging from the food chain to conservation. The goal is to encourage the visitors to become the animals in this nonanimal exhibit. The summer 1991 presentation, produced with assistance from staff at the Science Museum of Minnesota workshop, is "Nature's Magic." In this original work, which features three live animals, a young boy learns about the interrelatedness of living things from a "magician" (otherwise known as a keeper).

The Philadelphia troupe is still experimenting. Its next goal is to develop programming in which each actor has an individual repertoire of activities to complement and enhance the main plays. The program benefits from outside professional expertise through the Artist-in-Education program of the Pennsylvania Council on the Arts, which provides help in scripting and in theatrical techniques such as improvisation, puppetry, and creative drama. As the Treehouse staff become more skilled in the use of theater, they share these methods with the education staff, who in turn are able to enhance their classroom and auditorium presentations.

In addition to the Treehouse, the Philadelphia Zoo has experimented with other theater ideas in the main zoo: a puppet show, street theater in a variety of guises, and, in the summer of 1990, a first attempt at combining theater and an animal show. Zoowalk Theater, a summer program produced by the education department, won an award from the American Association of Zoological Parks and Aquariums in 1985.

An experimental program at the National Zoological Park in Washington, D.C., takes a multifaceted approach to theater, helping visitors see the animal exhibits with new eyes. This Improving Exhibit Interpretation program is exploring a variety of approaches: a professional actor performs a monologue about the young Charles Darwin; performing arts high school students enthusiastically involve visitors in street theater activities; visitors play a game to learn how bats navigate. The one-week summer showcase held in 1990 has been expanded to a whole summer of activities in 1991.

Exciting work is being done at the Minnesota Zoological Garden in Apple Valley, Minnesota, by the education department's Theater in Education (TIE) program. Started in 1983, this program has grown steadily. As costumed characters, the naturalist staff and volunteers interpret three of the five trails at the zoo using short, scripted monologues presented at various sites along the trails on themes such as adaptation and animal senses. TIE also presents 20-minute shows featuring giant puppets seen from a monorail ride; these shows take place on special event evenings such as Halloween and Arbor Day.

Projects such as these at the Philadelphia, National, and Minnesota zoos depend largely on outside funding and donations of time and material. But more important, the key to the success of these programs is a commitment to experiment and a willingness to hire the right personnel to perform or train others. So far, zoos have barely scratched the surface of what is possible. Theater is a perfect way to heighten zoo visitors' powers of observation. It helps them discover new ways of looking at animals. It can create a lasting image for the visitor, an image that can be the catalyst for further learning.

THINKING ABOUT OURSELVES
AND OUR FIELD

INTRODUCTION
On Professional Knowing

Teresa K. LaMaster

> In the varied topography of professional practice, there is a high, hard ground overlooking a swamp. On the high ground, manageable problems lend themselves to solution through the application of research-based theory and technique. In the swampy lowland, messy, confusing problems defy technical solution. . . . The practitioner must choose. Shall he remain on the high ground where he can solve relatively unimportant problems according to prevailing standards of rigor, or shall he descend to the swamp of important problems.
>
> —*Donald A. Schön*

"What do I or members of my staff need to know to do our jobs?" When was the last time you asked yourself this simple question? When beginning a major initiative with which you had little prior experience? When hiring a new staff person? When confronting a performance problem among existing staff? When imagining how to spend that smidgen of training money you had left in your budget at the end of the fiscal year? When restructuring your museum education department to take on new responsibilities in exhibition development or visitor services? When preparing a presentation on "the real world of work" for a group of museum education graduate students? Questions about the nature of professional competence enter our work under many guises.

At first glance it might seem easy to rattle off a list of skills and knowledge that make up what we call "professional expertise." Yet such lists rarely capture the increasingly complex work situations museum professionals confront. New technologies, changing patterns of financial support, a commitment to serving many audiences, and the desire to make intelligible the most pressing cultural and social issues of our time—these forces converge in the daily decisions of people who do museum work. The expertise museum work requires is not simply knowledge or skill in solving practical problems. Rather, today's professionals need the imaginative capacity to reconstruct the problems they encounter so as to open up new avenues for practice.

Donald A. Schön, in his books *The Reflective Practitioner* and *Educating the Reflective Practitioner*,[1] argues that the difficulty we encounter with questions of professional competence is rooted in a mistaken epistemology of professional work; we are held captive by a wrongheaded picture of the relationship between knowing and doing. Our usual notion is that professionals—doctors, lawyers, managers, and museum educators—are people who have a specialized theoretical knowledge and apply it to practical problems. For example, we think educators understand how people learn and apply that knowledge to the design of exhibitions. In this view training museum educators—or for that matter any effort at advancing professional practice—entails discovering new kinds of theoretical information and applying it to the practical problems the world presents to us. If, for example, visitors are not learning anything from our exhibitions it must be because we do not know enough about how people learn or because we have not correctly applied what we do know to the practice of exhibition development.

Schön agrees that some aspects of professional practice fit this model of the relationship between knowing and doing. He considers that we may in fact begin our professional development by learning to apply standard rules of practice and abstract knowledge in somewhat rote situations. As we encounter new and more problematic situations of practice, we learn to reason from general professional principles to practical cases. On the whole, however, or in the most critical professional situations, the world does not simply present us with problems to solve. Rather, Schön argues that the central feature of professional work is the construction and reconstruction of problems out of the uncertain, unique, and conflicted situations of practice itself.

For the last decade, we in museum education have consistently called for training in theoretical perspectives on how people learn. While there has long been a recognition that classroom-based research is not necessarily applicable to the museum setting, practitioners look with hope to research on how people learn in informal settings. In fact, the 1991 American Association of Museums Task Force on Museum Education recommended that museums develop "learning laboratories" to study and contribute to educational research. Schön's compelling work casts doubt on this appeal to abstract research as a solution to practical professional quandaries. At its best, his work points toward a new shape for "research"—and consequently training—for professional practice.

Rather than study how people learn in museums, I suggest the "learning laboratories" begin their work with a kind of anthropology of professional practice. To borrow from Clifford Geertz, museum education needs a "thick description" of both how we make decisions in shaping visitor experience and the kinds of decisions we make. From the rich, contrary stuff of practice—well articulated and reflected upon rigorously in conversation with colleagues—two products emerge. First, a new topography of problems of practice and new language for describing them takes shape. Second, the profession further develops a collective habit, new skills, and dissemination mechanisms for what Schön calls "reflective practice." From this grounding in practice, "learning laboratories" develop in Schön's model as "design and development studios." Problems are constructed and reconstructed from the situations of practice; solutions are attempted and modified; problems are reframed;

new solutions emerge from reinvented problems. Rather than searching out new theories to apply to practical problems, the studio invents and articulates problems framed anew. As a research and perhaps training environment, these studios maintain special responsibilities for documenting and disseminating this process of reflective practice.

Professional competence is not simply mastery of a body of knowledge coupled with skill in applying that knowledge in practice. Rather, it is a learned artistry in naming and reconstructing the problems of practice. From this swamp of daily decision making comes excellence in museum education.

Notes

The quotation in the epigraph is from Donald A. Schön, *Educating the Reflective Practitioner* (San Francisco: Jossey-Bass, 1987), p. 1.

1. Donald A. Schön, *The Reflective Practitioner* (New York: Basic Books, 1984).

INTRODUCTION
Your Private Temple: Fighting Change

Richard Mühlberger

Change has been a preoccupation of museum educators since the first ones got together to talk and compare notes. When educators have wanted change, they have caused change. In the 1980s much of the change was internal. With the help of museum organizations, academic programs, and in-house training, educators have bettered their qualifications and their status. Every day the typical museum educator has to maneuver programs through changes caused by cutbacks in museum funding and cutbacks in public education funding while designing new programs to help raise the standards of public education. To say the least, museum educators are experts in dealing with change and planning for change.

But an important part of educators' agenda in the 1990s might be fighting change. Indeed, there are insidious changes happening in museums. They derail educators more than anything else does, robbing them of energy, spirit, and motivation. They will eventually derail museums themselves. They must be squarely faced, and educators must find the inner resources to address them. They are not discussed because they involve the trustees of museums.

Like educators, trustees want change. Indeed, they do; but it is not the change that educators are talking about. Trustees couch their ambitions for the institutions they serve in terms that flatter education departments. What they do, however, frequently surprises and offends education departments. They say they want higher attendance, and then they institute admission fees or raise existing ones. They vote for programs that bring more school children into the museum, and then they levy the school departments for support. They agree to computerize the museum, but that really means the finance office. And when they decide to expand the staff (only months after severe cutbacks), a human resources manager is hired, along with a shop manager and a coordinator to oversee catering of parties. Of course, everything trustees do is justified under the rubric of public service—until the deficit becomes unacceptable (that means that two-thirds of the restricted endowment has been spent). Then the doors are closed Tuesdays and Wednesdays as well as Mondays, the closing time is an hour earlier, and evening hours are curtailed. (These are just a few examples from art museums during the past two years.)

The typical museum board member serves an indefinitely shorter term today than 20 years ago and serves on a board that is three or four times the size it was when the museum was founded. He or she therefore has less of a chance for involvement in the museum, except socially. In fact, a shocking number of new trustees have not been in the galleries of the institution they are about to serve, only in its "great hall" where they remember attending a "great party." The typical trustee is drawn from the professions, banking, business, and community service, and unless a collector or a teacher, he or she knows little about the mission or workings of a museum. The new trustee is probably a little irritated at having to sit on the board, because it is clear that money or access to money is what is wanted, though there is a pretense to need expertise. That should not come as a surprise. The director of the museum was selected because he or she resembles the profile of the board of trustees and will work hard to be one of them rather than to be their mentor.

If directors and board members are running museums as restaurants, ballrooms, and boutiques, who is left to struggle for their integrity as institutions for collecting, preserving, and educating? The task is noble and difficult: to protect museums, to keep them honest, to allow no compromises. Who but educators will take this on? Fortunately, there are others just as concerned about these matters as educators are, and that is when the task really becomes interesting. The people who want to help save museums from becoming a branch of the entertainment industry are colleagues on the staff. Conservators, curators, and educators must ally. By supporting one another they will support the high principles for which their institutions exist. This triumvirate of museum workers is the hope for the future of museums. Their specific task must be described in less than inspiring words: they must browbeat their bosses into being honest museum men and women, and they must aid them in influencing their communities to support museums for what they are.

Educators are different from conservators and curators in one dramatic way: they are continually being pulled deeper and deeper into services to the community. For the museum educator, the museum is not a temple. Visits to the exhibits and galleries do not inspire; they turn into planning sessions. Meetings are pep rallies or seminars that the educator must lead, not opportunities to be enriched by contact with bright, motivated people. Reading is cramming for something that happens tomorrow, not a chapter in life enhancement. Exhaustion at the end of the week is not unusual, and a career ending before the educator reaches 40 is all too common. (Conservators and curators work very hard, too, but their careers last much longer.) But what does this have to do with the larger problem of fighting change in museums?

The educator needs strength and inner tranquility to be truly effective as a moral force. It is mandatory to have an interior life that is regenerating in order to make any impact in this complicated world of profit into which museums have been pulled. The generosity to put aside one's own agenda in favor of a larger one is the first requirement. The humility to work with curators and conservators is the second. The American Association of Museums does not give workshops in developing these qualities, nor does any university in the world. You will have to learn them on your own. Find your own private temple, and you will have started changing yourself into the educator for the 1990s.

The development of an interior life demands the devotion of certain amounts of time on a daily basis, a model to follow, and exercises to arrive at the model. Start with your educator colleagues: What have they done? Which of your volunteers exudes qualities of inner peace and generosity? Do you work with someone in your town or city who has that special aura? Ask questions. Follow up by reading the books they tell you about. Do the exercises they do. And don't forget to look back to your own life. Is there a reason to consider trying to regain the spirituality that was taught to you as a young person? Select a program. Start it, learn it well, and keep it going. Your inner life is as important for your future as are your intelligence, creativity, and competence.

Your personal temple is a place where your interior life develops. At first it will not be a very private place. When you go there, others will come wandering in, figuratively speaking, of course—your husband, wife, or lover, your siblings and parents, friends and old teachers, people from work—all of them wanting to help you. But you will grow in spite of their presence. Good days will be measured by how many of them leave your temple. One by one, they will go away until you are left alone with your soul. And on those exceptional days, even you will leave. Then you are ready for anything. Even fighting change.

Getting It Down on Paper

Ken Yellis

Museum education seems to be a field that is populated by and attractive to people who either cannot write, are reluctant to write, do not like to write, fail to understand the importance of writing, do not see the relationship between writing and professionalism, do not see any relationship between writing and what they really like to do, have mental or emotional hangups about writing—or perhaps all of the above. Moreover, many of our colleagues around the country who do write may be doing highly innovative and even exciting work but somehow fail to communicate that in their prose. Many, too, have little familiarity with the existing museum education literature, apparently, since many of the methodological breakthroughs they announce were known to Charles Willson Peale.

Indeed, writing is the main method by which professionals secure advances in their disciplines, disseminate knowledge of superior techniques, and mark change over time. But museum educators seem rather unconscious of time, perhaps because so few of us remain long in the field or come to it from a systematic training program. However that may be, I do not write to decry the state of the profession, which actually seems fairly robust just now [1985]. My role [as editor-in-chief of the *Journal of Museum Education*] and that of the journal have been to try to provide both support and leadership to museum educators as they endeavor to communicate better. It is my intention to be supportive of that endeavor here by offering some concepts that may be helpful in thinking about writing.

It may not be possible to do anything about all the reasons museum educators do not write, but we may be able to work with some of the emotional and mechanical ones. It is liberating, I have found, for those of us who have problems with writing to confront these problems and to work with our negative feelings directly. The hang-ups that prevent us from writing well, or indeed at all, are often quite explicitly voiced, and here are some of them:

- Writing is a talent or gift.
- Writing is self-expression.
- Writing is an art form.
- Writing is highly technical.
- Writing is hard.

Journal of Museum Education 10, no. 2 (Spring 1985): 18–22.

I argue that none of these statements is entirely true and most are totally false, at least for ordinary purposes. I propose to take these obstacles in order and attempt to substitute a positive attitude for each.

First Fallacy: Writing Is a Talent or Gift

Some writers have what might be called a talent or gift, but most do perfectly well without it, getting by on industry and discipline. Just as most musicians do not have perfect pitch, most writers do not have an inborn ear for language. As with good musicianship, a good ear is helpful, certainly, but the ear can be tuned. Mozarts are as rare among writers as among composers. Writing is like the rest of life: it can be and, in fact, has to be learned; one gets better at it the more of it one does; it gets easier the more of it one does; practice is necessary to keep it sharp, and, unfortunately, late 20th-century Americans have had the luxury of being very lazy about it. It is no accident that we now speak of things being "authored" than "written"; words these days are manufactured, processed, not written.

Part of the reason for this fallacy's being so widespread is the confusion between writing and style; good prose can be serviceable and still fall well short of elegance. The master craftspersons of language are certainly few and far between; more important, for most of the uses of writing, they are not needed. Most of the purposes of writing are occasional and ephemeral, but many of us who experience writer's block do so because of our awe at writing for the ages, as if the ages cared. And, too, often, because we don't write enough, we don't have the good habits whose momentum can carry us through those patches where our sails catch no wind.

Writing, in fact, is itself a discipline, and it can be mastered with discipline. This is most easily done by linking it to as many other activities as possible. When you are to give a talk, however brief or however familiar a topic, write it first. If you give the same talk again, rewrite it, even if you were happy with how it went the first time. Write out your tours, even if you would never contemplate reading a tour; my minister writes out each of his sermons, even though he talks from notes. Write out your phone calls; write up things after they happen; write letters to your mother, your mentor, or me.

For most people and for most situations, writing is not a natural quality that one does or does not have. It is, rather, a skill one can do more or less well and one can work to strengthen. The best writers have to work at it all the time, experience writer's block, often have difficulty finding the right word or phrase, make glaring errors of commission or omission, commit howlers, lapse into clichés and the passive voice, and have all the other problems mere mortals have. Shall I not write because I am not Dostoevski or because I become blocked on the article? You don't stop breathing because your nose is stuffed; writing should be breath to us.

Second Fallacy: Writing Is Self-Expression

Good writing is often so very far from self-expression, it seems the polar opposite of it. It is transporation pure and simple, that is, a way of conveying an idea, a fact, or an insight from one place to another, from here to there, from my head to yours. This is not to say that writing is not a creative act; obviously it can and should be a creative process and part of the overall process of communication. Writing certainly is the means by which we express our ideas, feelings, experiences, plans, knowledge, and concerns, but it is usually not an end in itself. When it becomes an end in itself, usually something has gone wrong, often a malfunction in the writer's priority system. Writing, for most of us, is a means to an end, a vehicle of communication, transportation, not some mystical or mysterious act that has a life of its own, deeply rooted in our unconscious. The end—communication—counts, not the means.

Nor is writing a form of therapy, although it can be a highly therapeutic process. Mostly, it is a transaction, the exchange of thought between me and you, a way for us to connect. Communication consists of two parts: your understanding me and my understanding that you have understood me. Without that interaction, that exchange of understanding, we have no real communication; instead, we have performance, self-expression. Self-indulgence is one of the most painful kinds of bad writing and requires constant vigilance on the part of the writer to avoid.

Indeed, the main difference between writing and speaking is that in writing there is no immediate feedback—applause, laughter, looks of befuddlement, "um-hms," boos and hisses—to tell you how you are doing and whether you need to adjust. Time passes between the writing and the reading; the reader either understands or does not. More time must pass before the writer learns how well he has been understood or misunderstood. The instant, and constant, adjustments that speakers make to maintain contact are not possible in writing. You are long gone by the time I discover I need to win you back, and I may never get a second chance.

What difference does this make? It means that the first question is the most important: What is my objective in writing? It means that in writing I must be as conscious of how I will be read as of what I mean to say. Who am I writing for? What will these words mean to them? Will this sequence of thoughts be as comprehensible and logical to them as it is to me? What have I left out that they may not be aware of? What have I assumed that may be contradicted by the reader's beliefs? What have I included that may disguise or detract from my message or distract attention from it? What technical, obscure, colloquial, regional, archaic, foreign, or otherwise strange, unclear, or ambiguous words have I used? Have I manipulated language or stipulated definitions that defy common sense or common usage? What have I said that may anger, put off, bore, or puzzle the reader? What evidence have I produced for my arguments? Will the reader be persuaded by it? Have I been guilty of either overkill or understatement? Is there a secondary or tertiary audience that must be kept in mind, as well as the primary one? Is there an intermediate audience?

The key word in all this is discipline, especially self-discipline. So far is writing from self-expression that the less we think of ourselves when we write, the better off we are. It is the reader of whom we should think at all times—what the reader knows, believes, understands, wants, has time for, is interested in. We must write not so much from where we are as to where the reader is. It is all too easy to be misunderstood even so.

Third Fallacy: Writing Is an Art Form

To assert that writing is communication is to argue that ordinarily it does not exist for its own sake but to serve some other, more important purpose. In other words, writing is a craft rather than an art that needs no other justification. Of course, like other crafts, writing can be and often is artful in the right hands; one may cause pleasure with one's prose, and surely most of us find great satisfaction in the beautiful or well-crafted language of others. But if writing is an art, it is primarily a useful one, and our emphasis should be on its utility and appropriateness.

To paint my ceiling does not require Michelangelo's gifts or the time commitment necessitated by the Sistine Chapel. To take more time than the situation calls for, to labor excessively over the physical product, is a form of self-indulgence. It is also an unconscionable waste, diverting energies better spent on other activities, other thought, other writing. Think about the different kinds of tasks a museum educator performs: giving tours, designing programs, making up budgets, conducting workshops, preparing materials for classroom use, as well as writing printed programs for special events, publicity, and grant proposals, to name a few. Note that writing is the most basic tool of the trade, like the bicycle for the messenger. But like the messenger's bicycle it is not the end product; durability, moreover, not beauty, is the main virtue in both cases. Indeed, the most artful characteristic of most good writing is its selectivity, its self-effacement, its scrupulous omission of anything extraneous, superfluous, and supererogatory.

Fourth Fallacy: Writing Is Highly Technical

Of the crafts that come to mind, writing seems to me the least dependent for its successful execution on an understanding of its principles. Learning to write well has as much to do with knowledge of rules, grammar, or linguistics as learning to walk has to do with an understanding of the biomechanics of the foot. Good writing is organization, pure and simple. It is the expression of information and ideas as written words and their arrangement in a sensible, comprehensible, and logical sequence toward a specific purpose—nothing more. Some purposes present more difficulties or complexities in structuring than others, of course, just as some data and concepts are harder to verbalize, but the challenge remains organizational.

If one can perform any managerial task, one can teach oneself to write. To do that does not mean mounting an assault on the grammar, syntax, and diction of English, memorizing the rules of good communication and good prose, and killing to acquire an extensive vocabulary. All are good to have at your disposal, but none is so important as common sense.

Common sense is the very essence of the communication process, getting these data from you to me in more or less the same shape they were in when you still had them. There is no mystery or alchemy in any of this. In graduate school I was instructed to tell 'em what you're gonna say, say what you have to say, tell 'em what you said. Another way to say that is: don't be subtle, be clear. The point simply is that none of this has any more to do with the technical part of the language than taking apart a watch has to do with telling time. They are entirely different enterprises.

Final Fallacy: Writing Is Hard

To say one fails to write because writing is "hard" is to miss the point: it is also a cop-out. To say writing is hard does not excuse us from doing it; it actually underscores the importance of trying. The labor of bringing it forth may constitute the real contribution. In any case, organization may be hard, planning may be hard, self-discipline may be hard, rigorous, sequential thinking may be hard, finding time to document and to follow through to the finished product may all be very, very hard. But writing itself is a mere physical task, not in itself very difficult.

I am not trying to be cute or flip. These distinctions can help us to figure out what exactly it is about writing that is hard and where the barrier really is. By breaking writing up into its component parts, we render it less formidable, more straightforward, and nonthreatening. To be sure, a large or difficult writing assignment can be daunting, but surely the simple transcription of words from the orderly mind to the clean piece of paper or blank screen cannot be what makes it so for most of us. It must be something else in the process that hangs us up, and it is this something else we must identify and wrestle with. I cannot tell what that is for you, but I don't have to, do I? You already know.

Preventing Bad Writing

To this point, we have really been addressing matters of the spirit, the state of mind that subverts the readiness to write. I now offer some, I hope, simple rules, caveats, bits of advice, and helpful hints toward the prevention of bad writing. Everyone is occasionally guilty of bad writing, often in the same piece with excellent writing. Bad writing is not a crime; it is more often a mistake. Indeed, if what I have said is true, good writing is largely a negative condition, that is, the absence of anything that detracts from the ability of prose to communicate. In a word, good writing is writing that is not bad.

1. *Eschew clichés.* Clichés are intellectual shortcuts. Like the highway bypasses that enable you to drive through a city without stopping, clichés speed you past ideas without requiring you to think. Thoughtless writing invariably, inevitably, and by definition means bad writing. Of course, clichés appear to have the advantage of

universal acceptance and understanding, but often that appearance is quite deceptive. Universal use either renders them completely meaningless—in the best case—or ambiguous, that is, understood differently by user and listener, which is much worse. "I could care less" ought to mean an idea exactly contrary to "I couldn't care less." Similarly, "up tight" now means the opposite of what it meant when I first heard it, I think.

While half-dead clichés are the most dangerous, fully dead clichés are preferable to obscure phrases or new coinages, unless these are extremely vivid or carefully explained in context. Otherwise, only your very close friends will know what you mean. We are obliged to bring our readers along with us; few things in life are truly self-explanatory.

2. *Avoid mixed metaphors.* As *New Yorker* readers know, mixed metaphors are a sure sign that the author or speaker is not paying attention. Far from having more on his or her mind than words can express, the metaphor mixer usually has rather less. Unless one's images are clear, as well as vivid, it might be best to avoid them altogether. The best writing, like the best pool, is limpid: you can see right through the water to the bottom, you can see right through the words to the ideas. Similarly, be as explicit as you can manage without treating the reader as if he or she were newly arrived from Mars—or as if you were. What do we gain from being cryptic or elliptical?

3. *Avoid jargon, buzz words, euphemisms, foreign figures of speech, and Greek and Latin cognates where plain English will do.* Readers of George Orwell's "Politics and the English Language" will find this advice familiar. Jargon, like clichés, can be a two-edged sword. It is usually defended on the ground of precision and, indeed, it can be useful when it is confined to its technical meaning. Jargon serves as a verbal shorthand among initiates, a timesaving and explanation-saving device. But jargon has a way of leaking into common parlance, where it quickly loses its precision; it is often used vaguely, inappropriately, deceitfully, pretentiously, or dangerously.

An example from our own field is the phrase "inquiry method," which has been so diluted that it now refers to any exchange in which questions are asked and answers given. This depreciation of verbal coinage is probably inevitable, but that should make us even more wary of how we use pseudotechnical terms, and why. The pervasiveness of buzz words in museum education is perhaps no worse than in other fields, but it is certainly no better; think of "hands-on." Our native caution should be activated when we see buzz words in our own prose, or in anyone else's.

Euphemisms are a slightly different case, but only slightly. The justification is usually the "protection" of the reader's sensibilities. In reality, however, most of the time it is the posterior (note the euphemism) of the writer that is in jeopardy. My current favorite is "to share," a verb without which museum educators and religious leaders alike would be helpless. And in fact, to say, "I have something I would like to share with you," sounds very friendly, but more often it is an alert: "Put on your hard hat: I have something I want to dump on you." Euphemisms are not soft shoes intended to make the walk more pleasant; they are blinders intended to conceal the destination.

Foreign expressions, on the other hand, are indispensable when English is found wanting. *Chutzpah,* for example, is an idea so subtle, complex, and ineffable that even a short story cannot convey it, let along a phrase. But when your intent in using foreign formulation is to impress, beware. What, for example, have you gained when you say *mariage de convenance* instead of marriage of convenience? Do you really want what you have gained?

Jesse Jackson has reminded us of how evocative and moving the cadences of the King James Version of the Bible are. Vernacular English, with its clarity, specificity, and power, is still hard to beat as a medium of expression. Modern usage, heavily dependent on Greek and Latin cognates, is much less evocative, suggestive, rich, and interesting than, say, Elizabethan or Jacobean English. It is abstract, murky, dull, and vague, rather than concrete, lucid, vivid, and precise. No one should ever use a word he or she does not understand, or a big word where a small one will do, or a fancy one where the plain equivalent is at hand. Do as I say, not as I do.

4. *Choose the right word.* Writing is a little like love: there is no substitute for variety. It is not just that a fuller vocabulary makes for greater precision, it also makes for more satisfying, refreshing, enriching experience for the reader. A lot of the writing I see suffers from dull, limited vocabulary. Good writing is lively writing, which means that even if the ideas are not new the way they are couched should be. Shades of meaning are much easier to convey when there is a rich and subtle vocabulary at one's disposal: vocabulary is the writer's palette.

You can make your palette more luminous and varied. Write with a dictionary and a thesaurus close by, for instance. You lose no points for consulting them; no one need ever know. Most of us already have much larger vocabularies that we ordinarily use; we really have four vocabularies, two passive (reading and listening), two active (writing and speaking), in order of size. Good reading and alert listening can activate our passive vocabularies; we can expand the number of words at our disposal when needed. We can quite consciously upgrade our spoken or written vocabularies by pausing to search in our memory banks for different, more accurate words before we proceed to speak or write. We can also try to phrase things several different ways if we cannot decide on a preferred formulation. Reading your written work aloud can also help you flag the wrong words, the not-quite-right words, the fuzzy or off-the-mark phrases.

5. *Avoid the passive voice.* To change the image, if vocabulary carries the freight, verbs pull the cars. Things written in the passive voice, academia's preferred form of camouflage ("It is thought that. . .") may sound dignified, formal, impressive, scholarly, and detached, but as writing they are gutless and flat. The freight never leaves the warehouse. Active verbs provide the engines that carry the ideas to the reader.

6. *Avoid long sentences and watch out for repetitive sentence structure.* Sentence

structure, like vocabulary, must be varied to sustain interest. Too many long sentences—particularly ones where the subordinate clauses dominate, where the tail wags the dog—too many short sentences, too many sentences with the same rhythm, all can drain away the reader's interest. A speech delivered in a monotone can lose an audience, however interesting the content; sentence structure is the writer's equivalent of inflection and modulation in speech, changes in emotional intensity, voice level, and so on. Written prose is, in fact, very much like speech: it ought to have rhythms and cadences, natural pauses, turns, curves, and hops. Poor writing feels brittle and stiff, unable to mold itself to the shape of the idea; good writing is serpentine, supple, flexible, and sinuous, following the contours of the terrain it covers. Here again, reading your stuff aloud will reveal to you the repetitive patterns and rigid structures.

7. *Edit your writing mercilessly.* Read your prose as if you had never seen it before, or, better yet, as if you had seen it before and loathed it. Every good writer is either an instinctive self-editor or a compulsive one. Everything should be edited as often as time and patience permit; when you budget time for a writing assignment, allocate equal amounts for writing, rewriting, and allowing ideas to jell, perhaps the most important of the three. The reason for this is that one must learn to guard against false euphoria about a piece of writing and for this there is no substitute for psychic distance. The best means of attaining that is time away from the piece. Even an hour can make a big difference in your coolness and detachment.

Time can also help resolve difficult technical problems. There is no denying that some ideas are more reluctant to be expressed than others, some information harder to shape. Often sentences will seem not to respond to ministration, but in reality they are quite malleable. Usually a balky sentence will move right along if you turn it around, if you reverse the sequence of presentation. I often find it helpful, too, to break sentences up into their component parts and then recombine them: change the order of the sentences, change the order of the clauses within sentences, splice parts of several sentences into new ones, add transitions, add an adverb here or there, and you have done miracles. But the key to doing all this is detachment: if you love your writing too much, it will never bend to your will.

8. *Writing is storytelling.* As long as the subject of transitions has come up, think of them as what keeps the story moving and fluid. Stories have a beginning, a middle, and an end, more or less in that order; they start with a grabber or hook and end with a release; they have enough repetition to make sure the reader understands and remembers but not so much as to put him or her to sleep; they contain enough surprise to keep the reader interested but not so much as to make him or her edgy.

And, by the way, you needn't try to be subtle either. Subtlety is wasted on most people and you are probably subtler than you intend; we all are. People almost never understand us quite as we mean to be understood, however explicit we think we are. One way to ensure explicitness is to attend to the internal logic of the presentation, and for this no device is so useful as the outline. An outline is to writing what the chassis is to cars. The folks at General Motors do not start with the headlights, keep going until they come to the tailpipe, and then start on the next car. The shape, if not every last detail, of the finished product, is evident at every stage of the process.

The power of words—to move, to inspire, to explain, to arouse, to embrace, to evoke, to inform, to persuade, to provoke, to prod, to wound, and to heal—is wonderful and awesome. Why deprive yourself of such power? The mere ability to articulate in prose what one sees or understands with any clarity is a teaching tool of such extraordinary versatility and force a museum educator would be demented to forego it. Indeed, there is no tool more effective, and few so easy to acquire.

Education for Excellent Interpretation

Robert C. Birney

Introduction
William Tramposch

Each year the Colonial Williamsburg Foundation invests approximately $500,000 in educational programs for its interpretive staff, which numbers about 550 in the busy season. Presently, a department of 12 oversees the development of these programs.

When interpreters are hired at Colonial Williamsburg, they participate in a preliminary interpretive education program that introduces them to the role of the interpreter at Colonial Williamsburg, the significance of our historical site, and the mission of the Colonial Williamsburg Foundation. Interpreters then become involved in incremental training programs within the various departments in which they will interpret (crafts, performers, house interpreters, and escorted tours). Only after completing these programs do they put on period costumes and interpret to the public.

Veteran interpreters participate annually in an in-service training program, the "Core Curriculum." This sequential program consists of required courses and leads to elective courses very much like the elective options offered in a higher education curriculum. Plans are now under way for advanced tutorial sessions for our more senior interpreters as well as for independent study options for those who have a strong desire to pursue individual research topics.

When asked to write an article about the interpretive training philosophy at the Colonial Williamsburg Foundation, I thought immediately of a stimulating piece that Robert C. Birney had written for our interpretive newsletter in March 1984. Bob's thoughts were directed to the interpretive staff, but his message bears relevance to all historic site interpreters.

It is my purpose to offer guidelines for achieving excellence in the task of educating people to interpret historic sites to the public. A recent analysis of the service profile of Colonial Williamsburg Foundation interpreters shows that a sizable proportion have been with us for three to four years, an even larger proportion for more than

Journal of Museum Education 10, no. 3 (Summer 1985): 15, 17–18.

10 years, and the remainder for four to 10 years. Our interpreters mirror our adult visitors in terms of age, sex, education, and experience with Colonial Williamsburg. Therefore, Colonial Williamsburg interpreters are a most unusual student body, and their efforts to learn more to tell the public are unending. There is nothing as tiresome and boring for the interpreter and the visitor as an aging interpretation from yesteryear. Education for excellent interpretation requires constancy, attention, and, above all, enjoyment.

Education embraces a number of terms. I want to consider just two—training and study. *Webster's New Collegiate Dictionary* is obviously puzzled by the word "training": "I. the act, process, or method of one who trains; II. state of being trained." No help there. Let me try to extract meaning for the word "training" from its uses. Children are trained. Novices seek training programs. The military gives training. And as *Webster's* observes, you can be in training in athletics.

I submit that "training" is a useful word because it points to a certain kind of educational situation. I think the key lies in the fact that we have trainers and trainees. Oddly enough, not many of the trainers are so identified. Those who train animals and athletes are called trainers. Most of the true trainers in our society are called something else: coaches, masters, supervisors, and occasionally teachers. (However, I shall not address teachers as trainers.)

Most trainers have trainees. Trainees are usually thought of as novices. A novice is somebody who wants to learn, knows a negligible amount of what is to be learned, and is willing to be trained. The largest training establishment in the world has probably always been the military. The military practically monopolizes the word "training" because everyone understands that someone who joins the military will be trained. If we look at the military training situation, immediately we sense the central relationship between the trainer and the trainee. The trainee, willingly or unwillingly, volunteer or draftee, understands that the situation requires obedience, attention, and a high level of motivation to attempt the performance sought by the trainer. Trainers seem to face two kinds of situations. One is a selective situation in which it is understood that many are called but few will meet the standards of training. Piloting aircraft, operating sophisticated equipment, practicing certain types of medical work—these are understood to be sufficiently demanding and important that a high level of minimum performance is set. Large numbers of people are processed through the training program in order to get a few people who can do the job.

Let's consider what characterizes the desired performance. I am struck by what I call the convergent character of the performance. For many of the tasks I have been describing there is one right way, or at best there are a few right ways, to perform the task. Indeed there is not much latitude for variation in performance if the task is to operate an exotic piece of machinery, execute the mechanics of a particular performance, meet certain treatment requirements in a medical situation, and so forth.

There is another side to training. Sometimes trainers are not told that their task is to produce an elite corps who can perform at a difficult level; rather, trainers understand that their task is to see that a mass of people acquire the basics. And so we distinguish between basic training and advanced training. Trainers who handle basic training are expected to get everyone in their unit up to standard with only a few exceptions. Driver training is an example. Presumably driver training schools are excellent if they can teach anybody the rudiments of good driving.

How do we describe an excellent trainer? Such instructors maintain the trainee's motivation using a variety of techniques. They have sophisticated analytic skills as they follow the trainee's efforts. They usually follow a sequence of instruction that permits progressive building on what the trainee is doing well. They know how to set goals the trainee can reach in ascending order of difficulty. They try to modulate the effort required so the trainee has a sustained sense of progress, even if it is partial and unintegrated for a while. Somehow they combine patience with demand for improvement.

Both these roles lead to a kind of sophistication over time and situations. Experienced trainers and trainees meet for yet another round of training, quickly size each other up, adjust to each other, and get the job done. Opera singers and voice coaches, professional golfers and old pros, experienced computer programmers and representatives of the newest equipment are examples of this.

What does it take to be a good trainee? I suggested earlier that good trainees, first of all, are willing to undergo training. They value it. Second, good trainees concentrate on what they are being offered; they inhibit and restrain any tendencies to raise questions about the training itself. The best trainees are people who willingly place themselves in the hands of the trainer. The poorest trainees are those who persist in believing that they can actually learn the skill or the task without help from a trainer or that they can improve on what the trainer is doing. When we describe trainee behavior in this way, there is a great temptation to speculate as to whether some personalities are born trainees, others are born trainers, and others are born otherwise. I have no intention of pursuing that line of speculation except to comment that it is almost impossible to grow up in this society without being a trainee several times in the course of one's life. It is probable that to be a successful trainee does involve tolerance of frustration. Even if the trainee does not have faith in the trainer, he must act like a good trainee to maximize his benefits. Obviously it is better to be a volunteer than a draftee.

So, is the Colonial Williamsburg Department of Interpretive Education engaged in training? Before addressing that question, I want to put forth a second term—"study." Obviously, if trainees train, we expect students to study. *Webster's* is able to do much more with this word. Instead of two definitions, it offers seven. I suggest we are interested in the following: "application of the mental faculties to the acquisition of knowledge"; or "a careful examination or analysis of a phenomenon, development, or question." Of course *Webster's* cannot resist "the activity or work of a student." And then there are more specialized definitions.

Once again I suggest that *Webster's* is missing the mark, although the first definition points us in the right direction. What happens if we subject a particular phenomenon to a long and careful analysis? The answer lies in the observation that the more one studies in a field and the more one learns about the field, the more interesting the questions become that can be put to the field. I said earlier that the implication of training is that we finally master one of the several right ways of doing things. The implication of study is that if we carry it on long enough we become scholars. Scholars are people with a great breadth of comprehension and knowledge, which they expand year by year. Therefore, if one initiates studies and becomes a student, the implication is that the process is endless.

There is a second implication, too. As one masters the techniques of study, there is a progressive divergence of possibility, an opening up of creativity, a capacity for seeing things from more perspectives, of producing a wider range of questions and weaving the answers to those questions into an ever-larger understanding of the subject at hand. If we look at educational situations and ask what we expect people to get out of their educational efforts, it makes a big difference whether we think they are trainees or students. Just as all of us have had the experience of being trainees, many of us have been given the opportunity to become students. Students, too, have to be highly motivated. They, too, have to want to learn, but unlike trainees, students are more and more frequently in charge of their own educational programs. Students increasingly generate their studies for themselves.

Earlier I shied away from calling a teacher a trainer. Obviously, I hold that a teacher should face students and not trainees. What do we expect from a good teacher? First of all, one teaches by personal example, whether intentionally or not. Successful teachers are curious, probing, analytical, and always project a sense of wanting to know more, of informing others so as to set up for them important questions. Teachers listen to students, reward inquiry, and demand study. They challenge thought of poor quality, expose trivial questions, and, above all, hold the student intellectually responsible for personal utterance in speech and writing. Somehow they combine compassion with rigorous standards.

Not surprisingly, there are fewer students than trainees in the world. That is a pity, because study is much more personally rewarding than training. And oddly enough, there is a greater likelihood that study can be self-taught, and, once mastered, the arts of study sustain self-education.

I may have exaggerated this distinction between being a trainee and being a student, but I honestly don't think I've exaggerated it much. I do think there is an enormous amount of confusion in our institutions of higher learning about the balance between these two rather distinct educational activities. I think that people who try desperately to prepare themselves for a job are defining their opportunities in trainee terms. They may be doing themselves a great disservice if they find themselves in positions in which self-instruction on the job is the way to success. At any rate, we do have to ask what happens, finally, on the job as a consequence of training and study.

Here I think the results are fairly clear. For interpretation, at least, someone whose effort never gets much beyond that of a good trainee is probably going to perform for our visitors in fairly stereotyped ways. On the other hand, those who have combined their training with serious efforts to study the history of the colonial capital in all its many forms should be people who are constantly increasing what they can tell our visitors.

Where in our interpretive situations do we require training? Obviously we require it in communication and interpersonal skills in dealing with the public. These are skills that can be learned even by the shiest and most inhibited, to say nothing of those who don't know when to keep quiet. We certainly do have a large body of valid information that we expect everyone to master. In that sense, it takes a sizable amount of training to get all of this material straight. But, with that accomplished, one's study is ready to begin; and study follows along lines of personal interest and personal temperament. We never have to justify our interest in some particular part of the story.

Study is flexible. Study leads to comprehension. Study means that if we don't know the answer to the visitor's question as put, we can still respond to the question in a way that is helpful to the inquirer despite the fact that we can't provide a definite answer. Now, because the goal is to provide this experience to visitors, I have been concentrating on how training and study, which in my title I call "education," serve the visitor. But there is a marvelous payoff in all of this that is not often talked about. To the extent that an interpreter serves the visitors well, the chief beneficiary of that achievement is the interpreter himself or herself. There is simply nothing as satisfying as achieving confidence and a breadth of understanding—achieving command, if you will, of a body of material. It is a resource that can always be used for personal pleasure and the pleasure of others. It leads to acquaintanceship with a wide network of people who have similar interests and who are a resource for growth, who provide the critiques that must come from somebody else for us to improve. Earlier I referred to the unusual profile of our interpretive group at Colonial Williamsburg. Obviously we have a lot of people for whom the most productive role of the moment is trainee. But we also have a great many people who long since became students.

Concept, Method, and Professional Exchange

Candace T. Matelic

At many North American museums in the last few years, interpreter training has been the focus of much evaluation, rethinking, and new energy. We have long since come out of the dark ages, when guides and docents were handed a mountain of written material, told to learn it (memorize it if necessary), and be ready to meet the public when they reappeared. These "walking encyclopedias," who spieled off facts and facts and facts to unsuspecting and unprepared visitors, while always being gracious yet firmly in control, are being replaced by a new breed of interpreters. Training is no longer the icing on the cake, the last item to be added to budget if there is anything left over. Rather, it is recognized as a mandatory, integral part of developing a successful interpretive program. We've begun to implement a long-held conviction: interpretive training must include method as well as message. Content alone is not enough. Interpreters must also learn *how* to communicate their interpretive message and information to our wide variety of 20th-century audiences. We've also learned that ideas and concepts, not facts, provoke thought and inspiration in museum visitors. Thus, interpretive information and training should be conceptual in approach and focus. Finally, interpreters, discovering that they have much to share and learn from each other, have begun a series of large-scale and very fruitful professional exchanges. This article will explore the development of interpreter training at the Henry Ford Museum and Greenfield Village in Dearborn, Michigan, over the last few years and the recent series of interpreter seminars co-sponsored by the Midwest Open-Air Museums Coordinating Council (MOMCC) and the Association for Living Historical Farms and Agricultural Museums (ALHFAM).

At the Henry Ford Museum and Greenfield Village, the interpretive training process was totally revamped following an intensive self-study completed in 1981. This curriculum report identified collection strengths and proposed an overall interpretive focus for the museum. It also outlined several interpretive themes or subject areas through which the museum could communicate this interpretive message. This is where the interpretive training division of the education department came into the picture. To incorporate the new interpretive ideas into the daily

Journal of Museum Education 10, no. 3 (Summer 1985): 14, 16–17.

interpretive program, we had to redo all written information. This seemed like a formidable task, considering our size (the village has more than 100 historic structures and the museum houses 12 acres of collections) and the size of our interpretive manual (300 pages of undocumented facts and trivia).

First we organized a system for interpretive information consisting of separate manuals for introductory training, research, and on-site use by both staff and visitors. For the actual rewriting and compiling of information, we worked very closely with the staff in collections, library and archives, and photographic services and with other education department staff. The manuals contained different types of information and were designed for specific functions that corresponded to the sequence of interpretive training. For instance, the introductory manuals contained primarily conceptual and overview information, briefly summarizing basic facts but concentrating on interpretive significance and relationship to other collections and exhibits. The first and only place that an interpreter would find curatorial information was in the on-site manuals, located in the buildings or exhibits along with the artifacts. Likewise, research manuals were placed in the interpreter's library to be checked out once an interpreter felt ready to tackle this additional information.

After four years, six revisions of the introductory manual, and two years of work with on-site and research manuals, we were convinced that the system was flexible and worked. More important, we realized that we had to be translators of historical information for the facts to be usable for interpretation. If the program was to be of high quality, then a conscious, planned effort and an aggressive, responsive training program were necessary.

The training program was based on the following premises:

■ Interpretive training includes clarifying interpretive story line and significance; organizing and setting priorities for research information; preparing written materials; conducting classroom and on-site sessions; and following through with performance appraisals.

■ Interpretive training should be conceptual in approach and focus.

■ What occurs on site between interpretive staff and museum visitors is directly related to what occurs during interpretive training.

■ Learning is cumulative, and so, too, interpretive training must occur in stages and be ongoing.

■ Interpretation is a communication process between museum and visitor, and, when human staff are the communicators, interpretive training must include presentation skills as well as interpretive content.

For a new interpreter at the Henry Ford Museum and Greenfield Village, introductory training consists of three phases. The first phase is an introductory course held primarily in the classroom covering background of the museum, basic facts, interpretive significance, and an introductory workshop on communication skills. The second phase occurs primarily on site, with curators and lead interpreters teaching more detailed sessions on background and process information, interpretive technique, and working with visitors. (This is necessary because the interpretive approach changes from building to building and covers the entire spectrum from tours and uniformed staff in stations to process demonstrations and first-person role-playing.) Phase three covers all the specific process skills that staff need to interpret areas such as mills, farms, trades, domestic sites, role-playing, or hands-on programs. This entire process, which usually takes about three months, is completed before staff meet the public.

Following introductory training, interpreters become "students." They attend a continuous round of sessions and workshops offered throughout the year that highlight new research, seasonal changes in programs, and new installations. Staff do much of their own research in preparing characters for role-playing interpretation. They regularly consult the interpreters and research libraries for additional information and often submit questions for curatorial input when they cannot find the answers. Interpretive content is continually revised for staff both through sessions and by written information.

To balance content and to build on the introductory communication skills workshop, interpreters also attend an interpretive methods program that focuses on technique, particularly presentation skills. This methods program includes sessions on speech physiology, care of the vocal system, effective use of language, and body movement and gesture. These sessions are followed up with individual observation throughout the year. A special component of the first interpretive methods course was a dynamic participatory workshop taught by a team of actor-teachers, the California-based Free Association Theatre. The workshop, "Applied Theatre Techniques," covered physical and vocal warm-up, vocal inflection, working with the senses, making transitions, using open-ended questions, and working effectively with large groups of people. Our 200 interpreters were totally energized by these sessions and continue to refer back to them for presentation techniques and ideas. Now [1985] in initial planning stages are method sessions for working with children, senior citizens, and handicapped visitors. Too, plans are under way to videotape individual interpreters interacting with the public as an evaluative tool for presentation skills. This type of interpreter training, which focuses on method rather than message, is crucial to support effective interpretation with today's audience. Interpreters must help visitors develop a visual and sensory literacy to fully enjoy and understand the rich teaching resources that are museums.

Increasingly, interpreters are better understanding their role within museums and developing a professional awareness and sophistication. Many museums have lead interpreter programs that provide motivated and talented staff with an opportunity to get more involved in the behind-the-scenes and administrative aspects of interpretation. Lead interpreters participate in ongoing research, program planning and evaluation, and on-site supervision and evaluation of staff. They also actively serve as interpretive trainers. Many of them regularly read professional journals and literature and attend professional conferences and seminars.

Recently in the Midwest, interpreters participated in an unprecedented exchange. Since 1983, interpreters have gathered for an Interpreters Seminar, co-sponsored by MOMCC and ALHFAM. The gatherings are unique for a number of reasons. Each of the three seminars has had between 120 and 160 participants, the majority of whom were interpreters or volunteers who never before had had the opportunity to participate in a professional conference. Representatives from 30–50 museums located in eight states attended each seminar. Many of the seminar sessions were suggested, planned, and delivered by the interpreters themselves, often in teams from a variety of sites. Topics ranged from interpretive techniques and translating research into interpretation to using reproductions and developing a good period clothing program. There were numerous opportunities for informal sharing as well. The accommodations were dormitory-style, which fostered much discussion long after the formal sessions were completed. Each conference also included a period meal and dance, complete with appropriate music and the majority of interpreters clad in their best period attire. Thanks to in-kind contributions from the host institutions and long hours of volunteer service from many organizers, the conference registration fees were kept very low, which made the experience economically feasible for interpreters and volunteers. The participants' evaluations of the sessions were as perceptive as any professional conference, and the resulting content quality was very high. By far the most rewarding aspect of these conferences was the change in attitude of the participants. One could almost watch them grow as professionals as they shared and solved mutual concerns and problems. The excitement level and respect for interpretation increases steadily as this midwestern experiment becomes a regular tradition.

The ramifications for the larger museum field of these changes in interpretive training and interpreters' attitudes about their jobs are difficult to predict precisely. But the overall effect of interpretive programs on an individual-site basis can be measured. Museum visitors are already letting us know that they appreciate the change in treatment and attitude. Interpreters are more challenged and satisfied with their jobs, and more staff are taking a lifelong learning approach. We are also seeing many applicants to professional museum studies training programs who received that first spark of inspiration for museum work as interpreters. Thank goodness we've come out of the dark ages; this new emphasis on concept, method, and professional exchange is much more invigorating.

Training for Museum Education Professionals

Nina Jensen and Mary Ellen Munley

At the 1984 American Association of Museums annual meeting in Washington, D.C., a group of museum education professionals met to discuss possible responses to the then-anticipated report of the Commission on Museums for a New Century. At that meeting hopes ran high that the report would provide a strong mandate for increased attention to the educational responsibility of the museum.

As we now know, *Museums for a New Century* stresses the public side of the museum and in so doing emphatically claims that there are dual areas of responsibility for any museum—a responsibility to collections and a responsibility to learning. The commission calls for an expanded role for education in the museum. The report reframes the education issue by substituting the term "museum learning" for "museum education," and it observes that museums have not yet realized their potential as learning institutions.[1]

In light of the commission report and as a follow-up to the 1984 meeting, staff from the museum education training programs of George Washington University in Washington, D.C., and Bank Street College in New York City sponsored a colloquium on museum education training as a part of the 1985 AAM annual meeting in Detroit. It is evident that fundamental changes are in store for the field of museum education and that museum education training programs such as those at GWU and Bank Street should take a leadership position during this transition period. As programs that train future professionals, they are ideally situated to initiate change. They are also important because of their ties to academic communities and university-based departments of research.

Training programs cannot work successfully in isolation. When the museum education program was first designed at George Washington University, for instance, museum professionals offered advice on its focus, curriculum, and program elements. The same care was taken with the development of the Bank Street program. Current changes in thinking about museum education suggest that the time is once again right for conversations between these training programs and the profession as a whole. In her thoughtful article on the future of museum education, Laura Chapman observed that "the quality of thought and vision brought to museum education will shape its future."[2] The 1985 Detroit colloquium

Journal of Museum Education 10, no. 4 (Fall 1985): 12–15.

was designed to begin the process of developing a shared vision for the field of museum education. Specifically, the participants discussed these issues:

- What are the elements of the changing role and expectations for museum educators?
- Given the emerging focus on learning—as opposed to teaching—in museums, what are the implications for the museum education field?
- What are the desirable characteristics for the next generation of museum educators?

Discussion at the colloquium began with reactions to the commission report, moved to changing definitions of museum education, and ended with thoughts on directions for action—for training programs and for others. This article summarizes the key points of the discussion. For the sake of clarity, elaboration of some points has been provided by the authors.

Reactions to "Museums for a New Century"

The consensus of the colloquium was that *Museums for a New Century* pointed to a strong future for educators in museums. "The report," said one participant, "gives credibility to the idea of the museum as an educational environment." Discussants expressed satisfaction with the commission's insistence that learning is central to the definition of the museum and that collections care and learning are intricately intertwined functions for all museums.

Concerns were expressed about various interpretations of the commission's message. Some felt that the argument for a central role for education could be read as an endorsement for the abolition of departments of education. If education is a museum-wide concern, the argument goes, then all staff members are educators and there is no need for a special department. A concern about misinterpretation was again introduced when colloquium participants discussed the implications of the commission's use of the term "learning" rather than "education." While all understood the commission's intention to expand thinking about museum education by breaking loose from the legacy of museum educators as teachers of elementary school children, the report's separation of teaching in the museum and learning was questioned. Some participants worried that the report undermines the importance of teaching in the museum and could be read as an endorsement of the view that museum objects speak for themselves and are inherently educational. Colloquium participants advocated a more integrated and holistic view of the museum's educational responsibility. Ideally, teaching and learning are not unrelated and antithetical processes. In museums, concerted teaching efforts enhance the learning potential of objects and collections.

The key to realizing benefits from the commission report was seen to be the careful reading of the learning chapter by directors, trustees, and other decision makers. The report offers a powerful rationale for the role and functions of museum educators.

A Changing Role for the Museum Educator

Echoing the commission's recommendations, participants saw the major change in museum education as a shift in focus from programs and activities for school groups to larger issues concerning all aspects of museum learning. Specifically, museum educators need to turn their attention to programming for the unguided adult visitor and to the exhibit design process. Participants took the position that museum educators will be recognized as having a unique and irreplaceable role in the museum if they have an identifiable area of expertise comparable in depth and importance to the knowledge about the museum's collection that curators contribute. Developing and disseminating a substantive body of knowledge about museum learning will give educators the clout they seek.

Frequently museum educators find themselves wrestling with issues, unaware that pertinent information already exists on the topic. John Dewey's concepts of self-discovery and personal experience, for instance, are central to museum learning, but his writings have only recently been introduced to museum educators. Dewey's philosophy of education embraces many tenets attractive to museum educators. For Dewey, the educative experience is one that lives "fruitfully and creatively in subsequent experiences." If one accepts this philosophical framework and argues the importance of visitors' experiences, then a thorough understanding of the learner and the learning process are essential to responsible programming. The task for the educator is clear. In Dewey's words, the educator "must have that sympathetic understanding of individuals as individuals which gives him an idea of what is actually going on in the minds of those who are learning."[3]

Philosophers from Socrates to Sartre have written about education, and it would behoove museum educators to study these philosophers as they articulate their own perspectives, theories, and procedures. Generally, participants felt that the expanding role for museum education would come to fruition only if museum educators work to upgrade their competence. There was disagreement, however, about the nature of the expertise most appropriate for museum educators. Job descriptions, it was pointed out, call for subject matter experts to fill museum education positions.

Because of the demands of the job market, one is compelled to suggest upgrading the competence of museum educators by encouraging them to acquire additional training in content areas like history, anthropology, and art history. On the other hand, participants agreed that the jury is still out on the value of a communication-education expert to a museum staff. There was agreement that museum programming should be informed by knowledge about learning and communication. Museums and museum educators need to know more about human development, communication theory, information processing, the nature of nonverbal learning, group dynamics, cross-cultural learning, and human responses to built environments.

Currently there is a gap between what museum educators know they should know about learning and communication and what they actually know. The real contribution of the communication-learning specialist will be tested when museum educators bring to the museum knowledge about the audience, learning, and philosophies of education. If such expertise becomes the foundation for museum education work, then the long-standing images of the museum educator as either a content-free contributor or a second-rate curator could change.

Research about Visitor Learning

In addition to acquiring knowledge from other disciplines, museums need to know more about the interaction among programs, exhibits, and visitors. Time and again, discussion about the museum as a learning environment has turned to calls for audience research and evaluation studies. Participants endorsed the value of evaluation for all museums and advised training programs to include evaluation in their curriculums and to encourage students to design and carry out audience research studies. They acknowledged, however, that many museums are still reticent about evaluation studies and that museum educators are likely to find themselves in the position of having to defend the value of such activity.

Colloquium participants suggested a review of extant literature as a necessary first step. Audience studies and evaluations have been conducted in museums since the 1920s. A critical review of the literature would enable an integration of study findings in an effort to identify generalizations, concepts, and practices useful to the practitioner. The valuable results of evaluation studies is the single best justification for such a review. Past efforts need to be examined not only for their results but also for the lessons they provide about study designs and methodologies appropriate to the museum setting.

Meanwhile, colloquium participants encouraged museums to undertake evaluation studies to assess the success of their programs. One participant underscored the importance of evaluation activity by recommending that each museum undertake at least one evaluation study each year. Another recommended that museum educators work in teams with curators and exhibit designers to study the educational effectiveness of exhibits. Generally, participants saw value in viewing the museum as a learning laboratory where educators and others could test theories about learning and confirm through research the appropriateness of their practices. Museums must be cautious as they embark on evaluation programs, however, remembering that the museum environment is different from other learning environments and that models developed for those other settings will not necessarily be applicable to the museum setting.

Future Directions for Training Programs

Colloquium participants focused their recommendations for museum education training programs on four main points. Most important was their wish that these programs prepare professionals with bold vision, new ideas, and a more sophisticated knowledge of educational approaches. Some remarked that they looked to the training programs to produce "movers and shakers" who would be prepared to "hit the ground running"—able both to meet the current demands of the profession and lead it in new directions.

The issue of training in an academic discipline versus training in education was not entirely resolved. The consensus was that a well-prepared museum educator must have solid training in both areas. It was recommended that training programs be structured to encourage interaction among students studying for all areas of museum work. Future directors, curators, registrars, and educators need to talk with each other. This early introduction to varying perspectives on museum work could lead to better communication and increased sensitivity on the job.

Museum education programs and museum studies programs were applauded for offering a diverse set of training opportunities. Programs were encouraged to retain their individual differences and consider developing recognizable areas of specialization. Finally, graduate programs were asked to expand their offerings to include midcareer training, especially in the area of audience research and evaluation. University-based programs were asked to consider how they might provide services to the field by producing resources such as bibliographies, annotations of important books, and other publications.

Recommendations for Action

The need to consolidate existing information was the central theme of recommendations for immediate action. Specifically, participants agreed that the museum education field needs:

■ a bibliography of materials about audience and museum learning. A simple listing of article titles is not helpful to the practitioner. Museum educators need an annotated, critical review of the existing literature that they can use to inform their decision making.

■ publications about museum learning. Theories from other fields need to be reviewed for their usefulness to museum education practice. Museum educators should alert funding sources to the need for this research and the publication of important findings.

■ a clearinghouse for information about museum learning. Although scores of audience studies are conducted in museums each year, reports of the findings rarely go beyond the department sponsoring the research.

Increased interest in evaluation and learning suggests that many museums could benefit from these research efforts. A central location is needed for the cataloging, indexing, and dissemination of information from audience studies and other sources of information about museum learning.

Participants were encouraged to take actions within their own institutions and areas of influence. Ideas for reasonable action included adding a researcher to the museum staff and seeking funds to support evaluation efforts, inviting education specialists to deliver keynote addresses at professional meetings, and organizing a conference on the theme of visitor behavior in the museum. It is fair to say that each participant left the meeting with ideas for a personal agenda for action.

Notes

1. Commission on Museums for a New Century, *Museums for a New Century* (Washington, D.C.: American Association of Museums, 1984).
2. Laura H. Chapman, "The Future of Museum Education," *Museum News* 60, no. 6 (July/August 1982): 48–55.
3. John Dewey, *Experience and Education* (New York: Collier Books, 1938), p. 39.

Afterword
Nina Jensen

The discussion reported in this article took place in 1985, shortly after the publication of *Museums for a New Century*. The most recent Colloquium on Museum Learning sponsored by George Washington University, held in Denver in 1991, took a measure of the progress since then on our understanding about museum learning.

There was general agreement in Denver that museums today are much more accepting of the notion of visitor research and evaluation. Our growth in knowledge and sophistication concerning visitor studies has led to an awareness of the complexity and richness of the museum experience and to an expanded range of approaches to assessing its impact. The museum visit is now recognized as a highly personal and unique construction of the individual visitor, influenced by the physical and social context as well as by the visitor's cultural background and preferred learning style. In-depth, qualitative studies now explore changes in attitude, effect on long-term memory, and the development of museum literacy skills. The discussion has shifted in both subtle and profound ways from the museum's agenda to the visitor's experience. Projecting five years into the future (bringing us just four years short of the year 2000), some participants suggested that the trend toward including visitor perspectives could lead to the development of true partnerships with museum audiences. At the very least, awareness of the visitor's agenda is causing museum professionals to rethink and clarify their mission with increased focus on public service.

How far have museum educators come in developing the definable area of expertise in learning and communication called for in 1985? In addition to visitor studies, the literature informing museum educators has broadened to include such issues as learning styles, multiple intelligences, memory, linguistics, and reflective practice. We have moved beyond a strictly developmental view to an understanding of the key role of sociocultural context and of learning as a mediated activity. Terms such as "scaffolding" have entered the museum educator's vocabulary. Museum education students at Bank Street College, George Washington University, and other institutions are being asked to synthesize varied sources (the ideas of John Dewey continue as a seminal influence at Bank Street) into a coherent framework that informs the practice of museum education in its broadest sense. The ability to articulate a theoretical framework for our work, together with an expanding body of knowledge based on the empirical study of visitor behavior, has moved us significantly closer to our goal of professionalism. But "professionalism"—more moving target than final destination—implies continually contributing to as well as keeping abreast of ongoing research and development in the field. If we have begun to catch up, we will always need to keep on running!

What challenges lie ahead for the museum education profession? Rapid and profound changes on a global and national scale include increased cultural diversity and rising ethnic and racial tensions, the AIDS epidemic, grave environmental issues, and economic recession. In these troubled times, museums must respond to social needs or risk becoming irrelevant. Appropriately, the report of the AAM Task Force on Museum Education, *Excellence and Equity: Education and the Public Dimension of Museums* (1992), expands the term "museum education" to encompass the broader concept of public service. The report suggests a dual challenge for museums: to maintain intellectual rigor while reaching out to serve a broader spectrum of our culturally pluralistic society. On its most profound level, this challenge implies rethinking every aspect of museum operations, from the composition of board and staff to exposing the cultural biases and assumptions conveyed by museums in their exhibitions. Museum professionals, along with audiences, need to develop sophisticated cultural literacy skills that will enable them to understand and articulate the values, world views, and ways of life of other cultures. By drawing on the multiple perspectives of more culturally diverse students and faculty (a critical issue for museum professional training programs) and a broad range of disciplines including anthropology, ethnology, and philosophy, training programs have the potential to play a leading role in the future of museum education.

Preparation for Empowerment

Diane Brigham

Credentials alone do not make a competent art museum educator. But academic training combined with experience certainly make the road to competence easier to travel. At the Denver Meeting of Art Museum Educators, held in November 1987, we attempted to identify the unique combination of knowledge, attitudes, and skills that art museum educators need. Placing the question of training within the context of a broad definition of art museum education, we discussed a variety of issues related to the professional preparation of educators in our field. This article shares the group's thoughts and conclusions on some of the issues and, in an effort to stimulate continued dialogue, expands on three of the topics we discussed: the role of teaching, the empowerment of art museum educators, and recommendations for action.

Professional Preparation

When we think about the academic background and skills appropriate to a career in art museum education, we often recall our own preparation and consider its impact on our careers. We may conclude that our own academic major was the best training, or we may feel that we are being held back because we do not have a particular type or level of degree. This kind of thinking is limiting. It is more productive to consider the ideal types, proportions, and levels of knowledge, attitudes, and skills that are consistent with our individual goals as museum educators. Museum administrators need to ask the same questions about the experience and ability required for their educators. We need to think creatively about alternatives and untapped possibilities, not only about our own backgrounds.

What knowledge, attitudes, and skills should entry-level art museum educators bring to their work? Art museum educators must be able to create a bridge between people and art objects. We must be exemplary teachers who are committed to both people and art. We must strive to put people first in our teaching, as well as in our institutions.

The Denver group emphasized that the diversity of backgrounds museum educators bring to their work gives our field strength and richness. Several academic areas can provide useful preparation for museum educators. Ideally, an education

Journal of Museum Education 13, no. 3 (Fall 1988): 8–11.

department with several staff members would employ people with a mix of knowledge and experience. But all of them would share an attitude that puts people first, and they would have skills common to effective educators.

The group agreed that art museum educators must have master's degree–level competency in:

- the knowledge of art, as demonstrated by the study of esthetics, art criticism, art education, art history, the humanities, or studio art. Art museum educators must know how to interpret art objects. Our knowledge of an object is enhanced by an awareness of these various disciplines and by the points of view of the artists themselves.

- the knowledge of how people learn, as demonstrated by the study of art education, museum education, philosophy of education, developmental psychology, educational research and evaluation, curriculum development, or learning theory

- the ability to teach with objects. This special skill is essential and unique to educators in museums, where the focus is on using objects as a source of information, ideas, and esthetic pleasure. An internship or other preservice practice in teaching with objects is an essential component of the museum educator's preparation.

Museum educators need several additional skills in order to be a bridge between art and people. They must be able to:

- communicate well orally and in writing

- think creatively and then plan appropriate means (programs, installations, or publications) to connect people with art

- "read" the behavior of others and interact easily with people.

As they advance, educators usually need management skills, too. This need may occur alarmingly early for those who are thrust into a management role in small departments before they have a fully formed philosophy based on teaching experience. Supervision, advocacy, risk taking, strategic planning, analysis and decision making, and time and resource management are among the skills needed by the many educators who pursue administration.

The Denver group discussion of midcareer development concluded that three career development models should evolve. Art museum educators might aspire to be:

- museum education administrators and, in some cases, museum directors

- master teachers, who can pursue the highest-quality teaching without administrative burden

- researchers/visionaries, who focus on moving the field forward and are given the opportunity to pursue philosophical issues in museum education.

The Need for Teaching Experience

The Denver group agreed that the ability to teach with objects, while it may take many forms, is essential for an art museum educator. There is no substitute for live teaching in the galleries to provide that experience. Facing real people and trying to help them connect to works of art compel the teacher to plan, try, and alter his or her approaches. Learners' reactions provide quick feedback. Experience builds quickly as the teacher tries alternative strategies, expands the range of art subjects, and reaches diverse audiences.

New museum educators need experiences that help them articulate a philosophy and guide their program design. Internship opportunities that emphasize teaching are vital. Mortimer Adler stresses in *The Paideia Proposal* that teaching skill is "developed best by practice under supervision, that is, by coaching."[1] Coaching involves close supervision, directed criticism, and repeated effort. Interns should observe master teachers, practice teaching under their supervision, experiment with various teaching approaches, and receive frequent feedback that helps them improve their teaching skill.

What does the educator learn from teaching? Teaching in the gallery, in situations in which the educator facilitates more thoughtful visitor experiences with works of art, is the most direct and rewarding way to understand the potential and reality of museum education. The essential work of writing labels and gallery guides and of planning other kinds of interpretation is all informed by the experience of live teaching.

Teaching experiences offer the following insights:

■ Our audiences have diverse abilities and learning styles.

■ Our audiences have varying perceptions of specific objects and exhibitions, and even of the museum itself.

■ Effective teaching strategies can help others increase their ability to see more and learn more from works of art.

■ An understanding of human behavior patterns and an appreciation of the power of human ideas are important to effective teaching.

■ A myriad of seemingly unpredictable audiences, questions, and teaching situations can provide new insights that affect other interpretive methods and program planning.

■ The role of bridge between objects and people can be highly rewarding.

As a field, we need to reassess the value we place on teaching. Master teachers should be encouraged to hone their skills, share their expertise, and teach without the intrusion of administrative duties. We should devote research to the effectiveness of teaching strategies. Those who move into administrative roles must find ways to communicate the value of teaching, perhaps by continuing to teach on a limited basis and encouraging colleagues to become master teachers.

Empowerment

By identifying the essential components of art museum educator preparation, we can clarify our essential role within the museum framework. When we realize that we offer abilities that no one else in the museum can contribute, we are better able to offer leadership. We empower ourselves when we are clear about what we are and have prepared ourselves to practice our profession with rigor. If we believe that our role as audience advocate is not subordinate to the curatorial role, but its equal in the mission of the museum, then we know that our training cannot mimic that of curators. Our role is different. We cannot have second-rate or even first-rate curatorial training. We must have first-rate training in museum education.

Certainly there are political implications involved in the training of art museum educators. With our history of basement status, we must actively work to achieve parity with curators if our museums are to accomplish their missions. Academic degrees could be one avenue to increased status. Judith White commented thoughtfully in the *Journal of Museum Education* on the perceived need for Ph.D. programs that could make educators "comparable to curators." She concluded that, while there is a need for more research and scholarship, "a Ph.D. is only one way," and we must guard against forgetting the broad range of skills educators need. She discounted the value of a Ph.D. in achieving power within an institution and wondered if multifaceted approaches to innovative programming would suffer.[2] How well can we be served by earning terminal degrees in art history if we are only attempting to achieve the elusive parity with curators? For those who do pursue an advanced degree, the area of scholarly inquiry could address the process of learning in museums. The unique skills of educators and the rigorous pursuit of educational excellence—not just academic credentials—will make our voices strong in our institutions.

The Next Step

This outline of essential abilities provides a baseline that can be scrutinized, tested, and refined. Among the questions we should ask are: How do these translate into course work and internships? How can future educators best develop skill in teaching with objects? What is the ideal entry-level job? What experiences should supervisors provide for young professionals? What training and early experiences were pivotal for practicing educators? How can we provide these opportunities for aspiring educators today? What can the profession do for educators in one-person departments where there are no mentors from whom to learn? What can we learn about career preparation from educators in other types of museums?

Next, we need to refine our outline of basic preparation in light of our notion of branching career models for the midcareer professional. When would we encourage such specialization? What Ph.D.-level academic training could a museum educator pursue that would enrich his or her research abilities? How can we encourage educators to feel an obligation to move the field forward? There are larger questions to examine as well. How does the field foster rigor and the sense of a common ground while maintaining diversity?

Recommendations for Action

There are numerous steps we can take to improve the professional preparation of art museum educators. These recommendations have been expanded from suggestions voiced at the Denver Meeting:

■ Identify and track young educators as they progress. Consider what opportunities are needed to help them achieve their potential. Use the experience of seasoned educators to assist new members of the field.

■ Interview leaders in the field about the experiences and readings that have been pivotal to their professional development. Give this information to entering professionals, university faculty, and work supervisors.

■ Support multiple career models for art museum educators as administrators, master teachers, and visionaries.

■ Consider university-level research and the preparation of museum educators as alternative career models for museum educators.

■ Publish articles about art museum education more frequently in professional publications to foster intellectual rigor and discourse. Publish in popular publications to inform broader audiences about our work.

■ Compile a directory of expert resources in museum education.

■ Continue and expand the development of art museum education consortiums. These consortiums encourage interaction between experienced professionals and new educators; stimulate exchange among museum education professionals with similar and dissimilar concerns; enrich both professions by sharing expertise between museum educators and educational philosophers; and foster communication among relevant professional organizations such as the National Art Education Association and the American Association of Museums.

■ Gain institutional support for educators' professional activities, including research, sabbatical leaves, exchange visits between institutions, study trips, and formal and informal continuing education.

■ Offer graduate-level courses within the museum on museum teaching.

■ Persist in working for parity in salary and status with other administrative and curatorial positions within museum

■ Recognize and support visionaries in the field who can lead it forward.

■ Recognize and give awards for models of excellence in teaching, publications, research, and institutional leadership.

By working to improve the career preparation of art museum educators, we strengthen the field in several ways. We focus attention on the unique combinations of abilities that educators need. We clarify our role in the museum and foster parity with colleagues in other departments. We establish commmon expectations for entry-level professionals and then can develop the means to achieve these basic competencies. Most important, once empowered by the appropriate mix of training and practice, new art museum educators gain confidence in enhancing the visitor's experience.

Notes

1. Mortimer Adler, *The Paideia Proposal* (New York: Macmillan, 1982), p. 61.

2. Judith White, in " *The Uncertain Profession:* Perceptions and Directions," introd. Carol B. Stapp, *Journal of Museum Education* 12, no. 3 (Fall 1987): 6–8, reprinted in this volume as "Strength in Ambiguity," pp. 51–53.

The Whole Audience Catalogue

Introduction
George E. Hein

In August 1989 Elaine Gurian, [then] deputy assistant secretary for museums, Smithsonian Institution, and Mary Ellen Munley, chief of museum education, New York State Museum, Albany, wrote to a group of friends and associates asking them to contribute to an effort to gather and distribute materials that they have found useful in taking on the role of audience advocate. To quote from their letter:

> Some of us within the Education Committee of the American Association of Museums and on the staff of the Smithsonian Institution would like to investigate the gathering and eventual distribution of the most seminal or "just plain useful" materials that will help us all to become audience advocates. Additionally, we intend to design training mechanisms that will fit within the calendar of the already employed and overworked museum professional.
>
> As a step toward establishing a series of self-help forums in audience advocacy, we are inviting you to join us in suggesting baseline literature that we can read, understand, and integrate into our professional tasks. We would appreciate it if you would send us a short list of the most important and useful things you have read, since you are known to be an advocate within your museum. These suggestions can come from both literature within the field and external to us.

The responses include some careful bibliographies of literature primarily within the museum field as well as a number of lists that address broader topics and a wider field of reading. There is a remarkable overlap of suggestions from the fields of humanistic psychology, education, and environmental psychology. Reading preferences are, of course, idiosyncratic, but other people's lists at least give us insight into their thought processes and, at best, include items that may intrigue us. Selections from a few of the letters are published here to give a flavor of the literature that has inspired, educated, and entertained museum professionals. We have focused primarily on letters that mention publications beyond the professional literature about museum visitors.

Journal of Museum Education 15, no. 1 (Winter 1990): 22–24.

Questioning Premises
Carol B. Stapp

Quickly searching my mental bookcase to identify what have been influential readings for me, I came up with two categories, both of which helped me see human beings and museums in a new light. In the first category—which focuses on the needs and interests of regular folks—fall *Freedom to Learn,* by Carl R. Rogers (Columbus, Ohio: Merrill, 1969) and *All Our Kin: Strategies for Survival in a Black Community,* by Carol B. Stack (New York: Harper and Row, 1974). These two seemingly disparate books unblinkingly address issues of interaction and coping that stray from the middle-class norm. An article by Robert Coles—"The Art Museum and the Pressures of Society," in *On Understanding Art Museums,* edited by Sherman E. Lee (Englewood Cliffs, N.J.: Prentice Hall, 1975)—serves as a bridge between the first category and a look at the museum as an authoritative institution. My favorites in this category are "An Anti-Catalog," by Rudolf Baranik et al. (New York: Catalog Committee, 1977) and, of course, *The Visitor and the Museum,* edited by Linda Draper (Berkeley, Calif.: Lowie Museum of Anthropology, 1977). In the latter, the articles by Nelson Graburn and John Kinard stand in provocative juxtaposition.

What I have valued about all these readings is their effectiveness in causing me to question my premises about people and museums. Perhaps these readings don't provide much in terms of "hard data," but they pack a wallop intellectually and emotionally for educating ourselves and other museum practitioners about the barriers between the world view of the general public and that of the museum specialist. Although I was by no means to the manner born, by virtue of educational opportunity I have gradually moved away from my lower-middle-class origins, and I need reminders of that fact. The contact I once had with museum visitors on the floor for hours every day at the Philadelphia Museum of Art is no longer my privilege.

Let me mention also that knowing certain powerful personalities and undergoing significant experiences opened my eyes in ways that reading never could have equaled. Of course, there's been my wonderful mentor Marcella Brenner, who has shared with me her wisdom about being an agent of change. And then there were my two years abroad—in France and in India—where I felt cultural displacement rather acutely from time to time. I suspect that these served me well—again as a reminder—once I became part of an institutional establishment.

Touchstones
Dennis O'Toole

I circulated your letter among directors in the Colonial Williamsburg programs area, and I have a few titles to add to what I hope is a growing and by now impressive list. These titles, taken together, form what our education staff think are the "touchstone" works in the areas of evaluation theory and practice and the exhibition process:

Museum Visitor Evaluation, by Ross Loomis (Nashville, Tenn.: American Association for State and Local History, 1987)

The Design of Educational Exhibits, by Roger Miles et al. (Winchester, Mass.: Allen and Unwin, 1982). The author is head of the Public Services Department at the British Museum (Natural History).

Theory, Research and Practice, proceedings of the first annual Visitor Studies Conference, 1988, edited by Stephen Bitgood, James T. Roper, Jr., and Arlene Benefield (Jacksonville, Fla.: Center for Social Design, 1988).

All of our staff commented that little has been done so far on the most common educational experience for museum visitors—encounters with live interpretation. Here the best work comes from the marketing perspective, especially where focus groups have been used to get at visitor expectations and reactions to the museum experience. The J. Paul Getty Trust study, *Insights: Museums, Visitors, Attitudes, and Expectations* (Santa Monica, Calif.: J. Paul Getty Trust, 1991) and independent studies by Greenfield Village and Henry Ford Museum and Colonial Williamsburg are the best in this area so far. And to put all this in a theoretical framework, try Dean MacCannell's *The Tourist: A New Theory of the Leisure Class* (New York: Schocken Books, 1976).

Thomas J. Peters and Robert H. Waterman, Jr.'s *In Search of Excellence* (New York: Harper and Row, 1982) and the excellent videotapes Tom Peters has produced still offer, in my opinion, the best materials available on how to build and guide "consumer-oriented" organizations, teams, and groups. Probably my favorite tape in the series is the one that introduces the viewer to Stew Leonard's supermarket in Connecticut. Here's the last word in listening to and responding to the consumer.

Human development theory? There's a lot to choose from. But my personal favorite is Walker Percy's *The Message in the Bottle* (New York: Farrar Straus and Giroux, 1975), especially the chapters titled "The Loss of the Creature" and "The Message in the Bottle." The book's subtitle suggests the approach Percy takes: "How Queer Man Is, How Queer Language Is, and What One Has to Do with the Other." This is not Piaget, McCarthy, or Jung, but it rings true for me today just as it did in 1975.

A multicultural learning perspective can be gained in many ways. Contemplating the history of race and ethnic relations in this country works for me, as do stories (fiction and nonfiction) of men and women who have struggled to make meaningful lives for themselves and their people amid the hardships and depradations—and blessings—of their circumstances. In this regard, I have benefited greatly from having read Richard Rodriguez's *Hunger of Memory: The Education of Richard Rodriguez* (Boston: David R. Godine, 1982); John Edgar Wideman's *Brothers and Keepers* (New York: Holt, Rinehart and Winston, 1984); Harry Ashmore's *Hearts and Minds: A Personal Chronicle of Race in America* (rev. ed., Cabin John, Md.: Seven Locks Press, 1988); David Bradley's *The Chaneysville Incident* (New York: Harper and Row, 1981); and Winthrop Jordan's *White over Black: American Attitudes toward the Negro, 1550–1812* (New York: Norton, 1977).

Teaching and Learning and Being
Mary Worthington

On human development theory, *Childhood and Society,* by Erik Erikson (New York: Norton, 1964), contains the first developmental theory I ever read that stuck. I still use it, as I do *Toward a Psychology of Being,* by Abraham Maslow (Princeton, N.J.: Van Nostrand Reinhold, 1968). Piaget's theories have had a powerful influence on the field and on me, but I've never been able to read him in the original. David Elkind does a good job of interpreting in his *Children and Adolescents: Interpretive Essays on Jean Piaget* (New York: Oxford University Press, 1970), and Mary Ann Pulaski's *Understanding Piaget: An Introduction to Children's Cognitive Development* (New York: Harper and Row, 1971) is the most readable book about Piaget I know.

Other basic child development literature:

Frank and Theresa Caplan, *The Power of Play* (Garden City, N.Y.: Anchor Books, 1974)

Ronald W. Henderson and John R. Bergan, *The Cultural Context of Childhood* (Columbus, Ohio: Merrill, 1976), a textbook marked, as its title suggests, by a relativist approach.

Dorothy H. Cohen and Virginia Stern, *Observing and Recording the Behavior of Young Children* (New York: Teachers College Press, 1983). This little book was the text for my observing and recording classes when I taught at Pacific Oaks College. It's a comprehensive guide, useful for training museum staff in the techniques. We encourage our museum's staff to do written observations as part of training and for exhibit evaluation.

Dorothy Briggs's *Your Child's Self-Esteem* (New York: Doubleday, 1967) is a classic, though not as classic as Dr. Spock, which is still, I think, the best how-to-parent book around. The latest edition is co-authored with Michael Rothenberg and titled *Dr. Spock's Baby and Child Care: 40th Anniversary Edition* (New York: Dutton, 1985). This category continues to proliferate, of course, reflecting the trends and fashions in childrearing. They're useful books to dip into occasionally to stay current and for basic child development information.

My educational philosophy was formed during the 1960s and fueled by the writings of George Leonard, James Herndon, Herbert Kohl, Jonathan Kozol, and the like, who taught in urban elementary schools and were dedicated to freedom, reform, and making their principals crazy. All of them were, to one degree or another, influenced by A. S. Neill. From the same era, try *The Metaphoric Mind,* by Bob Samples (Reading, Mass.: Addison-Wesley, 1976).

When I think about adult learning I think of the writings of Mortimer Adler and Jerome Bruner and of Johan Huizinga's *Homo Ludens: A Study of the Play Element in Culture* (New York: Beacon Press, 1955), which I only recently read, though it is also a classic. I've also struggled through Howard Gardner's *Frames of Mind* (New York: Basic Books, 1983) and Mihaly Csikszentmihalyi's *Beyond Boredom and Anxiety* (San Francisco: Jossey-Bass, 1975), both of which offered exciting ideas and extended my thinking, but which I'm glad friends had read first and synthesized for me. They're hard sledding.

Museum Education Anthology (Washington, D.C.: Museum Education Roundtable, 1984) is a landmark, as is the Smithsonian's *Report of the Proceedings of the Children in Museums International Symposium, 1979* (Washington, D.C.: Smithsonian Institution Office of Museum Programs, 1982). Bruno Bettelheim's speech in particular stays with me and says some eloquent things about the sense of wonder.

I am particularly interested in how spaces influence learning and was glad to find *The Environment of Play,* by John Mason (West Point, N.Y.: Leisure Press, 1982). Although it is primarily about school and day care spaces, it offers many wise words about the importance of environment. An issue of *Children's Environments Quarterly* is devoted to children's museums (vol. 4, no. 4, spring 1987), and *Hand to Hand,* the newsletter of the Association of Youth Museums, has been publishing since 1986.

Teaching Adults: An Active Learning Approach (Washington, D.C.: National Association for the Education of Young Children, 1986), by my friend and mentor Elizabeth Jones of Pacific Oaks College, is a gem. It's a how-to manual for teaching a child development class, but it's also a treasury of wisdom about teaching and learning and being.

A Visitor's View
Arminta Neal

I must qualify my contribution by saying that when I retired as assistant director of the Denver Museum of Natural History in January 1982 I deliberately left professional involvement in the museum field behind me. My involvement now with museums is strictly as a visitor. So perhaps my views *can* contribute to an "audience advocate" approach. I will, however, list some of the publications I found useful while I was still in the field, for I think they provide continuing basic information.

Lest we think we are always coming up with new ideas, I think it is humbling to read:

"The Principles of Museum Administration," by George Brown Goode, published in a collection of his writings called *A Memorial of George Brown Goode* (Washington, D.C.: U.S. Government Printing Office, 1907)

Museum Ideals, by Benjamin Ives Gilman, 2d ed. (Cambridge: Harvard University Press, 1923)

I am almost always made aware of how exhibit designers continue to ignore the physical needs of visitors. Labels are often in type that is too small, with lines that are too long and too close together, making it hard for eyes to go from the end of one line to the beginning of the next, and placed too high or too low on a wall and flat on a horizontal surface instead of tilted at a right angle to the line of sight. Exhibit halls consistently are lacking in enough places to sit down or to rest a rump on a railing. I know lack of benches helps to speed traffic along, but is that what we're after? Exhibits should be places for contemplation.

I think my two books are still good references for designing with consideration of human anatomy: *Help! for the Small Museum* (2d ed., Boulder, Colo.: Pruett Press, 1987) and *Exhibits for the Small Museum* (Nashville, Tenn.: American Association for State and Local History, 1976). And *Anatomy for Interior Designers,* by Julius Panero (New York: Watson-Guptill, 1962) is fun to read as well as an excellent reference.

Principles of Visual Perception, by Carolyn M. Bloomer (New York: Van Nostrand Reinhold, 1976), is fascinating, with explanations in layperson's terms of *how* we see and process visual information.

Art and Visual Perception, by Rudolf Arnheim (Berkeley: University of California Press, 1974), subtitled "A Psychology of the Creative Eye, the New Version," also deals with how we see and process visual information.

Environmental Psychology, by Paul Bell, Jeffrey Fisher, and Ross Loomis (Philadelphia: W. B. Saunders, 1978), provides insights that can be adapted to the museum situation.

Three books by cultural anthropologist Edward T. Hall provide an excellent background for factors tangential to museum exhibit design:

The Silent Language (Garden City, N.Y.: Doubleday, 1959) may help museum people understand the ethnocentrism we often bring, unconsciously, to our interpretations of other people's cultures.

The Hidden Dimension (Garden City, N.Y.: Doubleday, 1966) treats different cultures' concepts of space, including intimate, personal, social, and public distance.

The Dance of Life (Garden City, N.Y.: Anchor Press, 1983), explores different cultures' concepts of time.

A couple of books by Kenneth Hudson are fun and informative: *A Social History of Museums: What the Visitors Thought* (London: Macmillan, 1975) and *Museums for the 1980s: A Survey of World Trends* (New York: Holmes and Meier, 1977).

And finally, in terms of the "team approach" but on a much broader basis, Riane Eisler's *The Chalice and the Blade* (San Francisco: Harper and Row, 1987) discusses the possibility of "partnership" societies rather than "dominator" societies.

Contributors

James Affolter is director of Cornell Plantations, Ithaca, New York, the botanical garden, arboretum, and natural areas of Cornell University, and associate professor in Cornell's Bailey Hortorium.

Nina Archabal is director of the Minnesota Historical Society, St. Paul. Prior to joining the historical society staff 15 years ago, she was assistant director for humanities at the University of Minnesota Art Museum.

Luke Baldwin is a member of the faculty at Lesley College Graduate School, Cambridge, Massachusetts.

Sharon Barry is on the staff of the graphics office, National Zoological Park, Smithsonian Institution, Washington, D.C.

Valorie Beer has consulted on educational programs for museums, including substantial work for the new Japanese American National Museum in Los Angeles. She works in the training department at Apple Computer, Inc., Palo Alto, California.

Barbara A. Birney has coordinated the visitor research and exhibit evaluation program at Brookfield Zoo, Brookfield, Illinois, for five years.

Robert C. Birney retired recently as senior vice-president for education, Colonial Williamsburg Foundation, Williamsburg, Virginia.

Joel N. Bloom is president emeritus of the Franklin Institute Science Museum, Philadelphia, past president of the Association of Science-Technology Centers, and past president of the American Association of Museums.

Minda Borun is director of museum programs at the Franklin Institute Science Museum, Philadelphia. She also conducts research on exhibit-based learning and serves as a consultant on exhibit and program evaluation.

Diane Brigham is senior museum educator at the J. Paul Getty Museum in Malibu, California, where she administers school, teacher, and public gallery programs. She was assistant curator of education at the Philadelphia Museum of Art.

Claudine K. Brown is deputy assistant secretary for museums, Smithsonian Institution, Washington, D.C. An attorney with a master's degree in museum education, she was formerly assistant director for government and community affairs at the Brooklyn Museum.

Barbara G. Carson teaches undergraduate survey courses in Western European and American decorative arts and graduate seminars exploring ways to use material culture to illuminate problems of social history at the College of William and Mary, Williamsburg, Virginia, and George Washington University, Washington, D.C.

Marlene Chambers has been director of publications at the Denver Art Museum since 1974.

Sharlene Cochrane is a member of the faculty at Lesley College Graduate School, Cambridge, Massachusetts.

Jon Charles Coe and his firm, Coe Lee Robinson Roesch, Inc., of Philadelphia, are zoo planning and design specialists with a nationwide practice. He was one of the originators of the "landscape immersion" approach to exhibit design in zoos.

Constance Counts is a member of the faculty at Lesley College Graduate School, Cambridge, Massachusetts.

Judy Diamond is an associate professor and curator for public programs at the University of Nebraska State Museum, Lincoln. A former staff member of the Exploratorium, San Francisco, and the Lawrence Hall of Science, Berkeley, California, she has been conducting programs and research in science museums for the past 15 years.

Amina J. Dickerson is director of the Elizabeth F. Cheney Center for Education and Public Programs at the Chicago Historical Society. She was president of the Du Sable Museum of African American History, Chicago, and assistant executive director of the Afro-American Historical and Cultural Museum, Philadelphia.

Lynn D. Dierking is an assistant professor in the College of Education at the University of Maryland, College Park. She is currently on leave to direct a national curriculum project, Science in American Life, at the National Museum of American History, Smithsonian Institution, Washington, D.C.

Joan Dolamore is a member of the faculty at Lesley College Graduate School, Cambridge, Massachusetts.

Eleanor Duckworth is professor of education at Harvard University, Cambridge, Massachusetts, where she gives courses on teaching and learning and their interrelationships.

Zora Felton is chief of the education department at the Anacostia Museum, Smithsonian Institution, Washington, D.C.

John Fines, a consultant in West Sussex, England, is director of the Nuffield Project History in Schools, which is implementing the new English National Curriculum. The former head of history at the West Sussex Institute of Higher Education, he held a fellowship at the Folger Shakespeare Library, Washington, D.C.

Barbara Franco is assistant director for museums at the Minnesota Historical Society, St. Paul, with responsibility for the educational programs, exhibitions, and museum collections that will be available to the public in the new History Center scheduled to open in the fall of 1992. She has worked at the Munson-Williams-

Proctor Institute, Utica, New York, and the Museum of Our National Heritage, Lexington, Massachusetts.

Edmund Barry Gaither has been director of the Museum of the National Center of Afro-American Artists, Boston, Massachusetts, since 1984. He has taught and lectured in Afro-American studies and art history and was special consultant/ adjunct curator at the Museum of Fine Arts, Boston.

Alberta Sebolt George is executive vice-president of Old Sturbridge Village, Sturbridge, Massachusetts. She is responsible for all interpretive and educational programs, publications, research, exhibitions, collections, security, and plant maintenance.

Mauricio Gonzalez is assistant vice-president for multicultural student development in the Office of Student Affairs, University of Toledo, Toledo, Ohio. He was director of the University of Texas at San Antonio Teaching Art Gallery.

Elaine Heumann Gurian is deputy director of the United States Holocaust Memorial Museum, Washington, D.C. She has been deputy director for public program planning at the National Museum of the American Indian, deputy assistant secretary for museums at the Smithsonian Institution, associate director of the Children's Museum, Boston, and director of education at the Institute of Contemporary Art, Boston.

John Gwynne is deputy director for design in the Exhibition and Graphic Arts Department of the New York Zoological Society, Bronx, New York.

Rosemary Harms is director of the Treehouse at the Philadelphia Zoological Garden.

George E. Hein, professor of education at Lesley College, Boston, carries out research on visitor learning in museums and other formal and informal settings. He is the author of a recent monograph on science assessment and was a Fulbright Research Fellow in England in 1990.

Carolyn Heinrich is a doctoral student at the University of Chicago Graduate School of Public Policy Studies and a research assistant in the Department of Visitor Research and Exhibit Evaluation, Brookfield Zoo, Brookfield, Illinois.

Paul G. Heltne is director of the Chicago Academy of Sciences. He was previously assistant professor, Department of Animal Medicine, School of Medicine, and Department of Pathobiology, School of Hygiene and Public Health, Johns Hopkins University, Baltimore, Maryland.

Karen A. Hensel is executive director of the East Hampton Historical Society Museums, East Hampton, New York. She was curator of education at the New York Zoological Society/New York Aquarium.

Janet S. Jackson-Gould is curator of education at the Zoological Society of Philadelphia.

Nina Jensen directs the master's degree program in museum education at Bank Street College, New York City, and is a consultant to museums on educational exhibitions and programs.

Merryl Kafka is senior instructor in the Education Department, New York Aquarium, Brooklyn, New York.

Sharon Kramer is creative director/graphics in the Exhibition and Graphic Arts Department of the New York Zoological Society, Bronx, New York.

Marcia Brumit Kropf is an educational consultant in New York City with a background in teaching, teacher training, reading education, and the design of educational materials.

Teresa K. LaMaster is deputy director of the Office of Museum Programs, Smithsonian Institution, Washington, D.C. Previously, she directed the Field Museum of Natural History's Kellogg project on expanding the public role of museums, "Museums: Agents for Public Education."

Judith Landau is assistant director of the Museum Education Program, George Washington University, Washington, D.C.

Jim LaVilla-Havelin the curator of education at the Staten Island Children's Museum, Staten Island, New York. He has written, consulted, evaluated, and developed programs and initiatives in intergenerational learning.

Howard Litwak is principal of Wetzel Associates, Boston, Massachusetts, an interpretive design firm specializing in informal public learning environments such as museums, zoos, and aquariums.

Joan C. Madden retired from her position as assistant director for education at the National Museum of Natural History, Smithsonian Institution, Washington, D.C., in June 1987. She lives in Exeter, New Hampshire.

Roger Mandle is deputy director of the National Gallery of Art, Washington, D.C. For 13 years he was associate director and then director of the Toledo Museum of Art, Toledo, Ohio. He is a member of the National Council on the Arts and cultural adviser to the Department of the Treasury Preservation Committee.

Dale Marcellini is curator of herpetology at the National Zoological Park, Smithsonian Institution, Washington, D.C.

Marian L. Martinello is professor of curriculum and instruction at the University of Texas at San Antonio. She works with museum educators to develop outreach and teacher education programs.

Candace T. Matelic is director and professor of museum studies, Cooperstown Graduate Program in History Museum Studies, Cooperstown, New York. She has worked in interpretive training, adult education, and interpretive programs at Henry Ford Museum and Greenfield Village, Dearborn, Michigan; Living History Farms, Des Moines, Iowa; and Old Sturbridge Village, Sturbridge, Massachusetts.

Susan M. Mayer is coordinator of education at the Archer M. Huntington Art Gallery and a member of the art faculty at the University of Texas at Austin, where she teaches graduate and undergraduate courses in museum education.

Martha McKenna is dean of the Liberal Studies and Adult Learning Division and associate professor of the arts at Lesley College, Boston, Massachusetts.

Patricia A. McNamara conducts exhibit and program evaluation at the Science Museum of Virginia, Richmond. She manages the museum's evaluation program, serves as consulting evaluator for the eight museums of the Exhibit Research Collaborative, and develops training workshops for other institutions.

Ann Mintz is special projects director at the Franklin Institute Science Museum, Philadelphia, where she is project director of the museum's multilayered, visitor-access, museum-wide computer system.

Richard Mühlberger writes books for young readers for the Metropolitan Museum of Art, New York City, and teaches the history of art at Western New England College, Springfield, Massachusetts. For 12 years, he was director of the Museum of Fine Arts and the G.W.V. Smith Art Museum, Springfield. He held museum education positions at the Metropolitan Museum of Art, the Detroit Institute of Arts, and the Worcester Art Museum.

Mary Ellen Munley is chief of museum education at the New York State Museum, Albany, New York. Before moving to Albany, she worked with the Museum Education Program, George Washington University; the Smithsonian Institution; and the American Association of Museums.

Arminta Neal was the assistant director of the Denver Museum of Natural History. She retired in 1982 and lives in Denver, Colorado. She is the author of *Help! for the Small Museum* (2d ed., 1987) and *Exhibits for the Small Museum* (1976).

Peter S. O'Connell is director of museum education at Old Sturbridge Village, Sturbridge, Massachusetts, where he and other museum staff continue to collaborate with schools in the development of educational programs and classroom materials.

Dennis O'Toole is vice-president and chief education officer for Colonial Williamsburg, Williamsburg, Virginia.

Anita Rui Olds is principal of Anita Olds & Associates, a consulting firm specializing in the design of facilities for children, and a lecturer at Tufts University, Medford, Massachusetts. Olds consults with architects, designers, and institutions throughout the United States and Canada and is writing a book on the design of child care facilities.

James F. Peterson is president of Bios:Inc., a Seattle, Washington, design firm specializing in zoo, aquarium, and nature center exhibits.

Bonnie Pitman is deputy director of the University Art Museum/Pacific Film Archive, University of California at Berkeley. She has worked at the Winnepeg Art Gallery, the New Orleans Museum of Art, and the Seattle Art Museum and has been an officer and board member of the American Association of Museums. In 1991 she was appointed chair of the AAM Accreditation Commission.

Vasundhara Prabhu is the first director of education at the Museum of Contemporary Art, Los Angeles, and was previously associated with the Cultural Education Collaborative, Boston; the Boston Children's Museum; and the Herbert F. Johnson Museum of Art, Cornell University, Ithaca, New York.

Danielle Rice is curator of education at the Philadelphia Museum of Art. She has worked as curator of education at the National Gallery of Art and at the Wadsworth Atheneum and has been active on the board of directors of the College Art Association.

Lisa Roberts is manager of public programs at the Chicago Botanical Garden. She is completing a doctoral thesis at the University of Chicago on the aims of education.

Patricia Rutowski coordinates the Outreach Education Department of the Monterey Bay Aquarium, Monterey, California, which takes live ocean animals and marine science theater to schools, libraries, and public events. She has worked in museum and school science for 12 years.

Suzanne B. Schell was a specialist in historic site interpretation and preservation education. During her career she worked for Sully Plantation in Fairfax County, Virginia, the National Endowment for the Humanities, the City of Alexandria, Virginia, and the National Park Service. She was actively involved in the Museum Education Roundtable and served as guest editor of several issues of the *Journal of Museum Education*. She died in 1989.

Thomas J. Schlereth is professor in the Department of American Studies at the University of Notre Dame, Notre Dame, Indiana. He is the author of 12 books, most recently *Cultural History and Material Culture* (1990), which won the Elsie Crews Parsons Prize, and *Victorian America: Transformations in Everyday Life, 1876–1915* (1991), which was a fall 1991 Book-of-the-Month Club selection.

Elizabeth M. Sharpe is deputy assistant director for public programs, National Museum of American History, Smithsonian Institution, Washington, D.C.

Anna Slafer is curator of education at the National Building Museum, Washington, D.C. For more than 10 years she has created education programs in the areas of design, social history, and the natural environment for a variety of institutions.

Carol B. Stapp is director of the Museum Education Program at the George Washington University, Washington, D.C. She has organized numerous professional events for museum practitioners and published on museum education theory and practice in several journals.

Kenneth Starr was director of the Milwaukee Public Museum, Milwaukee, Wisconsin, from 1970 to 1987. Following his retirement, he spent two and a half years at the National Science Foundation in Informal Science Education. Retiring again in 1990, he now divides his time between museums and Chinese studies. He is a past president of the American Association of Museums.

Mark St. John is the founder and president of Inverness Research Associates, an independent educational consulting firm in Inverness, California, specializing in evaluating private and public initiatives aimed at improving education through curriculum reform, professional development, or other capacity-building efforts.

Susan Stitt was director of the Museums at Stony Brook for 14 years until she resigned in September 1988 to give herself a sabbatical. In January 1990, she returned to the field as president and chief executive officer of the Historical Society of Pennsylvania, Philadelphia.

Joseph H. Suina is associate professor in the College of Education teacher training program at the University of New Mexico, Albuquerque. A member of the Cochita Pueblo tribe, he currently focuses his research efforts on literacy enhancement in the classrooms of Native-American pupils.

Robert Sullivan is associate director for public programs at the National Museum of Natural History, Smithsonian Institution, Washington, D.C. Previously he was director of museum services at the New York State Museum, Albany, and coordinator of museum education at the Rochester Museum and Science Center, Rochester, New York.

Scott T. Swank is director of Canterbury Shaker Village, Canterbury, New Hampshire. For 16 years he was a member of the management team at Winterthur Museum and Gardens, Winterthur, Delaware, most recently as deputy director of interpretation and administrator of Winterthur's historic site at Odessa, Delaware.

Linda Taylor is curator of exhibits and displays at the San Francisco Zoological Gardens, San Francisco, California.

Lonn Taylor is assistant director for public programs at the National Museum of American History, Smithsonian Institution, Washington, D.C.

Catherine Tompson is curator of education at the Baltimore Zoo, Baltimore, Maryland.

William Tramposch is the former executive director of the Oregon Historical Society, Portland. He was director of interpretation and special program officer at Colonial Williamsburg.

Ann Treadwell is executive director of the Creative ARTS Center, Pontiac, Michigan.

Barbara Vacarr is a member of the faculty at Lesley College Graduate School, Cambridge, Massachusetts.

Judith White is chief of the office of education, National Zoological Park, Smithsonian Institution, Washington, D.C., where she has developed three learning laboratories—ZOOlab, HERPlab, and BIRDlab. She is past president of the International Association of Zoo Educators.

Patterson B. Williams is dean of education at the Denver Art Museum, and she is also researching the museum's Asian collections to sharpen her skills as a master teacher.

Barbara L. Wolf is associate dean of the faculties at Indiana University, Bloomington, Indiana. For more than a decade, she collaborated with her husband, Robert L. Wolf. She continues to be an active consultant on museum evaluation, both at preprofessional and advanced professional levels.

Robert L. Wolf introduced the museum field to research and inquiry based on naturalistic, qualitative approaches. His contributions include a vocabulary and a methodology for looking at the wide range of visitor experiences and how that information could be used for policy and program planning. He died in 1988.

Mary Worthington is a writer, teacher, and consultant who lives in Santa Monica,

California. She is the former associate director of the Los Angeles Children's Museum and the author of *Where Are the Dinosaurs?*, a book about children's museums to be published by the Association of Youth Museums.

Ken Yellis is assistant director for public programs at the Peabody Museum of Natural History, Yale University, New Haven, Connecticut. He is review editor and former editor-in-chief (1980–87) of the *Journal of Museum Education* and principal of First Light Museum Consultants.

Philip Yenawine has been director of education at the Museum of Modern Art, New York City, since 1983. He has also had education positions at the Metropolitan Museum of Art and the Museum of Contemporary Art, Chicago. He is the author of *How to Look at Modern Art* (1991) and four books about art for young people.

Index

Accessibility. See Museum literacy

Adam, Thomas R., 114

Adler, Mortimer, 364, 372

Adolescent audiences, 6; as interpreters, 17, 279–85

Adult audiences, 6–7, 10; adult education 25, 74; programs for older adults, 262–75. See *also* Developmental psychology

Affolter, James, 83–86

African-American audiences, 4, 12–19, 75–76, 77, 249–50, 302

African-American museums, 10, 12–19, 249–50

African American Museums Association, 15–16

Afro-American Historical and Cultural Museum, 15, 16, 17, 18

Afro-American Museum (Detroit), 15, 16, 17

Alderson, William T., 29

Alexander, Edward P., 30

Alt, M. B., 37, 216

American Association for State and Local History, 16

American Association of Colleges for Teacher Education, 179

American Association of Museums (AAM), 16, 36, 366; accreditation, 29–30, 32, 46, 68–69, 306; annual meetings, Denver (1991), 9, 80, 366, Detroit (1985), 355–56, New Orleans (1989), 168, New York City (1926), 197, Philadelphia (1982), 41, Pittsburgh (1988), 157, Washington, D.C. (1984), 46, 129, 132, 355; *Code of Ethics for Museums,* 116; Commission on Museums for a New Century, 41–47, 72, 74, 75, 355; Education, Standing Professional Committee on, 47, 60–65, 368; *Historic House Museums,* 28; Historic Sites Committee of Accreditation

Commission, 29, 30, 32; *Museum Ethics,* 60; *Museums for a New Century,* 35, 38, 41–47, 79, 84, 85, 198, 355–57, 360; Task Force on Museum Education, 9, 71, 75, 77, 79–94, 116, 332, 361; visitor behavior research, 197–98

American Association of Zoological Parks and Aquariums, 324, 326

American Museum of Natural History, 76, 223

Amistad Research Center, 14, 17

Anacostia Museum, 8, 17, 69, 249–50

Anderson, Jay, 110n.7

Annis, Sheldon, 120

Appleton, William Sumner, 28

Aquariums, 233–39, 268–69, 279–85, 312–16

Aquinas, Thomas, 121

Archabal, Nina, 84–86

Aries, Philippe, 308

Arizona–Sonora Desert Museum, 236, 237

Arnheim, Rudolf, 373

Art centers, 299–306

Art museums, 48–59, 118–22, 144–52, 194, 230–32, 246–48, 273–74, 294–98, 334; preparation of educators in, 362–67; teacher training in, 286–93

Arts Awareness, 243

Ashmore, Harry, 370–71

Asian audiences, 262, 302

Association for Living Historical Farms and Agricultural Museums, 351, 354

Association of Youth Museums, 372

Atlanta University, 14

Audience advocacy, 62, 63, 64, 368, 372

Audience development, 3–8, 38, 62, 69, 83

Audience research. See Visitor demographics

Austin, Joy Ford, 15–16, 17

Baldwin, Luke, 162–67
Balling, John D., 187, 210, 223–29
Baltimore Museum of Art, 273–74
Bank Street College, 355, 361
Baranik, Rudolf, 369
Barry, Sharon, 276–78
Bates, Marilyn, 244
Beardsley, Monroe C., 231
Beer, Valorie, 193, 209–14
Behavioral psychology, 37, 38, 138–39
Bell, Paul, 373
Benefield, Arlene, 370
Bennett, William, 154
Benton, Deborah P., 222–29
Bergan, John R., 371
Bethune Museum and Archives of Black
    Women's History, 15
Bettelheim, Bruno, 372
Bierstadt, Albert, 8
Birney, Barbara A., 194, 233–39
Birney, Robert C., 346–50
Bitgood, Stephen, 370
Black American West Museum, 15
Bloom, Allan, 154–58
Bloom, Joel N., 9, 71–78, 79
Bloomer, Carolyn M., 373
Borun, Minda, 36, 159–61, 188
Botanical gardens, 83–86
Bourdieu, Pierre, 113
Bradley, David, 371
Brennan, T. J., 235
Brenner, Marcella, 47, 369
Briggs, Dorothy, 371
Brigham, Diane, 362–67
British Museum, 93
British Museum (Natural History), 37, 160,
    161, 218, 370
Bronx Zoo, 222, 317–19, 321
Brookfield Zoo, 235, 236, 237
Brooklyn Children's Museum, 222
Brown, Claudine K., 3–8
Bruner, Jerome, 119, 372
Buffalo Museum of Science, 197
Burroughs, Margaret, 15
Butler, Robert, 264

Cameron, Duncan, 15
Campbell, Mary Schmidt, 157
Camron-Stanford House, 106

Caplan, Frank, 371
Caplan, Theresa, 371
Career development and training, 46–47, 51–
    53, 57, 63–65, 67, 82, 229, 355–61,
    368–73; in art museums, 362–67; in
    research and evaluation, 51, 200–201,
    202. *See also* Interpreter training,
    Professionalism, Teacher training
Caribbean Cultural Center, 13
Carnegie Corporation, 197
Carson, Barbara G., 129–33
Centennial Exposition, Philadelphia, 28, 104
Center for African Art, 157
Chambers, Marlene, 194, 230–32
Chapman, Laura, 355
Chapman, Samuel, 13
Cherry, Schroeder, 17
Children in Museums International
    Symposium, 372
Children's Environments Quarterly, 372
Children's Museum of Manhattan, 310
Children's museums and programs, 37, 179–
    84, 249, 272–74, 300–301, 307–11, 372.
    See also Developmental psychology,
    School programs
Churilla, Jacqueline, 264
Cincinnati Historical Society, 109
Cincinnati Zoo, 321
Cleveland Museum of Art, 244
Cloisters Children's Museum, 272–73
Cochrane, Sharlene, 162–67
Coe, Jon Charles, 319–20
Cohen, Dorothy H., 371
Coleman, Laurence Vail, 28
Coles, Robert, 369
Collaborations, 17–18, 65, 82, 250, 271–72,
    300–306
Collecting, 16–17, 54, 82–83, 104, 122, 124
Colonial Williamsburg, 27, 28, 29, 77, 346–
    50, 369–71
Communication, 64, 67–68, 157, 158, 357–
    58. *See also* Interpretation, Publications
Community audiences, 3–8, 10, 18, 62, 246,
    249–50, 299–306
Community Folk Art Museum, 15
Compton Gallery (MIT), 105
Conner Prairie Pioneer Settlement, 28
Conway, William, 321
Counts, Constance, 162–67

Cousins, Norman, 68
Cranbrook Museums, 299
Creative ARTS Center, 304–6. *See also*
  Pontiac Art Center
Crocker, Margaret, 309
Csikszentmihalyi, Mihaly, 107–8, 194, 231,
  309, 372
Cultural pluralism. *See* Multiculturalism
Cunningham, Ann Pamela, 27
Curriculum, 193, 209–14, 252

d'Harnoncourt, René, 76
Damas, Leon, 14
Dana, John Cotton, 9, 114
Darwin, Charles, 327
Deetz, James, 105, 109
Delaware Art Museum, 109
Denver Art Museum, 115, 120–22, 124, 230
Denver Colloquium on Museum Learning,
  360
Denver Meeting of Art Museum Educators,
  144, 362–67
Denver Museum of Natural History, 372
Denver Zoo, 237
Detroit Colloquium on Museum Learning,
  355–60
Detroit Institute of Arts, 299
Deutsches Museum, 37
Developmental psychology, 64, 188, 370;
  adult development, 162–67, 372; child
  development, 168–73, 253–55, 371, 372
Dewey, John, 21, 38, 164, 253–54, 357, 361
Diamond, Judy, 187–90, 218, 222–29
Diaz, Carlos, 305
Dickerson, Amina J., 10, 12–19
Dierking, Lynn D., 187, 193–94, 216–22
Disabled audiences, 4, 25, 38, 62, 301
Discovery Center of the Southern Tier, 309
Discovery Hall Museum. *See* Studebaker
  National Museum
Dobbs, Stephen M., 48–59
Docents. *See* Interpretation
Dolamore, Joan, 162–67
Douglas, Mary, 108
Dow, George Francis, 28
Draper, Linda, 369
DuBois, W.E.B., 14
Duchamp, Marcel, 55
Duckworth, Eleanor, 168–73

Duke, Leilani Lattin, 49
Duncan, Isadora, 105
Dunlap, J., 234, 236
DuSable Museum, 15

Education departments: diversity in, 4, 68–
  69, 79, 82, 88, 94, 372; in museum
  organizational structure, 10, 43–44, 45–
  46, 50, 53–57, 63, 84, 245, 334, 355;
  status of museum education, 10, 41–59,
  84, 334–36
Educational theory, 10, 38–39, 118–22, 125,
  126–28, 137–39, 187–90, 371; need for
  research and training in learning, 38, 42,
  44, 45–46, 47, 51, 53, 63, 64, 73, 97,
  191–203, 292–93, 331–33, 357–59
Edwards, Betty, 244
Eisler, Riane, 373
Eisner, Elliot W., 48–59
Elementary and Secondary Education Act of
  1965, 21
Elkind, David, 371
Environmental psychology, 174–78, 372
Erikson, Erik, 107, 371
Essex Institute, 28, 29
Estes, W., 38–39
Ethics, 55, 60–65, 67
Ethnic audiences, 3–8, 12–19, 38, 75, 262,
  302
Ethnic museums, 75
Evaluation, 36–37, 67–68, 189, 191–203,
  204–208, 361, 370; need for research and
  training in, 51, 64, 194, 198–203, 358
*Excellence and Equity: Education and the
  Public Dimension of Museums,* 9, 79–94,
  116, 361. *See also* American Association of
  Museums, Task Force on Museum
  Education
Exhibit design, 38–39, 125, 140–43, 159–61,
  174–78, 189, 191–95, 370, 373; in zoos,
  317–27
Exhibit development, 63, 159–61, 204–8,
  319–20; team approach to, 10–11, 35–
  40, 63, 198, 277–78, 319–20
Exploratorium, 9, 37, 72, 188, 222–23
Expositions, 14, 28, 104

Fairmount Park, 28
Falk, John H., 187, 218, 220–21

Family audiences, 5–6, 10, 84, 276–78; research on, 187, 193–94, 215–19
Fanon, Frantz, 18
Farmer's Museum, 28
Feher, Elsa, 160, 161, 187
Felton, Zora, 17, 249–50
Ferguson, Eugene, 110n.11
Field Museum of Natural History, 157–58
Fines, John, 97–98
Finlay, Jan, 99
Fischer, Daryl, 115
Fisher, Jeffrey, 373
Fisk University, 14
Fiske, Richard, 45–46
Fleming, E. McClung, 114
Flint Institute of Arts, 299
Florida State Museum, 217
Ford, Henry, 28
Formal education, 68, 209–14; failures in, 71–78, 86, 144, 154–58. *See also* School programs
Franco, Barbara, 9–11
Franklin Institute Science Museum, 160, 161
Free Association Theatre, 353
Friedlander, Max, 118
Friedman, Renée, 132
Furlong, Harold, 299

Gaither, Edmund Barry, 3, 13, 86
Gardner, Howard, 244, 311, 372
Geertz, Clifford, 332
Genesee Valley Indian Center, 302
George, Alberta Sebolt, 20–26
George Washington University, Museum Education Program, 45, 49, 355, 361
Getty Center for Education in the Arts, 48–59, 144, 149
Gibran, Kahlil, 69
Gilman, Benjamin Ives, 9, 114, 373
Glassie, Henry, 105
Gombrich, Ernst, 120
Gonzalez, Mauricio, 286–93
Goode, George Brown, 113–14, 372
Goodlad, John I., 209–10, 211
Goodwin, William, 29
Gould, Stephen Jay, 231
Graburn, Nelson, 113, 253, 369
Greene, M., 235, 237
Greenfield Village, 28, 370. *See also* Henry Ford Museum and Greenfield Village

Griggs, Stephan, 160, 161
Gurian, Elaine Heumann, 46, 88–89, 368
Gwynne, John, 317–19

Haas, Malka, 169
Hagley Museum, 106
Haley, Alex, 14
Hall, Edward T., 373
Hamlin, Chauncey J., 197
Hampton Institute, College Museum, 13–14
Hand to Hand, 372
Handicapped audiences. *See* Disabled audiences
Hands-on exhibits, 37–38, 73, 159–61, 188–89, 256–57, 276–78, 322–23. *See also* Interactive video exhibits
Harlem Renaissance, 13, 14
Harmon Collection, 13
Harms, Rosemary, 325–27
Hasbrouck House, 27
Hawkins, David, 172
Hazelius, Arthur, 28
Hein, George E., 368
Heinrich, Carolyn, 194, 233–39
Heltne, Paul G., 90–91
Henderson, Ronald W., 371
Henry Ford Museum and Greenfield Village, 305, 351–54, 370
Hensel, Karen A., 279–85
Herndon, James, 371
Hicks, Ellen. *See* Hirzy, Ellen Cochran
Hilke, D. D., 223–29
Hindle, Brooke, 105
Hine, Lewis, 8
Hirsch, E. D., 147–48, 151n.9, 152
Hirzy, Ellen Cochran, 44–45, 80, 81
Hispanic audiences, 76, 262, 302
Historic sites, 27–34, 97–98, 346–54.
History museums, 20–26, 97–98, 102–11, 129–33, 251–67, 270–71, 274–75.
History of museums, 13–15, 27–34, 54, 72, 74–75, 93, 99–100, 113–14; of exhibit design, 125; of research, 187, 197–98, 201
Hodgson, Judith, 286
Holt, John, 39
Hudson, Kenneth, 373
Hughes, Langston, 14
Huizinga, Johan, 372

I. P. Stanback Museum and Planetarium, 18
Informal learning, 38–39, 73, 187–90, 243–
  45, 249
Inhelder, Barbel, 170
Institute of Museum Services, 29
Interactive video exhibits, 247, 320–22
International Council of Museums, 60
Interpretation, 62, 156–58. *See also museums
  by type*
Interpreter training, 229, 279–85, 304,
  346–54

J. Paul Getty Trust, 370. *See also* Getty
  Center for Education in the Arts
Jackson, Jesse, 343
Jackson-Gould, Janet S., 317
Jarrell, Randall, 307
Jefferson, Thomas, 71
Jennings, Gretchen, 46, 57
Jensen, Nina, 355–61
John Ball Zoo, 278
John Ward House, 28, 29
Jones, Elizabeth, 372
Jones, Stephen, 14
Jordan, Winthrop, 371

Kafka, Merryl, 279–85
Kegan, Robert, 163
Keirsey, David, 244
Kellert, Stephen, 234, 236–39
Kelsey, E., 236
Kennedy, John F., 305
Kiefer, Anselm, 77
Kimball, Fiske, 28, 197
Kinard, John, 69, 369
Klein, Frances, 209–10, 211
Knowles, Malcolm, 263
Kohl, Herbert, 371
Kolb, David, 164
Koran, John J., 188
Koran, Mary Lou, 188
Kozol, Jonathan, 371
Kramer, Sharon, 317–19
Kropf, Marcia Brumit, 187, 193–94, 216
Kuhn, Thomas, 231

Labels, 92, 125, 225–26, 228, 318, 323–25,
  373
Lakota, Robert, 36
LaMaster, Teresa K., 331–33

Landau, Judith, 55–57
Larkin, Jill H., 189
LaVilla-Havelin, Jim, 307–11
Lawrence Hall of Science, 222–23
Lawrence, Jacob, 8
Leadership, 42, 68–69, 75, 79–80, 248
Learning styles, 10, 37–38, 134–43, 164–66,
  177, 180, 187, 219, 244, 360
Learning theory. *See* Educational theory
Lee, Sherman E., 244, 369
Leonard, George, 371
Lesley College Graduate School, 162, 166–67
Levi-Strauss, Claude, 108, 253
Levinson, Daniel, 162
Lewis, Peirce, 108
Lewis, Sinclair, 107
Lichtenstein, Roy, 247
Lifelong learning. *See* Adult audiences
Lilla, Mark, 39
Lincoln, Crawford, 21
Lincoln's New Salem, 28
Linn, Marcia C., 210
Litwak, Howard, 320–22
Living collections, 83–84. *See also* Aquariums,
  Botanical gardens, Zoos
Living history, 104, 105, 129–33, 274
Loomis, Ross, 36, 142n.1, 370, 373
Los Angeles Zoo, 321
Low, Shirley Payne, 29
Low, Theodore, 114
Lowell Institute, 268
Lowenfeld, Viktor, 244
Lowie Museum of Anthropology, 109
Lyceum, 270–71

MacCannell, Dean, 370
Madden, Joan C., 35–40, 46, 123–25
Malraux, André, 146
Management, 64, 334
Mandle, Roger, 91–93
Marcellini, Dale, 276–78
Margaret Woodbury Strong Museum, 103
Martinello, Marian L., 286–93
Marzio, Peter, 118
Maslow, Abraham, 371
Mason, John, 372
Matelic, Candace T., 351–54
Material culture, 102–11
Maxim, G. W., 180
Mayer, Susan M., 243–45

McDermott, Melora, 230, 232
McKenna, Martha, 162–67
McManus, Paulette, 160, 161
McNamara, Patricia A., 189, 193, 204–8
Meinig, D. W., 107
Melton, Arthur, 187, 197–98
Metro Washington Park Zoo, 236
Metropolitan Museum of Art, 222, 243, 244
Meyer, Karl, 114
Midwest Open-Air Museums Coordinating
    Council, 351, 354
Miles, Roger S., 37, 38, 160, 161, 370
Minnesota Historical Society, 85, 132
Minnesota Zoological Garden, 327
Minorities. *See* Ethnic audiences, Ethnic
    museums, Women, *ethnic groups by name*
Mintz, Ann, 9, 71–78
Minuchin, Patricia P., 308
Mission of museums, 3–8, 45, 53–55, 61,
    79–94, 99–101, 192, 246–48, 315–16,
    356. *See also* Public service
Monterey Bay Aquarium, 312–16
Monticello, 27
Moorland-Spingarn Research Center,
    Howard University, 14
Mother Bethel African Methodist Episcopal
    (AME) Church, 14
Mount Vernon, 27, 28; Mount Vernon
    Ladies' Association, 27
Mühlberger, Richard, 334–36
Multiculturalism, 3–8, 10, 74–78, 81, 87, 88,
    99–101, 179–84, 373
Munley, Mary Ellen, 45, 46, 115, 187, 192–
    93, 196–203, 368
Museum Assessment Programs, 94, 116
Museum Education Anthology, 372
Museum Education Roundtable, 41, 44, 48,
    56, 66–70
Museum literacy, 90–91, 102–28, 134–43
Museum News, 37, 48, 286
Museum of Fine Arts, Boston, 9, 105, 114
Museum of Man (Ottawa), 104
Museum of Modern Art, 76, 244
Museum of Science and Industry (Chicago),
    37, 75–76
Museum of the National Center of Afro-
    American Artists, 13, 17

National Air and Space Museum, 250

National Aquarium in Baltimore, 236
National Art Education Association, 366
National Council on the Aging, 269–70
National Endowment for the Arts, 12, 21,
    144, 149, 251
National Endowment for the Humanities,
    12, 16, 21, 30, 251, 252, 269
National Museum of African Art, 18, 271–72
National Museum of American History, 49,
    57, 106, 114–15, 262–66
National Museum of Natural History, 45, 46,
    124, 217, 271–72
National Negro Business Association, 14
National Park Service, 30
National Portrait Gallery, 56
National Science Foundation, 68, 276
National Zoological Park, 49, 222, 276–78,
    271–72, 327
Native American audiences, 76, 262, 302
Natural history museums, 99–101, 124, 157–
    58, 312–16
Neal, Arminta, 372–73, 379
Neal, Larry, 13
Neisser, Ulrich, 188
New England Aquarium, 268–69
New York Aquarium, 279–85
New York City Board of Education, 18
New York Public Library, 14
New York State Museum, 203
New York Zoological Society, 317
New Yorker, 342
Newark Museum, 197
Norman, Donald A., 189
Northeast Museums Conference, 41

O'Connell, Peter S., 251–61
O'Toole, Dennis, 369–71
Object-based learning, 73, 91–93, 102–11,
    118–33. *See also* Hands-on exhibits,
    Museum literacy, Visual literacy
Old Sturbridge Village, 20–26, 251–61,
    274–75
Olds, Anita Rui, 174–78
Oppenheimer, Frank, 9, 72, 188–89
Orientation, 103, 134–43, 217
Orwell, George, 342

Pacific Oaks College, 371, 372
Panero, Julius, 373

Panofsky, Erwin, 114
Parr, A. E., 36
Peabody Museum of Natural History, 197
Pennsylvania Museum. *See* Philadelphia
    Museum of Art
Percy, Walker, 370
Perry, William, 163
Peters, Thomas J., 370
Peterson, James F., 322–23
Philadelphia Museum of Art, 28, 49, 75, 119,
    120, 121, 197, 369
Philadelphia Zoo, 236, 237, 278, 326–27
Phillips Collection, 220n.10
Piaget, Jean, 47, 168–73, 187, 371
Piatt, Margaret, 132
Picasso, Pablo, 77
Pitman, Bonnie, 79–81
Plimoth Plantation, 105
Pontiac Art Center, 299–306
Porter, Dorothy, 14
Prabhu, Vasundhara, 246–48
Professional standards, 9–11, 15–17, 43, 82,
    88–89
Professionalism, 41–65, 68, 331–33, 361,
    362–67, 368–73. *See also* Career
    development and training
Psychology. *See* Behavioral psychology,
    Developmental psychology,
    Environmental psychology
Public service, 9–11, 62, 79–94, 112–17,
    153–58, 361. *See also* Mission of
    museums
Publications, 39, 359; educational materials,
    251–61; writing skills, 337–45
Pulaski, Mary Ann, 371

Rea, Paul, 114
Reger, Lawrence L., 46
Reid Park Zoo, 236
Research, 187–204, 231–32. *See also*
    Educational theory, Evaluation, Visitor
    demographics
Reuben H. Fleet Science Center, 160, 161
Rice, Danielle, 43–44, 49, 53–55, 56–57,
    144–52
Richardson, Cindy, 268–69
Riznik, Barnes, 21
Roberts, Lisa, 153–58
Robinson, Edward S., 187, 197–98, 201

Robinson, Marilynne, 108
Rochberg-Halton, Eugene, 107–8
Rochester Museum and Science Center, 99
Rockefeller, John D., Jr., 28
Rodriguez, Richard, 370
Rogers, Carl, 203, 369
Roper, James T., Jr., 370
Rosenfeld, Sherman B., 187, 218, 223–29
Rothenberg, Michael, 371
Rutowski, Patricia, 312–16

Samples, Bob, 371
San Antonio Zoo, 236
San Diego Zoo, 235–36, 237
San Francisco State University, 48
San Francisco Zoo, 222, 321, 323–25
Santa Barbara Zoo, 236
Santini, Helen, 220n.10
Schell, Suzanne B., 27–34
Schiffer, Michael, 108
Schlereth, Thomas J., 123–28
Schomburg, Arthur A., 14
Schomburg Center for Research in Black
    Culture, 14
Schön, Donald A., 331–32
School programs, 6–7, 25, 69, 74, 150, 251–
    61, 286–93, 303, 312–16.*See also* Formal
    education
Science and technology centers, 37, 159–61,
    188–89, 194, 230–32
Science Museum of Minnesota, 326
Science Museum of Virginia, 160, 161,
    204–8
Screven, Chandler G., 36, 213, 287
Sedgwick Zoo, 236, 237
Sendak, Maurice, 310
Serrell, Beverly, 235
Sharpe, Elizabeth M., 262–67
Sheeler, Charles, 305
Shelburne Museum, 28, 106
Sheppard, William, 13–14
Shettel, Harris, 36, 37
Shiffrin, R., 38–39
Simon, H., 38–39
Skansen (Stockholm, Sweden), 28
Slafer, Anna, 44–46
Smith, Cyril Stanley, 105
Smith, E., 38–39
Smithsonian Institution, 16, 35, 37, 57, 124.

See also Anacostia Museum, National Museum of African Art, National Museum of American History, National Museum of Natural History, National Zoological Park
Society, museums and. *See* Public service
Society for the Preservation of New England Antiquities, 27–28
Spinney, Frank, 21
Spock, Benjamin, 371
St. John, Mark, 187, 191–95
St. Louis Zoo, 321
Stack, Carol B., 369
Stanford University, 48, 53, 154
Stapp, Carol B., 46–47, 48–49, 112–17, 126–28, 369
Starr, Kenneth, 66–70
Staten Island Children's Museum, 309, 310, 311
Steinhart Aquarium, 223
Stern, Virginia, 371
Stillman, Dianne, 57
Stitt, Susan, 41–43
Studebaker National Museum, 103–4
Studio Museum in Harlem, 17
Suina, Joseph H., 179–84
Sullivan, Robert, 99–101
Swank, Scott T., 93–94

Tanner, Henry O., 14
Tappan, Lewis, 14
Taylor, Francis Henry, 114
Taylor, Linda, 323–25
Taylor, Lonn, 49, 56
Taylor, Samuel M., 187, 223–29
Teacher training, 24–25, 251–61, 286–93
Templeton, Michael, 70
Theater, 133, 312–16, 325–27, 353; role playing, 307–11
Thomas Jefferson Memorial Foundation, 27
Thorndike, Edward, 197
Tilden, Freeman, 30
Tompson, Catherine, 325–27
Tramposch, William, 346
Treadwell, Ann, 299–306
Trustees, 82, 94, 334–35
Tuskegee Institute, 14
Twain, Mark, 69
Tye, Kenneth, 210–11, 212

Tymitz, Barbara. *See* Barbara L. Wolf

United Way, 299, 300, 301, 305
University galleries, 286–93
University of California Botanical Garden, 84
University of Chicago, 154
University of Texas at San Antonio Teaching Art Gallery, 286–93

Vacarr, Barbara, 162–67
Van Gogh, Vincent, 8
Van Rennes, Eve E., 208
Vancouver Aquarium, 236
Vega, Marta, 13
Visitor comfort, 38, 143, 175–76, 178, 216, 224, 246–47, 248, 373
Visitor demographics, 35, 38, 233–39
Visitor Studies Conference, 370
Visual literacy, 43–44, 118–22, 144–52, 156–57, 292, 297–98
Vukelich, Ronald, 188

Wall, Alexander, 21
Walsh, John, 244
Walton, William, 160, 161
Waterman, Robert H., Jr., 370
Watkin, C. Malcolm, 106
Watkins, Carleton, 109
Wells, Ruth, 21
Western States Black Research Center, 14
Westervelt, M. O., 234
Wetherell, W. D., 108
White, Judith, 46, 49, 56, 57, 276–78, 365
Wideman, John Edgar, 370
Williams, Patterson B., 48, 60–61, 118–22, 123–28
Witteborg, Lothar, 15, 37
Wittlin, Alma, 113
Wolf, Barbara L., 36–37, 142–43, 222–29
Wolf, Robert L., 36–37, 134–42, 142, 222–29
Women, 42, 68–69, 76
Woods, Tom, 132
Worthington, Mary, 371–72
Wright, Charles, 15
Wrye, Harriet, 264

Yale University, 197
Yale University Art Gallery, 110n.12

Yellis, Ken, 56, 57, 126–28, 337–45
Yenawine, Philip, 58, 294–98
Yosemite National Park, 109–10

Zeller, Terry, 48
Zoos, 51, 233–39, 276–78, 317–27